COPS FOR CRIMINALS

LEGENDARY

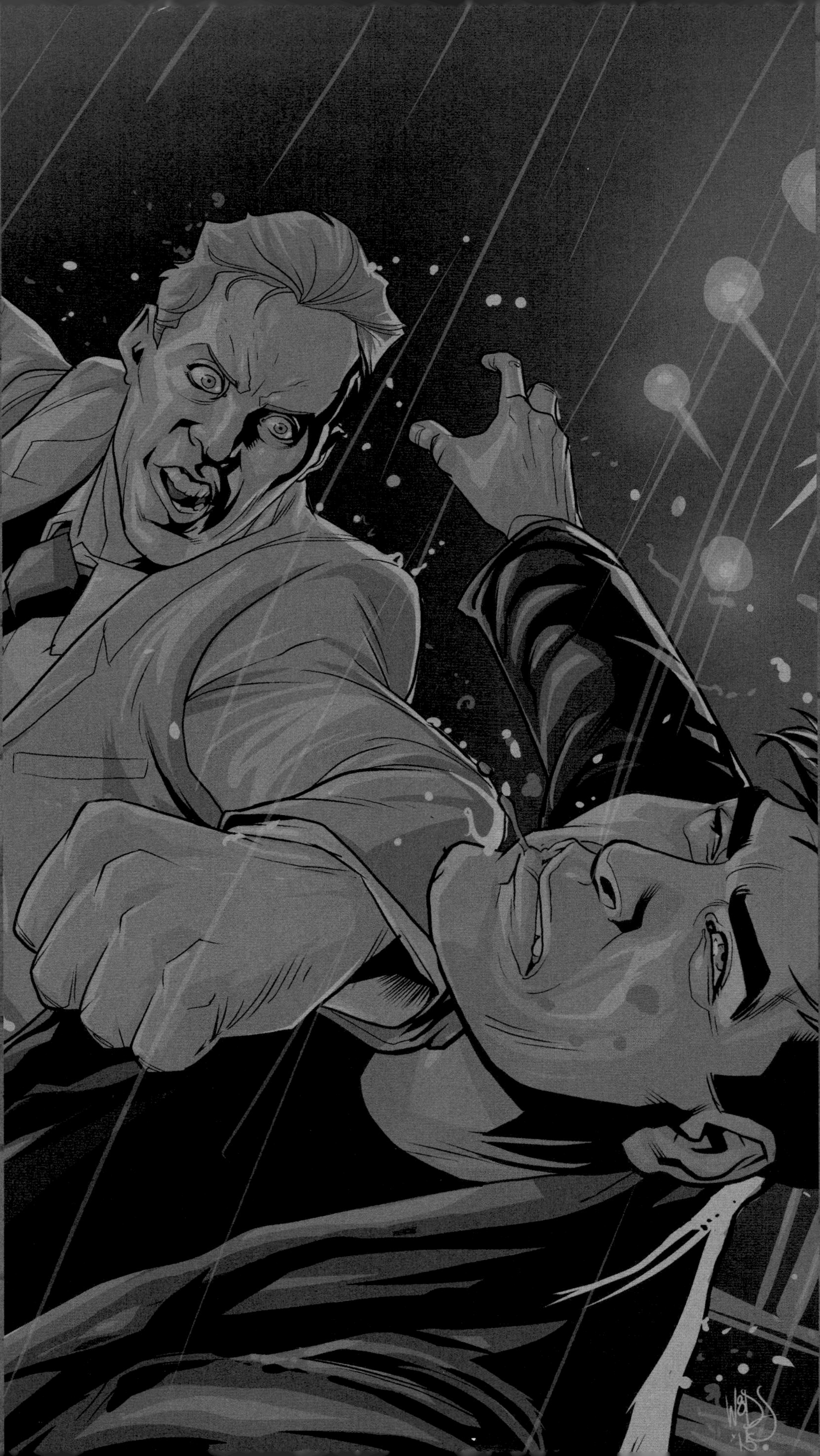

COPS FOR CRIMINALS

STEVEN GRANT
WRITER

PETE WOODS
ARTIST

SEAN KONOT
LETTERER

DAVE JOHNSON
PETE WOODS
ORIGINAL SERIES COVERS

NICOLAS SIENTY
PRE-PRESS & PRODUCTION

JOHN J. HILL
BOOK & LOGO DESIGNER

GREG TUMBARELLO
EDITOR

CREATED BY
THOMAS TULL

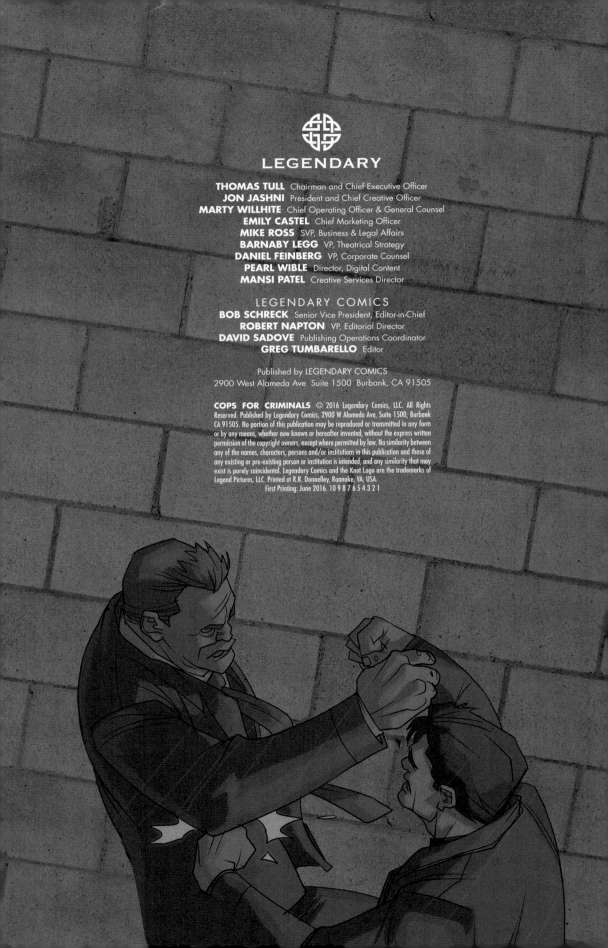

LEGENDARY

THOMAS TULL Chairman and Chief Executive Officer
JON JASHNI President and Chief Creative Officer
MARTY WILLHITE Chief Operating Officer & General Counsel
EMILY CASTEL Chief Marketing Officer
MIKE ROSS SVP, Business & Legal Affairs
BARNABY LEGG VP, Theatrical Strategy
DANIEL FEINBERG VP, Corporate Counsel
PEARL WIBLE Director, Digital Content
MANSI PATEL Creative Services Director

LEGENDARY COMICS

BOB SCHRECK Senior Vice President, Editor-in-Chief
ROBERT NAPTON VP, Editorial Director
DAVID SADOVE Publishing Operations Coordinator
GREG TUMBARELLO Editor

Published by LEGENDARY COMICS
2900 West Alameda Ave Suite 1500 Burbank, CA 91505

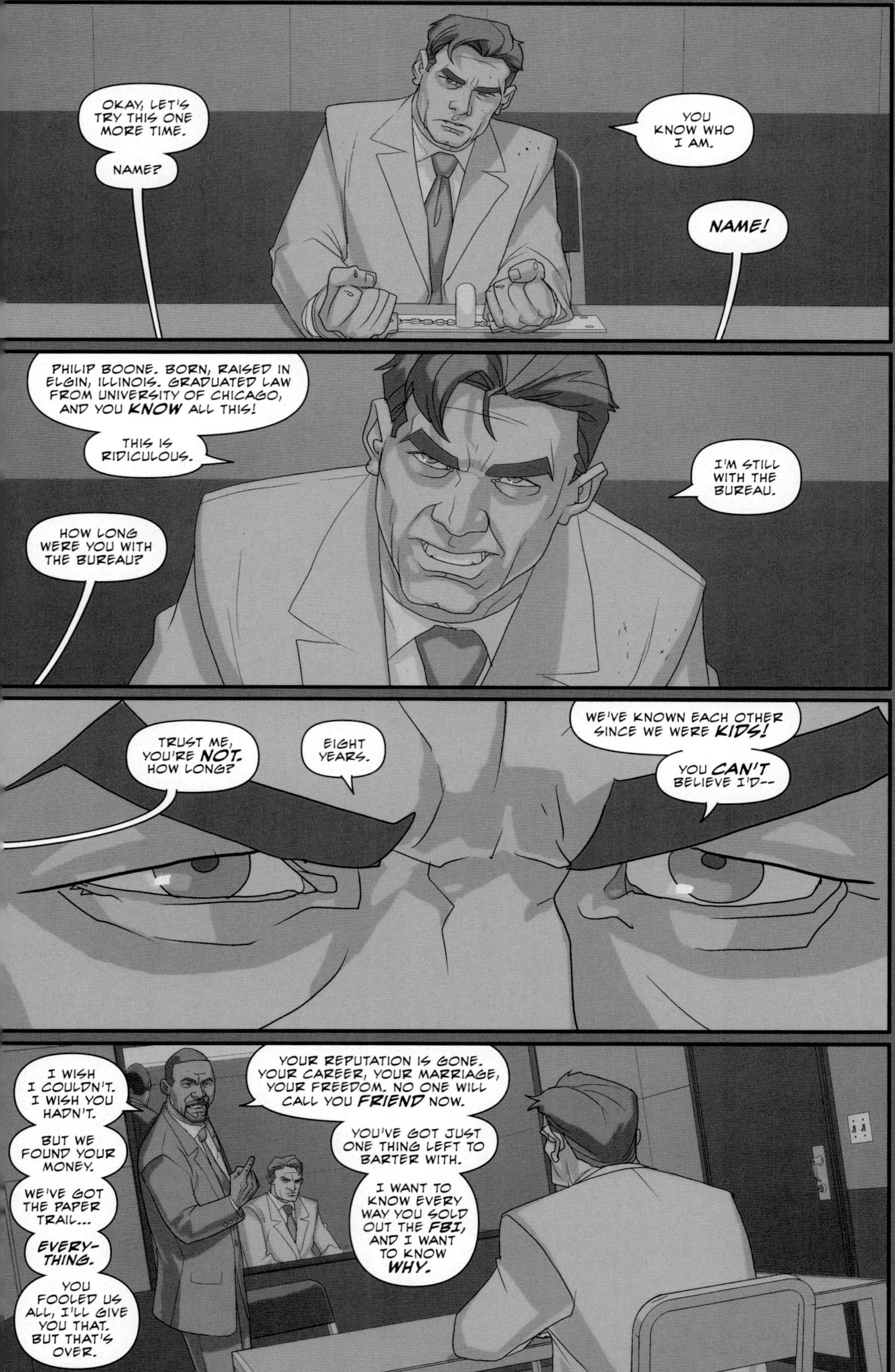
OKAY, LET'S TRY THIS ONE MORE TIME.
NAME?
YOU KNOW WHO I AM.
NAME!
PHILIP BOONE. BORN, RAISED IN ELGIN, ILLINOIS. GRADUATED LAW FROM UNIVERSITY OF CHICAGO, AND YOU KNOW ALL THIS!
THIS IS RIDICULOUS.
I'M STILL WITH THE BUREAU.
HOW LONG WERE YOU WITH THE BUREAU?
TRUST ME, YOU'RE NOT. HOW LONG?
EIGHT YEARS.
WE'VE KNOWN EACH OTHER SINCE WE WERE KIDS!
YOU CAN'T BELIEVE I'D--
I WISH I COULDN'T. I WISH YOU HADN'T.
BUT WE FOUND YOUR MONEY.
WE'VE GOT THE PAPER TRAIL...
EVERY-THING.
YOU FOOLED US ALL, I'LL GIVE YOU THAT. BUT THAT'S OVER.
YOUR REPUTATION IS GONE. YOUR CAREER, YOUR MARRIAGE, YOUR FREEDOM. NO ONE WILL CALL YOU FRIEND NOW.
YOU'VE GOT JUST ONE THING LEFT TO BARTER WITH.
I WANT TO KNOW EVERY WAY YOU SOLD OUT THE FBI, AND I WANT TO KNOW WHY.

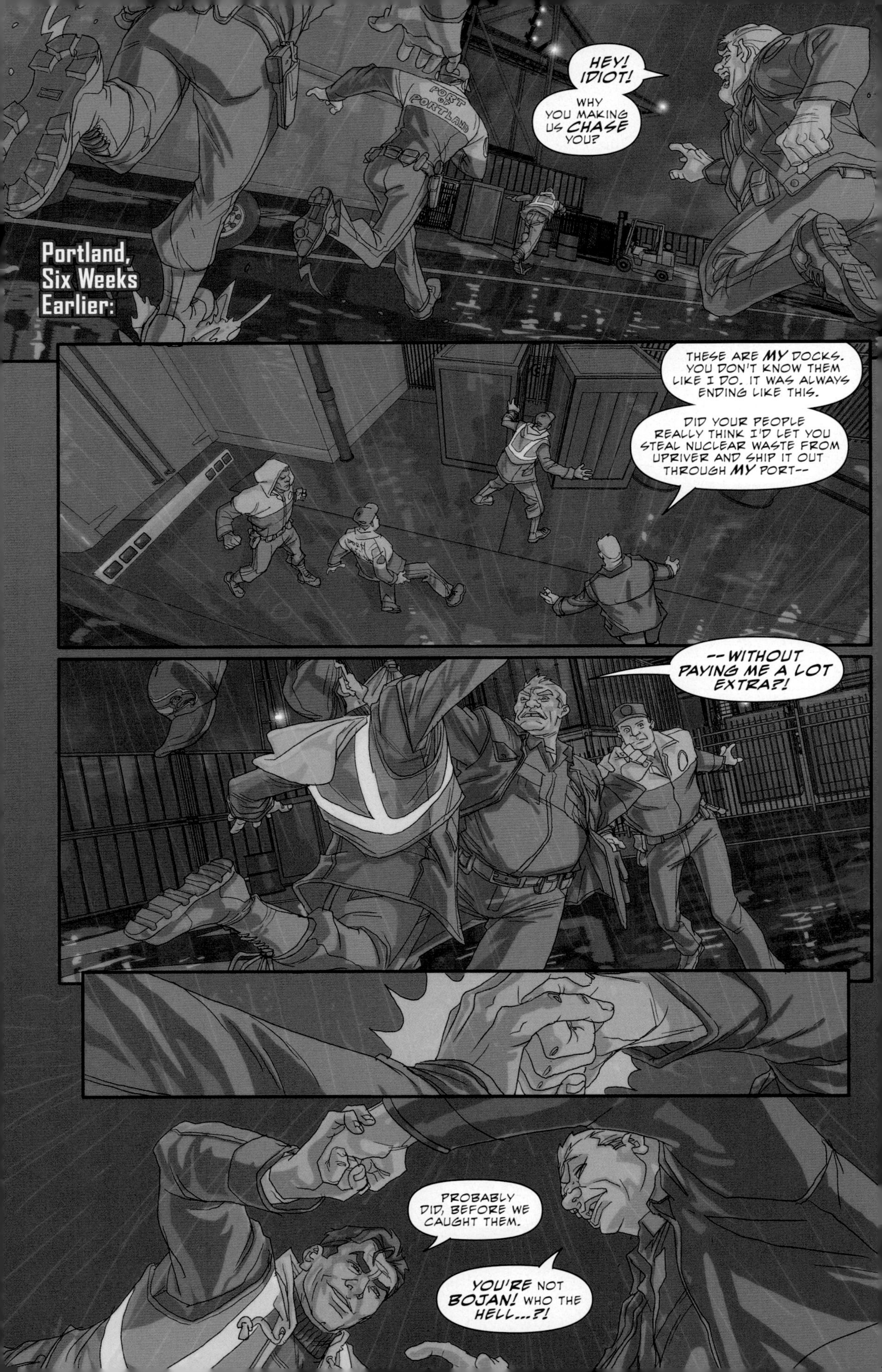
HEY! IDIOT!
WHY YOU MAKING US CHASE YOU?
PORT OF PORTLAND
Portland, Six Weeks Earlier:
THESE ARE MY DOCKS. YOU DON'T KNOW THEM LIKE I DO. IT WAS ALWAYS ENDING LIKE THIS.
DID YOUR PEOPLE REALLY THINK I'D LET YOU STEAL NUCLEAR WASTE FROM UPRIVER AND SHIP IT OUT THROUGH MY PORT--
--WITHOUT PAYING ME A LOT EXTRA?!
PROBABLY DID, BEFORE WE CAUGHT THEM.
YOU'RE NOT BOJAN! WHO THE HELL...?!

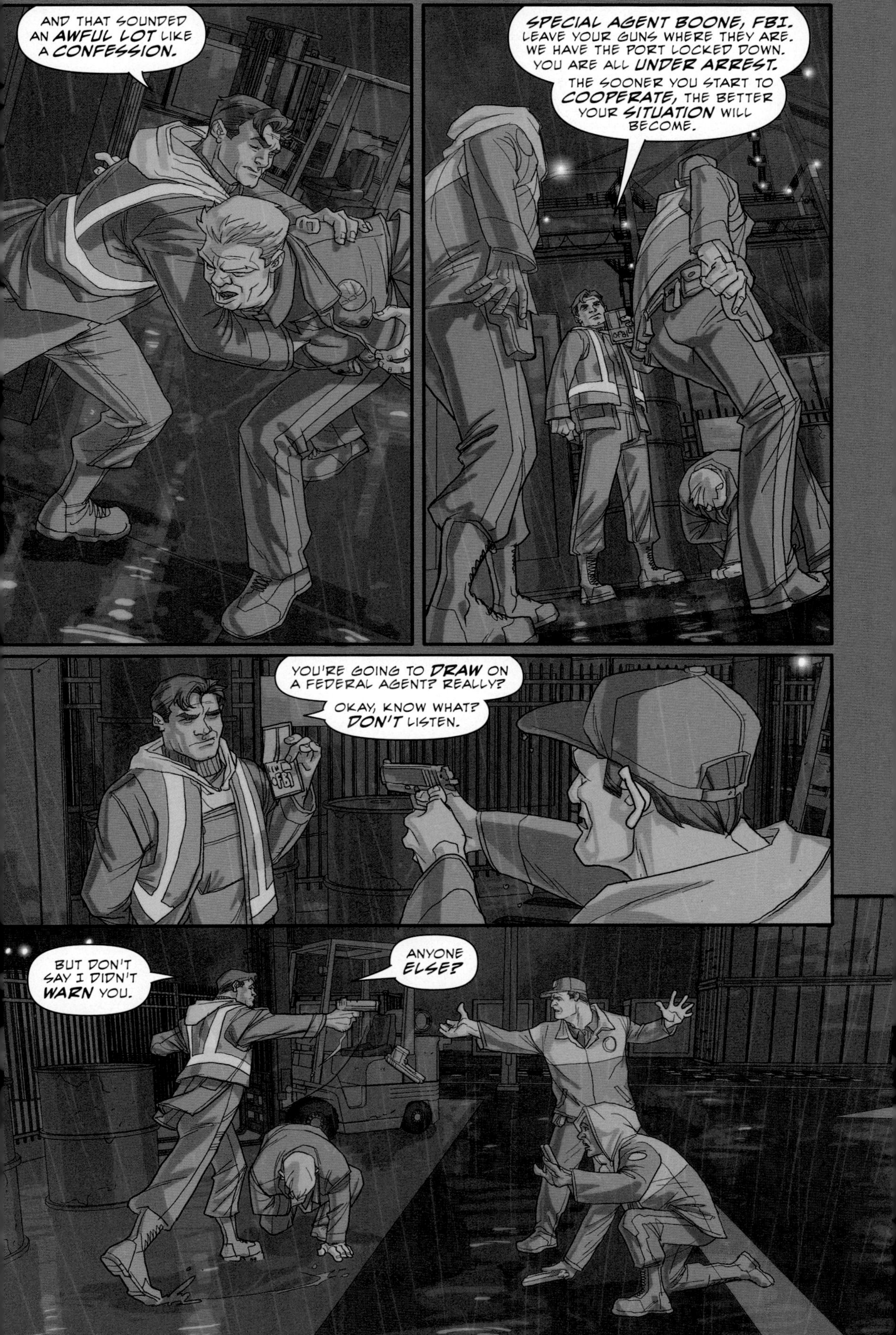
AND THAT SOUNDED AN AWFUL LOT LIKE A CONFESSION.
SPECIAL AGENT BOONE, FBI. LEAVE YOUR GUNS WHERE THEY ARE. WE HAVE THE PORT LOCKED DOWN. YOU ARE ALL UNDER ARREST.
THE SOONER YOU START TO COOPERATE, THE BETTER YOUR SITUATION WILL BECOME.
FBI
YOU'RE GOING TO DRAW ON A FEDERAL AGENT? REALLY?
OKAY, KNOW WHAT? DON'T LISTEN.
BUT DON'T SAY I DIDN'T WARN YOU.
ANYONE ELSE?

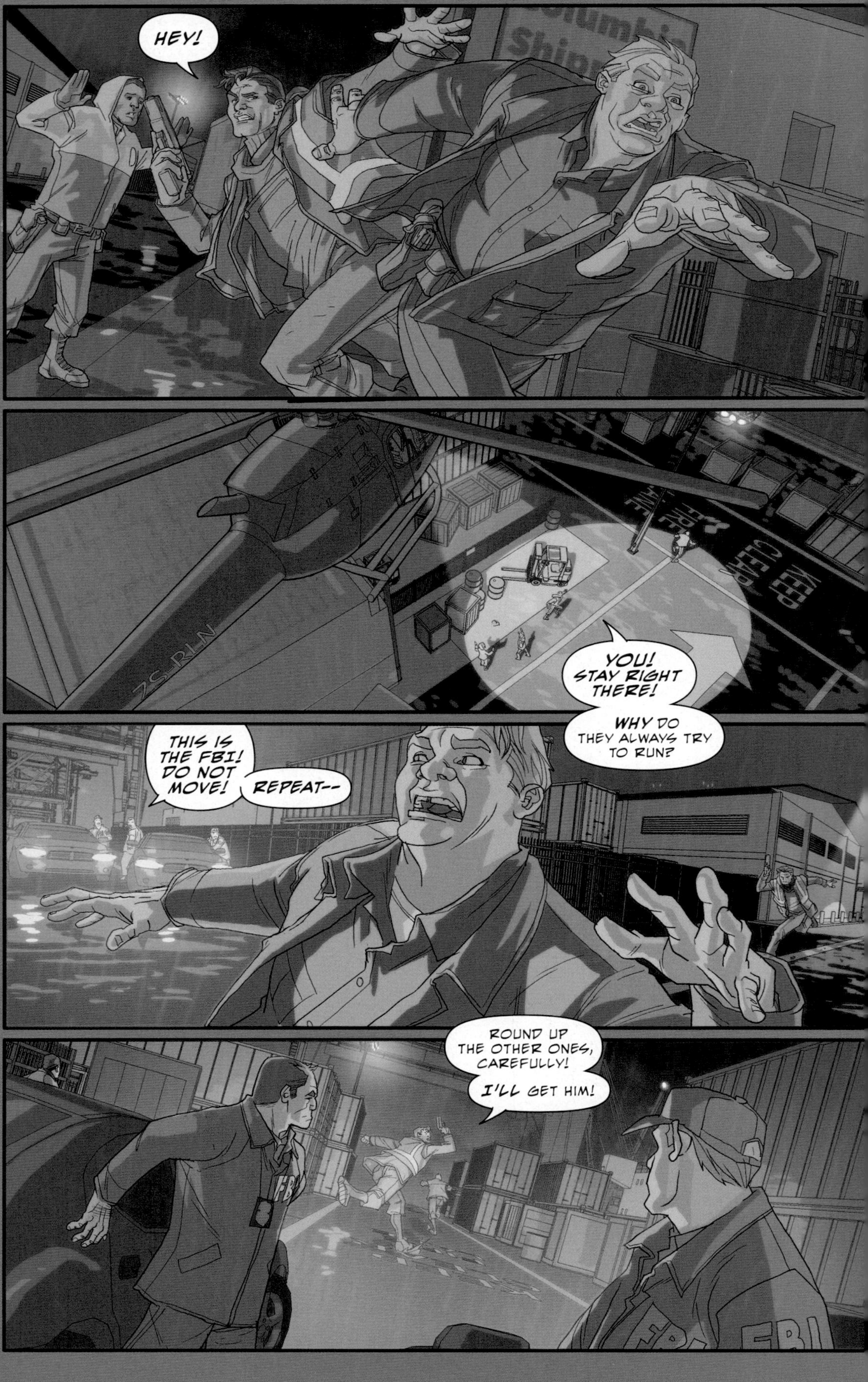
HEY!
YOU! STAY RIGHT THERE!
WHY DO THEY ALWAYS TRY TO RUN?
THIS IS THE FBI! DO NOT MOVE!
REPEAT--
ROUND UP THE OTHER ONES, CAREFULLY!
I'LL GET HIM!
KEEP CLEAR
FIRE LANE
FBI

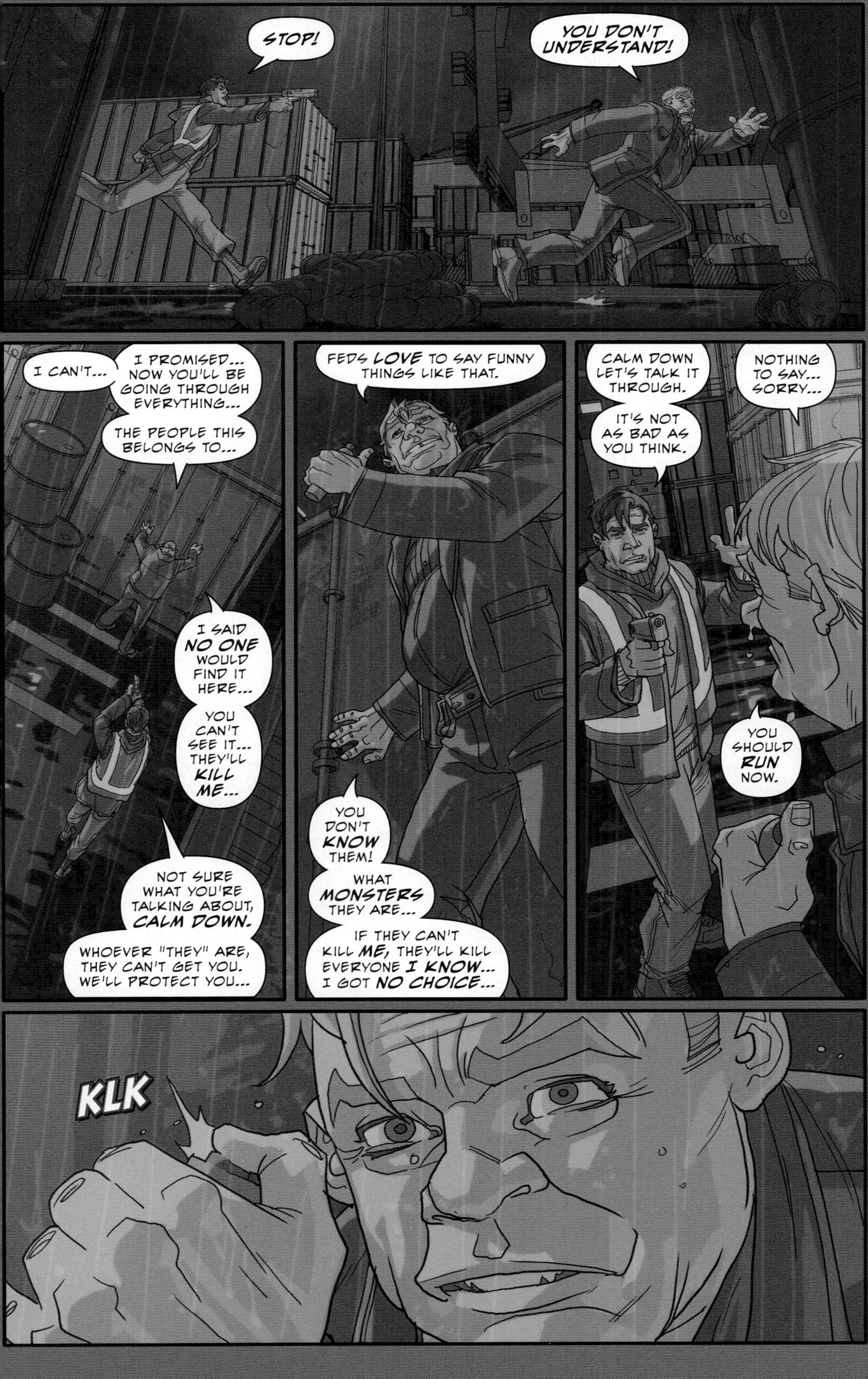

STOP!
YOU DON'T UNDERSTAND!
I CAN'T...
I PROMISED... NOW YOU'LL BE GOING THROUGH EVERYTHING...
THE PEOPLE THIS BELONGS TO...
I SAID NO ONE WOULD FIND IT HERE...
YOU CAN'T SEE IT... THEY'LL KILL ME...
NOT SURE WHAT YOU'RE TALKING ABOUT, CALM DOWN.
WHOEVER "THEY" ARE, THEY CAN'T GET YOU. WE'LL PROTECT YOU...
FEDS LOVE TO SAY FUNNY THINGS LIKE THAT.
YOU DON'T KNOW THEM!
WHAT MONSTERS THEY ARE...
IF THEY CAN'T KILL ME, THEY'LL KILL EVERYONE I KNOW... I GOT NO CHOICE...
CALM DOWN LET'S TALK IT THROUGH.
IT'S NOT AS BAD AS YOU THINK.
NOTHING TO SAY... SORRY...
YOU SHOULD RUN NOW.
KLK

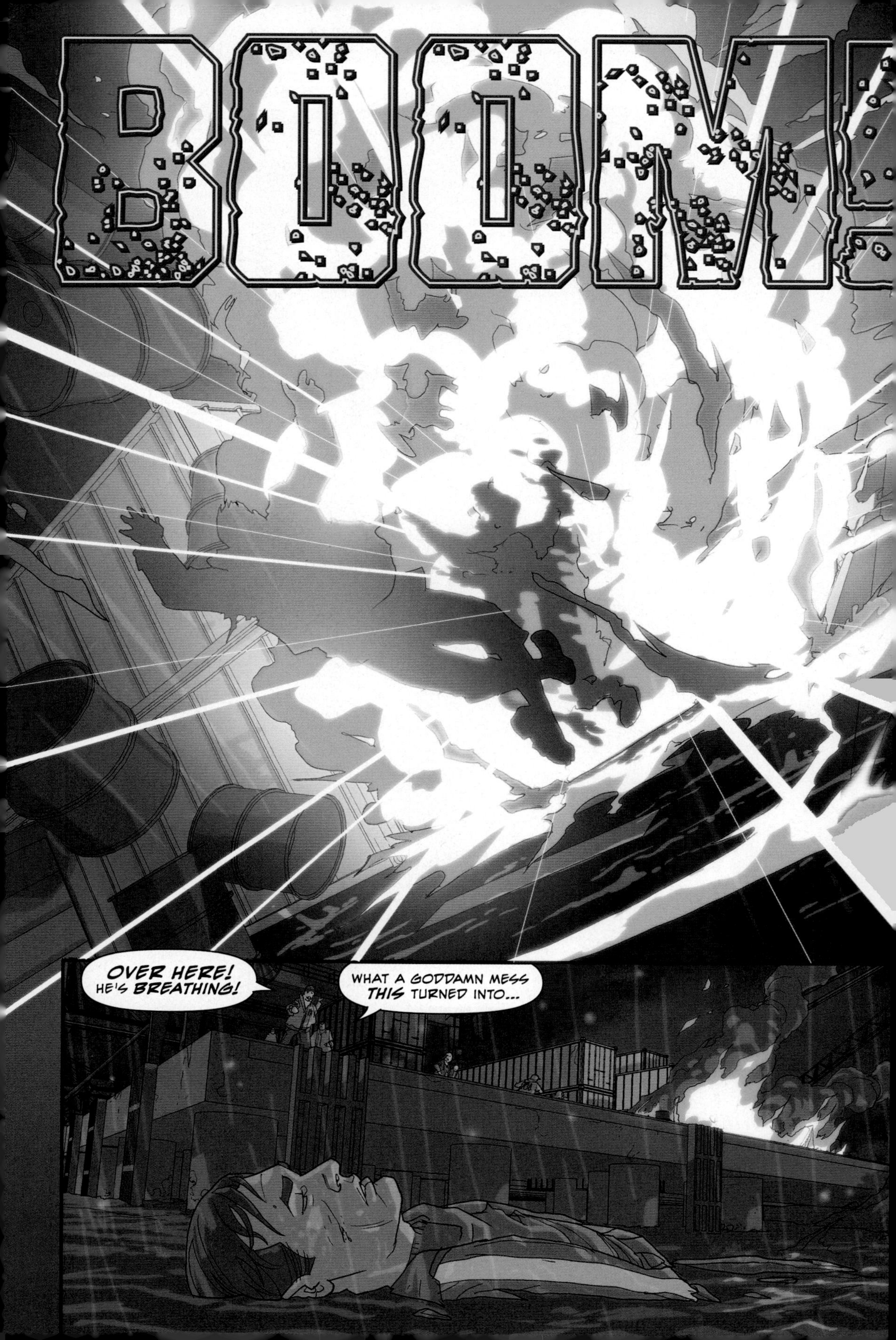
BOOM
OVER HERE! HE'S BREATHING!
WHAT A GODDAMN MESS THIS TURNED INTO...

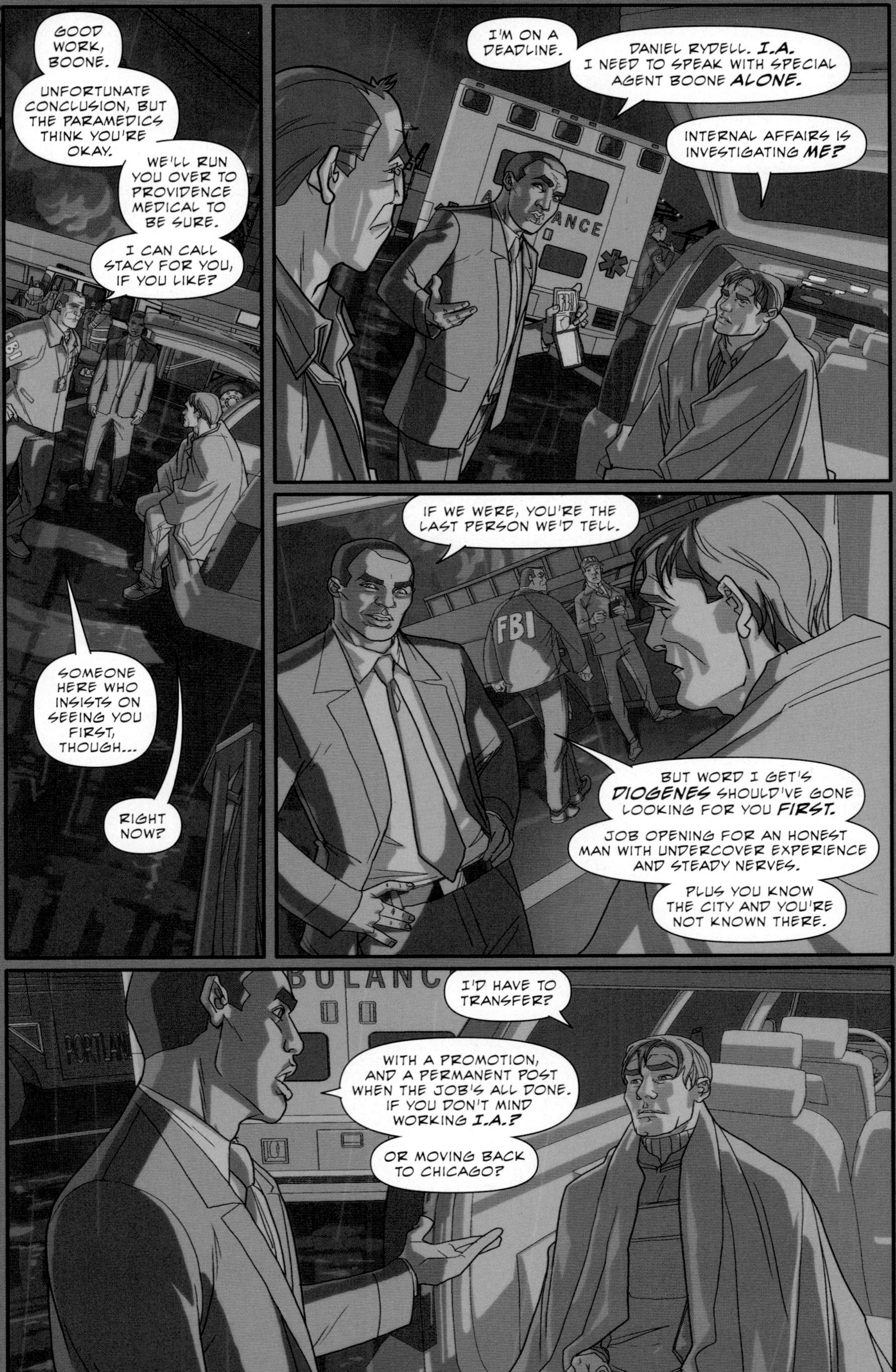
GOOD WORK, BOONE.
UNFORTUNATE CONCLUSION, BUT THE PARAMEDICS THINK YOU'RE OKAY.
WE'LL RUN YOU OVER TO PROVIDENCE MEDICAL TO BE SURE.
I CAN CALL STACY FOR YOU, IF YOU LIKE?
SOMEONE HERE WHO INSISTS ON SEEING YOU FIRST, THOUGH...
RIGHT NOW?
I'M ON A DEADLINE.
DANIEL RYDELL. I.A. I NEED TO SPEAK WITH SPECIAL AGENT BOONE ALONE.
INTERNAL AFFAIRS IS INVESTIGATING ME?
IF WE WERE, YOU'RE THE LAST PERSON WE'D TELL.
BUT WORD I GET'S DIOGENES SHOULD'VE GONE LOOKING FOR YOU FIRST.
JOB OPENING FOR AN HONEST MAN WITH UNDERCOVER EXPERIENCE AND STEADY NERVES.
PLUS YOU KNOW THE CITY AND YOU'RE NOT KNOWN THERE.
I'D HAVE TO TRANSFER?
WITH A PROMOTION, AND A PERMANENT POST WHEN THE JOB'S ALL DONE. IF YOU DON'T MIND WORKING I.A.?
OR MOVING BACK TO CHICAGO?

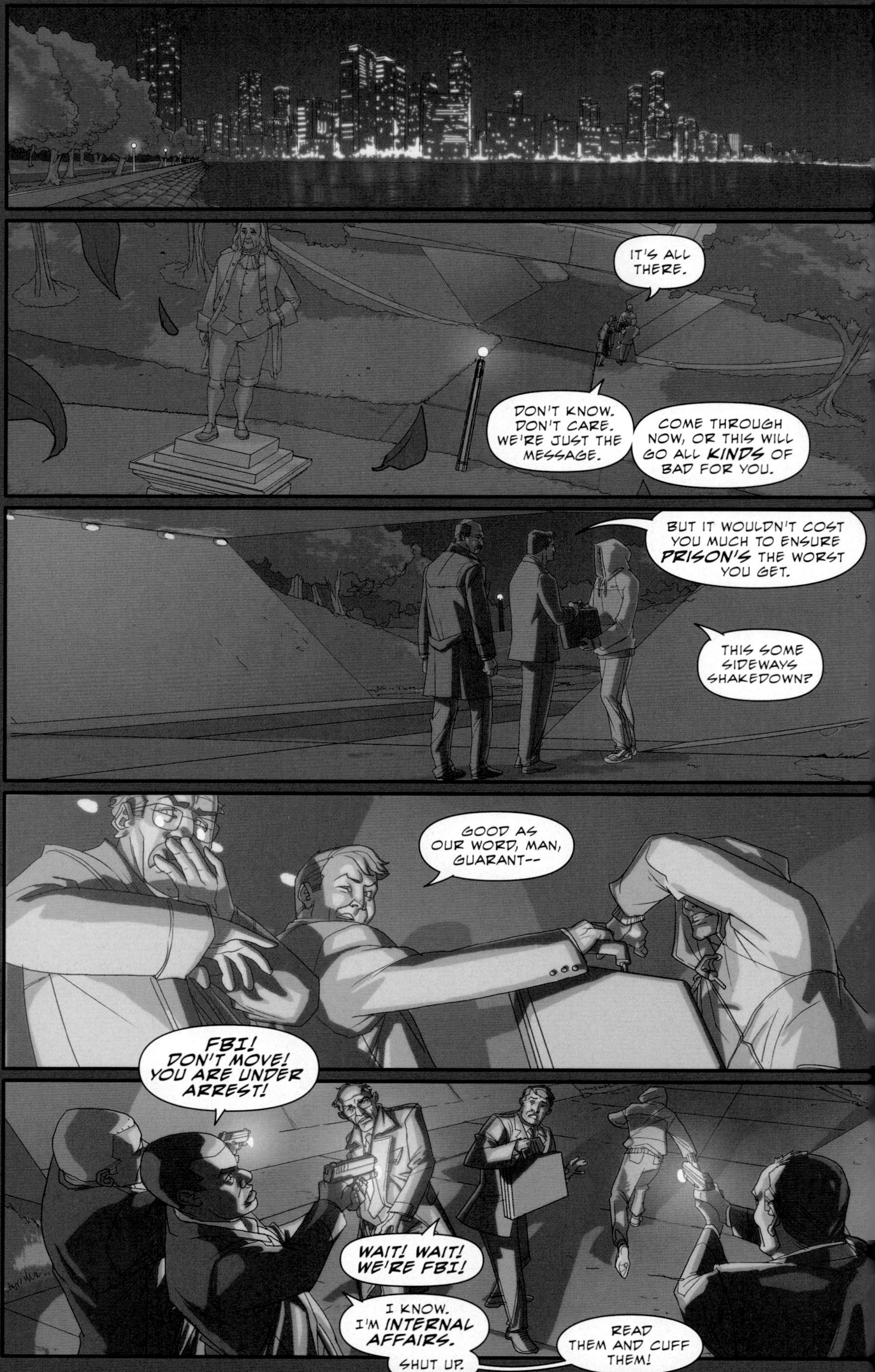
IT'S ALL THERE.
DON'T KNOW. DON'T CARE. WE'RE JUST THE MESSAGE.
COME THROUGH NOW, OR THIS WILL GO ALL KINDS OF BAD FOR YOU.
BUT IT WOULDN'T COST YOU MUCH TO ENSURE PRISON'S THE WORST YOU GET.
THIS SOME SIDEWAYS SHAKEDOWN?
GOOD AS OUR WORD, MAN, GUARANT--
FBI! DON'T MOVE! YOU ARE UNDER ARREST!
WAIT! WAIT! WE'RE FBI!
I KNOW. I'M INTERNAL AFFAIRS.
SHUT UP.
READ THEM AND CUFF THEM!

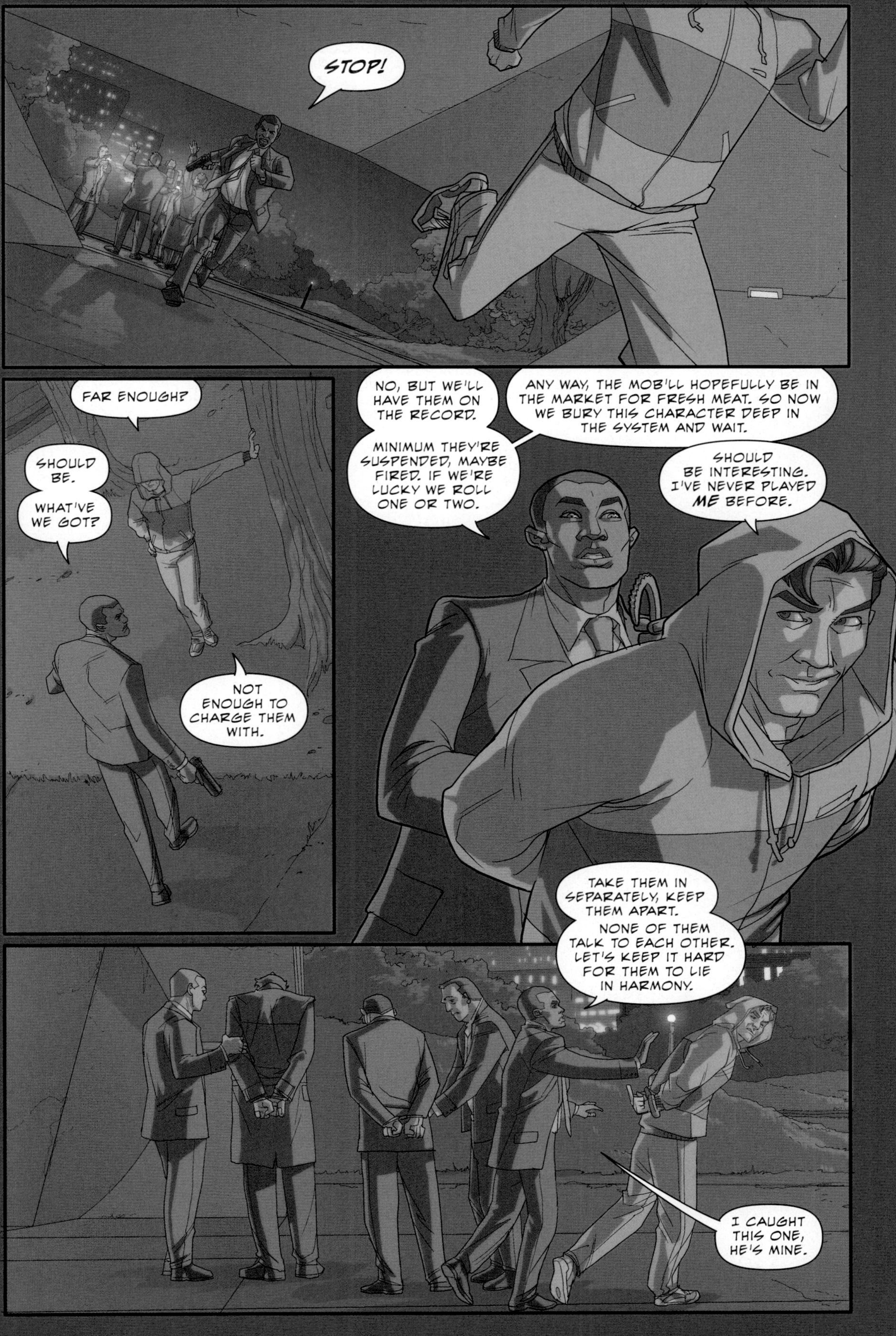
STOP!
FAR ENOUGH?
SHOULD BE.
WHAT'VE WE GOT?
NOT ENOUGH TO CHARGE THEM WITH.
NO, BUT WE'LL HAVE THEM ON THE RECORD.
MINIMUM THEY'RE SUSPENDED, MAYBE FIRED. IF WE'RE LUCKY WE ROLL ONE OR TWO.
ANY WAY, THE MOB'LL HOPEFULLY BE IN THE MARKET FOR FRESH MEAT. SO NOW WE BURY THIS CHARACTER DEEP IN THE SYSTEM AND WAIT.
SHOULD BE INTERESTING. I'VE NEVER PLAYED ME BEFORE.
TAKE THEM IN SEPARATELY, KEEP THEM APART.
NONE OF THEM TALK TO EACH OTHER. LET'S KEEP IT HARD FOR THEM TO LIE IN HARMONY.
I CAUGHT THIS ONE, HE'S MINE.

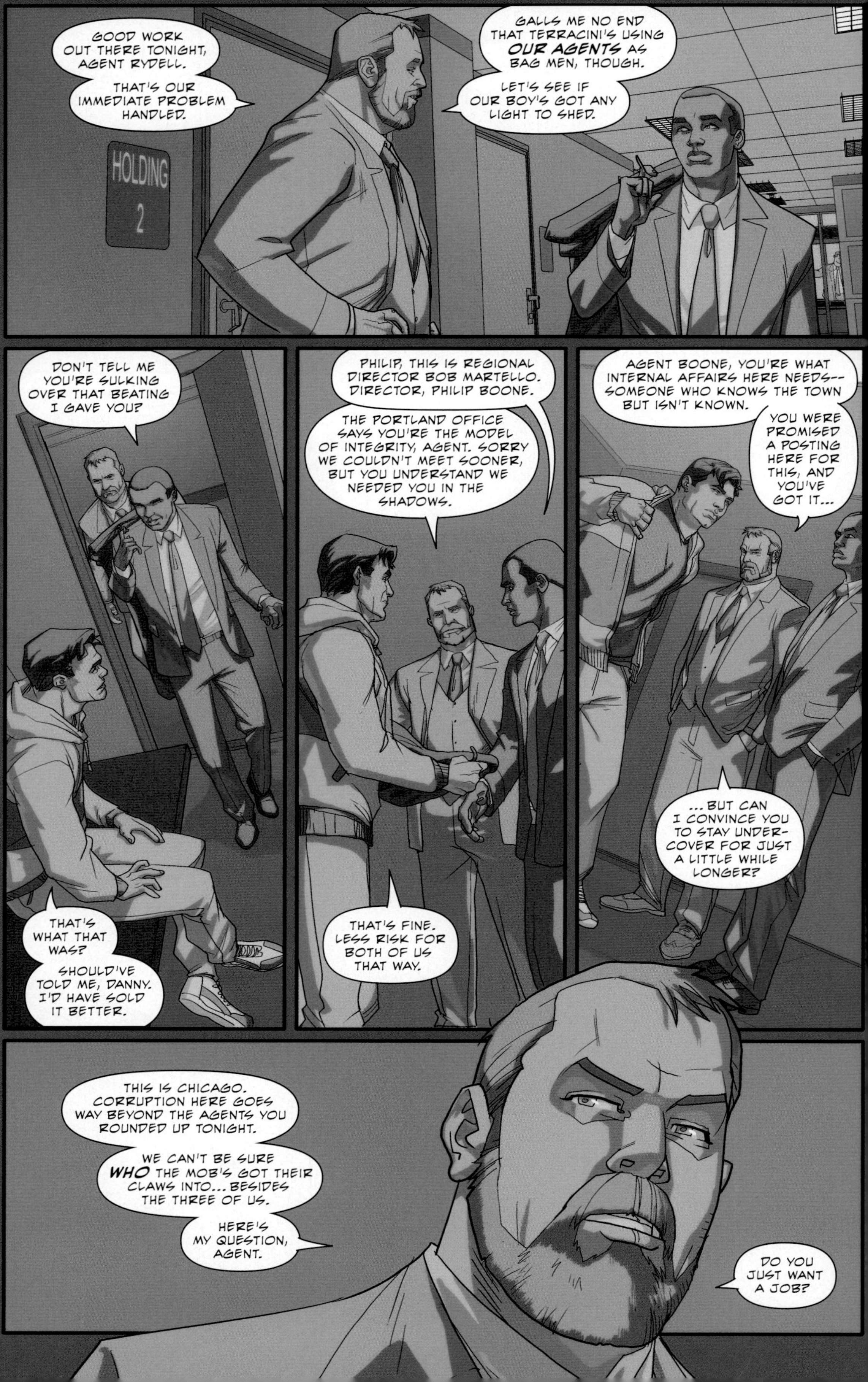
GOOD WORK OUT THERE TONIGHT, AGENT RYDELL.
THAT'S OUR IMMEDIATE PROBLEM HANDLED.
HOLDING 2
GALLS ME NO END THAT TERRACINI'S USING OUR AGENTS AS BAG MEN, THOUGH.
LET'S SEE IF OUR BOY'S GOT ANY LIGHT TO SHED.
DON'T TELL ME YOU'RE SULKING OVER THAT BEATING I GAVE YOU?
THAT'S WHAT THAT WAS?
SHOULD'VE TOLD ME, DANNY. I'D HAVE SOLD IT BETTER.
PHILIP, THIS IS REGIONAL DIRECTOR BOB MARTELLO. DIRECTOR, PHILIP BOONE.
THE PORTLAND OFFICE SAYS YOU'RE THE MODEL OF INTEGRITY, AGENT. SORRY WE COULDN'T MEET SOONER, BUT YOU UNDERSTAND WE NEEDED YOU IN THE SHADOWS.
THAT'S FINE. LESS RISK FOR BOTH OF US THAT WAY.
AGENT BOONE, YOU'RE WHAT INTERNAL AFFAIRS HERE NEEDS-- SOMEONE WHO KNOWS THE TOWN BUT ISN'T KNOWN.
YOU WERE PROMISED A POSTING HERE FOR THIS, AND YOU'VE GOT IT...
...BUT CAN I CONVINCE YOU TO STAY UNDER-COVER FOR JUST A LITTLE WHILE LONGER?
THIS IS CHICAGO. CORRUPTION HERE GOES WAY BEYOND THE AGENTS YOU ROUNDED UP TONIGHT.
WE CAN'T BE SURE WHO THE MOB'S GOT THEIR CLAWS INTO... BESIDES THE THREE OF US.
HERE'S MY QUESTION, AGENT.
DO YOU JUST WANT A JOB?

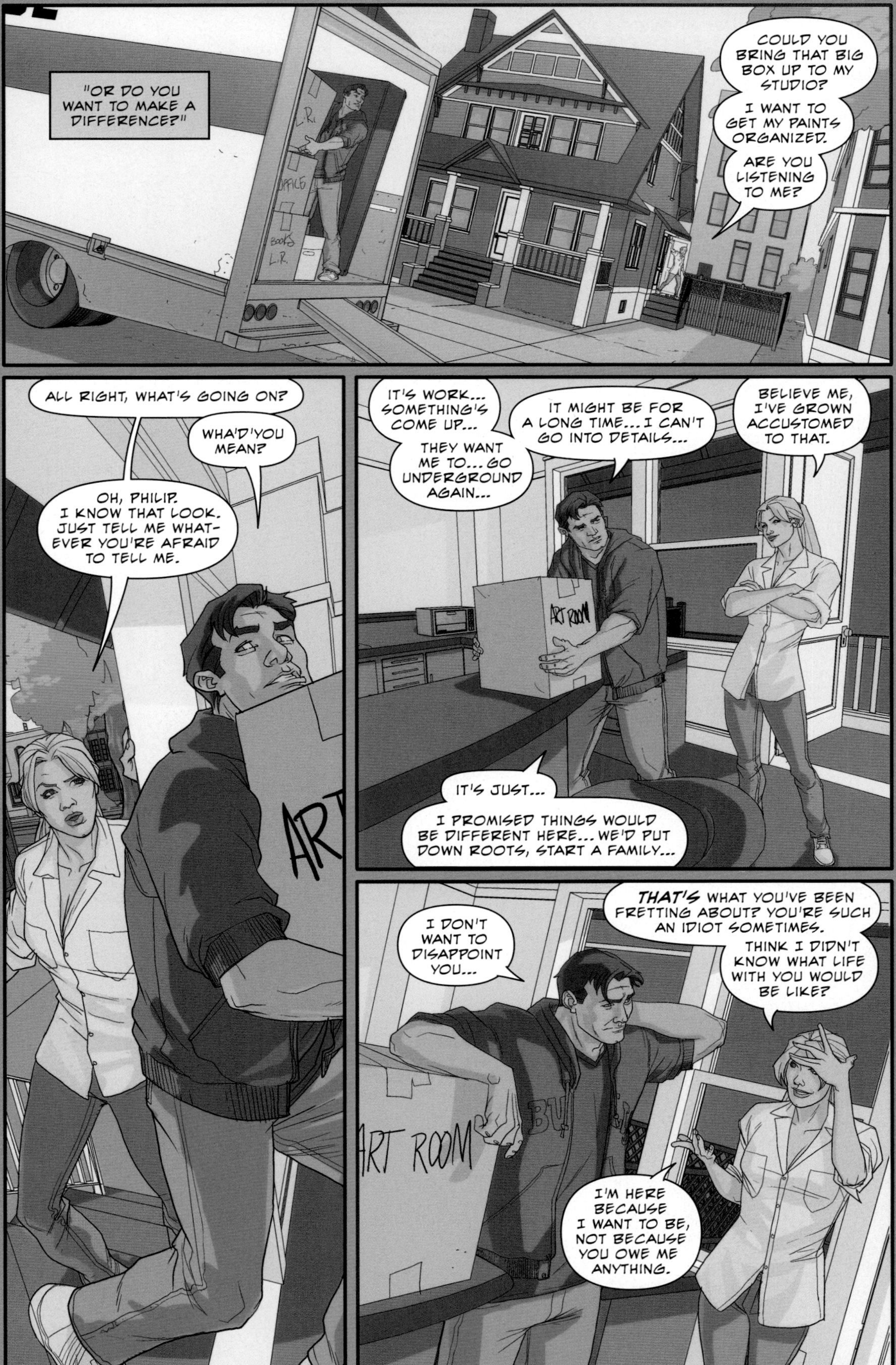
"OR DO YOU WANT TO MAKE A DIFFERENCE?"
COULD YOU BRING THAT BIG BOX UP TO MY STUDIO?
I WANT TO GET MY PAINTS ORGANIZED.
ARE YOU LISTENING TO ME?
ALL RIGHT, WHAT'S GOING ON?
WHA'D'YOU MEAN?
OH, PHILIP. I KNOW THAT LOOK. JUST TELL ME WHAT-EVER YOU'RE AFRAID TO TELL ME.
IT'S WORK... SOMETHING'S COME UP...
THEY WANT ME TO... GO UNDERGROUND AGAIN...
IT MIGHT BE FOR A LONG TIME... I CAN'T GO INTO DETAILS...
BELIEVE ME, I'VE GROWN ACCUSTOMED TO THAT.
IT'S JUST...
I PROMISED THINGS WOULD BE DIFFERENT HERE... WE'D PUT DOWN ROOTS, START A FAMILY...
I DON'T WANT TO DISAPPOINT YOU...
THAT'S WHAT YOU'VE BEEN FRETTING ABOUT? YOU'RE SUCH AN IDIOT SOMETIMES.
THINK I DIDN'T KNOW WHAT LIFE WITH YOU WOULD BE LIKE?
I'M HERE BECAUSE I WANT TO BE, NOT BECAUSE YOU OWE ME ANYTHING.

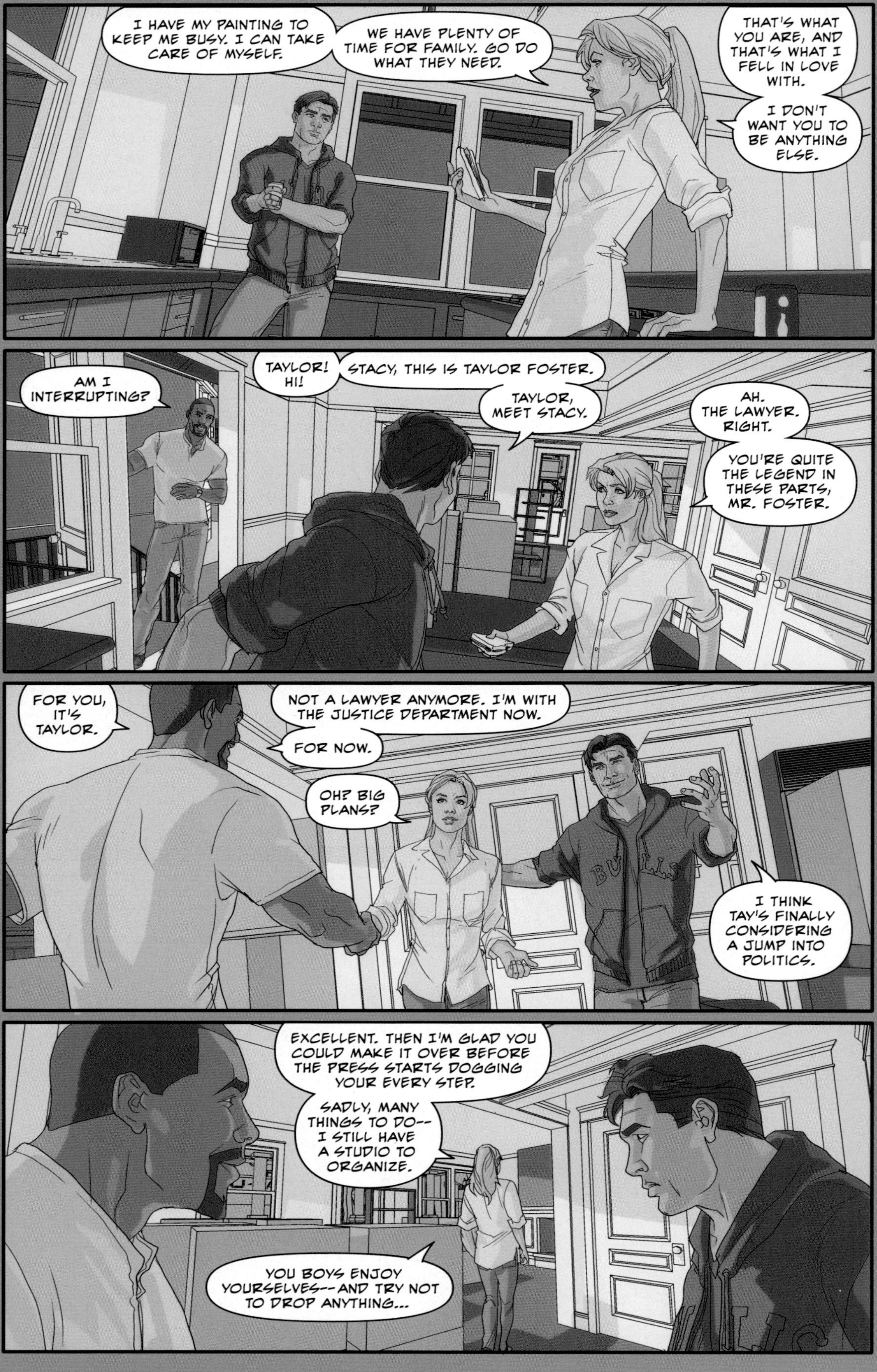
I HAVE MY PAINTING TO KEEP ME BUSY. I CAN TAKE CARE OF MYSELF.
WE HAVE PLENTY OF TIME FOR FAMILY. GO DO WHAT THEY NEED.
THAT'S WHAT YOU ARE, AND THAT'S WHAT I FELL IN LOVE WITH.
I DON'T WANT YOU TO BE ANYTHING ELSE.
AM I INTERRUPTING?
TAYLOR! HI!
STACY, THIS IS TAYLOR FOSTER.
TAYLOR, MEET STACY.
AH. THE LAWYER. RIGHT.
YOU'RE QUITE THE LEGEND IN THESE PARTS, MR. FOSTER.
FOR YOU, IT'S TAYLOR.
NOT A LAWYER ANYMORE. I'M WITH THE JUSTICE DEPARTMENT NOW.
FOR NOW.
OH? BIG PLANS?
I THINK TAY'S FINALLY CONSIDERING A JUMP INTO POLITICS.
EXCELLENT. THEN I'M GLAD YOU COULD MAKE IT OVER BEFORE THE PRESS STARTS DOGGING YOUR EVERY STEP.
SADLY, MANY THINGS TO DO-- I STILL HAVE A STUDIO TO ORGANIZE.
YOU BOYS ENJOY YOURSELVES--AND TRY NOT TO DROP ANYTHING...

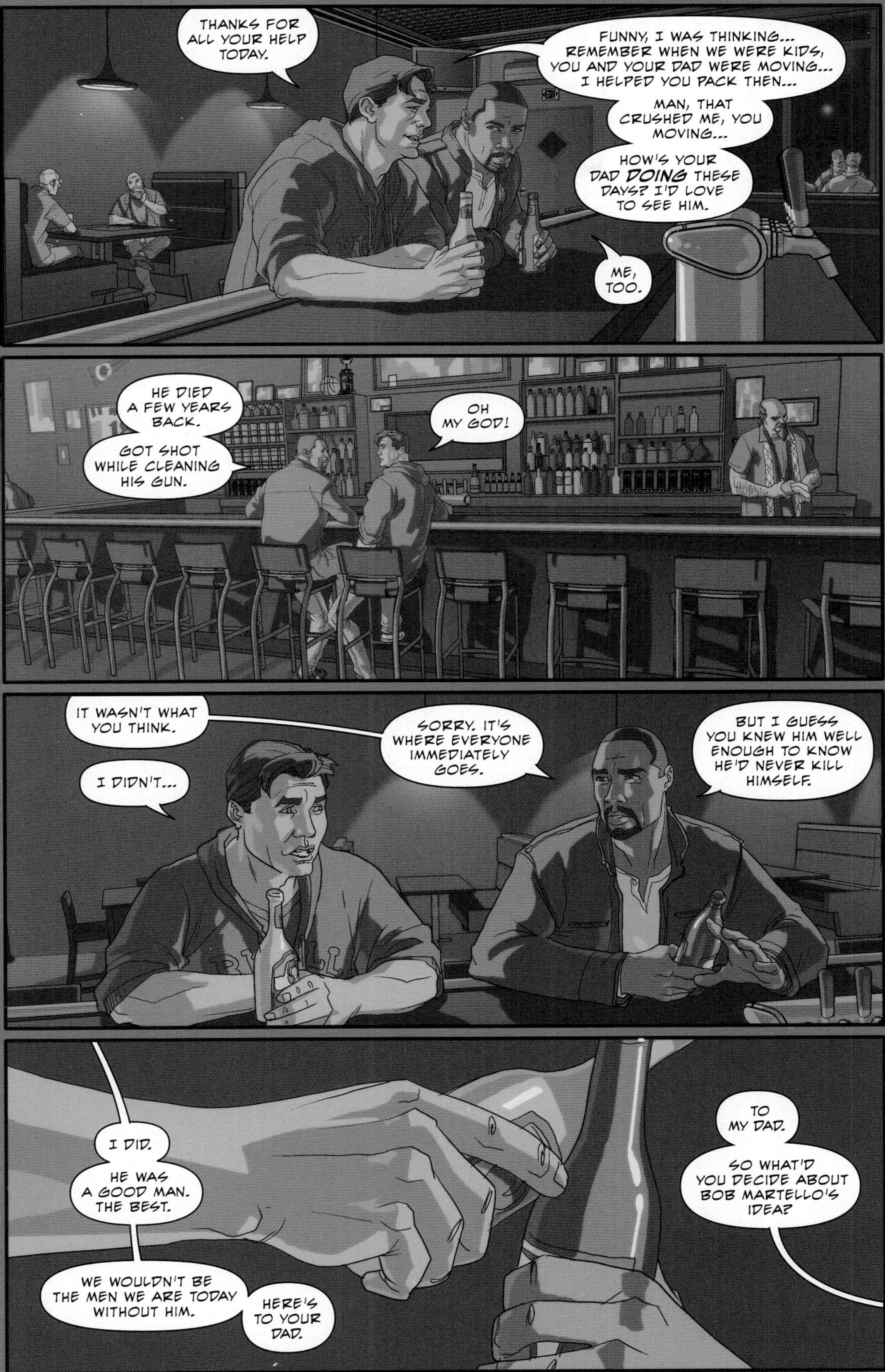
THANKS FOR ALL YOUR HELP TODAY.
FUNNY, I WAS THINKING... REMEMBER WHEN WE WERE KIDS, YOU AND YOUR DAD WERE MOVING... I HELPED YOU PACK THEN...
MAN, THAT CRUSHED ME, YOU MOVING...
HOW'S YOUR DAD DOING THESE DAYS? I'D LOVE TO SEE HIM.
ME, TOO.
HE DIED A FEW YEARS BACK.
GOT SHOT WHILE CLEANING HIS GUN.
OH MY GOD!
IT WASN'T WHAT YOU THINK.
I DIDN'T...
SORRY. IT'S WHERE EVERYONE IMMEDIATELY GOES.
BUT I GUESS YOU KNEW HIM WELL ENOUGH TO KNOW HE'D NEVER KILL HIMSELF.
I DID.
HE WAS A GOOD MAN. THE BEST.
WE WOULDN'T BE THE MEN WE ARE TODAY WITHOUT HIM.
HERE'S TO YOUR DAD.
TO MY DAD.
SO WHAT'D YOU DECIDE ABOUT BOB MARTELLO'S IDEA?

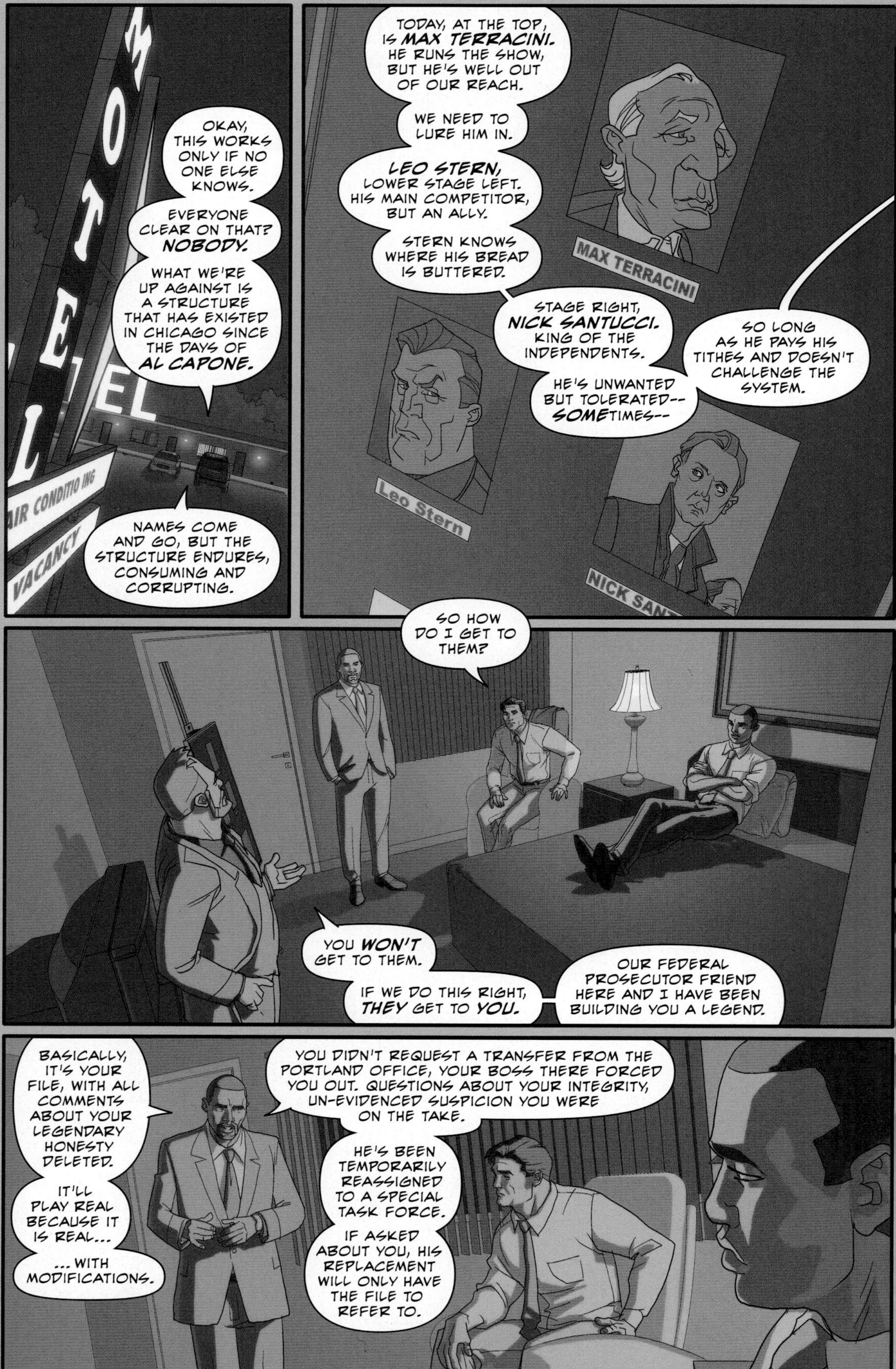
MOTEL
OKAY, THIS WORKS ONLY IF NO ONE ELSE KNOWS.
EVERYONE CLEAR ON THAT? NOBODY.
WHAT WE'RE UP AGAINST IS A STRUCTURE THAT HAS EXISTED IN CHICAGO SINCE THE DAYS OF AL CAPONE.
AIR CONDITIO ING
VACANCY
NAMES COME AND GO, BUT THE STRUCTURE ENDURES, CONSUMING AND CORRUPTING.
TODAY, AT THE TOP, IS MAX TERRACINI. HE RUNS THE SHOW, BUT HE'S WELL OUT OF OUR REACH.
WE NEED TO LURE HIM IN.
LEO STERN, LOWER STAGE LEFT. HIS MAIN COMPETITOR, BUT AN ALLY.
STERN KNOWS WHERE HIS BREAD IS BUTTERED.
MAX TERRACINI
STAGE RIGHT, NICK SANTUCCI. KING OF THE INDEPENDENTS.
HE'S UNWANTED BUT TOLERATED-- SOMETIMES--
SO LONG AS HE PAYS HIS TITHES AND DOESN'T CHALLENGE THE SYSTEM.
Leo Stern
SO HOW DO I GET TO THEM?
YOU WON'T GET TO THEM.
IF WE DO THIS RIGHT, THEY GET TO YOU.
OUR FEDERAL PROSECUTOR FRIEND HERE AND I HAVE BEEN BUILDING YOU A LEGEND.
BASICALLY, IT'S YOUR FILE, WITH ALL COMMENTS ABOUT YOUR LEGENDARY HONESTY DELETED.
IT'LL PLAY REAL BECAUSE IT IS REAL...
...WITH MODIFICATIONS.
YOU DIDN'T REQUEST A TRANSFER FROM THE PORTLAND OFFICE, YOUR BOSS THERE FORCED YOU OUT. QUESTIONS ABOUT YOUR INTEGRITY, UN-EVIDENCED SUSPICION YOU WERE ON THE TAKE.
HE'S BEEN TEMPORARILY REASSIGNED TO A SPECIAL TASK FORCE.
IF ASKED ABOUT YOU, HIS REPLACEMENT WILL ONLY HAVE THE FILE TO REFER TO.

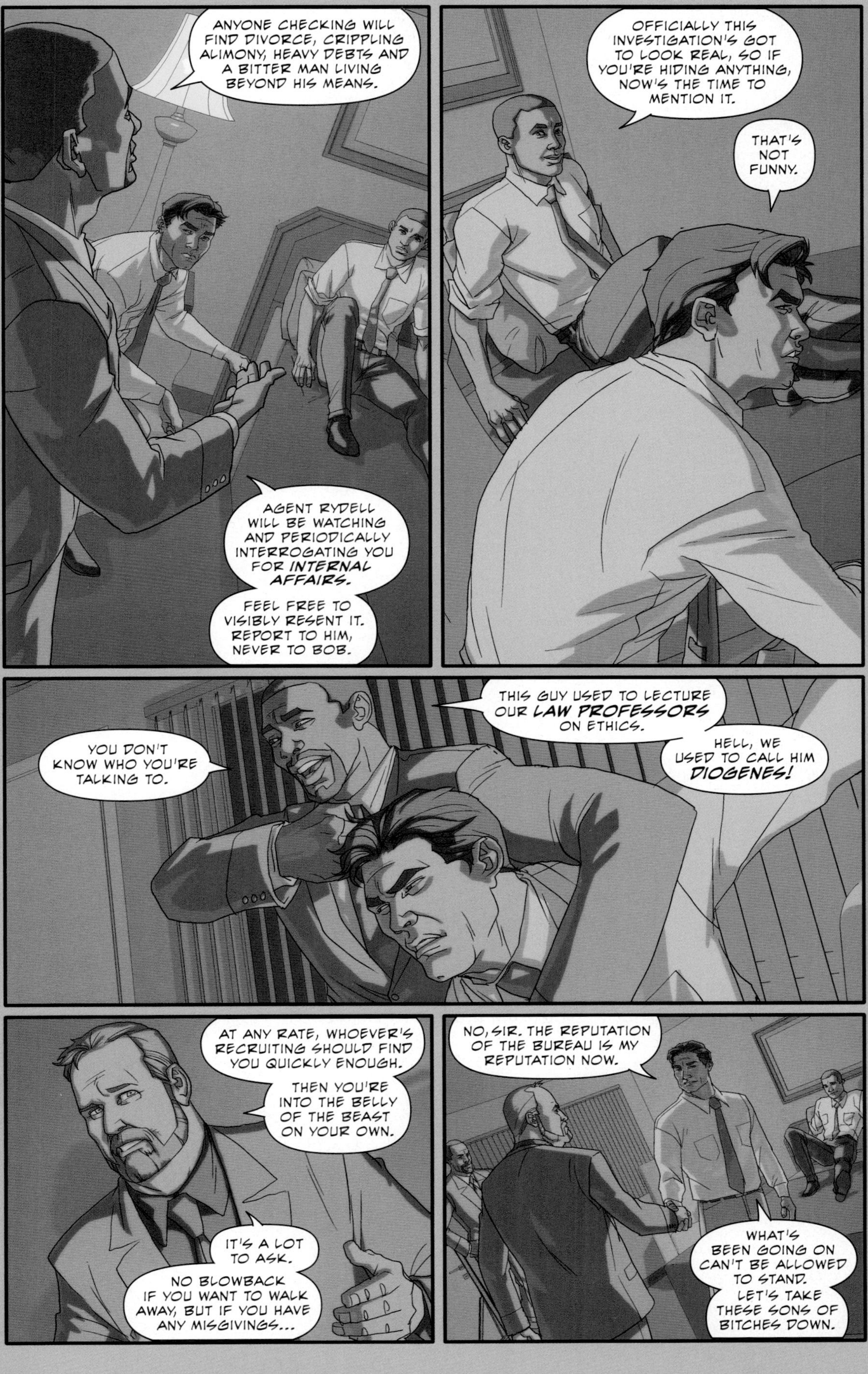
ANYONE CHECKING WILL FIND DIVORCE, CRIPPLING ALIMONY, HEAVY DEBTS AND A BITTER MAN LIVING BEYOND HIS MEANS.
AGENT RYDELL WILL BE WATCHING AND PERIODICALLY INTERROGATING YOU FOR INTERNAL AFFAIRS.
FEEL FREE TO VISIBLY RESENT IT. REPORT TO HIM, NEVER TO BOB.
OFFICIALLY THIS INVESTIGATION'S GOT TO LOOK REAL, SO IF YOU'RE HIDING ANYTHING, NOW'S THE TIME TO MENTION IT.
THAT'S NOT FUNNY.
YOU DON'T KNOW WHO YOU'RE TALKING TO.
THIS GUY USED TO LECTURE OUR LAW PROFESSORS ON ETHICS.
HELL, WE USED TO CALL HIM DIOGENES!
AT ANY RATE, WHOEVER'S RECRUITING SHOULD FIND YOU QUICKLY ENOUGH.
THEN YOU'RE INTO THE BELLY OF THE BEAST ON YOUR OWN.
IT'S A LOT TO ASK.
NO BLOWBACK IF YOU WANT TO WALK AWAY, BUT IF YOU HAVE ANY MISGIVINGS...
NO, SIR. THE REPUTATION OF THE BUREAU IS MY REPUTATION NOW.
WHAT'S BEEN GOING ON CAN'T BE ALLOWED TO STAND.
LET'S TAKE THESE SONS OF BITCHES DOWN.

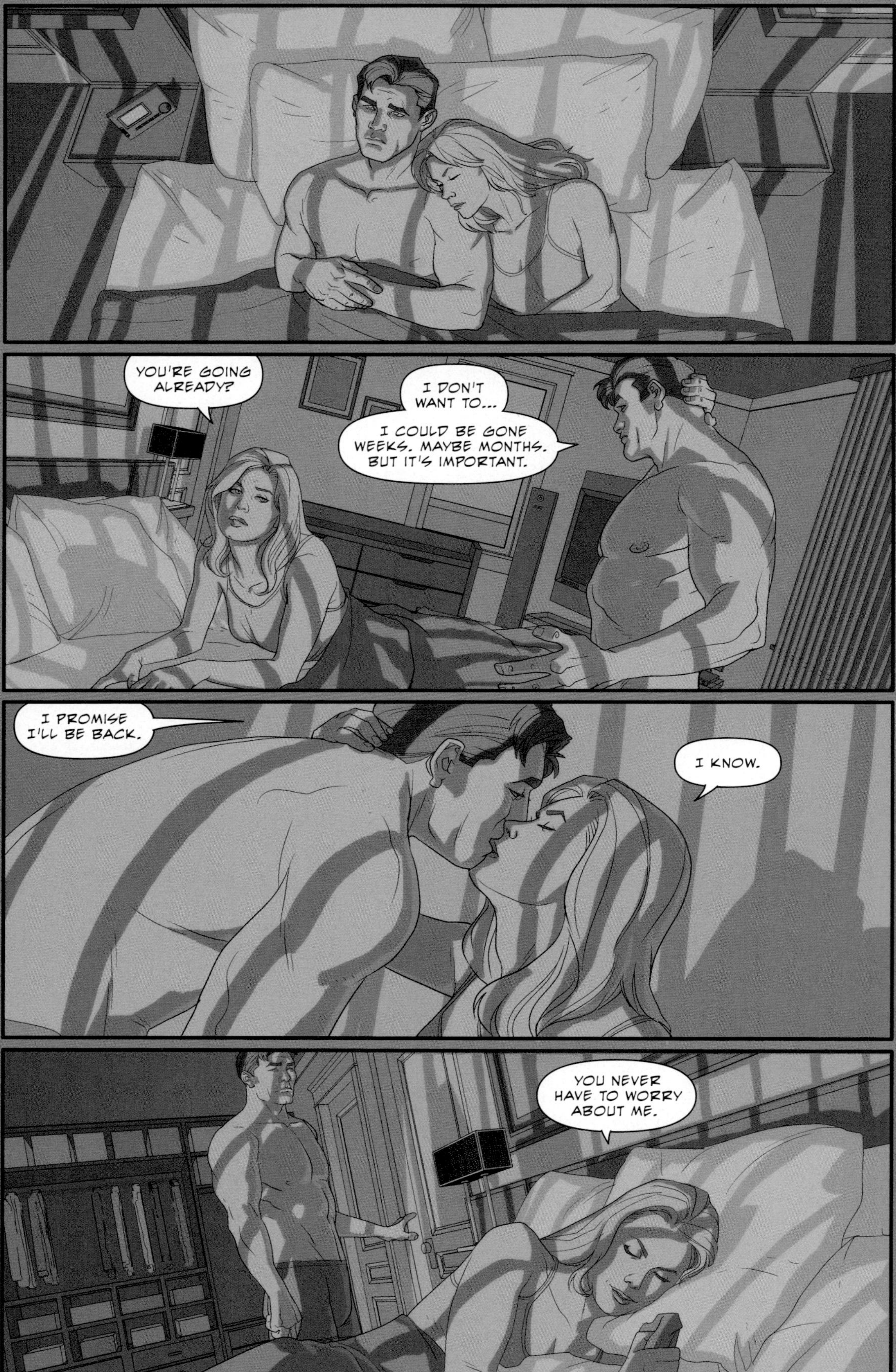
YOU'RE GOING ALREADY?
I DON'T WANT TO...
I COULD BE GONE WEEKS. MAYBE MONTHS. BUT IT'S IMPORTANT.
I PROMISE I'LL BE BACK.
I KNOW.
YOU NEVER HAVE TO WORRY ABOUT ME.

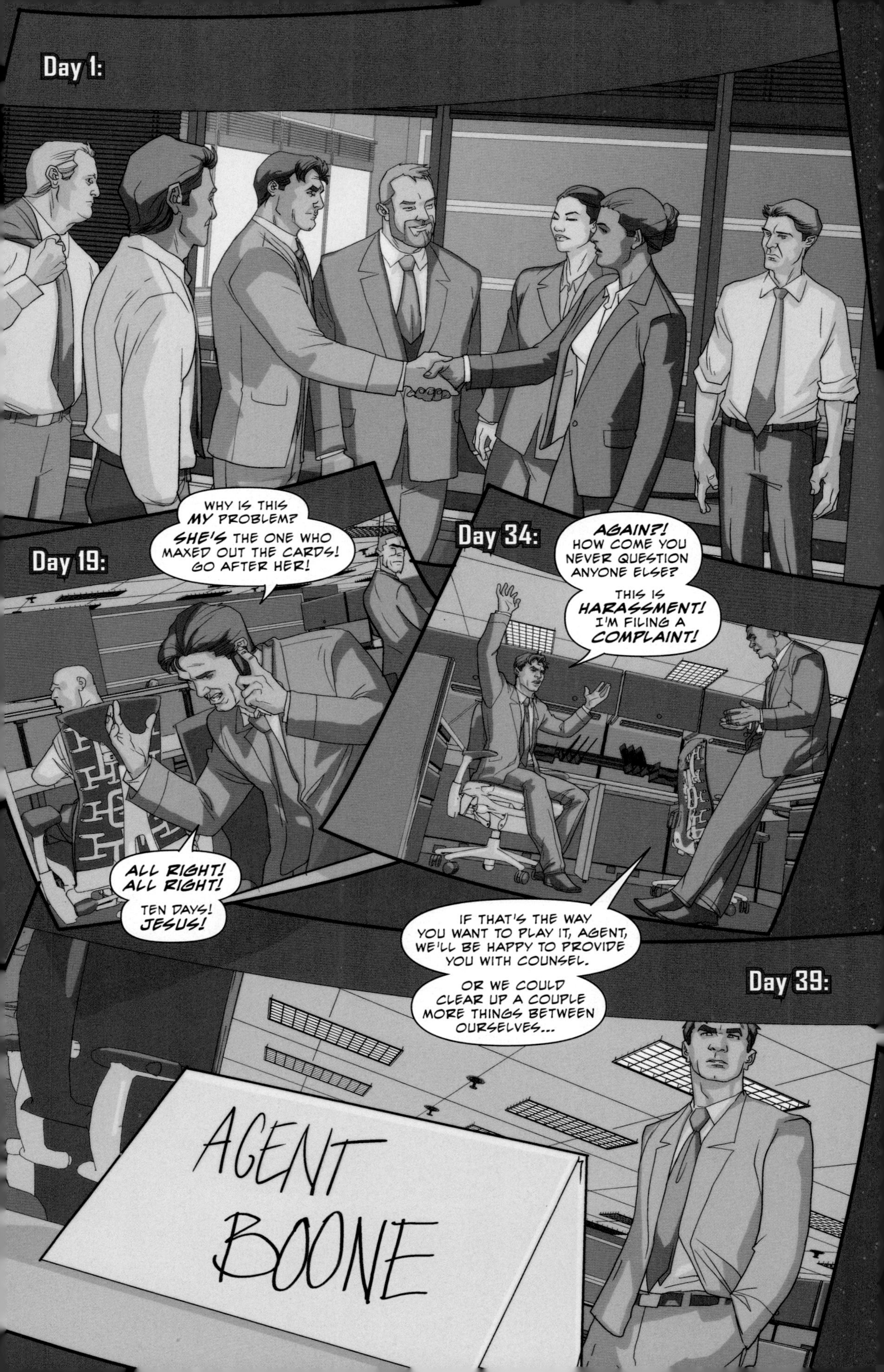

Day 1:
Day 19:
WHY IS THIS MY PROBLEM? SHE'S THE ONE WHO MAXED OUT THE CARDS! GO AFTER HER!
ALL RIGHT! ALL RIGHT! TEN DAYS! JESUS!
Day 34:
AGAIN?! HOW COME YOU NEVER QUESTION ANYONE ELSE? THIS IS HARASSMENT! I'M FILING A COMPLAINT!
IF THAT'S THE WAY YOU WANT TO PLAY IT, AGENT, WE'LL BE HAPPY TO PROVIDE YOU WITH COUNSEL.
OR WE COULD CLEAR UP A COUPLE MORE THINGS BETWEEN OURSELVES...
Day 39:
AGENT BOONE

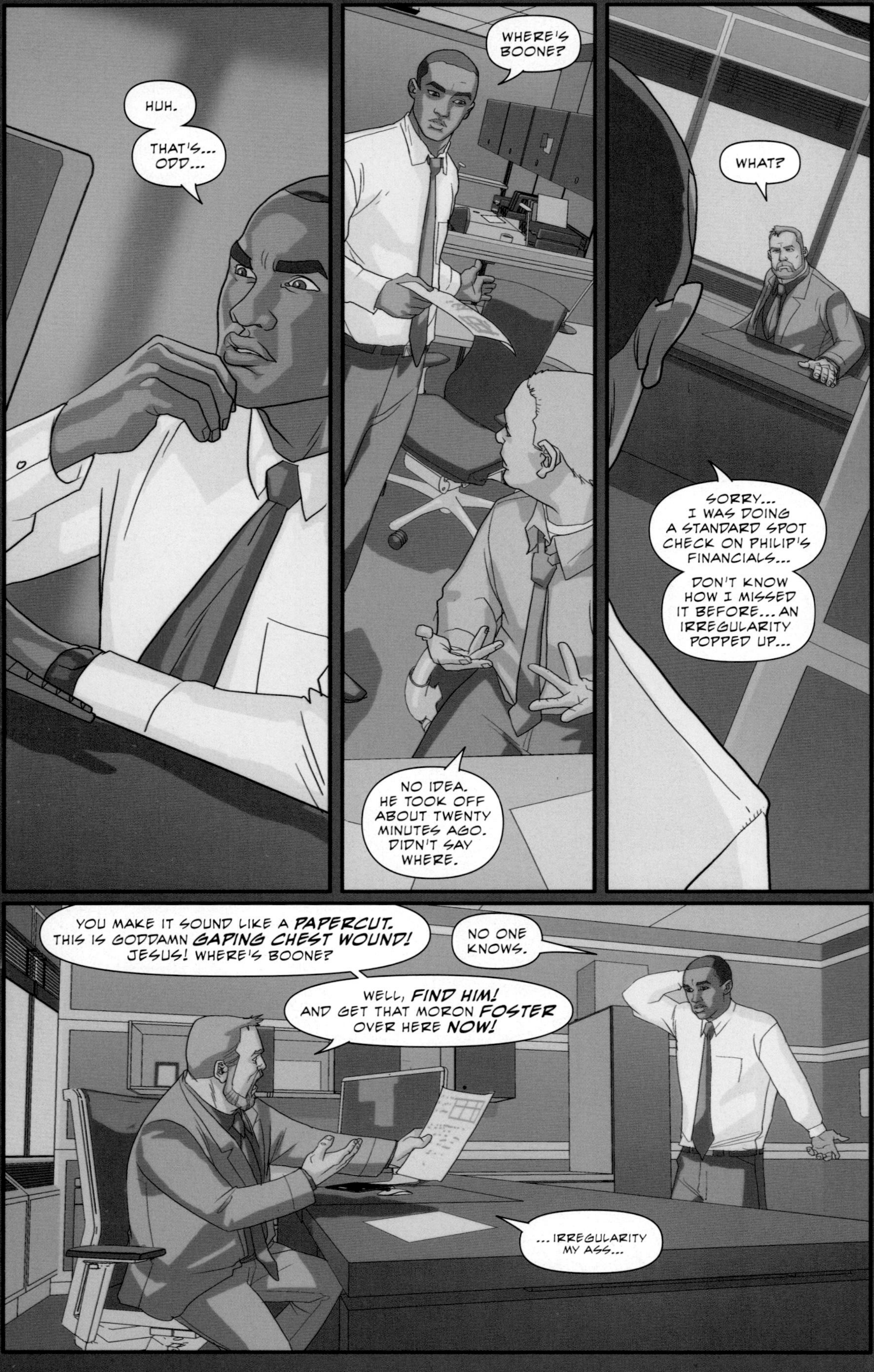
HUH.
THAT'S... ODD...
WHERE'S BOONE?
NO IDEA. HE TOOK OFF ABOUT TWENTY MINUTES AGO. DIDN'T SAY WHERE.
WHAT?
SORRY... I WAS DOING A STANDARD SPOT CHECK ON PHILIP'S FINANCIALS...
DON'T KNOW HOW I MISSED IT BEFORE... AN IRREGULARITY POPPED UP...
YOU MAKE IT SOUND LIKE A PAPERCUT. THIS IS GODDAMN GAPING CHEST WOUND! JESUS! WHERE'S BOONE?
NO ONE KNOWS.
WELL, FIND HIM! AND GET THAT MORON FOSTER OVER HERE NOW!
...IRREGULARITY MY ASS...

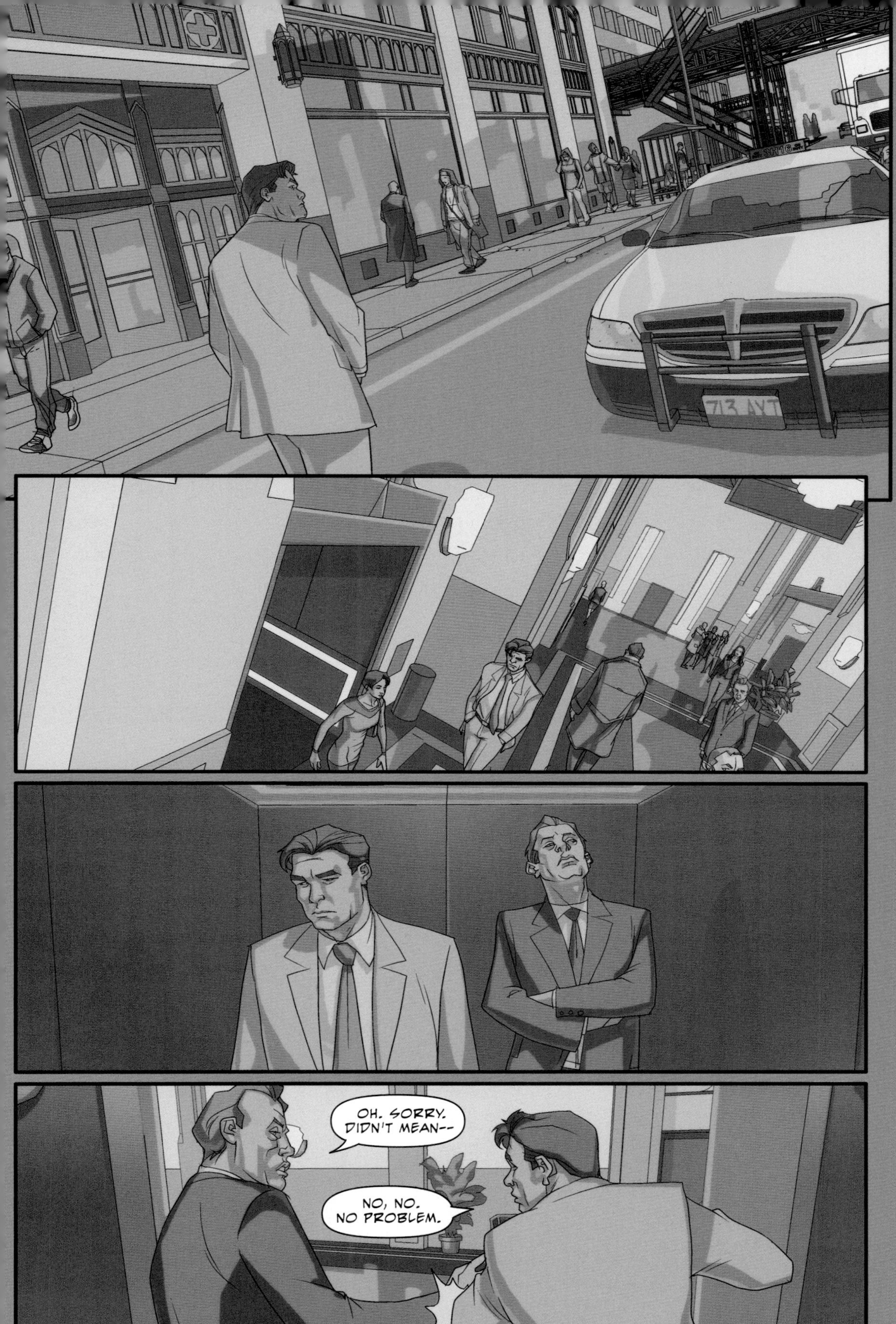

713 AYT
OH. SORRY. DIDN'T MEAN--
NO, NO. NO PROBLEM.

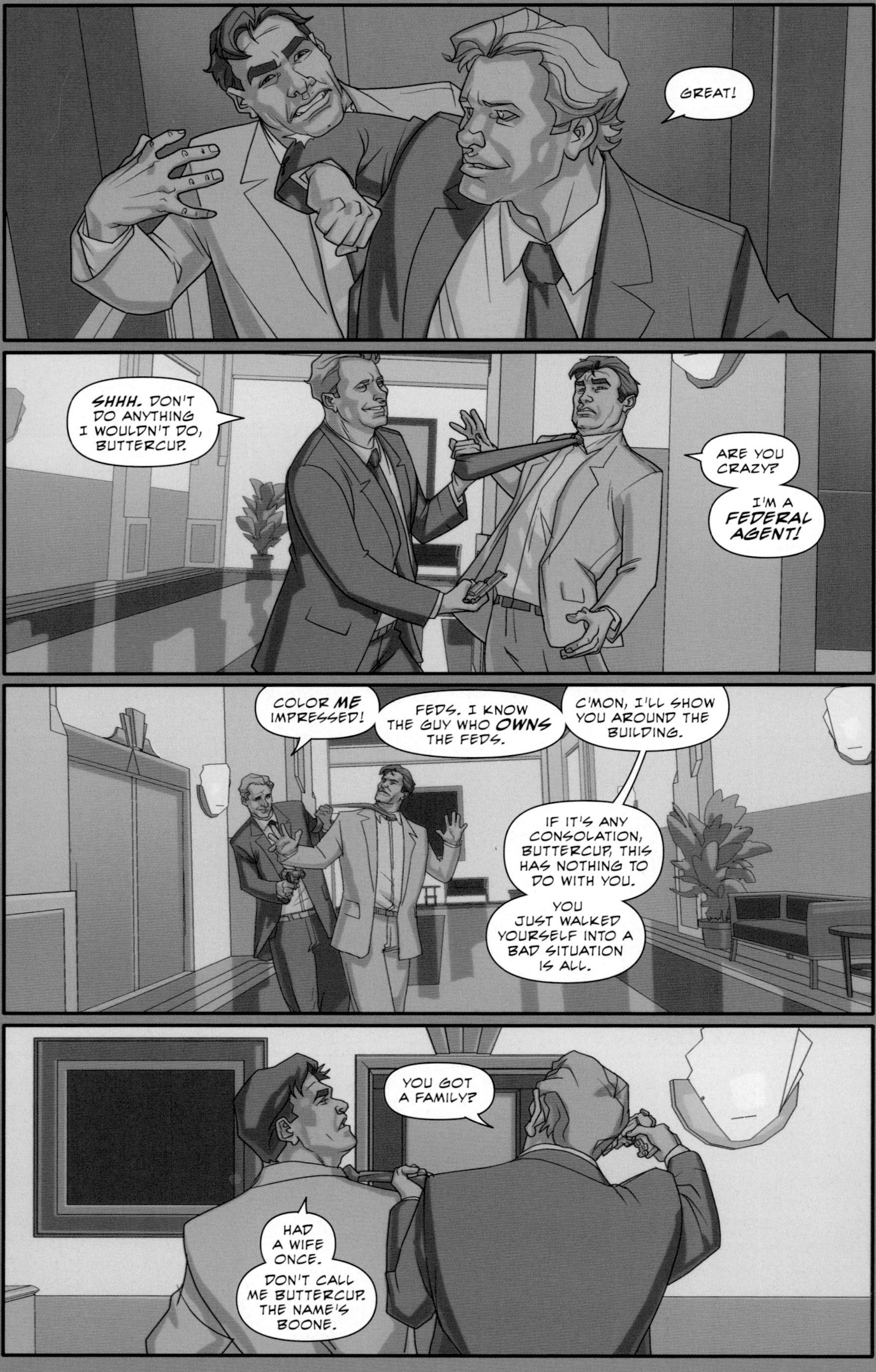
GREAT!
SHHH. DON'T DO ANYTHING I WOULDN'T DO, BUTTERCUP.
ARE YOU CRAZY?
I'M A FEDERAL AGENT!
COLOR ME IMPRESSED!
FEDS. I KNOW THE GUY WHO OWNS THE FEDS.
C'MON, I'LL SHOW YOU AROUND THE BUILDING.
IF IT'S ANY CONSOLATION, BUTTERCUP, THIS HAS NOTHING TO DO WITH YOU.
YOU JUST WALKED YOURSELF INTO A BAD SITUATION IS ALL.
YOU GOT A FAMILY?
HAD A WIFE ONCE.
DON'T CALL ME BUTTERCUP. THE NAME'S BOONE.

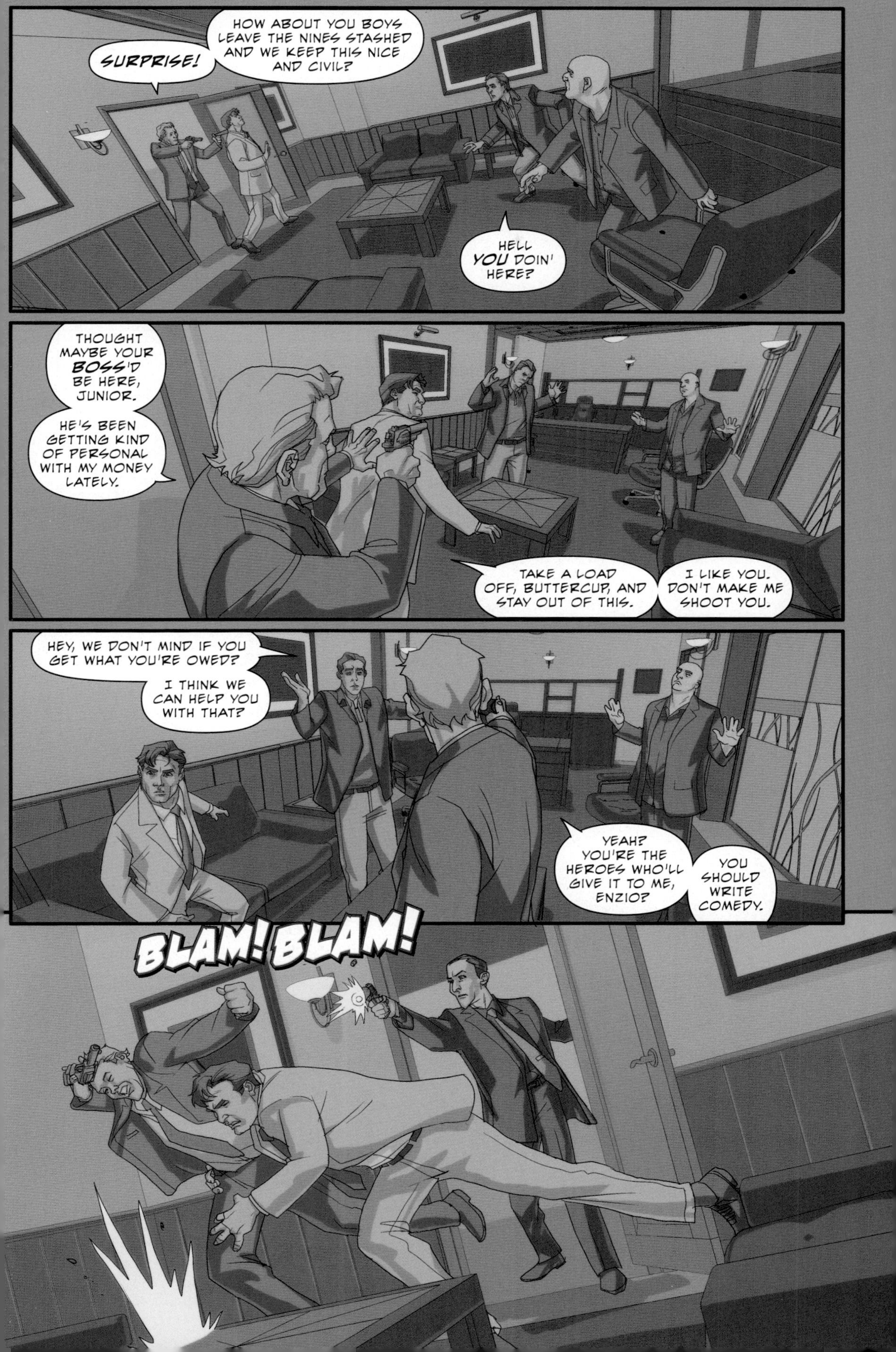
SURPRISE!
HOW ABOUT YOU BOYS LEAVE THE NINES STASHED AND WE KEEP THIS NICE AND CIVIL?
HELL YOU DOIN' HERE?
THOUGHT MAYBE YOUR BOSS'D BE HERE, JUNIOR.
HE'S BEEN GETTING KIND OF PERSONAL WITH MY MONEY LATELY.
TAKE A LOAD OFF, BUTTERCUP, AND STAY OUT OF THIS.
I LIKE YOU. DON'T MAKE ME SHOOT YOU.
HEY, WE DON'T MIND IF YOU GET WHAT YOU'RE OWED?
I THINK WE CAN HELP YOU WITH THAT?
YEAH? YOU'RE THE HEROES WHO'LL GIVE IT TO ME, ENZIO?
YOU SHOULD WRITE COMEDY.
BLAM! BLAM!

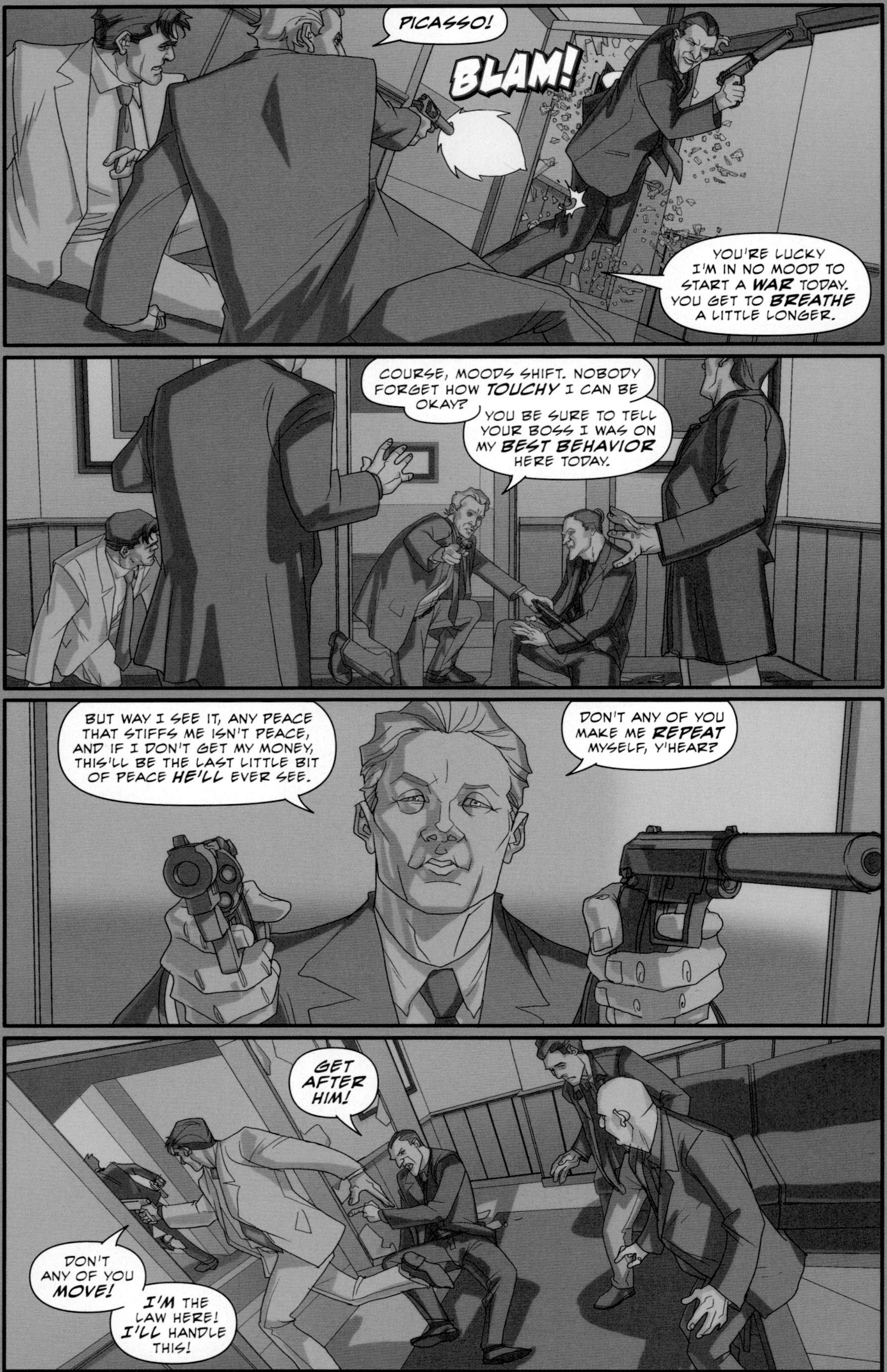
PICASSO!
BLAM!
YOU'RE LUCKY I'M IN NO MOOD TO START A WAR TODAY. YOU GET TO BREATHE A LITTLE LONGER.
COURSE, MOODS SHIFT. NOBODY FORGET HOW TOUCHY I CAN BE OKAY?
YOU BE SURE TO TELL YOUR BOSS I WAS ON MY BEST BEHAVIOR HERE TODAY.
BUT WAY I SEE IT, ANY PEACE THAT STIFFS ME ISN'T PEACE, AND IF I DON'T GET MY MONEY, THIS'LL BE THE LAST LITTLE BIT OF PEACE HE'LL EVER SEE.
DON'T ANY OF YOU MAKE ME REPEAT MYSELF, Y'HEAR?
GET AFTER HIM!
DON'T ANY OF YOU MOVE!
I'M THE LAW HERE! I'LL HANDLE THIS!

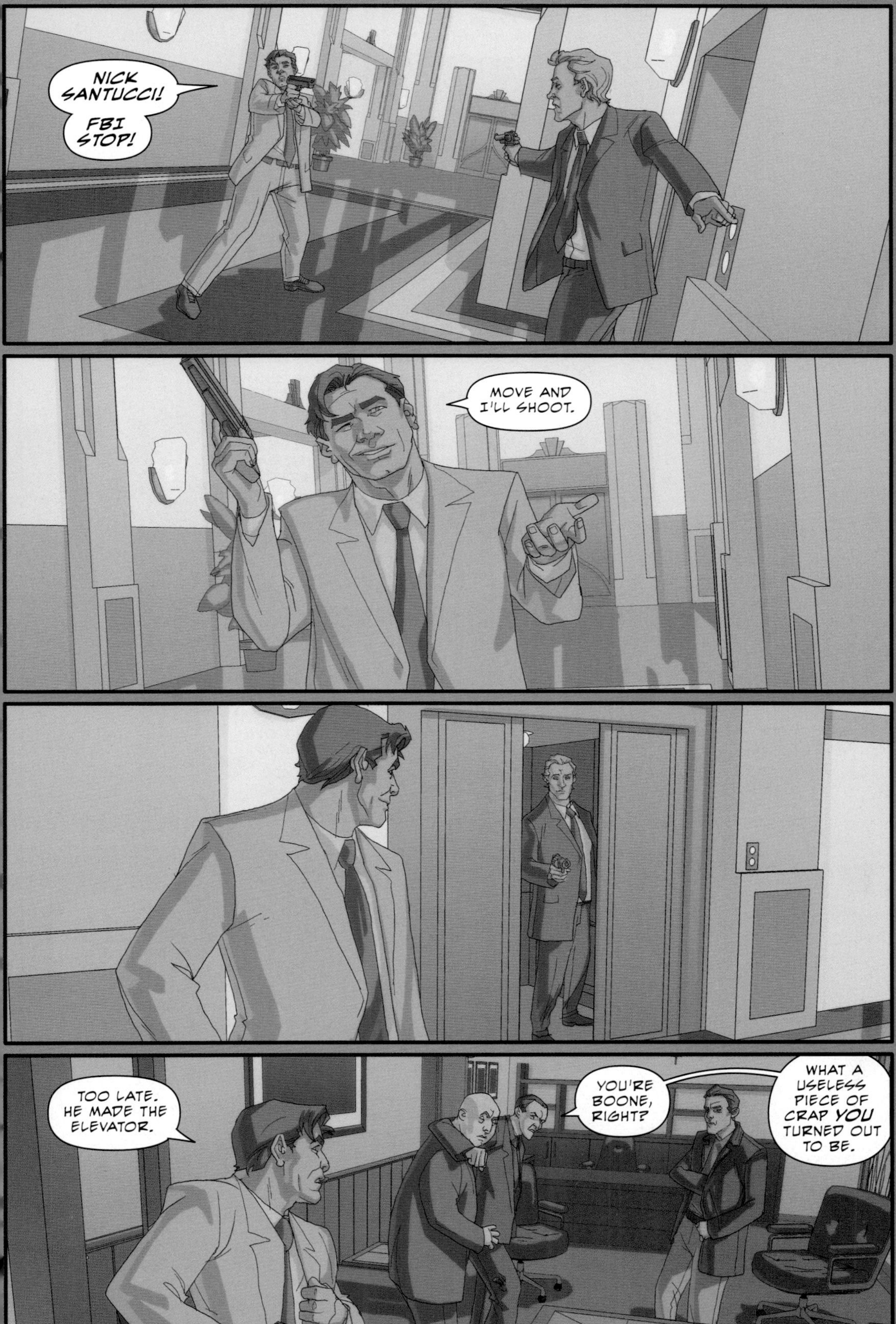
NICK SANTUCCI!
FBI STOP!
MOVE AND I'LL SHOOT.
TOO LATE. HE MADE THE ELEVATOR.
YOU'RE BOONE, RIGHT?
WHAT A USELESS PIECE OF CRAP YOU TURNED OUT TO BE.

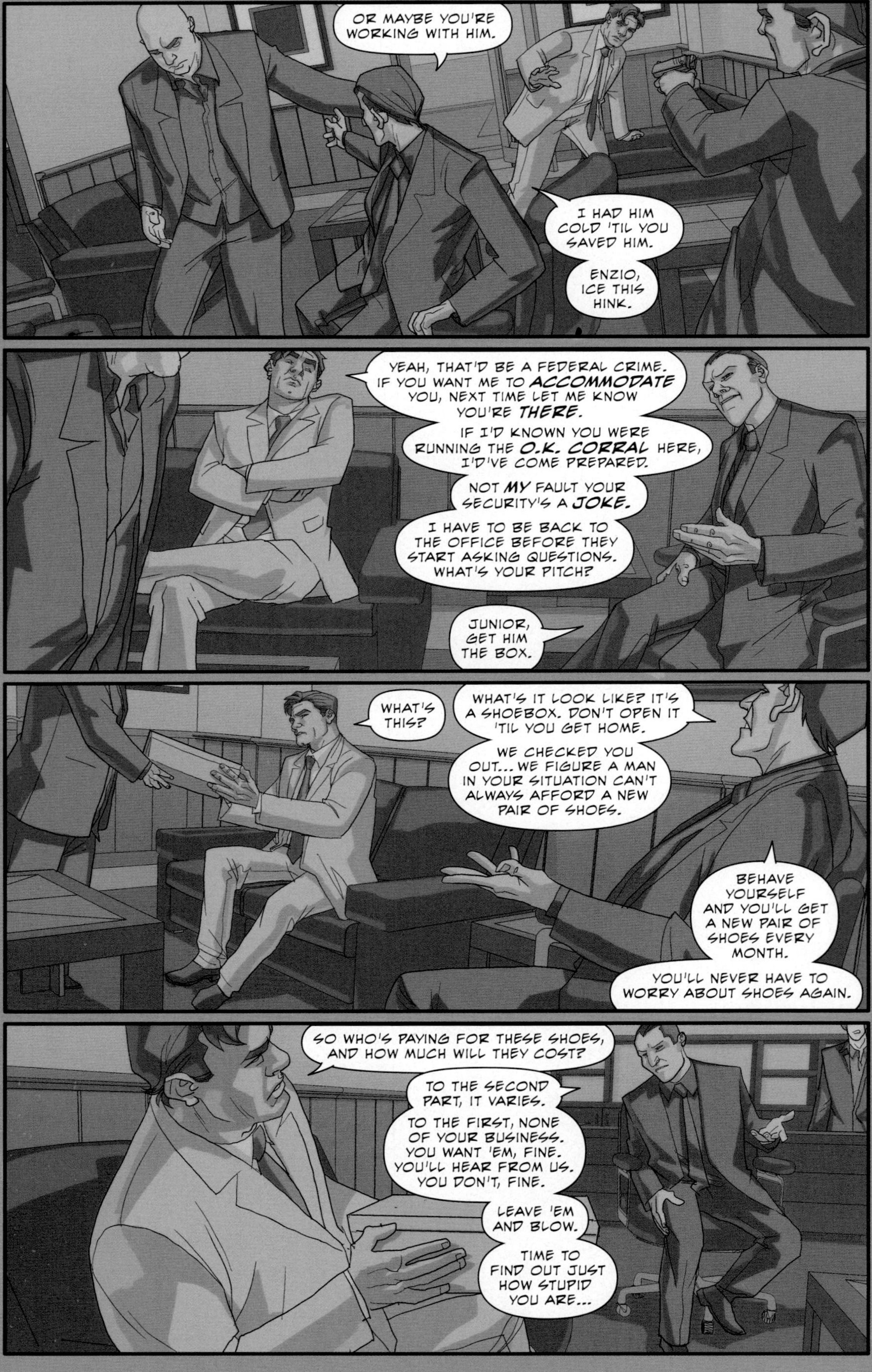
OR MAYBE YOU'RE WORKING WITH HIM.
I HAD HIM COLD 'TIL YOU SAVED HIM.
ENZIO, ICE THIS HINK.
YEAH, THAT'D BE A FEDERAL CRIME. IF YOU WANT ME TO ACCOMMODATE YOU, NEXT TIME LET ME KNOW YOU'RE THERE.
IF I'D KNOWN YOU WERE RUNNING THE O.K. CORRAL HERE, I'D'VE COME PREPARED.
NOT MY FAULT YOUR SECURITY'S A JOKE.
I HAVE TO BE BACK TO THE OFFICE BEFORE THEY START ASKING QUESTIONS. WHAT'S YOUR PITCH?
JUNIOR, GET HIM THE BOX.
WHAT'S THIS?
WHAT'S IT LOOK LIKE? IT'S A SHOEBOX. DON'T OPEN IT 'TIL YOU GET HOME.
WE CHECKED YOU OUT... WE FIGURE A MAN IN YOUR SITUATION CAN'T ALWAYS AFFORD A NEW PAIR OF SHOES.
BEHAVE YOURSELF AND YOU'LL GET A NEW PAIR OF SHOES EVERY MONTH.
YOU'LL NEVER HAVE TO WORRY ABOUT SHOES AGAIN.
SO WHO'S PAYING FOR THESE SHOES, AND HOW MUCH WILL THEY COST?
TO THE SECOND PART, IT VARIES.
TO THE FIRST, NONE OF YOUR BUSINESS. YOU WANT 'EM, FINE. YOU'LL HEAR FROM US. YOU DON'T, FINE.
LEAVE 'EM AND BLOW.
TIME TO FIND OUT JUST HOW STUPID YOU ARE...

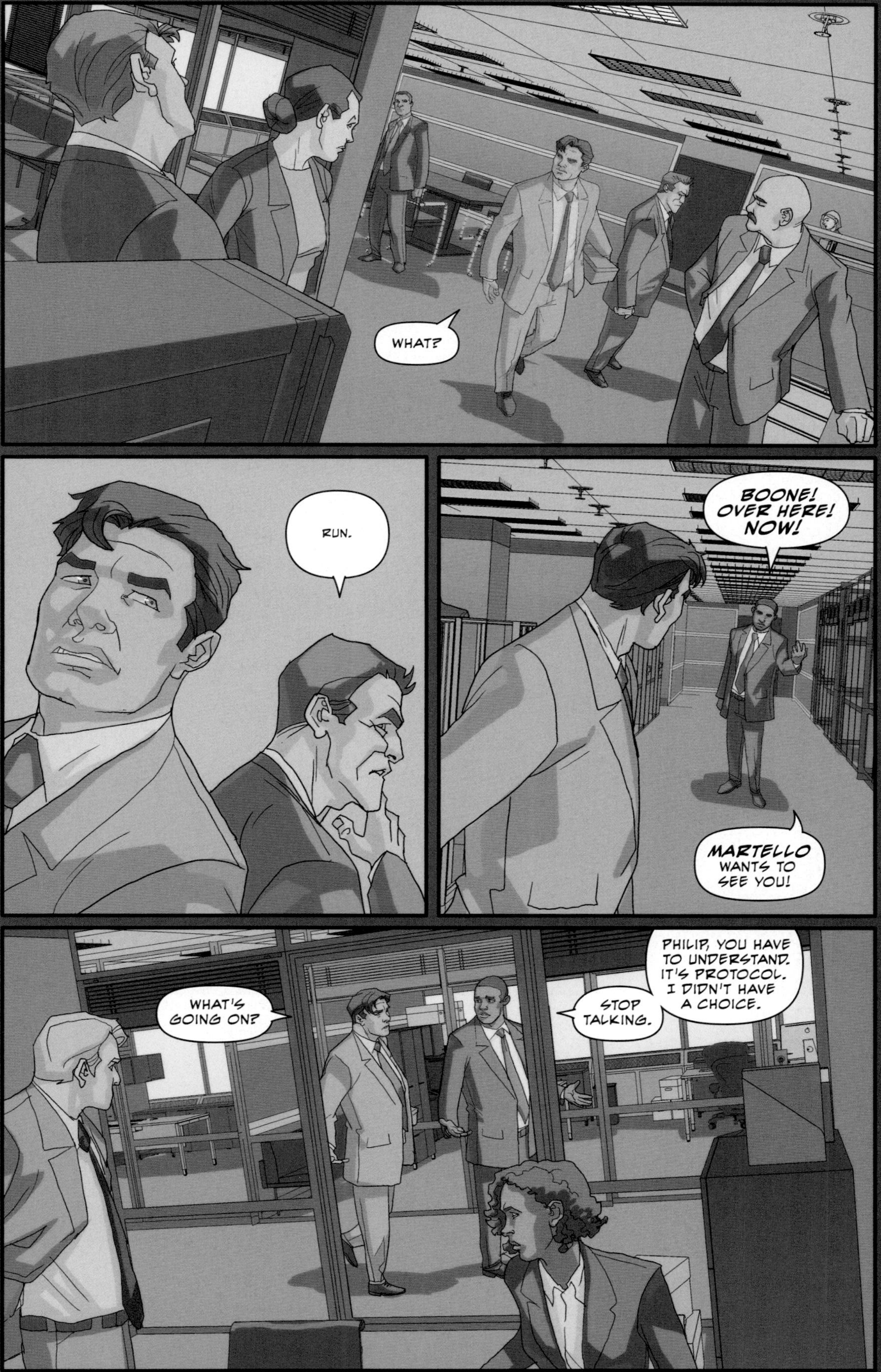
WHAT?
RUN.
BOONE! OVER HERE! NOW!
MARTELLO WANTS TO SEE YOU!
WHAT'S GOING ON?
PHILIP, YOU HAVE TO UNDERSTAND. IT'S PROTOCOL. I DIDN'T HAVE A CHOICE.
STOP TALKING.

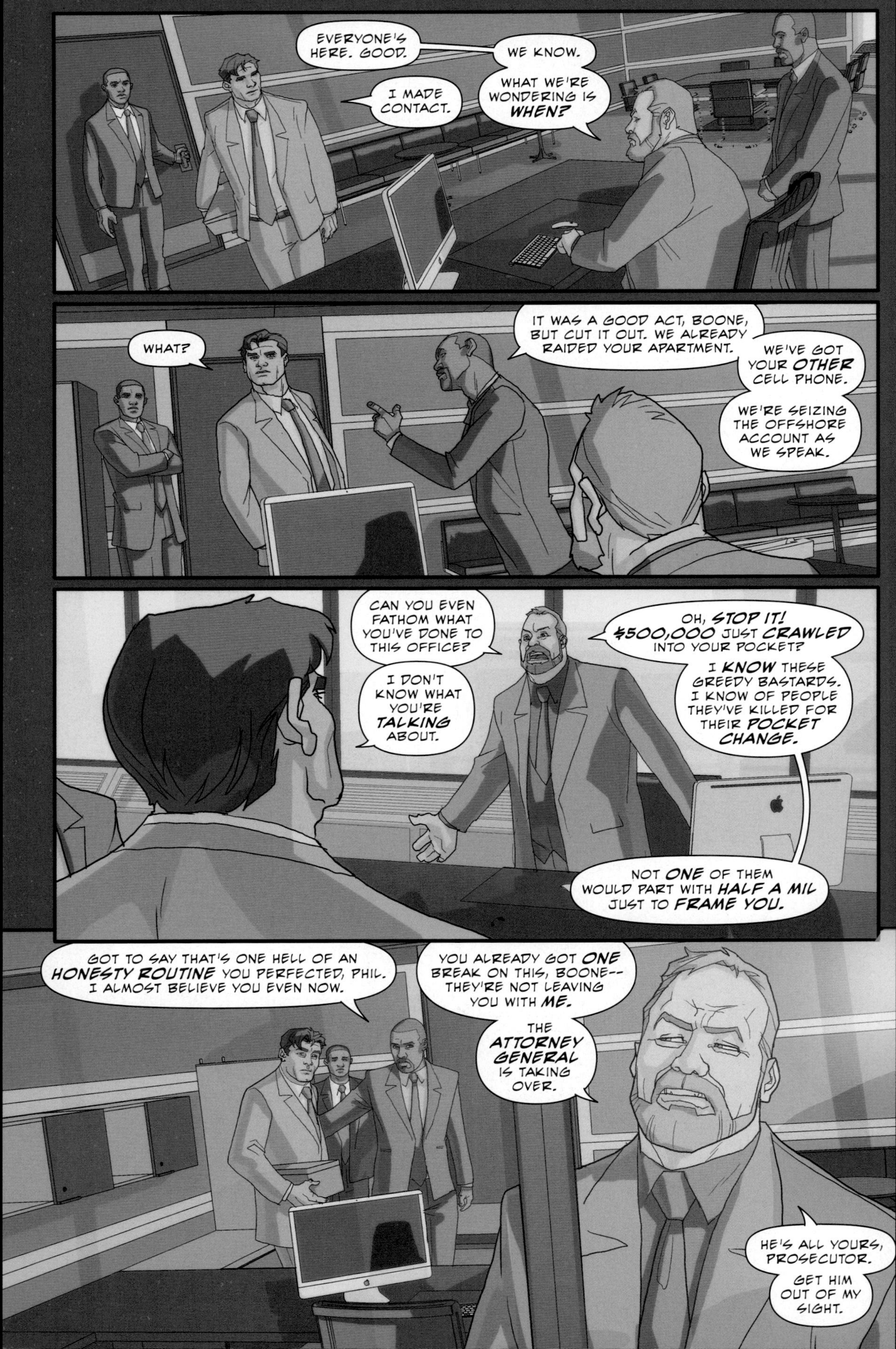
EVERYONE'S HERE. GOOD.
I MADE CONTACT.
WE KNOW.
WHAT WE'RE WONDERING IS *WHEN?*
WHAT?
IT WAS A GOOD ACT, BOONE, BUT CUT IT OUT. WE ALREADY RAIDED YOUR APARTMENT.
WE'VE GOT YOUR *OTHER* CELL PHONE.
WE'RE SEIZING THE OFFSHORE ACCOUNT AS WE SPEAK.
CAN YOU EVEN FATHOM WHAT YOU'VE DONE TO THIS OFFICE?
I DON'T KNOW WHAT YOU'RE *TALKING* ABOUT.
OH, *STOP IT! $500,000* JUST *CRAWLED* INTO YOUR POCKET?
I *KNOW* THESE GREEDY BASTARDS. I KNOW OF PEOPLE THEY'VE KILLED FOR THEIR *POCKET CHANGE.*
NOT *ONE* OF THEM WOULD PART WITH *HALF A MIL* JUST TO *FRAME YOU.*
GOT TO SAY THAT'S ONE HELL OF AN *HONESTY ROUTINE* YOU PERFECTED, PHIL. I ALMOST BELIEVE YOU EVEN NOW.
YOU ALREADY GOT *ONE* BREAK ON THIS, BOONE-- THEY'RE NOT LEAVING YOU WITH *ME.*
THE *ATTORNEY GENERAL* IS TAKING OVER.
HE'S ALL YOURS, PROSECUTOR.
GET HIM OUT OF MY SIGHT.

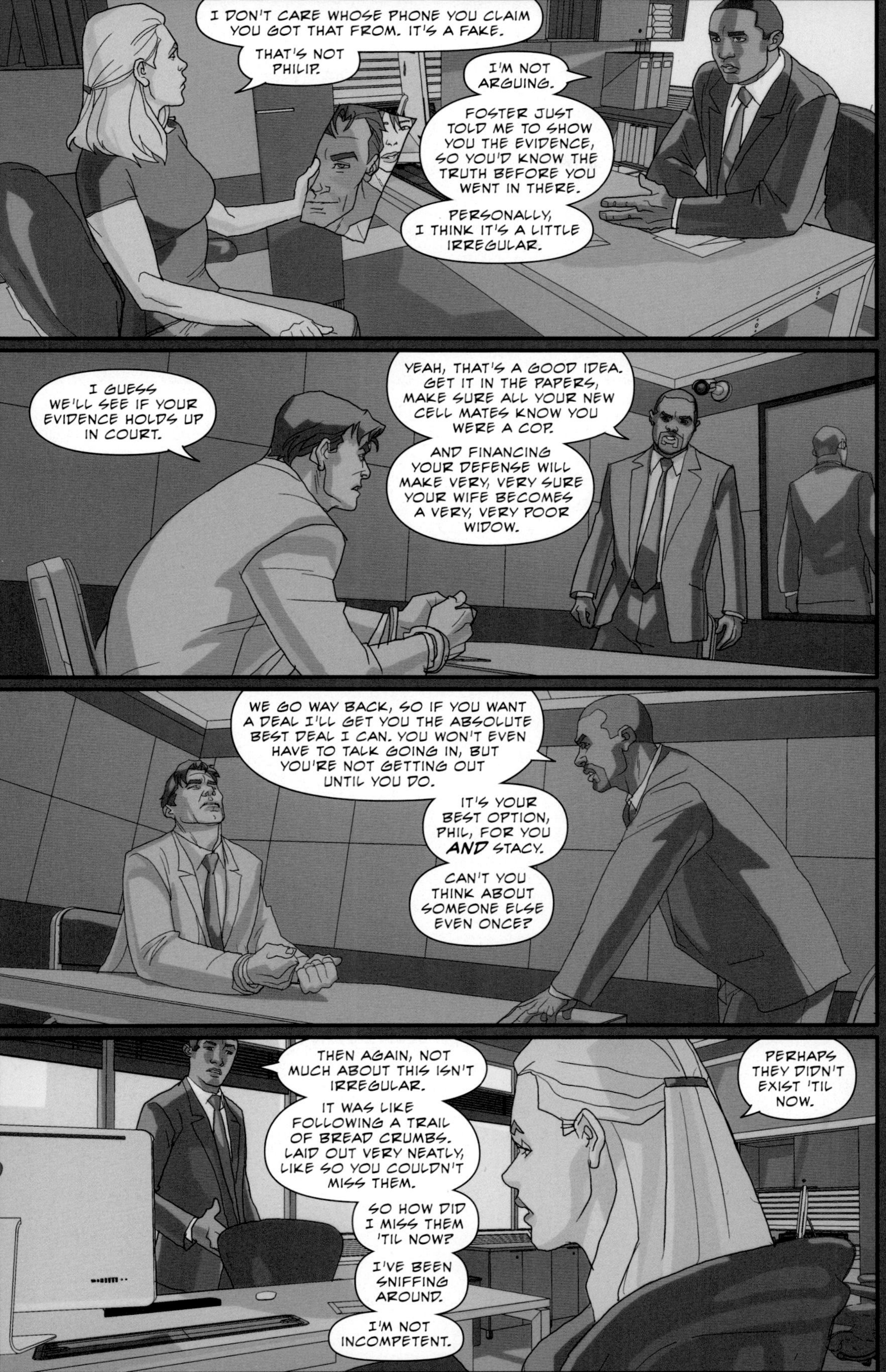
I DON'T CARE WHOSE PHONE YOU CLAIM YOU GOT THAT FROM. IT'S A FAKE.
THAT'S NOT PHILIP.
I'M NOT ARGUING.
FOSTER JUST TOLD ME TO SHOW YOU THE EVIDENCE, SO YOU'D KNOW THE TRUTH BEFORE YOU WENT IN THERE.
PERSONALLY, I THINK IT'S A LITTLE IRREGULAR.
I GUESS WE'LL SEE IF YOUR EVIDENCE HOLDS UP IN COURT.
YEAH, THAT'S A GOOD IDEA. GET IT IN THE PAPERS, MAKE SURE ALL YOUR NEW CELL MATES KNOW YOU WERE A COP.
AND FINANCING YOUR DEFENSE WILL MAKE VERY, VERY SURE YOUR WIFE BECOMES A VERY, VERY POOR WIDOW.
WE GO WAY BACK, SO IF YOU WANT A DEAL I'LL GET YOU THE ABSOLUTE BEST DEAL I CAN. YOU WON'T EVEN HAVE TO TALK GOING IN, BUT YOU'RE NOT GETTING OUT UNTIL YOU DO.
IT'S YOUR BEST OPTION, PHIL, FOR YOU **AND** STACY.
CAN'T YOU THINK ABOUT SOMEONE ELSE EVEN ONCE?
THEN AGAIN, NOT MUCH ABOUT THIS ISN'T IRREGULAR.
IT WAS LIKE FOLLOWING A TRAIL OF BREAD CRUMBS. LAID OUT VERY NEATLY, LIKE SO YOU COULDN'T MISS THEM.
SO HOW DID I MISS THEM 'TIL NOW?
I'VE BEEN SNIFFING AROUND.
I'M NOT INCOMPETENT.
PERHAPS THEY DIDN'T EXIST 'TIL NOW.

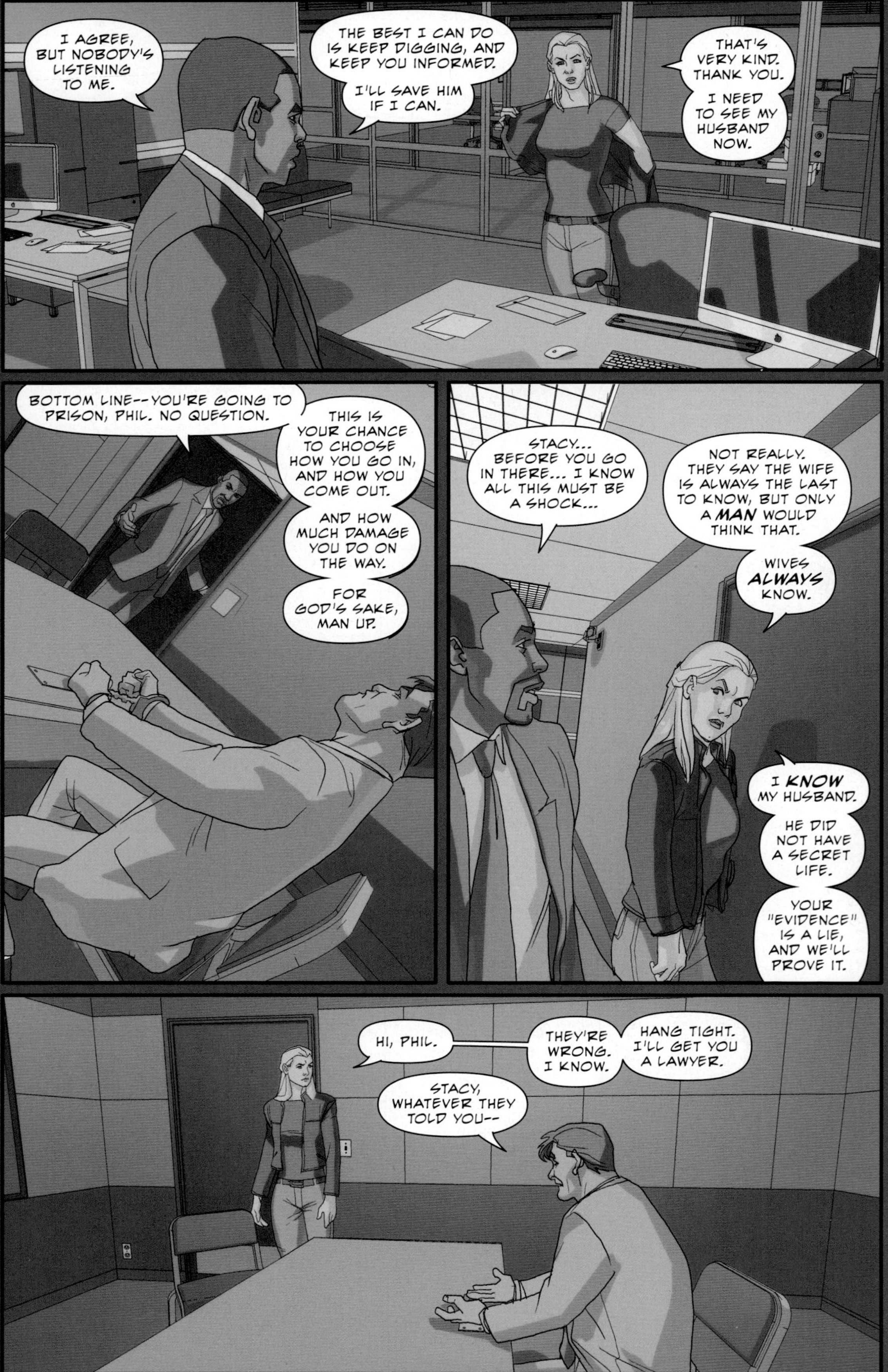
I AGREE, BUT NOBODY'S LISTENING TO ME.
THE BEST I CAN DO IS KEEP DIGGING, AND KEEP YOU INFORMED.
I'LL SAVE HIM IF I CAN.
THAT'S VERY KIND. THANK YOU.
I NEED TO SEE MY HUSBAND NOW.
BOTTOM LINE--YOU'RE GOING TO PRISON, PHIL. NO QUESTION.
THIS IS YOUR CHANCE TO CHOOSE HOW YOU GO IN, AND HOW YOU COME OUT.
AND HOW MUCH DAMAGE YOU DO ON THE WAY.
FOR GOD'S SAKE, MAN UP.
STACY... BEFORE YOU GO IN THERE... I KNOW ALL THIS MUST BE A SHOCK...
NOT REALLY. THEY SAY THE WIFE IS ALWAYS THE LAST TO KNOW, BUT ONLY A **MAN** WOULD THINK THAT.
WIVES **ALWAYS** KNOW.
I **KNOW** MY HUSBAND.
HE DID NOT HAVE A SECRET LIFE.
YOUR "EVIDENCE" IS A LIE, AND WE'LL PROVE IT.
HI, PHIL.
THEY'RE WRONG. I KNOW.
HANG TIGHT. I'LL GET YOU A LAWYER.
STACY, WHATEVER THEY TOLD YOU--

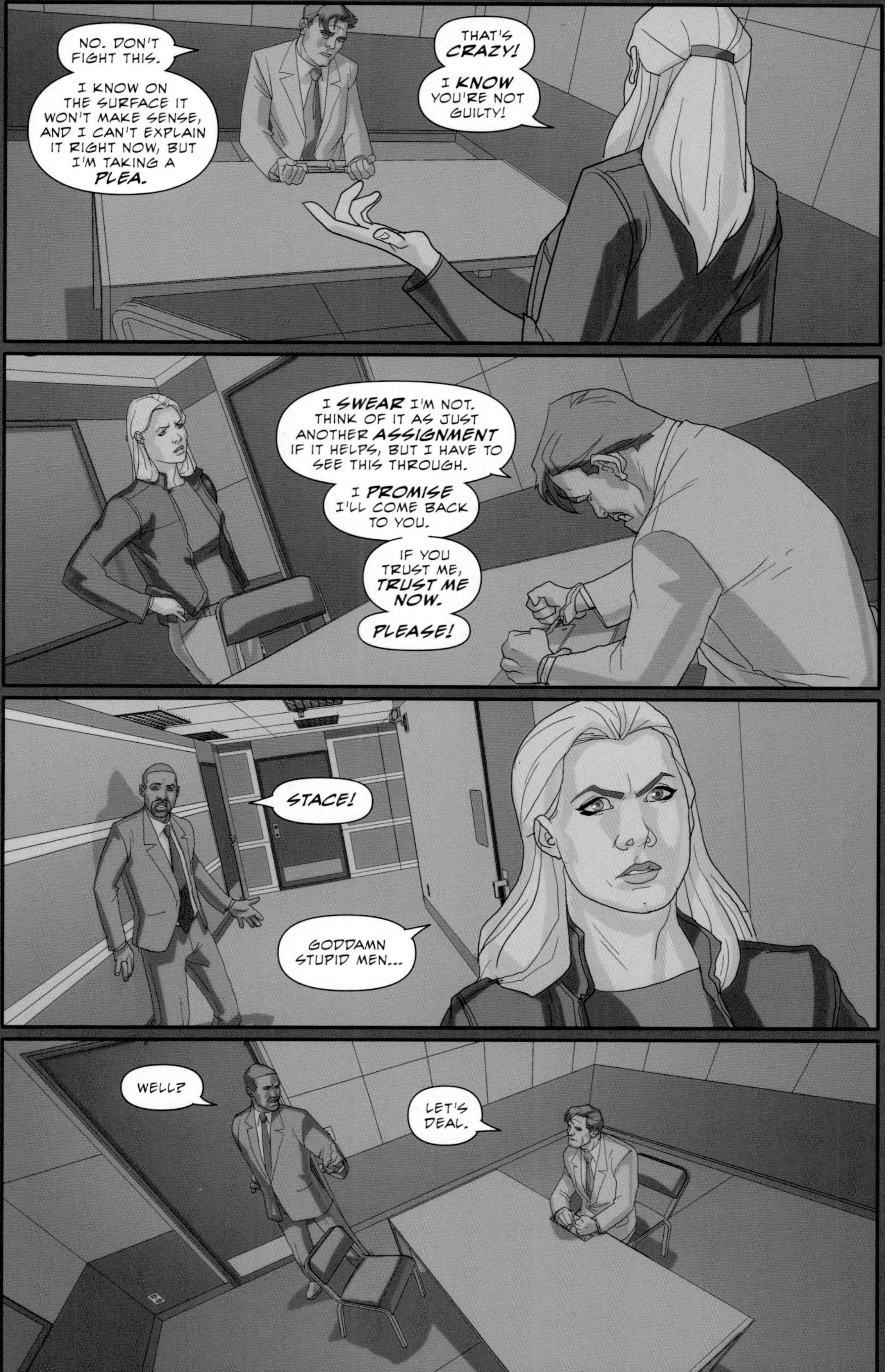
NO. DON'T FIGHT THIS.
I KNOW ON THE SURFACE IT WON'T MAKE SENSE, AND I CAN'T EXPLAIN IT RIGHT NOW, BUT I'M TAKING A PLEA.
THAT'S CRAZY!
I KNOW YOU'RE NOT GUILTY!
I SWEAR I'M NOT. THINK OF IT AS JUST ANOTHER ASSIGNMENT IF IT HELPS, BUT I HAVE TO SEE THIS THROUGH.
I PROMISE I'LL COME BACK TO YOU.
IF YOU TRUST ME, TRUST ME NOW.
PLEASE!
STACE!
GODDAMN STUPID MEN...
WELL?
LET'S DEAL.

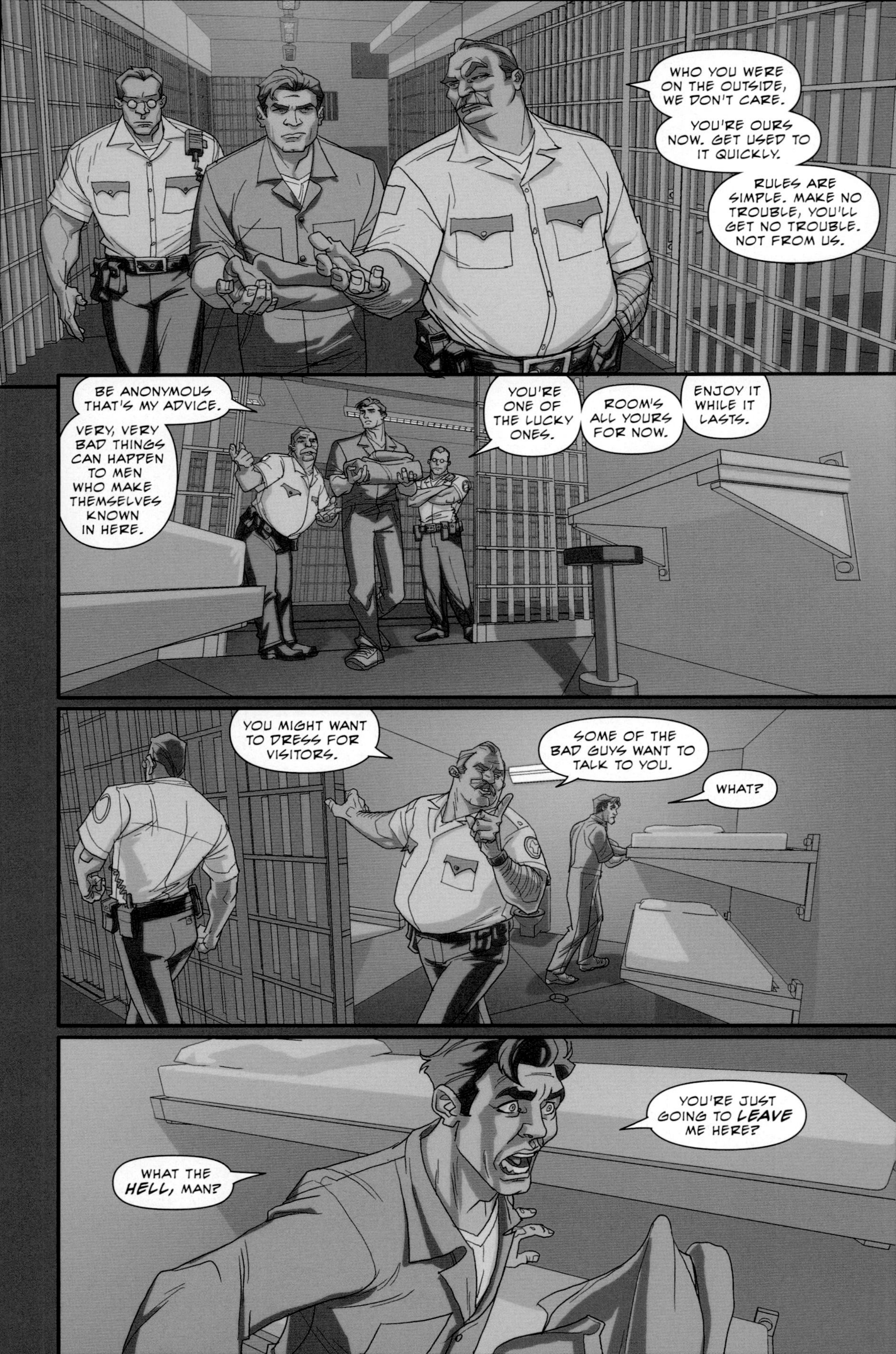
WHO YOU WERE ON THE OUTSIDE, WE DON'T CARE.
YOU'RE OURS NOW. GET USED TO IT QUICKLY.
RULES ARE SIMPLE. MAKE NO TROUBLE, YOU'LL GET NO TROUBLE. NOT FROM US.
BE ANONYMOUS THAT'S MY ADVICE.
VERY, VERY BAD THINGS CAN HAPPEN TO MEN WHO MAKE THEMSELVES KNOWN IN HERE.
YOU'RE ONE OF THE LUCKY ONES.
ROOM'S ALL YOURS FOR NOW.
ENJOY IT WHILE IT LASTS.
YOU MIGHT WANT TO DRESS FOR VISITORS.
SOME OF THE BAD GUYS WANT TO TALK TO YOU.
WHAT?
YOU'RE JUST GOING TO LEAVE ME HERE?
WHAT THE HELL, MAN?

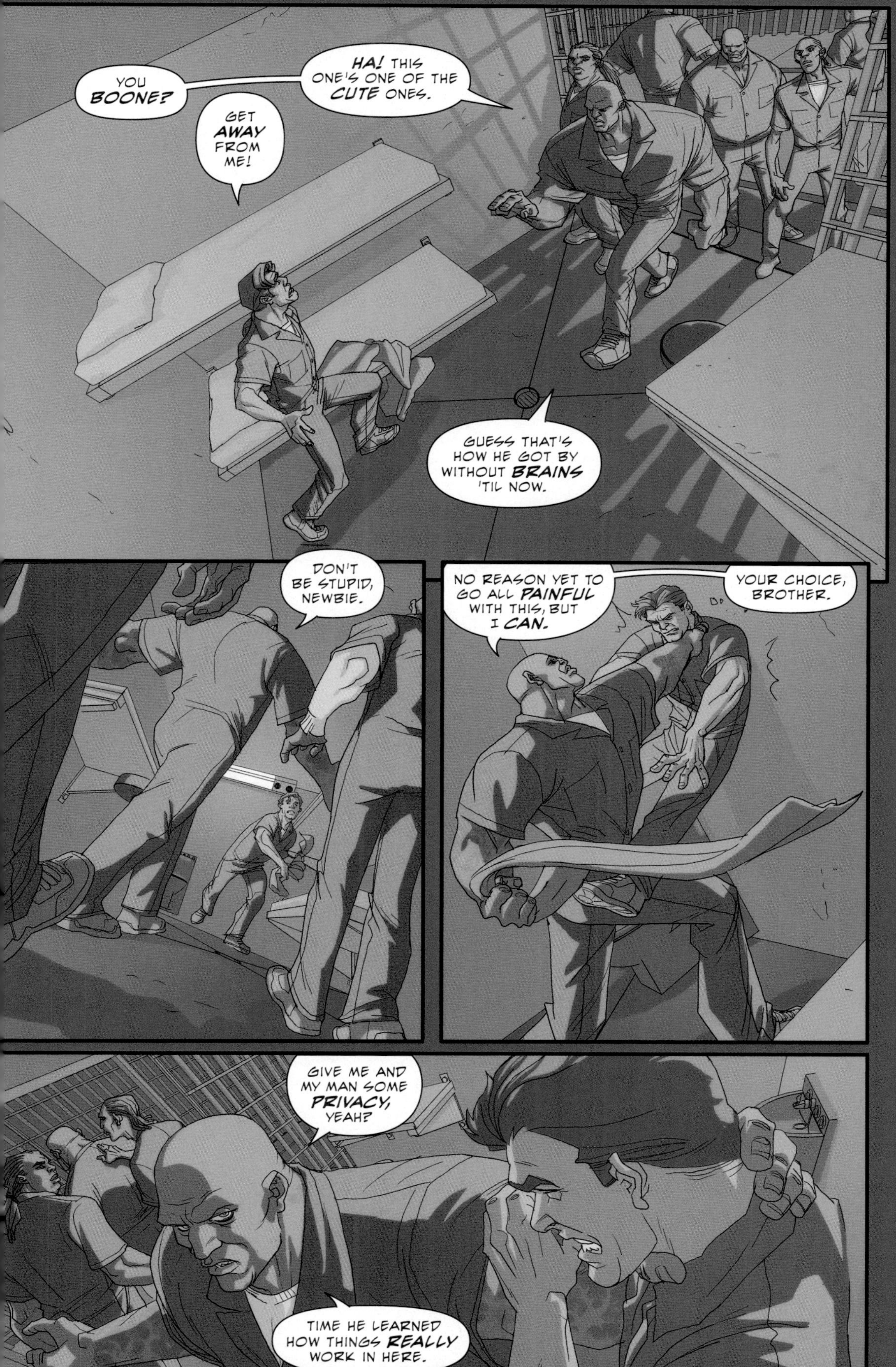
YOU BOONE?
HA! THIS ONE'S ONE OF THE CUTE ONES.
GET AWAY FROM ME!
GUESS THAT'S HOW HE GOT BY WITHOUT BRAINS 'TIL NOW.
DON'T BE STUPID, NEWBIE.
NO REASON YET TO GO ALL PAINFUL WITH THIS, BUT I CAN.
YOUR CHOICE, BROTHER.
GIVE ME AND MY MAN SOME PRIVACY, YEAH?
TIME HE LEARNED HOW THINGS REALLY WORK IN HERE.

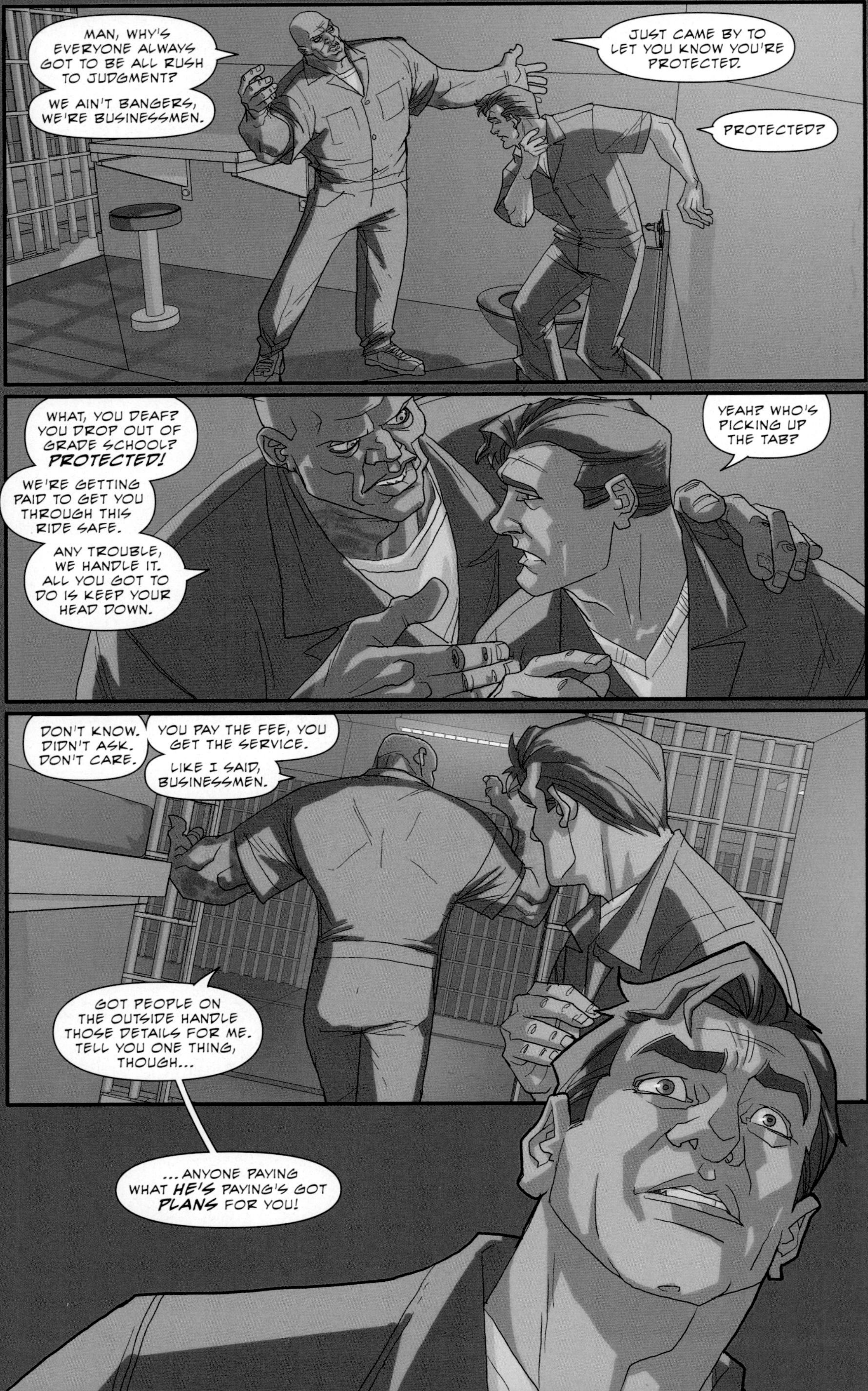
MAN, WHY'S EVERYONE ALWAYS GOT TO BE ALL RUSH TO JUDGMENT?
WE AIN'T BANGERS, WE'RE BUSINESSMEN.
JUST CAME BY TO LET YOU KNOW YOU'RE PROTECTED.
PROTECTED?
WHAT, YOU DEAF? YOU DROP OUT OF GRADE SCHOOL? PROTECTED!
WE'RE GETTING PAID TO GET YOU THROUGH THIS RIDE SAFE.
ANY TROUBLE, WE HANDLE IT. ALL YOU GOT TO DO IS KEEP YOUR HEAD DOWN.
YEAH? WHO'S PICKING UP THE TAB?
DON'T KNOW. DIDN'T ASK. DON'T CARE.
YOU PAY THE FEE, YOU GET THE SERVICE.
LIKE I SAID, BUSINESSMEN.
GOT PEOPLE ON THE OUTSIDE HANDLE THOSE DETAILS FOR ME. TELL YOU ONE THING, THOUGH...
...ANYONE PAYING WHAT HE'S PAYING'S GOT PLANS FOR YOU!

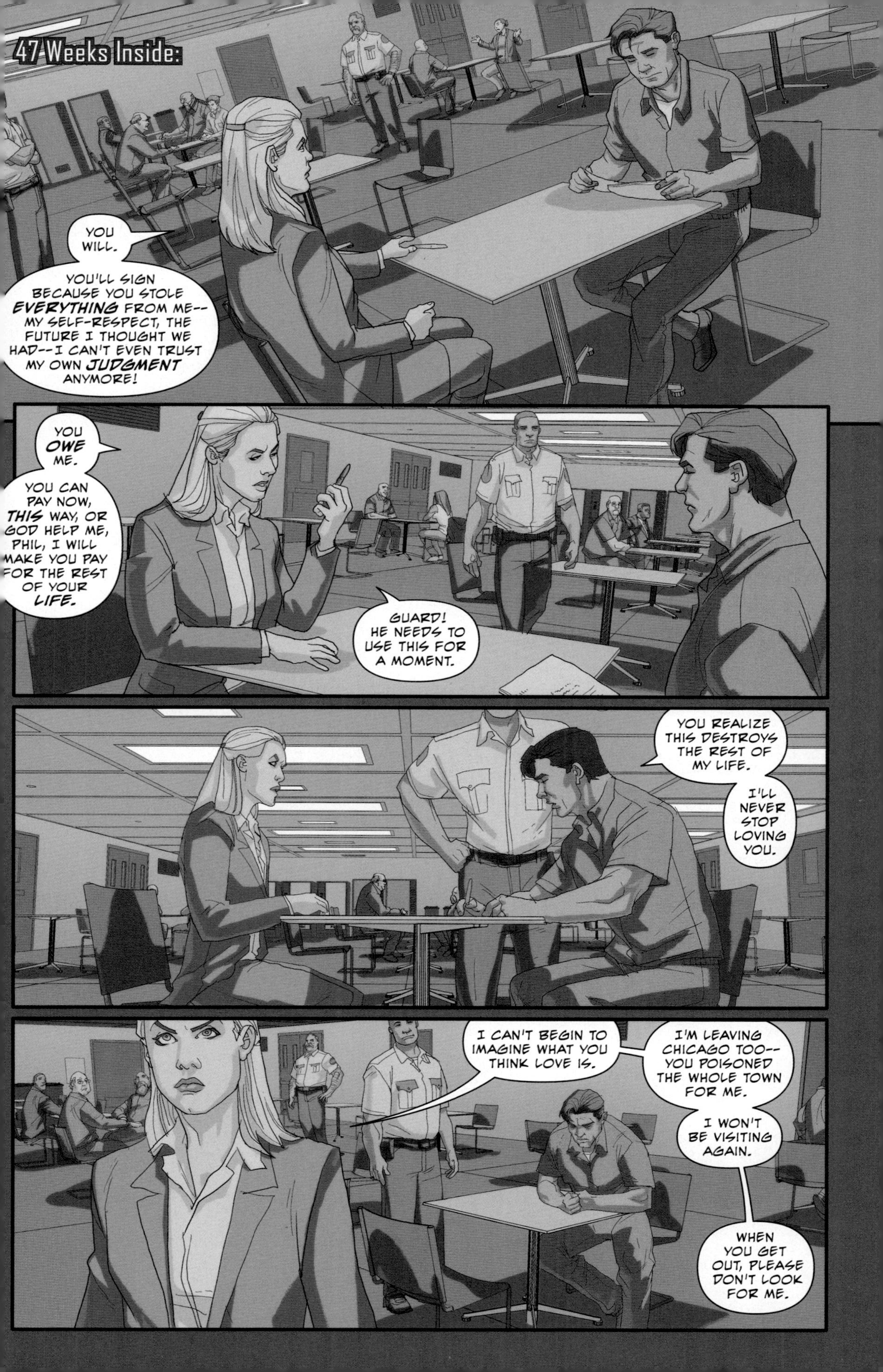

47 Weeks Inside:
YOU WILL.
YOU'LL SIGN BECAUSE YOU STOLE EVERYTHING FROM ME--MY SELF-RESPECT, THE FUTURE I THOUGHT WE HAD--I CAN'T EVEN TRUST MY OWN JUDGMENT ANYMORE!
YOU OWE ME.
YOU CAN PAY NOW, THIS WAY, OR GOD HELP ME, PHIL, I WILL MAKE YOU PAY FOR THE REST OF YOUR LIFE.
GUARD! HE NEEDS TO USE THIS FOR A MOMENT.
YOU REALIZE THIS DESTROYS THE REST OF MY LIFE.
I'LL NEVER STOP LOVING YOU.
I CAN'T BEGIN TO IMAGINE WHAT YOU THINK LOVE IS.
I'M LEAVING CHICAGO TOO--YOU POISONED THE WHOLE TOWN FOR ME.
I WON'T BE VISITING AGAIN.
WHEN YOU GET OUT, PLEASE DON'T LOOK FOR ME.

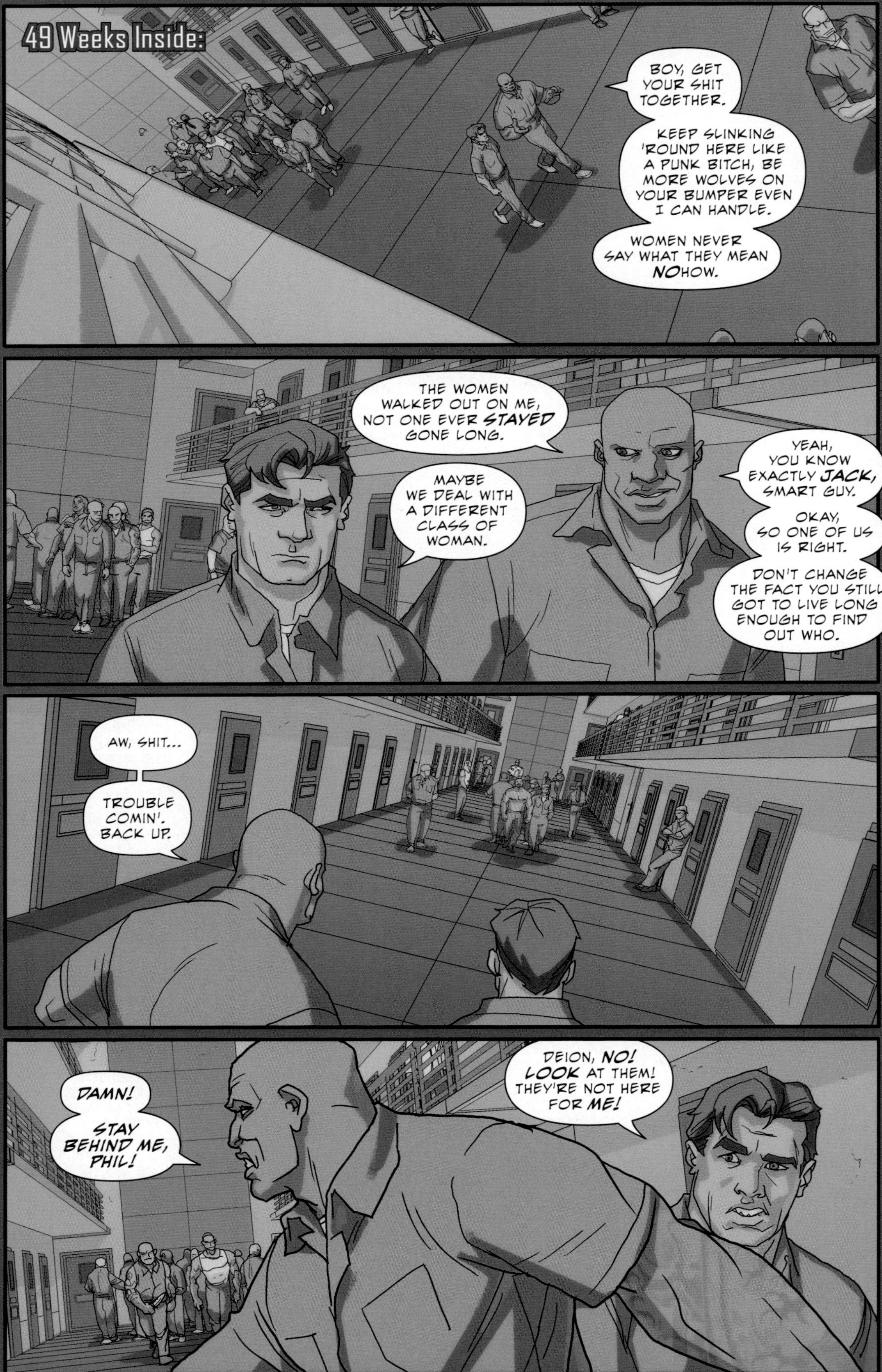
49 Weeks Inside:
BOY, GET YOUR SHIT TOGETHER.
KEEP SLINKING 'ROUND HERE LIKE A PUNK BITCH, BE MORE WOLVES ON YOUR BUMPER EVEN I CAN HANDLE.
WOMEN NEVER SAY WHAT THEY MEAN NOHOW.
THE WOMEN WALKED OUT ON ME, NOT ONE EVER STAYED GONE LONG.
MAYBE WE DEAL WITH A DIFFERENT CLASS OF WOMAN.
YEAH, YOU KNOW EXACTLY JACK, SMART GUY.
OKAY, SO ONE OF US IS RIGHT.
DON'T CHANGE THE FACT YOU STILL GOT TO LIVE LONG ENOUGH TO FIND OUT WHO.
AW, SHIT...
TROUBLE COMIN'. BACK UP.
DAMN!
STAY BEHIND ME, PHIL!
DEION, NO! LOOK AT THEM! THEY'RE NOT HERE FOR ME!

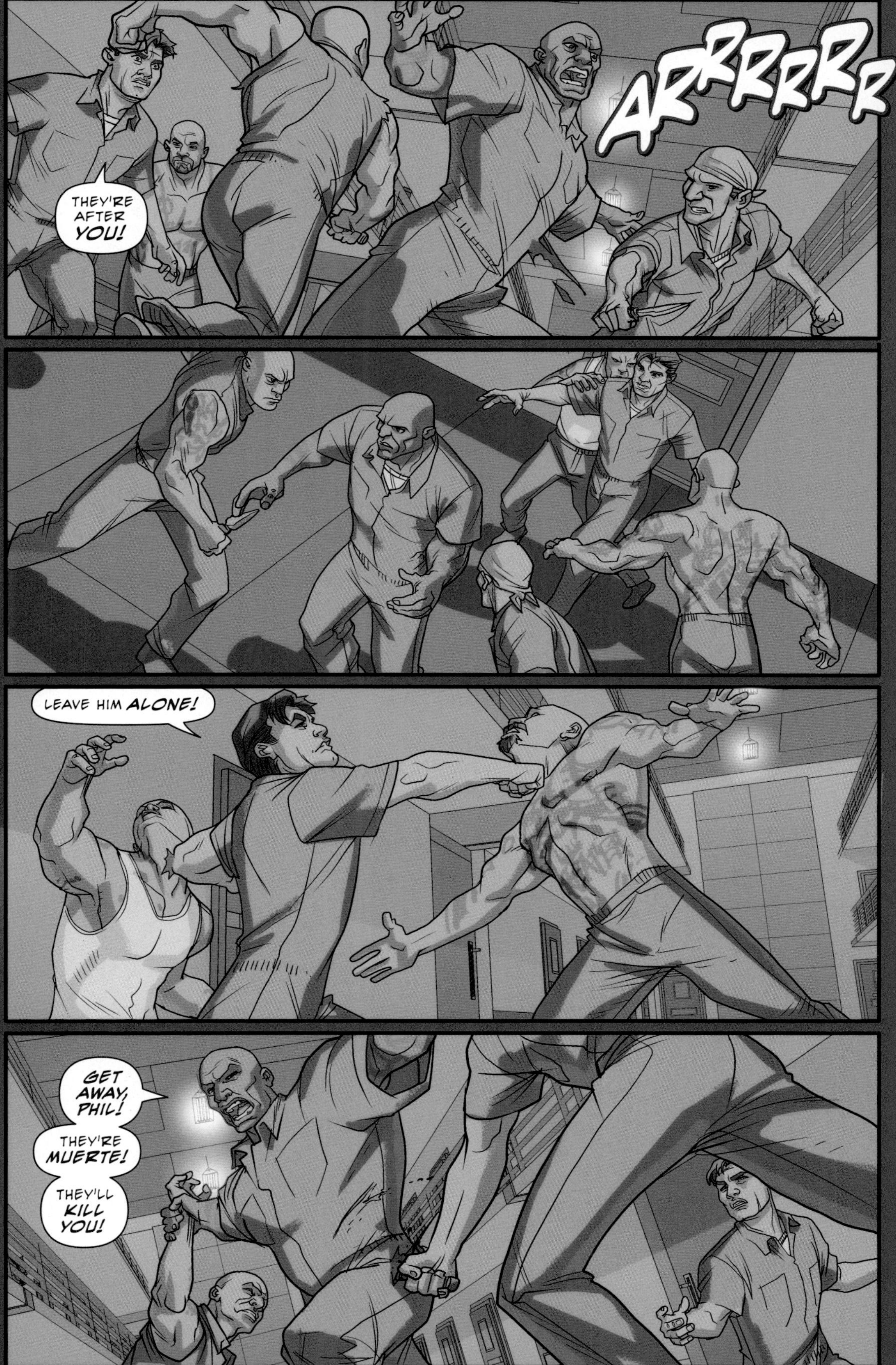
ARRRRRR
THEY'RE AFTER YOU!
LEAVE HIM ALONE!
GET AWAY, PHIL!
THEY'RE MUERTE!
THEY'LL KILL YOU!

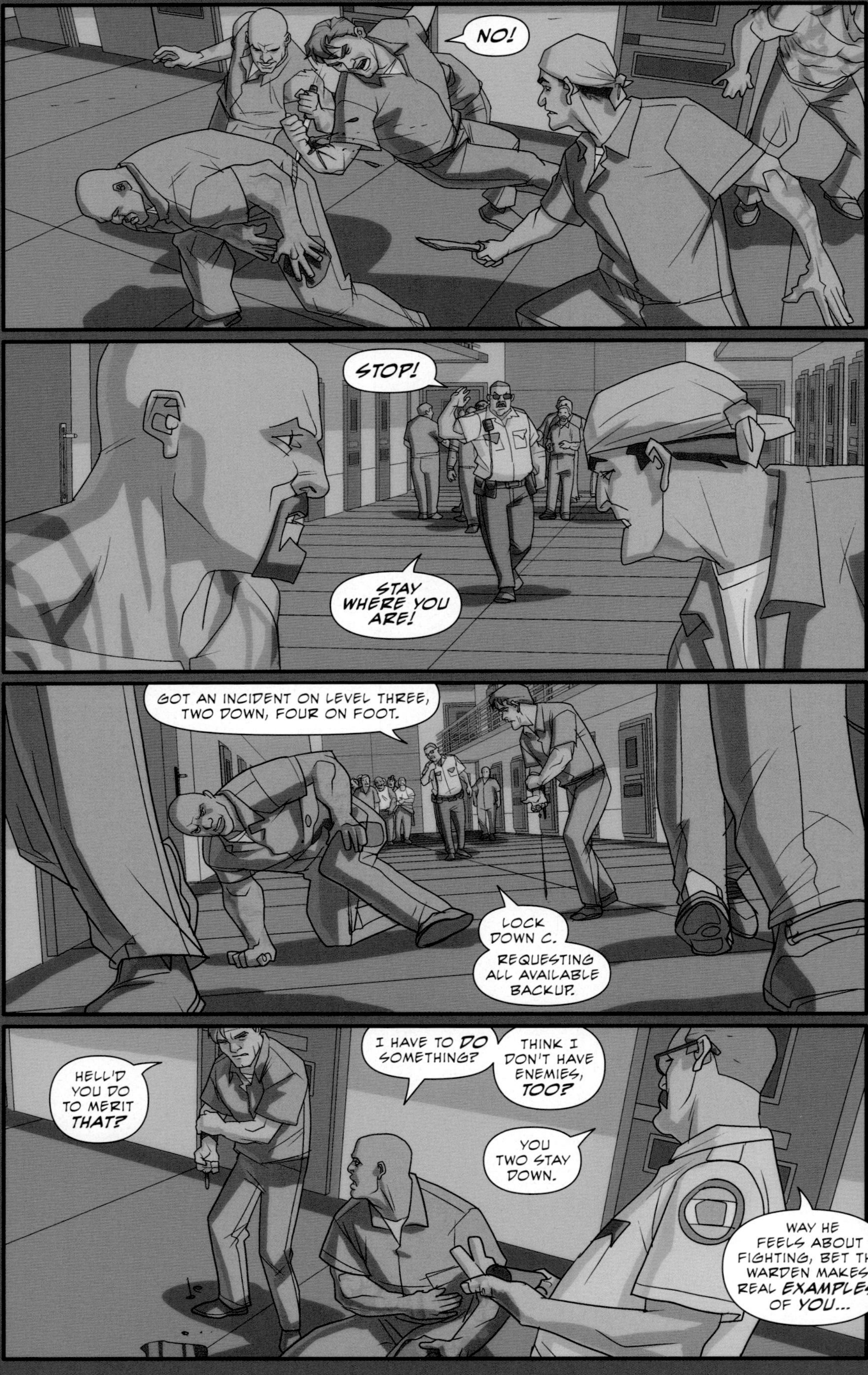
NO!
STOP!
STAY WHERE YOU ARE!
GOT AN INCIDENT ON LEVEL THREE, TWO DOWN, FOUR ON FOOT.
LOCK DOWN C.
REQUESTING ALL AVAILABLE BACKUP.
HELL'D YOU DO TO MERIT THAT?
I HAVE TO DO SOMETHING?
THINK I DON'T HAVE ENEMIES, TOO?
YOU TWO STAY DOWN.
WAY HE FEELS ABOUT FIGHTING, BET THE WARDEN MAKES REAL EXAMPLES OF YOU...

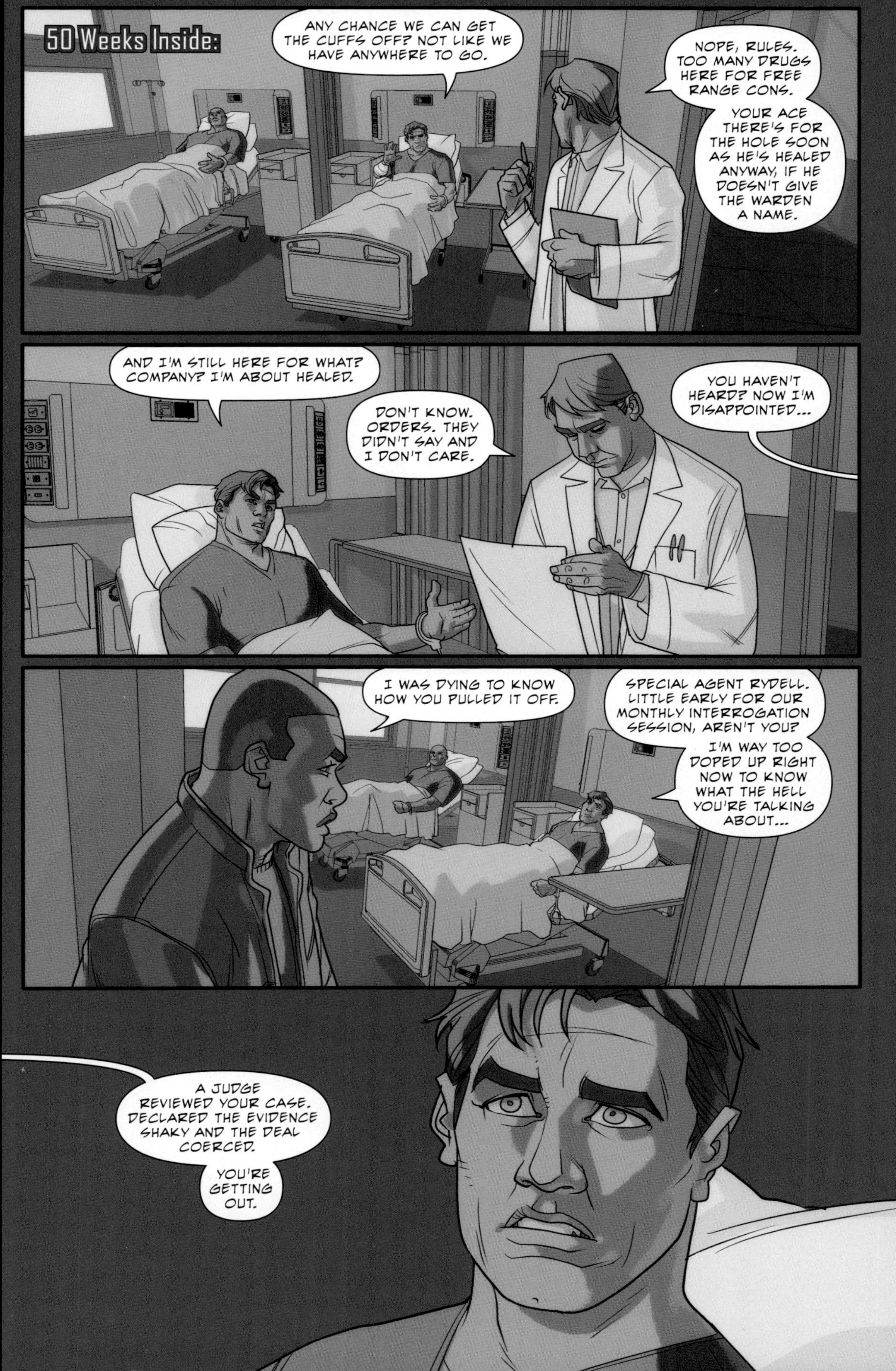
50 Weeks Inside:
ANY CHANCE WE CAN GET THE CUFFS OFF? NOT LIKE WE HAVE ANYWHERE TO GO.
NOPE, RULES. TOO MANY DRUGS HERE FOR FREE RANGE CONS.
YOUR ACE THERE'S FOR THE HOLE SOON AS HE'S HEALED ANYWAY, IF HE DOESN'T GIVE THE WARDEN A NAME.
AND I'M STILL HERE FOR WHAT? COMPANY? I'M ABOUT HEALED.
DON'T KNOW. ORDERS. THEY DIDN'T SAY AND I DON'T CARE.
YOU HAVEN'T HEARD? NOW I'M DISAPPOINTED...
I WAS DYING TO KNOW HOW YOU PULLED IT OFF.
SPECIAL AGENT RYDELL. LITTLE EARLY FOR OUR MONTHLY INTERROGATION SESSION, AREN'T YOU?
I'M WAY TOO DOPED UP RIGHT NOW TO KNOW WHAT THE HELL YOU'RE TALKING ABOUT...
A JUDGE REVIEWED YOUR CASE. DECLARED THE EVIDENCE SHAKY AND THE DEAL COERCED.
YOU'RE GETTING OUT.

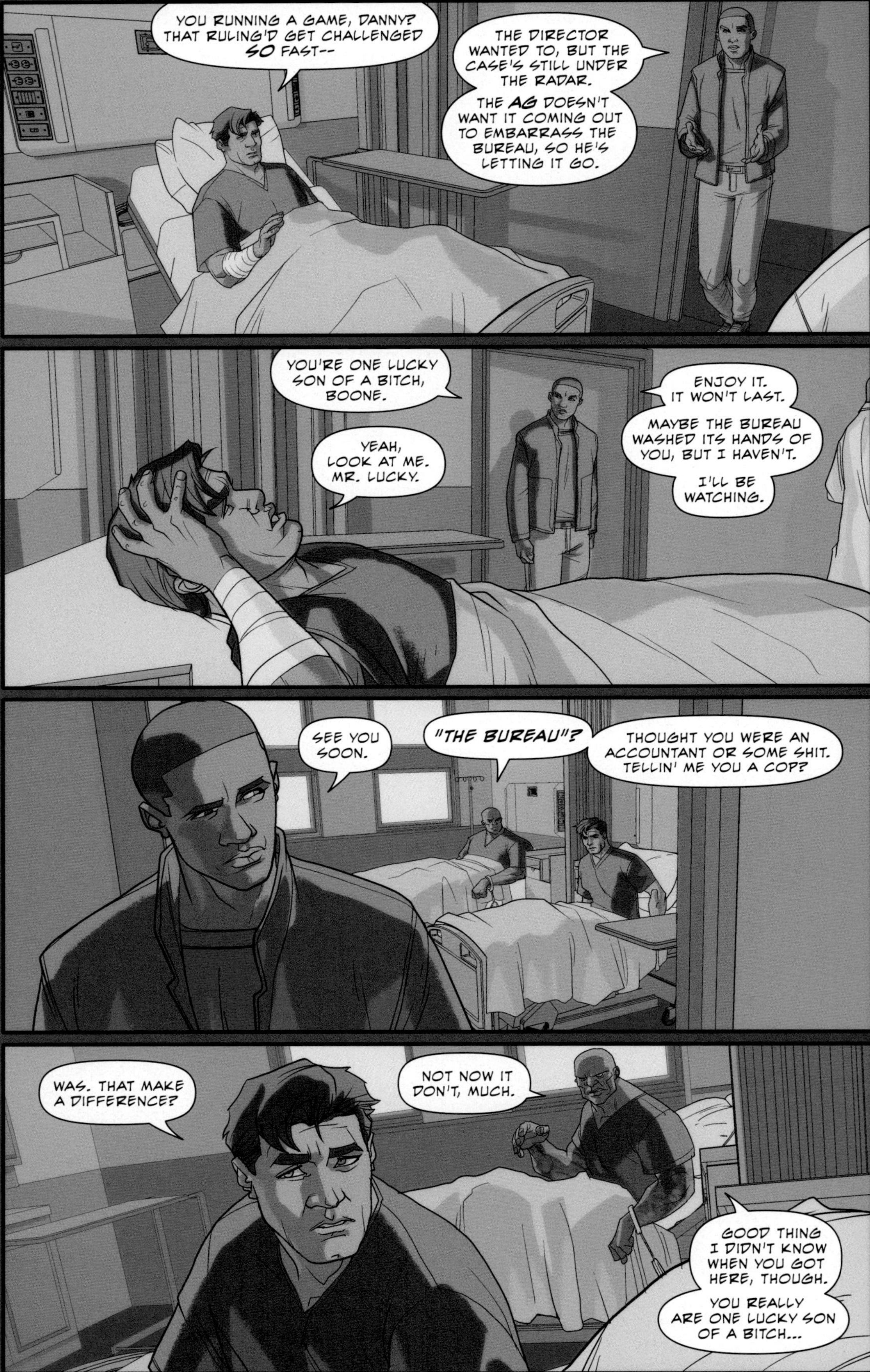
YOU RUNNING A GAME, DANNY? THAT RULING'D GET CHALLENGED SO FAST--
THE DIRECTOR WANTED TO, BUT THE CASE'S STILL UNDER THE RADAR.
THE AG DOESN'T WANT IT COMING OUT TO EMBARRASS THE BUREAU, SO HE'S LETTING IT GO.
YOU'RE ONE LUCKY SON OF A BITCH, BOONE.
YEAH, LOOK AT ME. MR. LUCKY.
ENJOY IT. IT WON'T LAST.
MAYBE THE BUREAU WASHED ITS HANDS OF YOU, BUT I HAVEN'T.
I'LL BE WATCHING.
SEE YOU SOON.
"THE BUREAU"?
THOUGHT YOU WERE AN ACCOUNTANT OR SOME SHIT. TELLIN' ME YOU A COP?
WAS. THAT MAKE A DIFFERENCE?
NOT NOW IT DON'T, MUCH.
GOOD THING I DIDN'T KNOW WHEN YOU GOT HERE, THOUGH.
YOU REALLY ARE ONE LUCKY SON OF A BITCH...

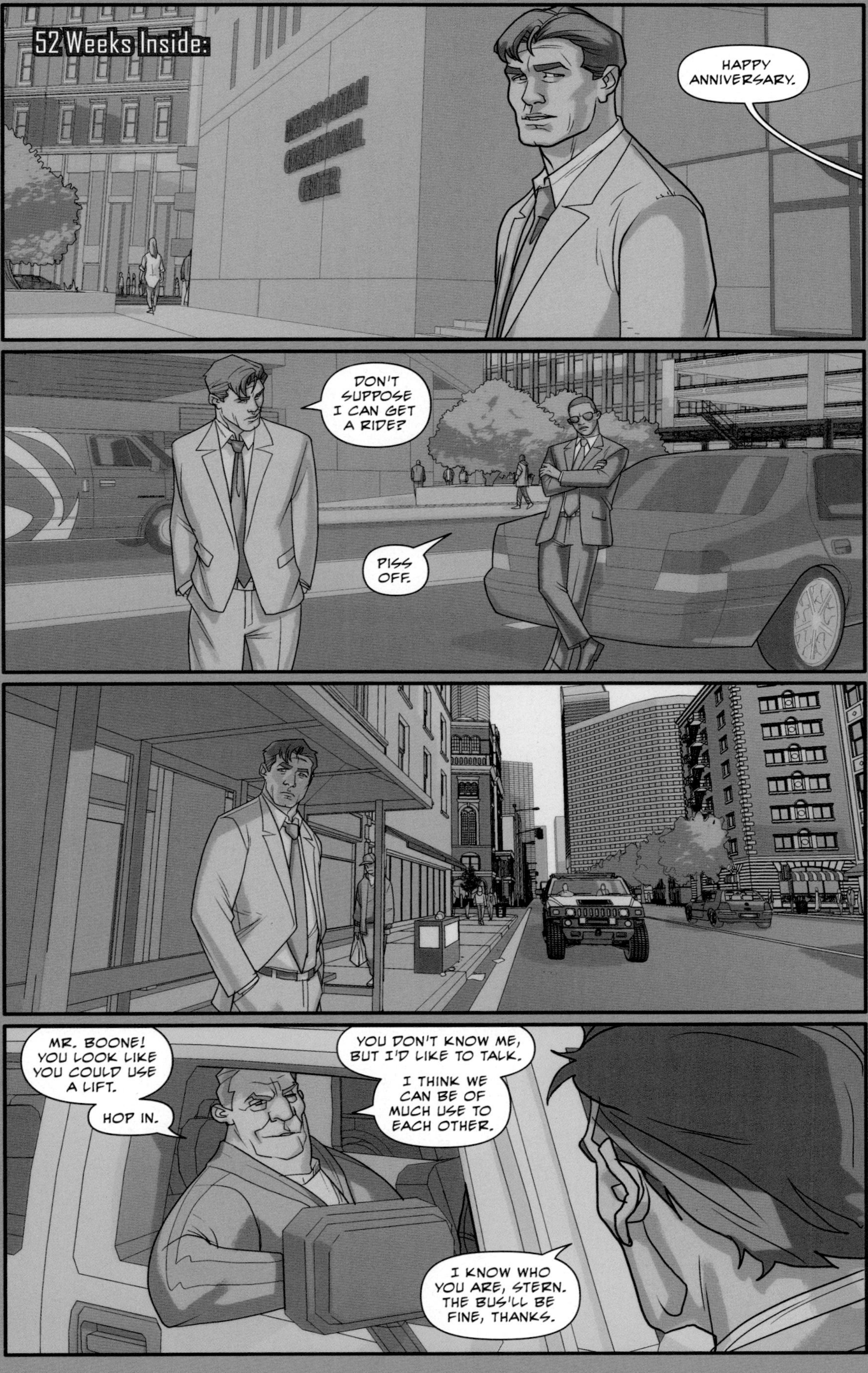
52 Weeks Inside:
METROPOLITAN CORRECTIONAL CENTER
HAPPY ANNIVERSARY.
DON'T SUPPOSE I CAN GET A RIDE?
PISS OFF.
MR. BOONE! YOU LOOK LIKE YOU COULD USE A LIFT.
HOP IN.
YOU DON'T KNOW ME, BUT I'D LIKE TO TALK.
I THINK WE CAN BE OF MUCH USE TO EACH OTHER.
I KNOW WHO YOU ARE, STERN. THE BUS'LL BE FINE, THANKS.

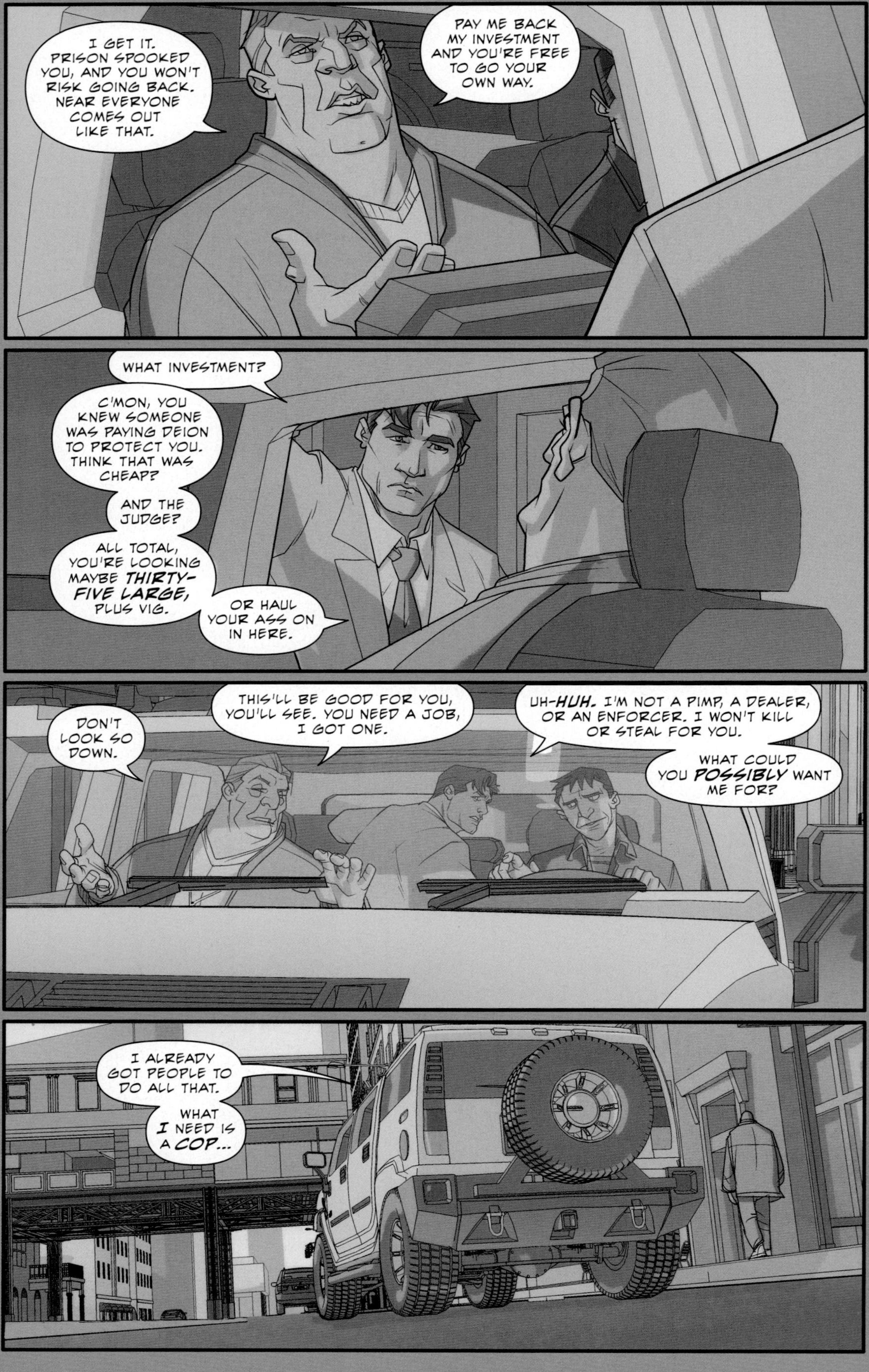
I GET IT. PRISON SPOOKED YOU, AND YOU WON'T RISK GOING BACK. NEAR EVERYONE COMES OUT LIKE THAT.
PAY ME BACK MY INVESTMENT AND YOU'RE FREE TO GO YOUR OWN WAY.
WHAT INVESTMENT?
C'MON, YOU KNEW SOMEONE WAS PAYING DEION TO PROTECT YOU. THINK THAT WAS CHEAP?
AND THE JUDGE?
ALL TOTAL, YOU'RE LOOKING MAYBE *THIRTY-FIVE LARGE,* PLUS VIG.
OR HAUL YOUR ASS ON IN HERE.
DON'T LOOK SO DOWN.
THIS'LL BE GOOD FOR YOU, YOU'LL SEE. YOU NEED A JOB, I GOT ONE.
UH-*HUH.* I'M NOT A PIMP, A DEALER, OR AN ENFORCER. I WON'T KILL OR STEAL FOR YOU.
WHAT COULD YOU *POSSIBLY* WANT ME FOR?
I ALREADY GOT PEOPLE TO DO ALL THAT.
WHAT *I* NEED IS A *COP...*

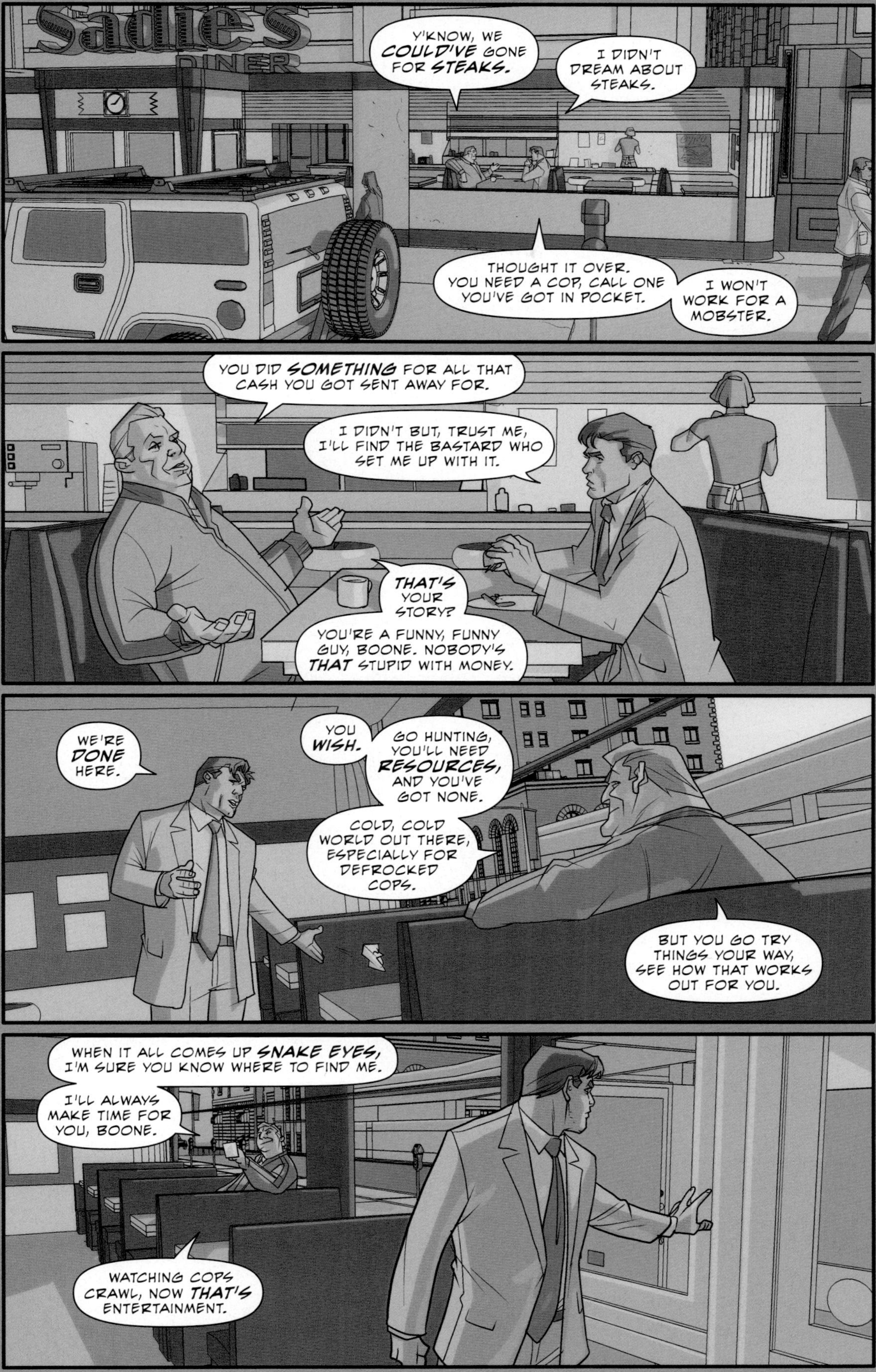
Sadie's
DINER
Y'KNOW, WE COULD'VE GONE FOR STEAKS.
I DIDN'T DREAM ABOUT STEAKS.
THOUGHT IT OVER. YOU NEED A COP, CALL ONE YOU'VE GOT IN POCKET.
I WON'T WORK FOR A MOBSTER.
YOU DID SOMETHING FOR ALL THAT CASH YOU GOT SENT AWAY FOR.
I DIDN'T BUT, TRUST ME, I'LL FIND THE BASTARD WHO SET ME UP WITH IT.
THAT'S YOUR STORY?
YOU'RE A FUNNY, FUNNY GUY, BOONE. NOBODY'S THAT STUPID WITH MONEY.
WE'RE DONE HERE.
YOU WISH.
GO HUNTING, YOU'LL NEED RESOURCES, AND YOU'VE GOT NONE.
COLD, COLD WORLD OUT THERE, ESPECIALLY FOR DEFROCKED COPS.
BUT YOU GO TRY THINGS YOUR WAY, SEE HOW THAT WORKS OUT FOR YOU.
WHEN IT ALL COMES UP SNAKE EYES, I'M SURE YOU KNOW WHERE TO FIND ME.
I'LL ALWAYS MAKE TIME FOR YOU, BOONE.
WATCHING COPS CRAWL, NOW THAT'S ENTERTAINMENT.

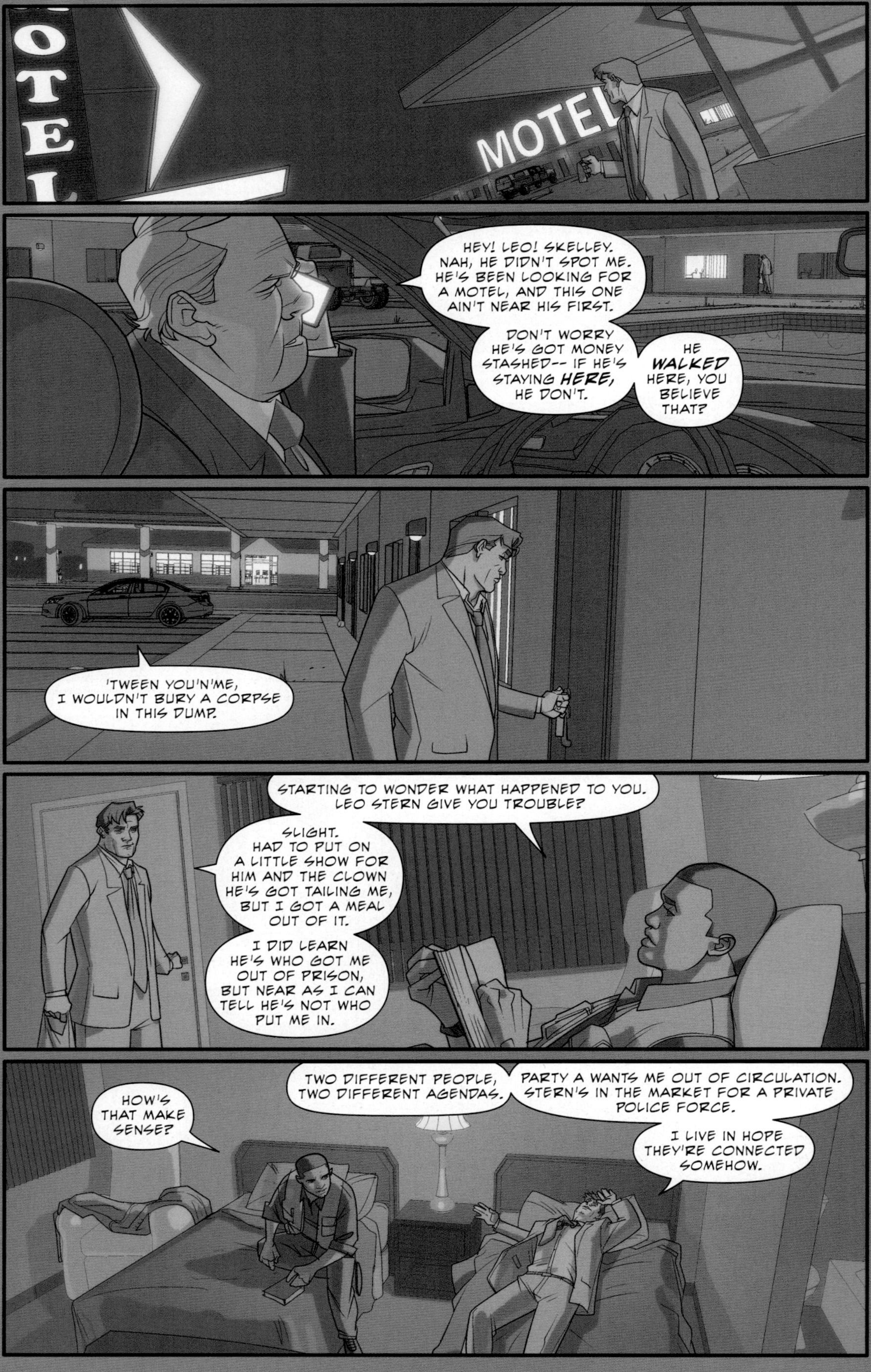
MOTEL
MOTEL
HEY! LEO! SKELLEY. NAH, HE DIDN'T SPOT ME. HE'S BEEN LOOKING FOR A MOTEL, AND THIS ONE AIN'T NEAR HIS FIRST.
DON'T WORRY HE'S GOT MONEY STASHED-- IF HE'S STAYING HERE, HE DON'T.
HE WALKED HERE, YOU BELIEVE THAT?
'TWEEN YOU'N'ME, I WOULDN'T BURY A CORPSE IN THIS DUMP.
STARTING TO WONDER WHAT HAPPENED TO YOU. LEO STERN GIVE YOU TROUBLE?
SLIGHT. HAD TO PUT ON A LITTLE SHOW FOR HIM AND THE CLOWN HE'S GOT TAILING ME, BUT I GOT A MEAL OUT OF IT.
I DID LEARN HE'S WHO GOT ME OUT OF PRISON, BUT NEAR AS I CAN TELL HE'S NOT WHO PUT ME IN.
HOW'S THAT MAKE SENSE?
TWO DIFFERENT PEOPLE, TWO DIFFERENT AGENDAS.
PARTY A WANTS ME OUT OF CIRCULATION. STERN'S IN THE MARKET FOR A PRIVATE POLICE FORCE.
I LIVE IN HOPE THEY'RE CONNECTED SOMEHOW.

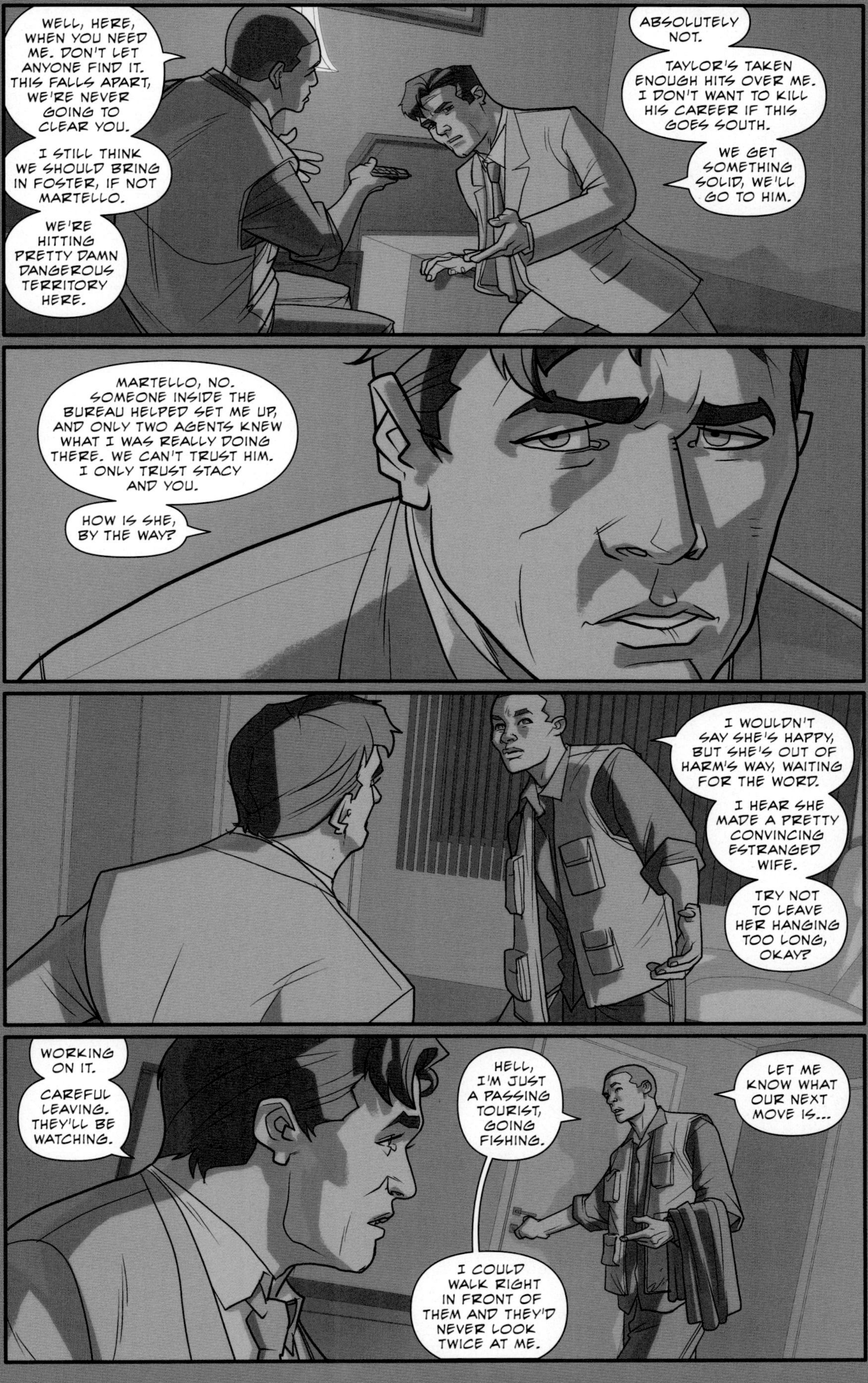
WELL, HERE, WHEN YOU NEED ME. DON'T LET ANYONE FIND IT. THIS FALLS APART, WE'RE NEVER GOING TO CLEAR YOU.
I STILL THINK WE SHOULD BRING IN FOSTER, IF NOT MARTELLO.
WE'RE HITTING PRETTY DAMN DANGEROUS TERRITORY HERE.
ABSOLUTELY NOT.
TAYLOR'S TAKEN ENOUGH HITS OVER ME. I DON'T WANT TO KILL HIS CAREER IF THIS GOES SOUTH.
WE GET SOMETHING SOLID, WE'LL GO TO HIM.
MARTELLO, NO. SOMEONE INSIDE THE BUREAU HELPED SET ME UP, AND ONLY TWO AGENTS KNEW WHAT I WAS REALLY DOING THERE. WE CAN'T TRUST HIM. I ONLY TRUST STACY AND YOU.
HOW IS SHE, BY THE WAY?
I WOULDN'T SAY SHE'S HAPPY, BUT SHE'S OUT OF HARM'S WAY, WAITING FOR THE WORD.
I HEAR SHE MADE A PRETTY CONVINCING ESTRANGED WIFE.
TRY NOT TO LEAVE HER HANGING TOO LONG, OKAY?
WORKING ON IT.
CAREFUL LEAVING. THEY'LL BE WATCHING.
HELL, I'M JUST A PASSING TOURIST, GOING FISHING.
I COULD WALK RIGHT IN FRONT OF THEM AND THEY'D NEVER LOOK TWICE AT ME.
LET ME KNOW WHAT OUR NEXT MOVE IS...

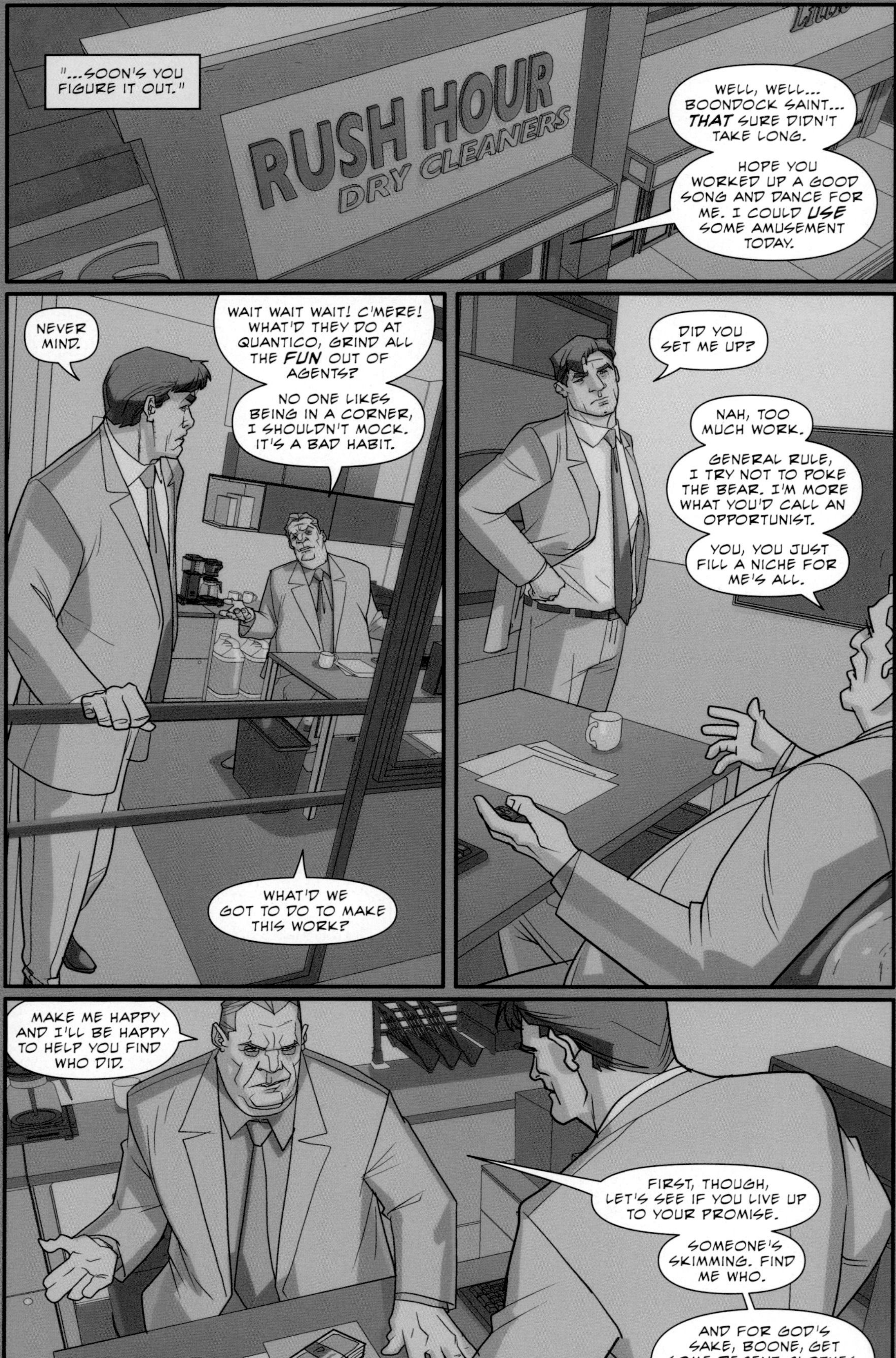
"...SOON'S YOU FIGURE IT OUT."
RUSH HOUR DRY CLEANERS
WELL, WELL... BOONDOCK SAINT... THAT SURE DIDN'T TAKE LONG.
HOPE YOU WORKED UP A GOOD SONG AND DANCE FOR ME. I COULD USE SOME AMUSEMENT TODAY.
NEVER MIND.
WAIT WAIT WAIT! C'MERE! WHAT'D THEY DO AT QUANTICO, GRIND ALL THE FUN OUT OF AGENTS?
NO ONE LIKES BEING IN A CORNER, I SHOULDN'T MOCK. IT'S A BAD HABIT.
WHAT'D WE GOT TO DO TO MAKE THIS WORK?
DID YOU SET ME UP?
NAH, TOO MUCH WORK.
GENERAL RULE, I TRY NOT TO POKE THE BEAR. I'M MORE WHAT YOU'D CALL AN OPPORTUNIST.
YOU, YOU JUST FILL A NICHE FOR ME'S ALL.
MAKE ME HAPPY AND I'LL BE HAPPY TO HELP YOU FIND WHO DID.
FIRST, THOUGH, LET'S SEE IF YOU LIVE UP TO YOUR PROMISE.
SOMEONE'S SKIMMING. FIND ME WHO.
AND FOR GOD'S SAKE, BOONE, GET SOME DECENT CLOTHES. YOU LOOK LIKE A COP.

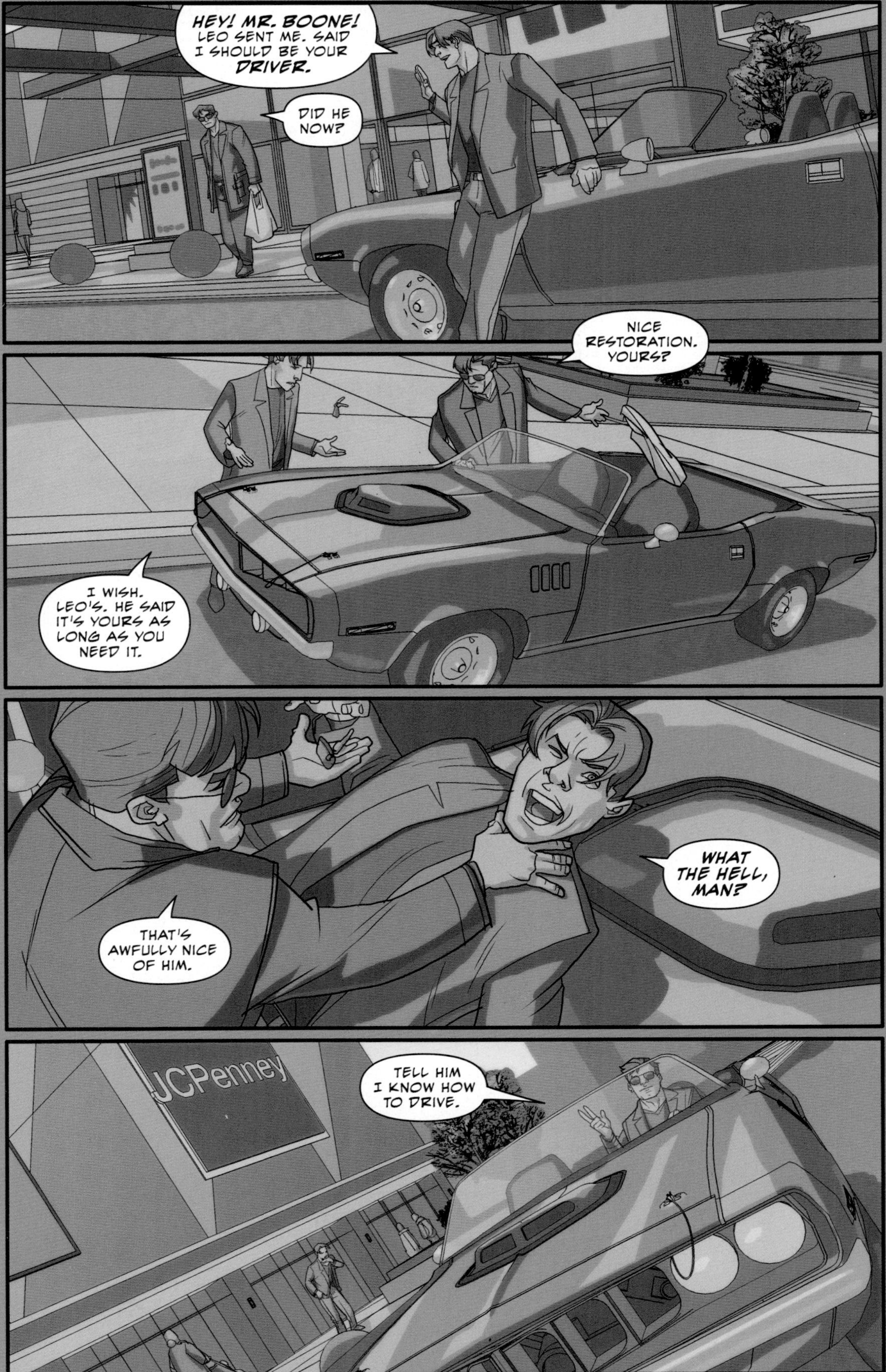
HEY! MR. BOONE! LEO SENT ME. SAID I SHOULD BE YOUR DRIVER.
DID HE NOW?
NICE RESTORATION. YOURS?
I WISH. LEO'S. HE SAID IT'S YOURS AS LONG AS YOU NEED IT.
THAT'S AWFULLY NICE OF HIM.
WHAT THE HELL, MAN?
JCPenney
TELL HIM I KNOW HOW TO DRIVE.

HE GAVE YOU A *LIST* OF ALL OF HIS OPERATIONS

JUST LIKE THAT?

HALF-DOZEN, CAN'T BE ALL.

A *TEST*, I'M PRETTY SURE, TO SEE IF I DO THE JOB OR GIVE HIM UP. HE'S A CUTE ONE.

STILL NOT SURE WHAT HE WANTS A COP FOR. THIS ONE SEEMS A PRETTY STRAIGHT-FORWARD SHAKE, RATTLE AND ROLL. ANY BEAT COP ON THE PAD COULD DO THAT FOR HIM.

MIGHT HAVE SOME NAMES FOR YOU TO RUN THROUGH THE DATABASE BY THE END OF THIS, IF YOU'RE WILLING.

ACCESS WITHOUT AUTHORIZATION, STRICTLY VERBOTEN. YOU KNOW THAT, PHILIP.

FORTUNATELY, INTERNAL AFFAIRS GETS A LITTLE MORE LEEWAY.

LET ME KNOW WHAT YOU NEED, AND STAY SAFE.

NOT TO WORRY. STERN'S MAKING SURE I HAVE PLENTY OF COMPANY.

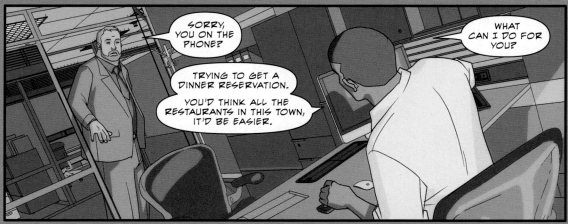

SORRY, YOU ON THE PHONE?

WHAT CAN I DO FOR YOU?

TRYING TO GET A DINNER RESERVATION.

YOU'D THINK ALL THE RESTAURANTS IN THIS TOWN, IT'D BE EASIER.

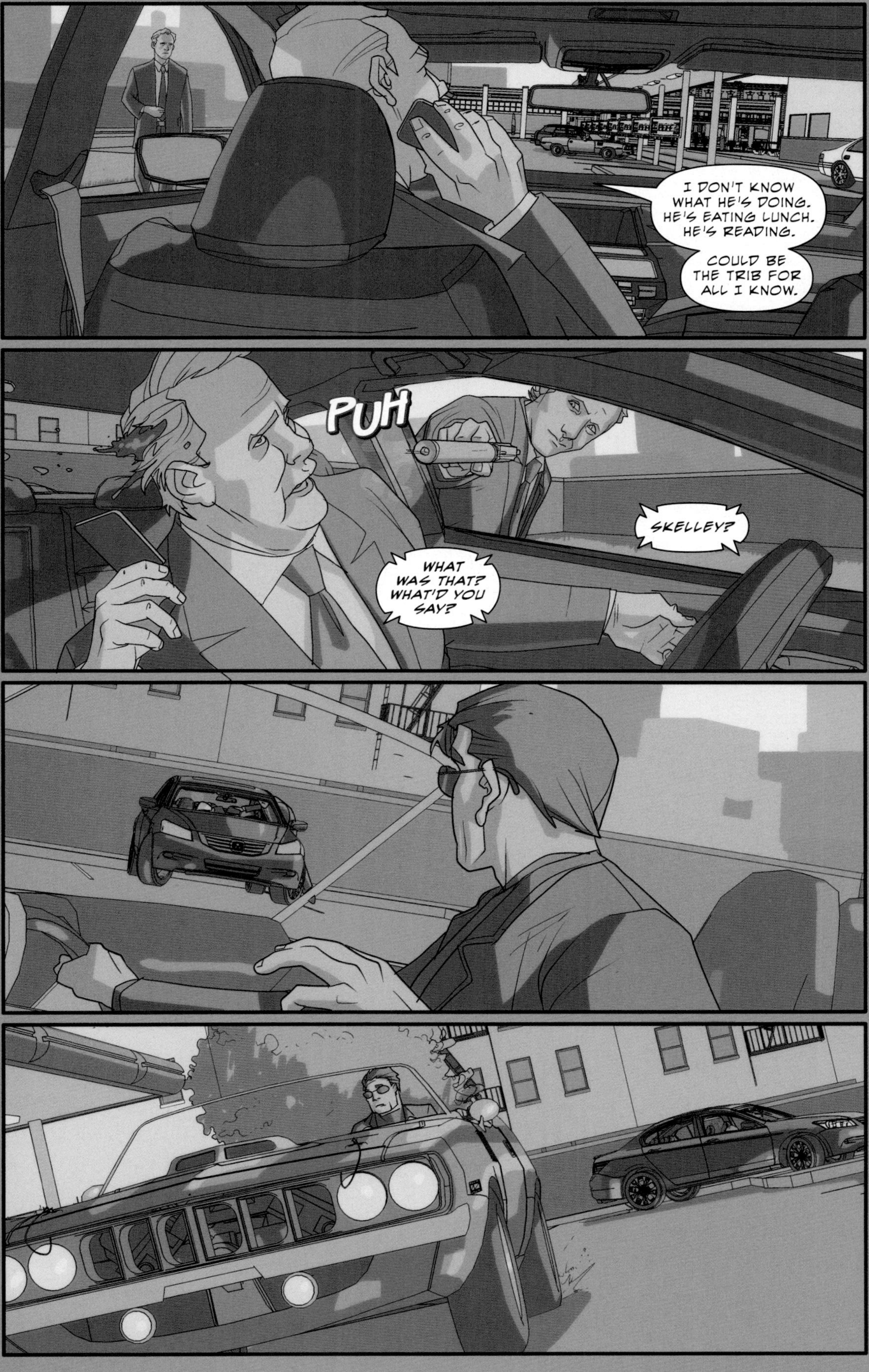
I DON'T KNOW WHAT HE'S DOING. HE'S EATING LUNCH. HE'S READING.
COULD BE THE TRIB FOR ALL I KNOW.
PUH
SKELLEY?
WHAT WAS THAT? WHAT'D YOU SAY?

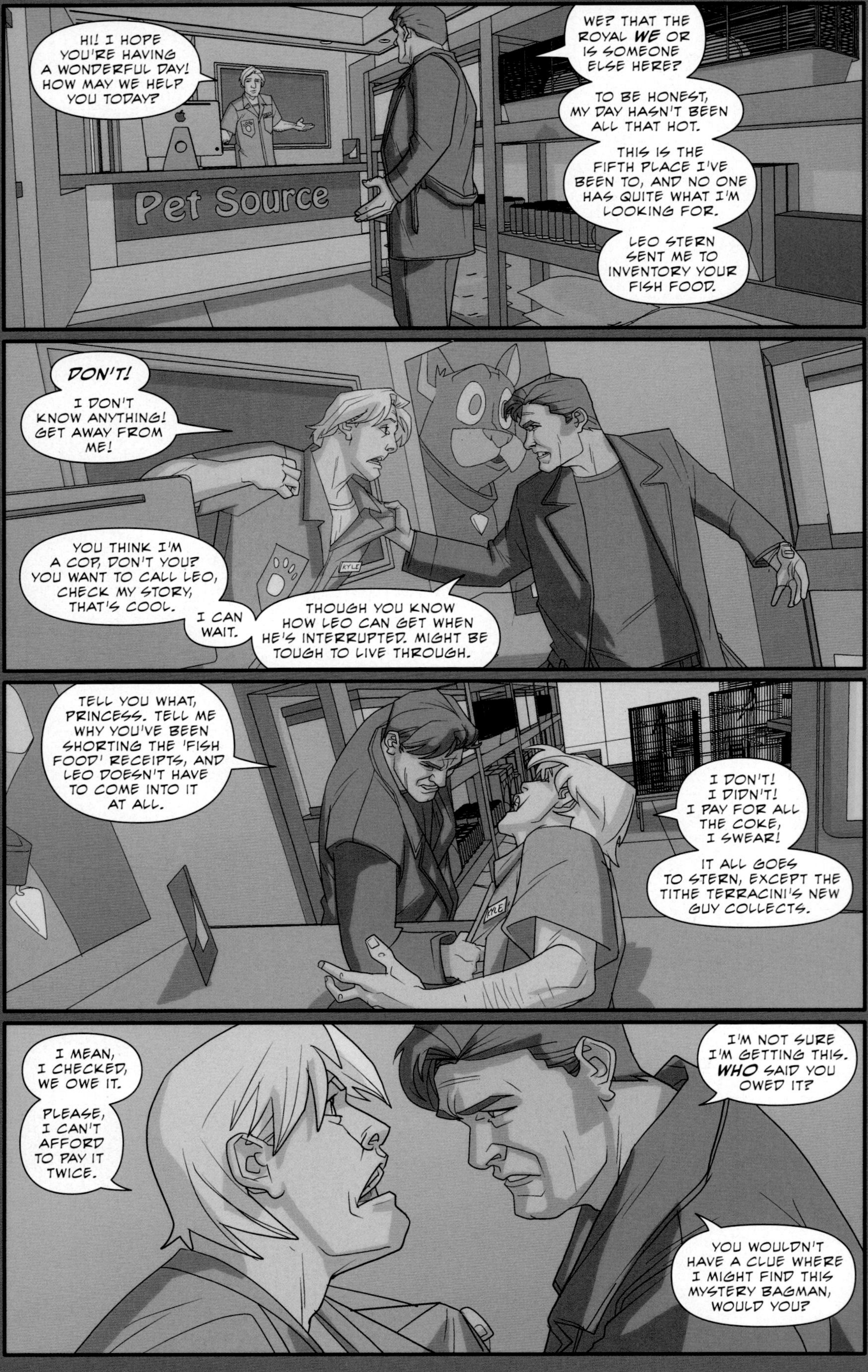
HI! I HOPE YOU'RE HAVING A WONDERFUL DAY! HOW MAY WE HELP YOU TODAY?
WE? THAT THE ROYAL WE OR IS SOMEONE ELSE HERE?
TO BE HONEST, MY DAY HASN'T BEEN ALL THAT HOT.
THIS IS THE FIFTH PLACE I'VE BEEN TO, AND NO ONE HAS QUITE WHAT I'M LOOKING FOR.
LEO STERN SENT ME TO INVENTORY YOUR FISH FOOD.
Pet Source
DON'T!
I DON'T KNOW ANYTHING! GET AWAY FROM ME!
YOU THINK I'M A COP, DON'T YOU? YOU WANT TO CALL LEO, CHECK MY STORY, THAT'S COOL.
I CAN WAIT.
THOUGH YOU KNOW HOW LEO CAN GET WHEN HE'S INTERRUPTED. MIGHT BE TOUGH TO LIVE THROUGH.
KYLE
TELL YOU WHAT, PRINCESS. TELL ME WHY YOU'VE BEEN SHORTING THE 'FISH FOOD' RECEIPTS, AND LEO DOESN'T HAVE TO COME INTO IT AT ALL.
I DON'T! I DIDN'T! I PAY FOR ALL THE COKE, I SWEAR!
IT ALL GOES TO STERN, EXCEPT THE TITHE TERRACINI'S NEW GUY COLLECTS.
KYLE
I MEAN, I CHECKED, WE OWE IT.
PLEASE, I CAN'T AFFORD TO PAY IT TWICE.
I'M NOT SURE I'M GETTING THIS. WHO SAID YOU OWED IT?
YOU WOULDN'T HAVE A CLUE WHERE I MIGHT FIND THIS MYSTERY BAGMAN, WOULD YOU?

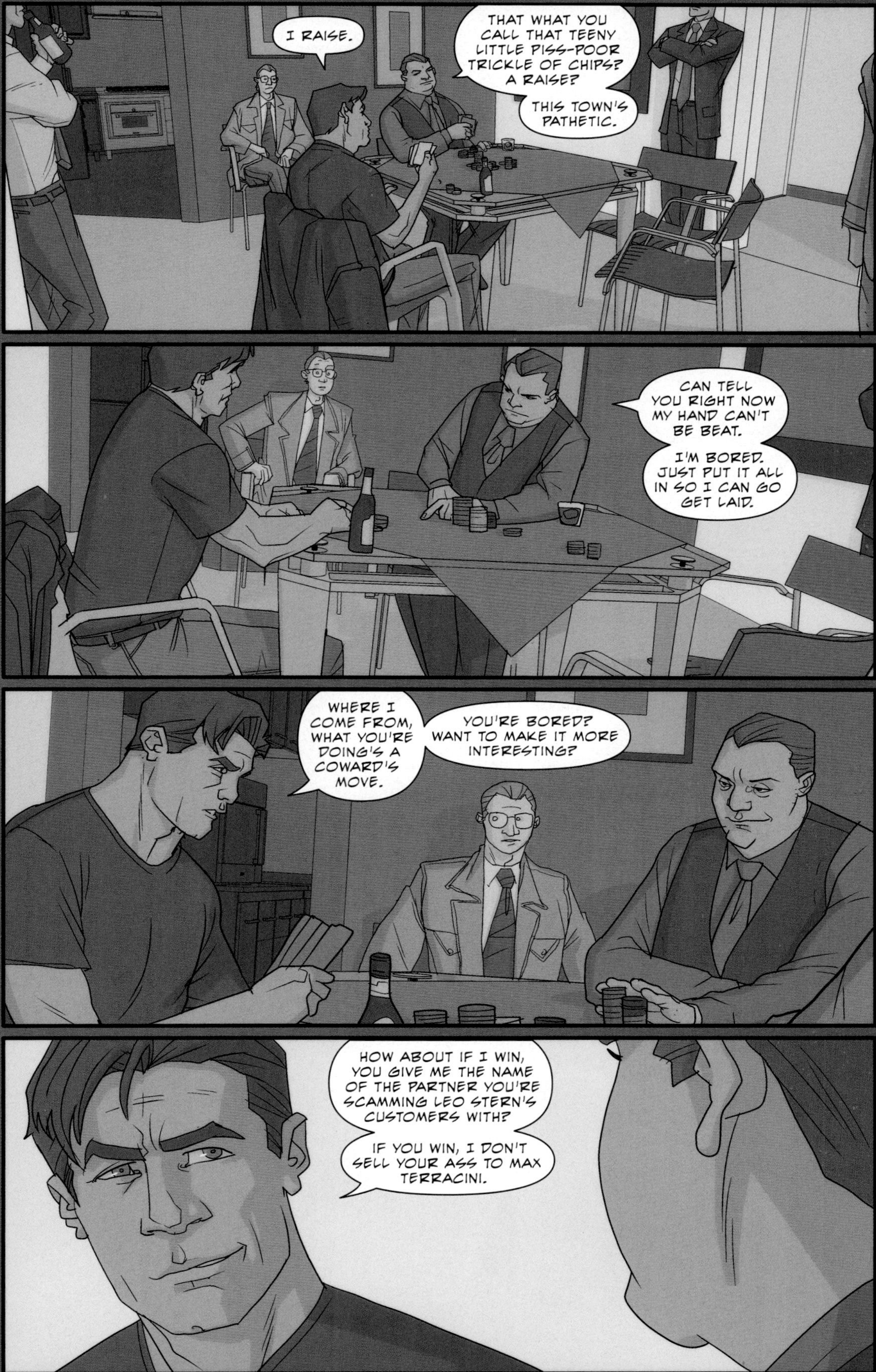
I RAISE.
THAT WHAT YOU CALL THAT TEENY LITTLE PISS-POOR TRICKLE OF CHIPS? A RAISE?
THIS TOWN'S PATHETIC.
CAN TELL YOU RIGHT NOW MY HAND CAN'T BE BEAT.
I'M BORED. JUST PUT IT ALL IN SO I CAN GO GET LAID.
WHERE I COME FROM, WHAT YOU'RE DOING'S A COWARD'S MOVE.
YOU'RE BORED? WANT TO MAKE IT MORE INTERESTING?
HOW ABOUT IF I WIN, YOU GIVE ME THE NAME OF THE PARTNER YOU'RE SCAMMING LEO STERN'S CUSTOMERS WITH?
IF YOU WIN, I DON'T SELL YOUR ASS TO MAX TERRACINI.

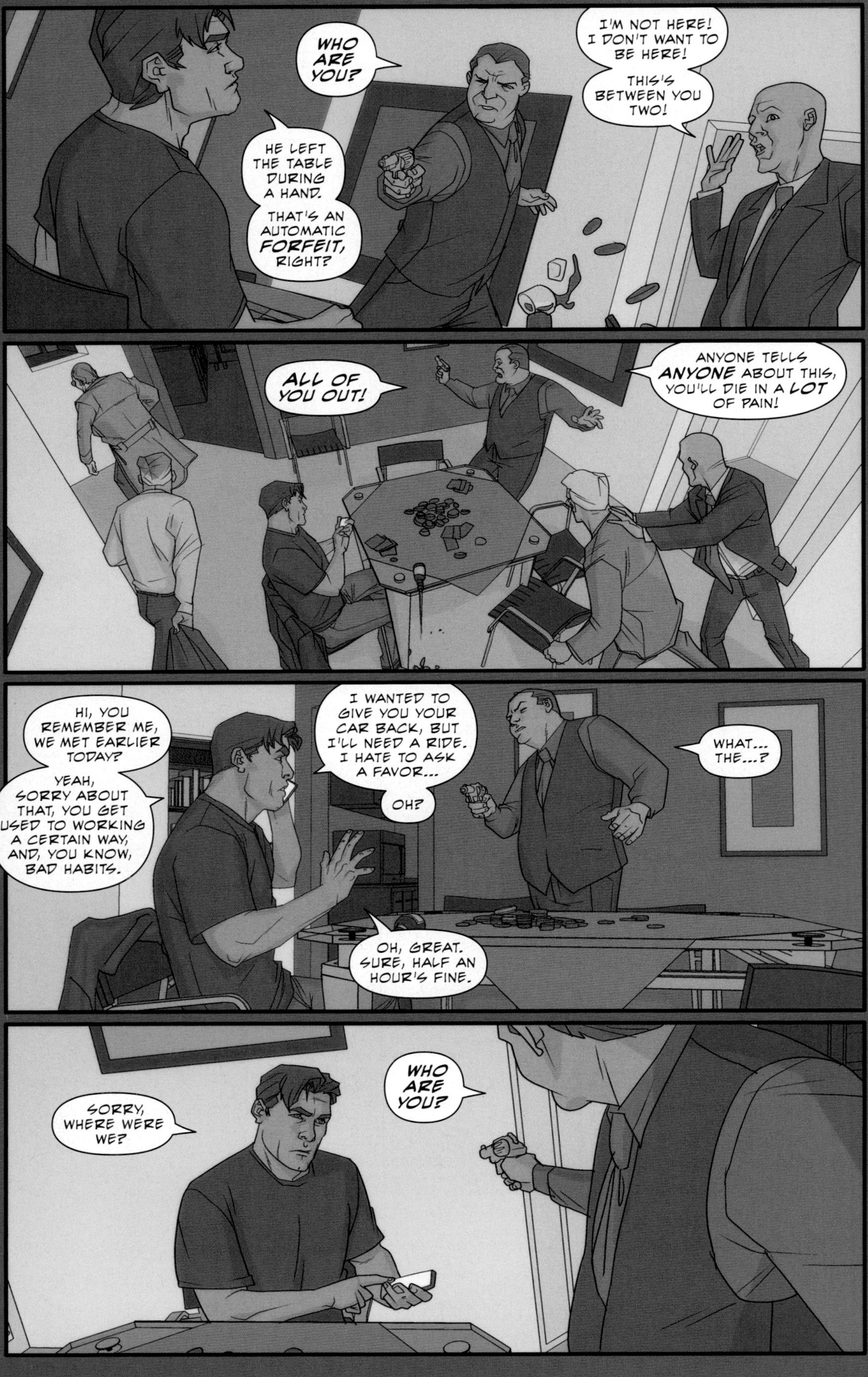
WHO ARE YOU?
HE LEFT THE TABLE DURING A HAND.
THAT'S AN AUTOMATIC FORFEIT, RIGHT?
I'M NOT HERE! I DON'T WANT TO BE HERE!
THIS'S BETWEEN YOU TWO!
ALL OF YOU OUT!
ANYONE TELLS ANYONE ABOUT THIS, YOU'LL DIE IN A LOT OF PAIN!
HI, YOU REMEMBER ME, WE MET EARLIER TODAY?
YEAH, SORRY ABOUT THAT, YOU GET USED TO WORKING A CERTAIN WAY, AND, YOU KNOW, BAD HABITS.
I WANTED TO GIVE YOU YOUR CAR BACK, BUT I'LL NEED A RIDE. I HATE TO ASK A FAVOR...
OH?
OH, GREAT. SURE, HALF AN HOUR'S FINE.
WHAT... THE...?
SORRY, WHERE WERE WE?
WHO ARE YOU?

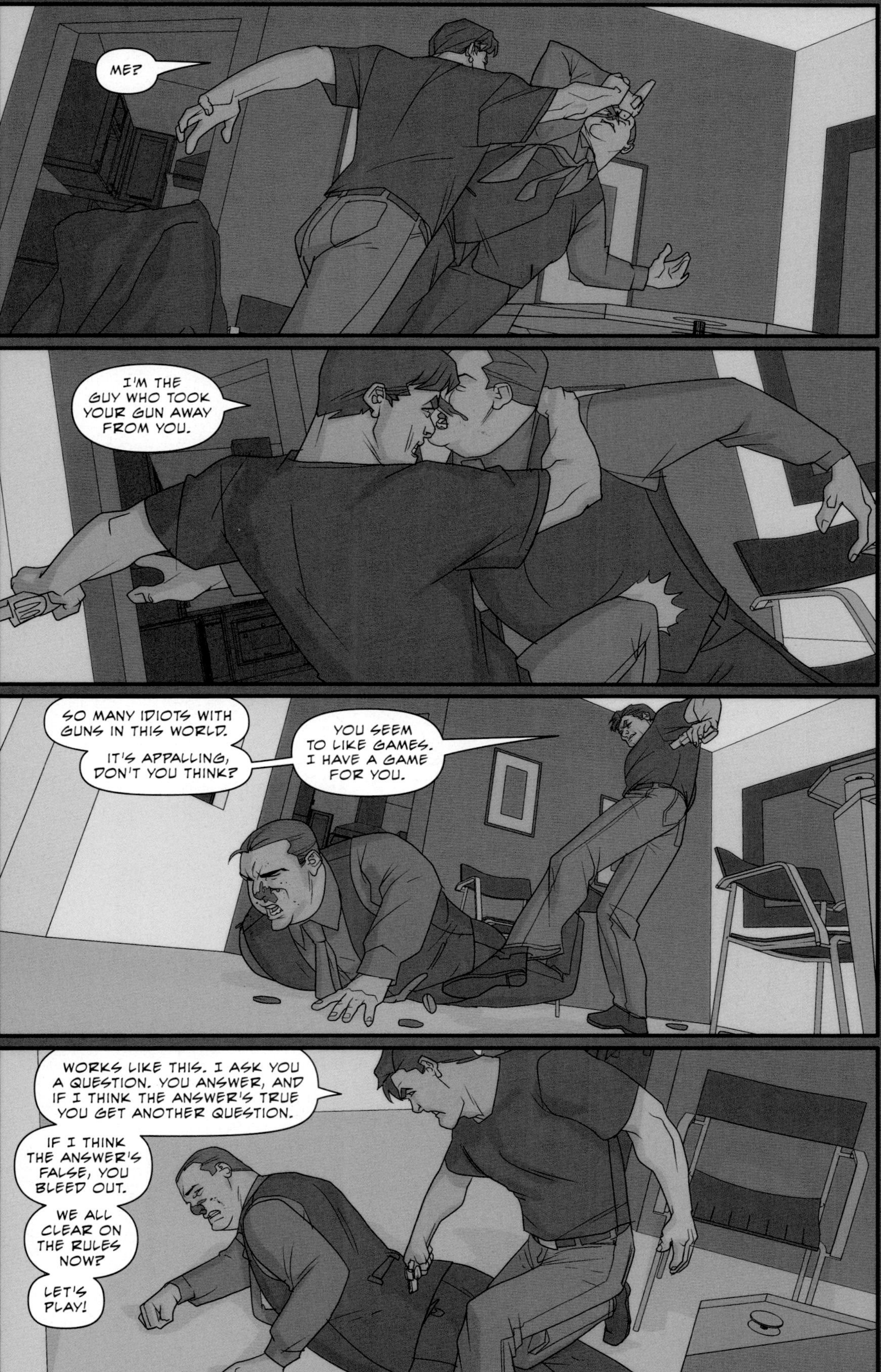
ME?
I'M THE GUY WHO TOOK YOUR GUN AWAY FROM YOU.
SO MANY IDIOTS WITH GUNS IN THIS WORLD.
IT'S APPALLING, DON'T YOU THINK?
YOU SEEM TO LIKE GAMES. I HAVE A GAME FOR YOU.
WORKS LIKE THIS. I ASK YOU A QUESTION. YOU ANSWER, AND IF I THINK THE ANSWER'S TRUE YOU GET ANOTHER QUESTION.
IF I THINK THE ANSWER'S FALSE, YOU BLEED OUT.
WE ALL CLEAR ON THE RULES NOW?
LET'S PLAY!

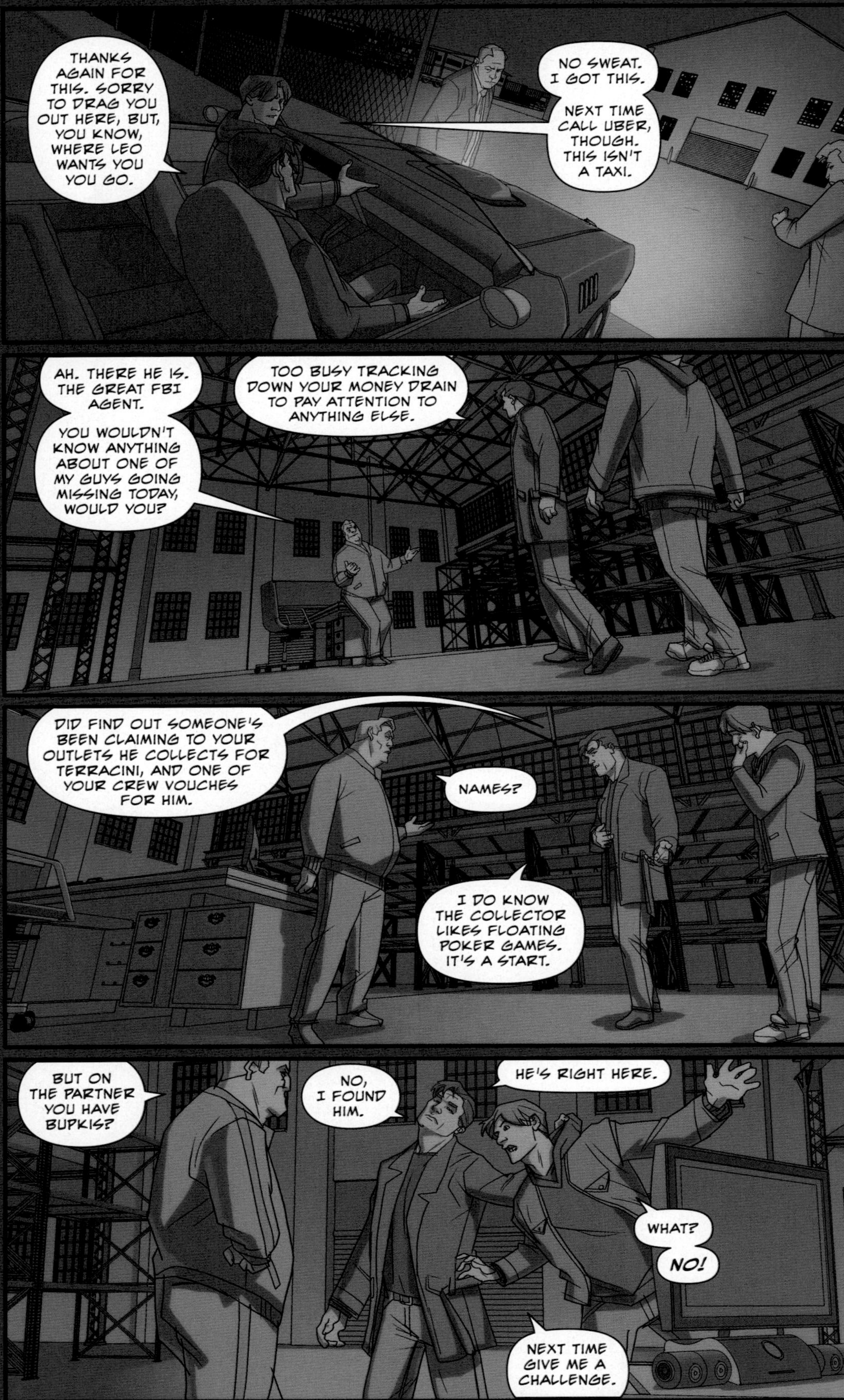
THANKS AGAIN FOR THIS. SORRY TO DRAG YOU OUT HERE, BUT, YOU KNOW, WHERE LEO WANTS YOU YOU GO.
NO SWEAT. I GOT THIS.
NEXT TIME CALL UBER, THOUGH. THIS ISN'T A TAXI.
AH. THERE HE IS. THE GREAT FBI AGENT.
YOU WOULDN'T KNOW ANYTHING ABOUT ONE OF MY GUYS GOING MISSING TODAY, WOULD YOU?
TOO BUSY TRACKING DOWN YOUR MONEY DRAIN TO PAY ATTENTION TO ANYTHING ELSE.
DID FIND OUT SOMEONE'S BEEN CLAIMING TO YOUR OUTLETS HE COLLECTS FOR TERRACINI, AND ONE OF YOUR CREW VOUCHES FOR HIM.
NAMES?
I DO KNOW THE COLLECTOR LIKES FLOATING POKER GAMES. IT'S A START.
BUT ON THE PARTNER YOU HAVE BUPKIS?
NO, I FOUND HIM.
HE'S RIGHT HERE.
WHAT?
NO!
NEXT TIME GIVE ME A CHALLENGE.

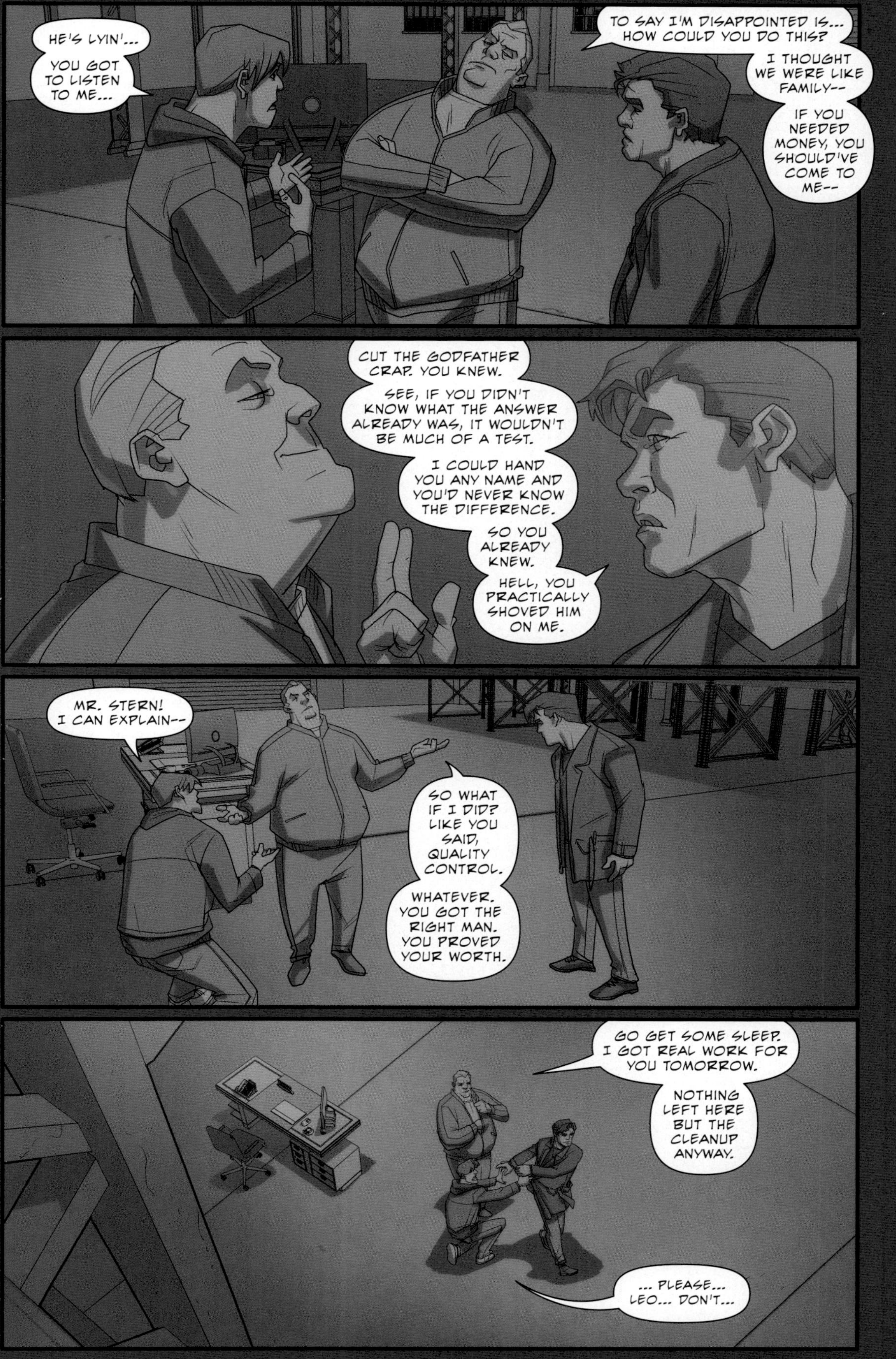
HE'S LYIN'...
YOU GOT TO LISTEN TO ME...
TO SAY I'M DISAPPOINTED IS... HOW COULD YOU DO THIS?
I THOUGHT WE WERE LIKE FAMILY--
IF YOU NEEDED MONEY, YOU SHOULD'VE COME TO ME--
CUT THE GODFATHER CRAP. YOU KNEW.
SEE, IF YOU DIDN'T KNOW WHAT THE ANSWER ALREADY WAS, IT WOULDN'T BE MUCH OF A TEST.
I COULD HAND YOU ANY NAME AND YOU'D NEVER KNOW THE DIFFERENCE.
SO YOU ALREADY KNEW.
HELL, YOU PRACTICALLY SHOVED HIM ON ME.
MR. STERN! I CAN EXPLAIN--
SO WHAT IF I DID? LIKE YOU SAID, QUALITY CONTROL.
WHATEVER. YOU GOT THE RIGHT MAN. YOU PROVED YOUR WORTH.
GO GET SOME SLEEP. I GOT REAL WORK FOR YOU TOMORROW.
NOTHING LEFT HERE BUT THE CLEANUP ANYWAY.
... PLEASE... LEO... DON'T...

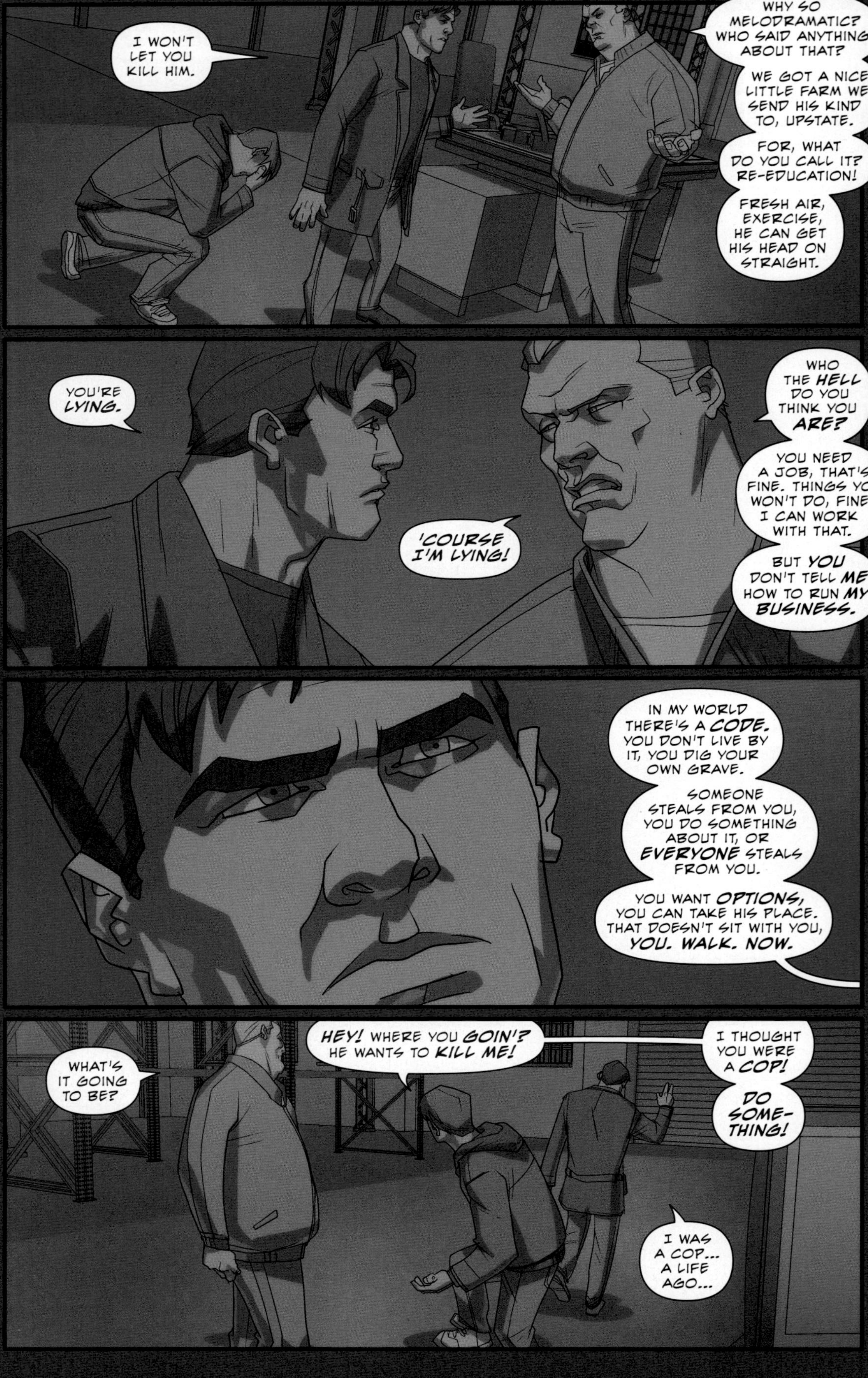
I WON'T LET YOU KILL HIM.
WHY SO MELODRAMATIC? WHO SAID ANYTHING ABOUT THAT?
WE GOT A NICE LITTLE FARM WE SEND HIS KIND TO, UPSTATE.
FOR, WHAT DO YOU CALL IT? RE-EDUCATION!
FRESH AIR, EXERCISE, HE CAN GET HIS HEAD ON STRAIGHT.
YOU'RE *LYING.*
'COURSE I'M LYING!
WHO THE *HELL* DO YOU THINK YOU *ARE?*
YOU NEED A JOB, THAT'S FINE. THINGS YOU WON'T DO, FINE, I CAN WORK WITH THAT.
BUT *YOU* DON'T TELL *ME* HOW TO RUN *MY BUSINESS.*
IN MY WORLD THERE'S A *CODE.* YOU DON'T LIVE BY IT, YOU DIG YOUR OWN GRAVE.
SOMEONE STEALS FROM YOU, YOU DO SOMETHING ABOUT IT, OR *EVERYONE* STEALS FROM YOU.
YOU WANT *OPTIONS,* YOU CAN TAKE HIS PLACE. THAT DOESN'T SIT WITH YOU, *YOU. WALK. NOW.*
WHAT'S IT GOING TO BE?
HEY! WHERE YOU *GOIN'?* HE WANTS TO *KILL ME!*
I THOUGHT YOU WERE A *COP!*
DO SOME-THING!
I WAS A COP... A LIFE AGO...

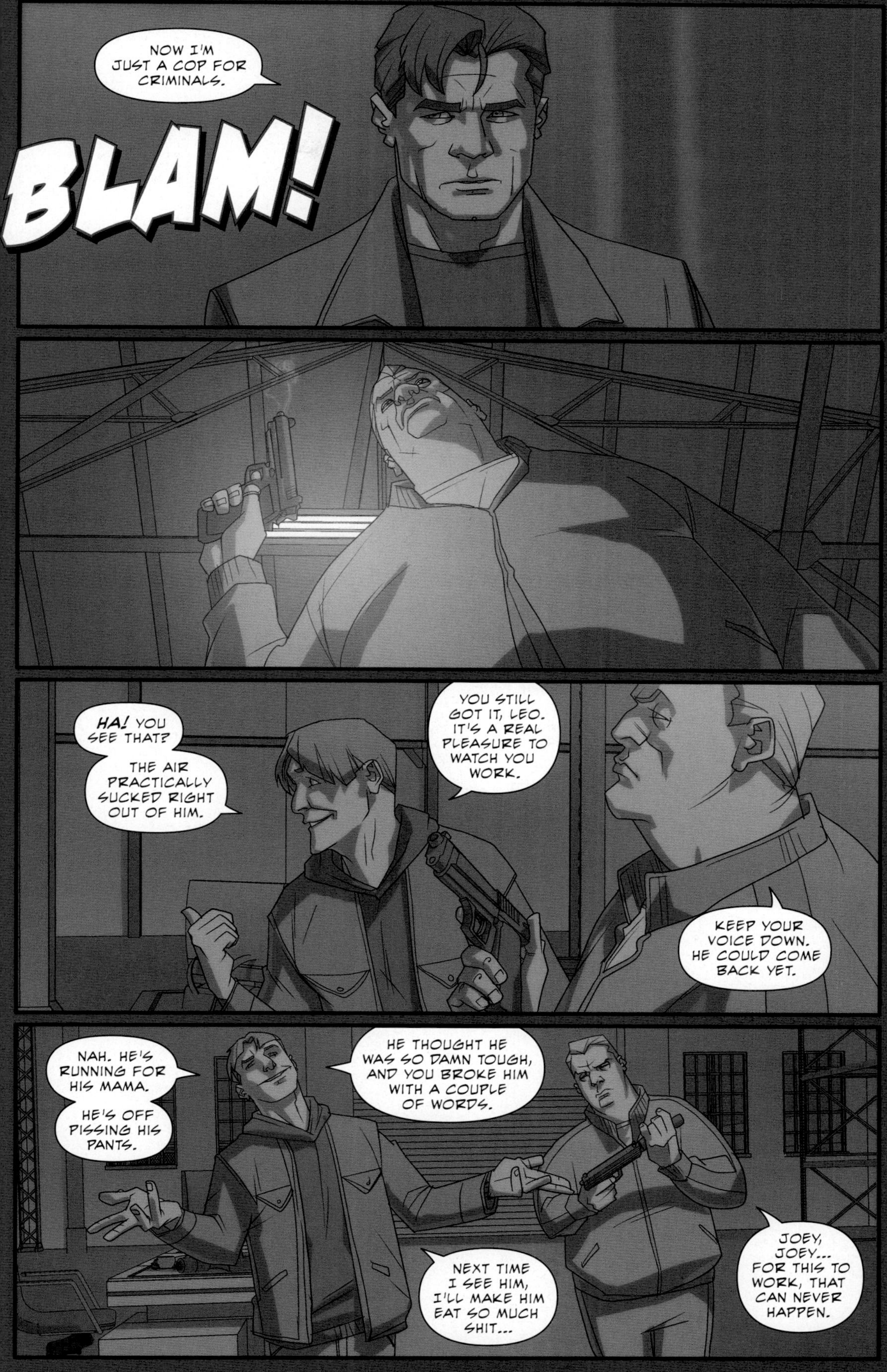
NOW I'M JUST A COP FOR CRIMINALS.
BLAM!
HA! YOU SEE THAT?
THE AIR PRACTICALLY SUCKED RIGHT OUT OF HIM.
YOU STILL GOT IT, LEO. IT'S A REAL PLEASURE TO WATCH YOU WORK.
KEEP YOUR VOICE DOWN. HE COULD COME BACK YET.
NAH. HE'S RUNNING FOR HIS MAMA.
HE'S OFF PISSING HIS PANTS.
HE THOUGHT HE WAS SO DAMN TOUGH, AND YOU BROKE HIM WITH A COUPLE OF WORDS.
NEXT TIME I SEE HIM, I'LL MAKE HIM EAT SO MUCH SHIT...
JOEY, JOEY... FOR THIS TO WORK, THAT CAN NEVER HAPPEN.

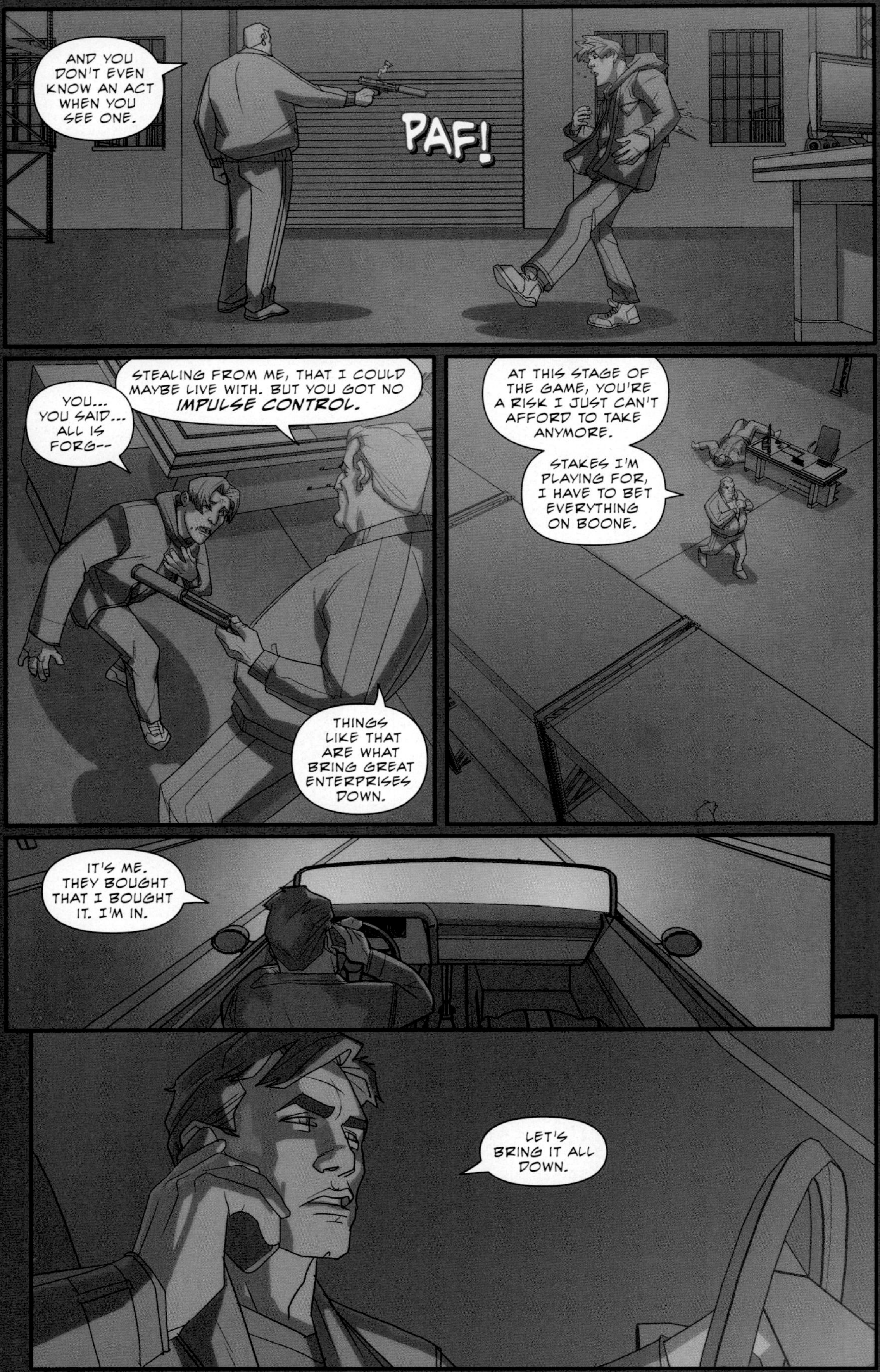
AND YOU DON'T EVEN KNOW AN ACT WHEN YOU SEE ONE.
PAF!
STEALING FROM ME, THAT I COULD MAYBE LIVE WITH. BUT YOU GOT NO IMPULSE CONTROL.
YOU... YOU SAID... ALL IS FORG--
THINGS LIKE THAT ARE WHAT BRING GREAT ENTERPRISES DOWN.
AT THIS STAGE OF THE GAME, YOU'RE A RISK I JUST CAN'T AFFORD TO TAKE ANYMORE.
STAKES I'M PLAYING FOR, I HAVE TO BET EVERYTHING ON BOONE.
IT'S ME. THEY BOUGHT THAT I BOUGHT IT. I'M IN.
LET'S BRING IT ALL DOWN.

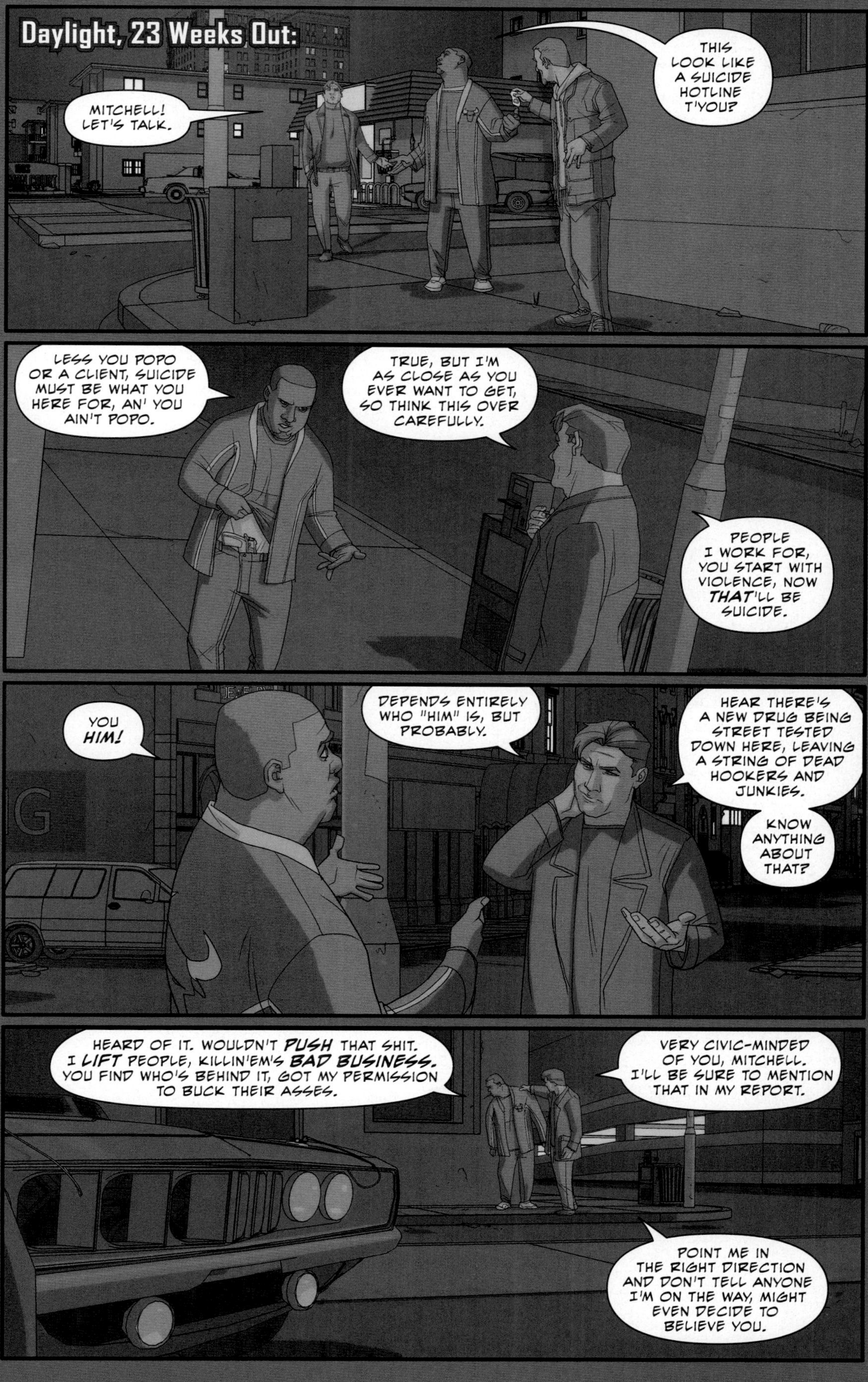
Daylight, 23 Weeks Out:
MITCHELL! LET'S TALK.
THIS LOOK LIKE A SUICIDE HOTLINE T'YOU?
LESS YOU POPO OR A CLIENT, SUICIDE MUST BE WHAT YOU HERE FOR, AN' YOU AIN'T POPO.
TRUE, BUT I'M AS CLOSE AS YOU EVER WANT TO GET, SO THINK THIS OVER CAREFULLY.
PEOPLE I WORK FOR, YOU START WITH VIOLENCE, NOW *THAT*'LL BE SUICIDE.
YOU *HIM!*
DEPENDS ENTIRELY WHO "HIM" IS, BUT PROBABLY.
HEAR THERE'S A NEW DRUG BEING STREET TESTED DOWN HERE, LEAVING A STRING OF DEAD HOOKERS AND JUNKIES.
KNOW ANYTHING ABOUT THAT?
HEARD OF IT. WOULDN'T *PUSH* THAT SHIT. I *LIFT* PEOPLE, KILLIN'EM'S *BAD BUSINESS.* YOU FIND WHO'S BEHIND IT, GOT MY PERMISSION TO BUCK THEIR ASSES.
VERY CIVIC-MINDED OF YOU, MITCHELL. I'LL BE SURE TO MENTION THAT IN MY REPORT.
POINT ME IN THE RIGHT DIRECTION AND DON'T TELL ANYONE I'M ON THE WAY, MIGHT EVEN DECIDE TO BELIEVE YOU.

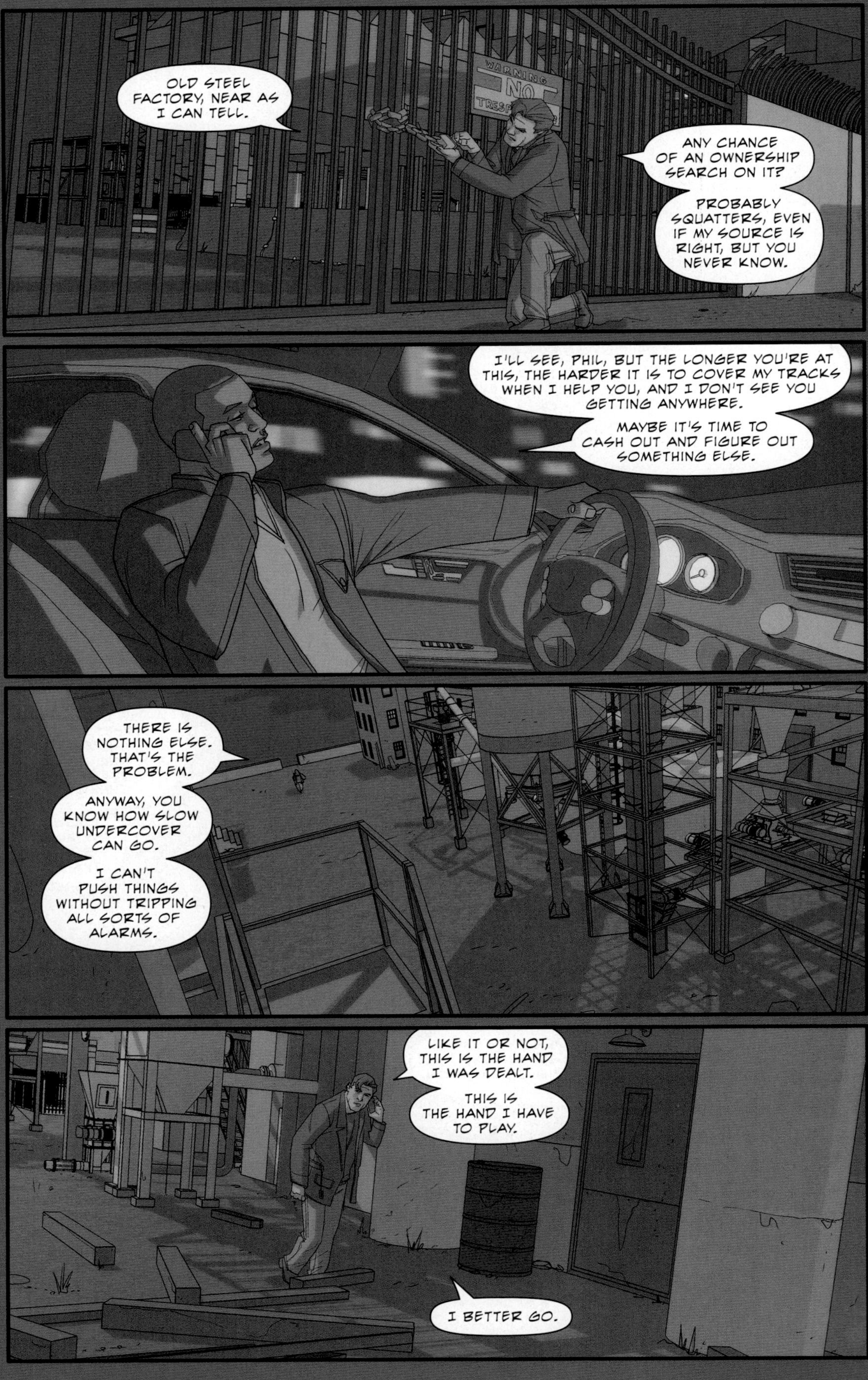
WARNING NO TRESP
OLD STEEL FACTORY, NEAR AS I CAN TELL.
ANY CHANCE OF AN OWNERSHIP SEARCH ON IT?
PROBABLY SQUATTERS, EVEN IF MY SOURCE IS RIGHT, BUT YOU NEVER KNOW.
I'LL SEE, PHIL, BUT THE LONGER YOU'RE AT THIS, THE HARDER IT IS TO COVER MY TRACKS WHEN I HELP YOU, AND I DON'T SEE YOU GETTING ANYWHERE.
MAYBE IT'S TIME TO CASH OUT AND FIGURE OUT SOMETHING ELSE.
THERE IS NOTHING ELSE. THAT'S THE PROBLEM.
ANYWAY, YOU KNOW HOW SLOW UNDERCOVER CAN GO.
I CAN'T PUSH THINGS WITHOUT TRIPPING ALL SORTS OF ALARMS.
LIKE IT OR NOT, THIS IS THE HAND I WAS DEALT.
THIS IS THE HAND I HAVE TO PLAY.
I BETTER GO.

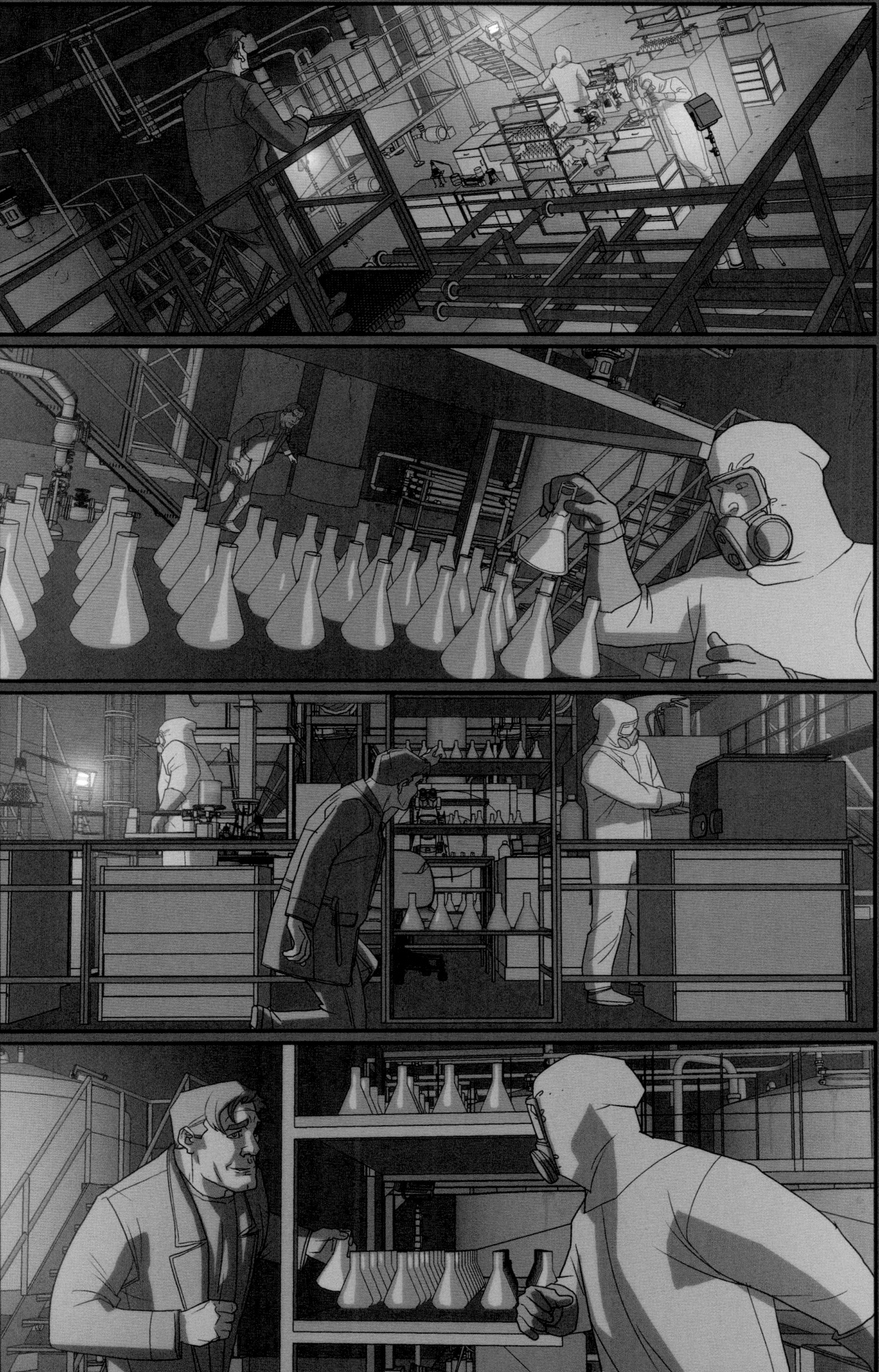

TROUBLE!
GET HIM!
BLAM! BLAM! BLAM!
SHIT!
WHAT'D WE DO NOW?
YOU KNOW THE RULES.
I DON'T WANT TO.
ME NEITHER.
WHAT CHOICE DO WE HAVE?

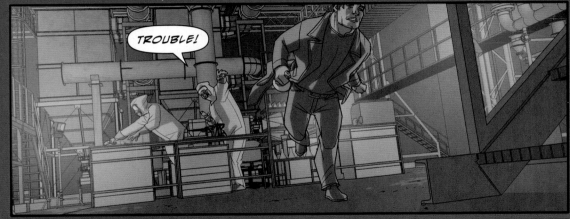

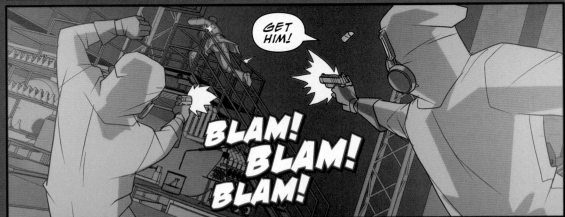

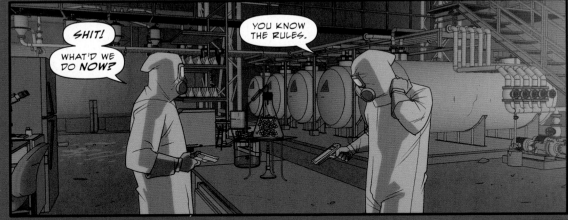

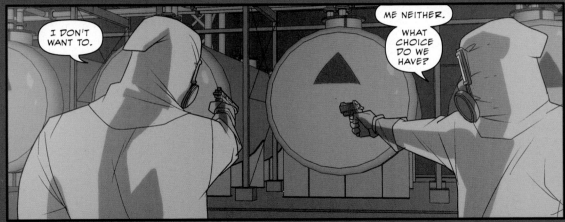

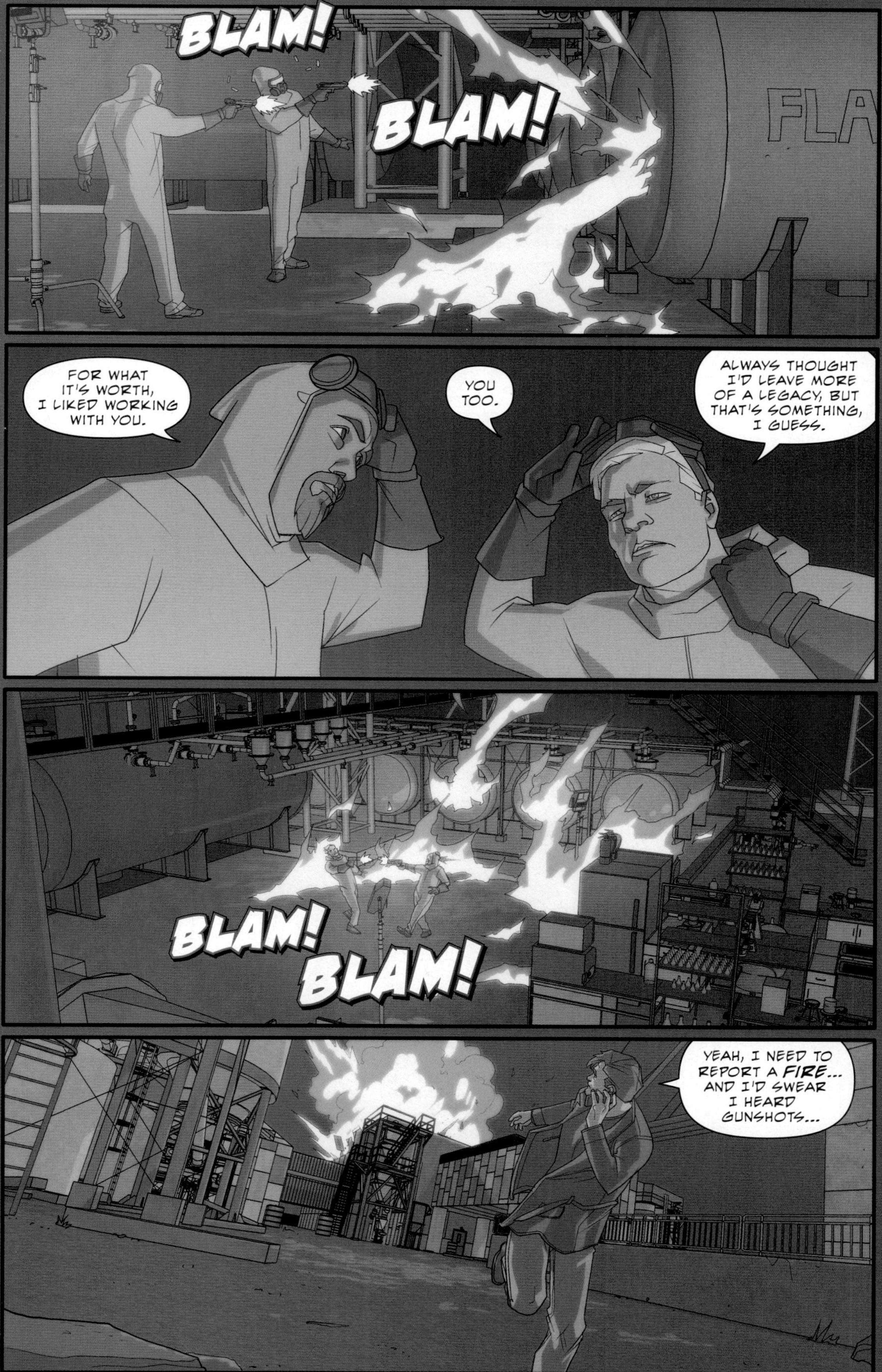
BLAM!
BLAM!
FLA
FOR WHAT IT'S WORTH, I LIKED WORKING WITH YOU.
YOU TOO.
ALWAYS THOUGHT I'D LEAVE MORE OF A LEGACY, BUT THAT'S SOMETHING, I GUESS.
BLAM!
BLAM!
YEAH, I NEED TO REPORT A *FIRE*... AND I'D SWEAR I HEARD GUNSHOTS...

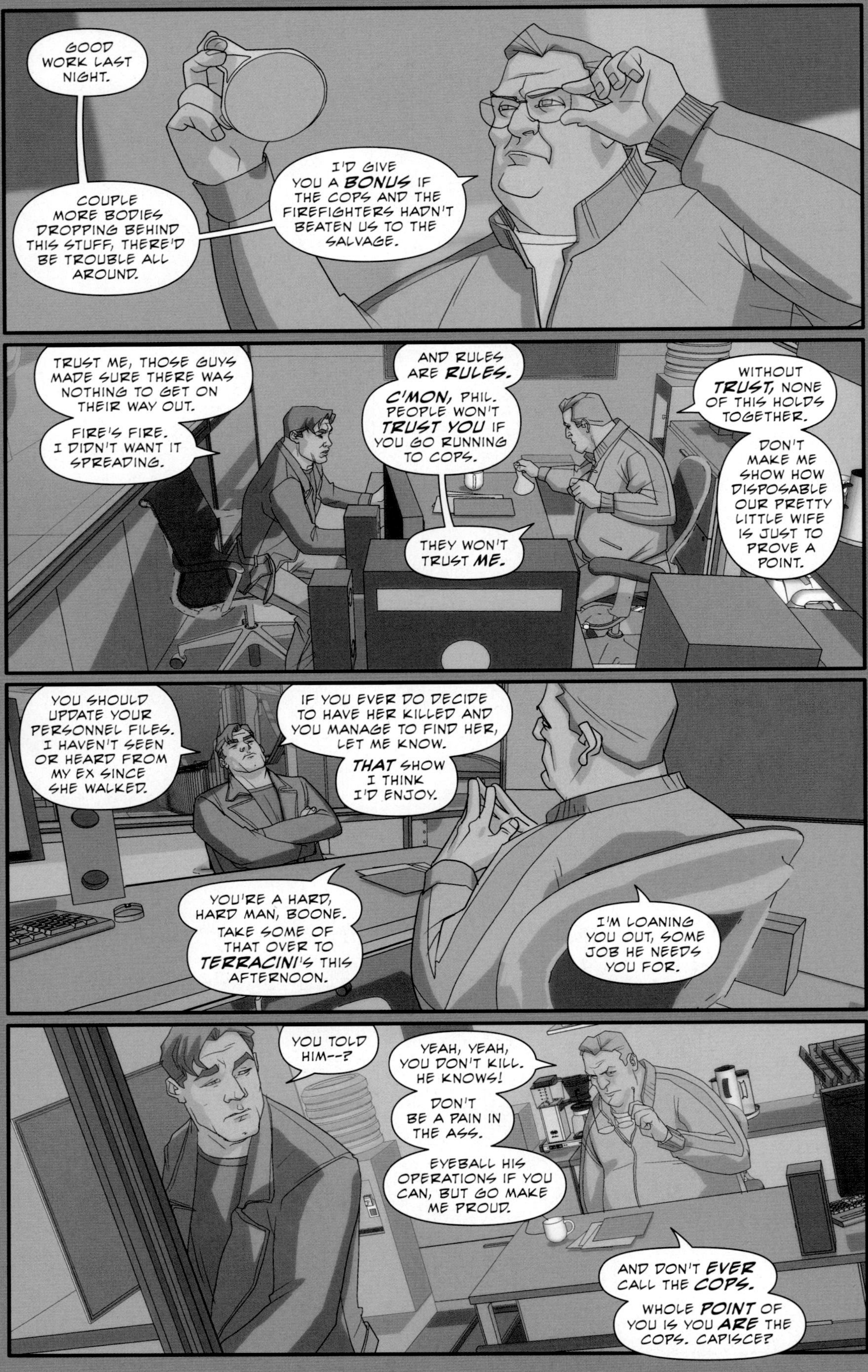
GOOD WORK LAST NIGHT.
COUPLE MORE BODIES DROPPING BEHIND THIS STUFF, THERE'D BE TROUBLE ALL AROUND.
I'D GIVE YOU A BONUS IF THE COPS AND THE FIREFIGHTERS HADN'T BEATEN US TO THE SALVAGE.
TRUST ME, THOSE GUYS MADE SURE THERE WAS NOTHING TO GET ON THEIR WAY OUT.
FIRE'S FIRE. I DIDN'T WANT IT SPREADING.
AND RULES ARE RULES.
C'MON, PHIL. PEOPLE WON'T TRUST YOU IF YOU GO RUNNING TO COPS.
THEY WON'T TRUST ME.
WITHOUT TRUST, NONE OF THIS HOLDS TOGETHER.
DON'T MAKE ME SHOW HOW DISPOSABLE OUR PRETTY LITTLE WIFE IS JUST TO PROVE A POINT.
YOU SHOULD UPDATE YOUR PERSONNEL FILES. I HAVEN'T SEEN OR HEARD FROM MY EX SINCE SHE WALKED.
IF YOU EVER DO DECIDE TO HAVE HER KILLED AND YOU MANAGE TO FIND HER, LET ME KNOW.
THAT SHOW I THINK I'D ENJOY.
YOU'RE A HARD, HARD MAN, BOONE.
TAKE SOME OF THAT OVER TO TERRACINI'S THIS AFTERNOON.
I'M LOANING YOU OUT, SOME JOB HE NEEDS YOU FOR.
YOU TOLD HIM--?
YEAH, YEAH, YOU DON'T KILL. HE KNOWS!
DON'T BE A PAIN IN THE ASS.
EYEBALL HIS OPERATIONS IF YOU CAN, BUT GO MAKE ME PROUD.
AND DON'T EVER CALL THE COPS.
WHOLE POINT OF YOU IS YOU ARE THE COPS. CAPISCE?

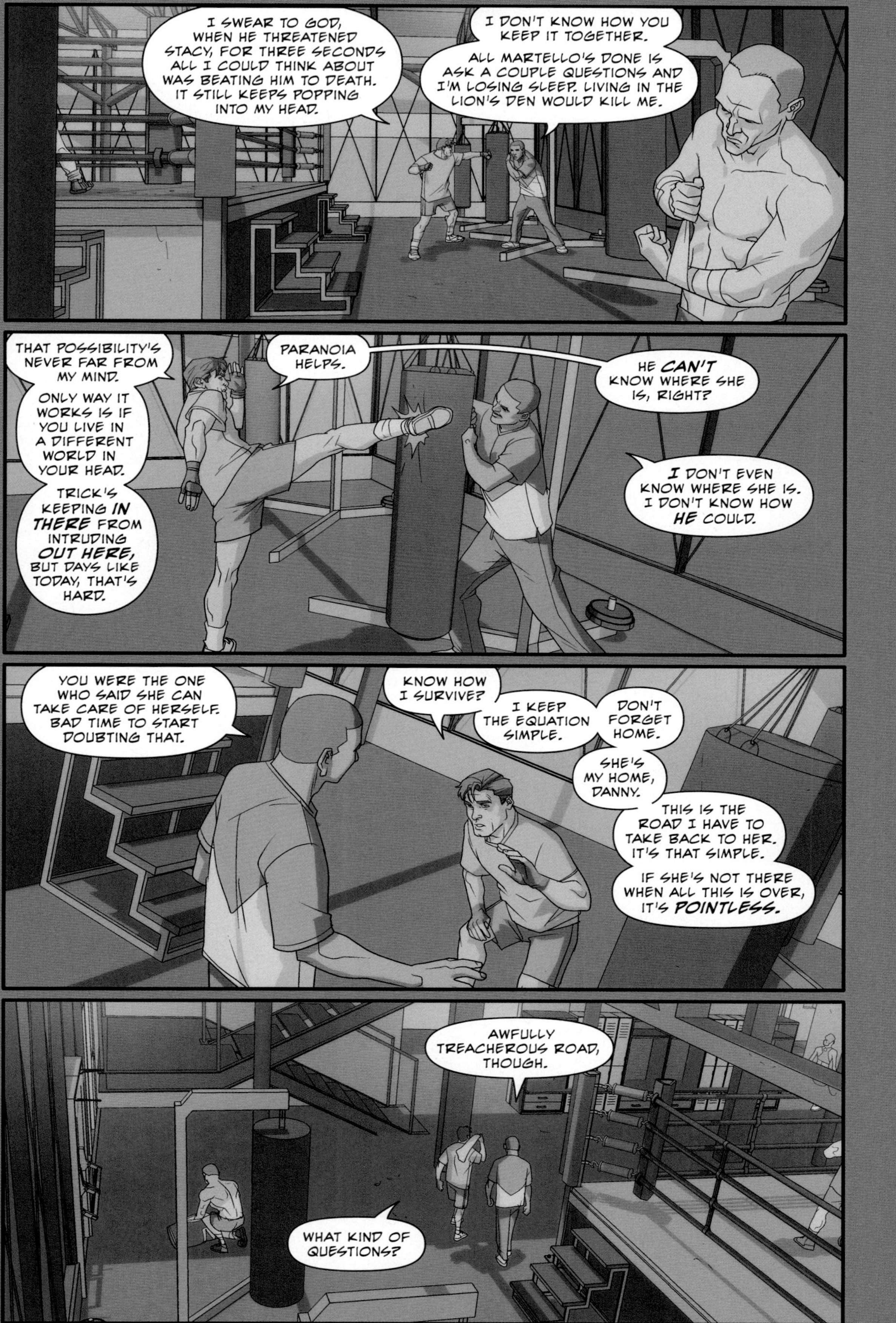

I SWEAR TO GOD, WHEN HE THREATENED STACY, FOR THREE SECONDS ALL I COULD THINK ABOUT WAS BEATING HIM TO DEATH. IT STILL KEEPS POPPING INTO MY HEAD.
I DON'T KNOW HOW YOU KEEP IT TOGETHER.
ALL MARTELLO'S DONE IS ASK A COUPLE QUESTIONS AND I'M LOSING SLEEP. LIVING IN THE LION'S DEN WOULD KILL ME.
THAT POSSIBILITY'S NEVER FAR FROM MY MIND.
ONLY WAY IT WORKS IS IF YOU LIVE IN A DIFFERENT WORLD IN YOUR HEAD.
TRICK'S KEEPING *IN THERE* FROM INTRUDING *OUT HERE,* BUT DAYS LIKE TODAY, THAT'S HARD.
PARANOIA HELPS.
HE *CAN'T* KNOW WHERE SHE IS, RIGHT?
I DON'T EVEN KNOW WHERE SHE IS. I DON'T KNOW HOW *HE* COULD.
YOU WERE THE ONE WHO SAID SHE CAN TAKE CARE OF HERSELF. BAD TIME TO START DOUBTING THAT.
KNOW HOW I SURVIVE?
I KEEP THE EQUATION SIMPLE.
DON'T FORGET HOME.
SHE'S MY HOME, DANNY.
THIS IS THE ROAD I HAVE TO TAKE BACK TO HER. IT'S THAT SIMPLE.
IF SHE'S NOT THERE WHEN ALL THIS IS OVER, IT'S *POINTLESS.*
AWFULLY TREACHEROUS ROAD, THOUGH.
WHAT KIND OF QUESTIONS?

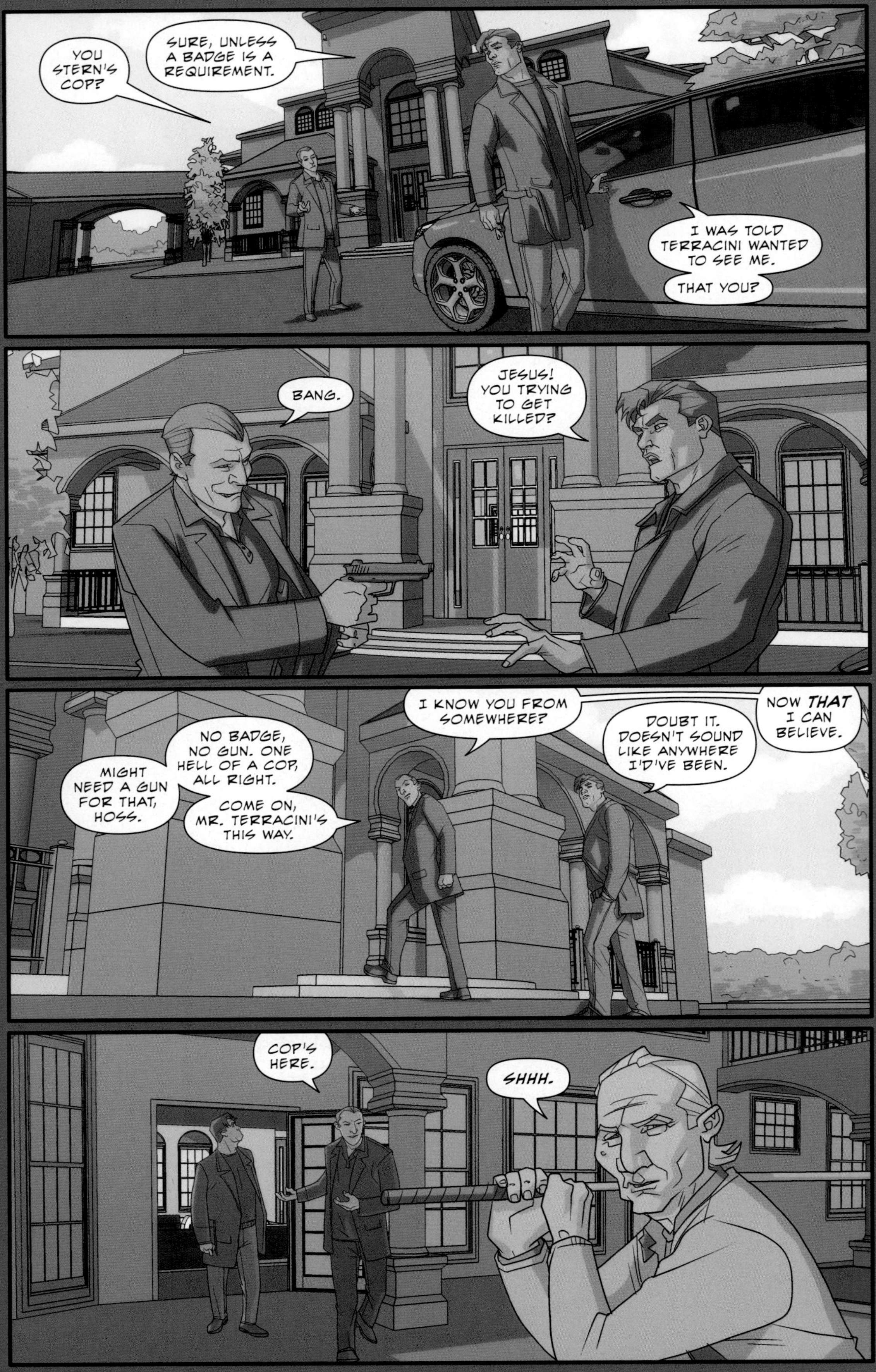
YOU STERN'S COP?
SURE, UNLESS A BADGE IS A REQUIREMENT.
I WAS TOLD TERRACINI WANTED TO SEE ME.
THAT YOU?
BANG.
JESUS! YOU TRYING TO GET KILLED?
MIGHT NEED A GUN FOR THAT, HOSS.
NO BADGE, NO GUN. ONE HELL OF A COP, ALL RIGHT.
COME ON, MR. TERRACINI'S THIS WAY.
I KNOW YOU FROM SOMEWHERE?
DOUBT IT. DOESN'T SOUND LIKE ANYWHERE I'D'VE BEEN.
NOW THAT I CAN BELIEVE.
COP'S HERE.
SHHH.

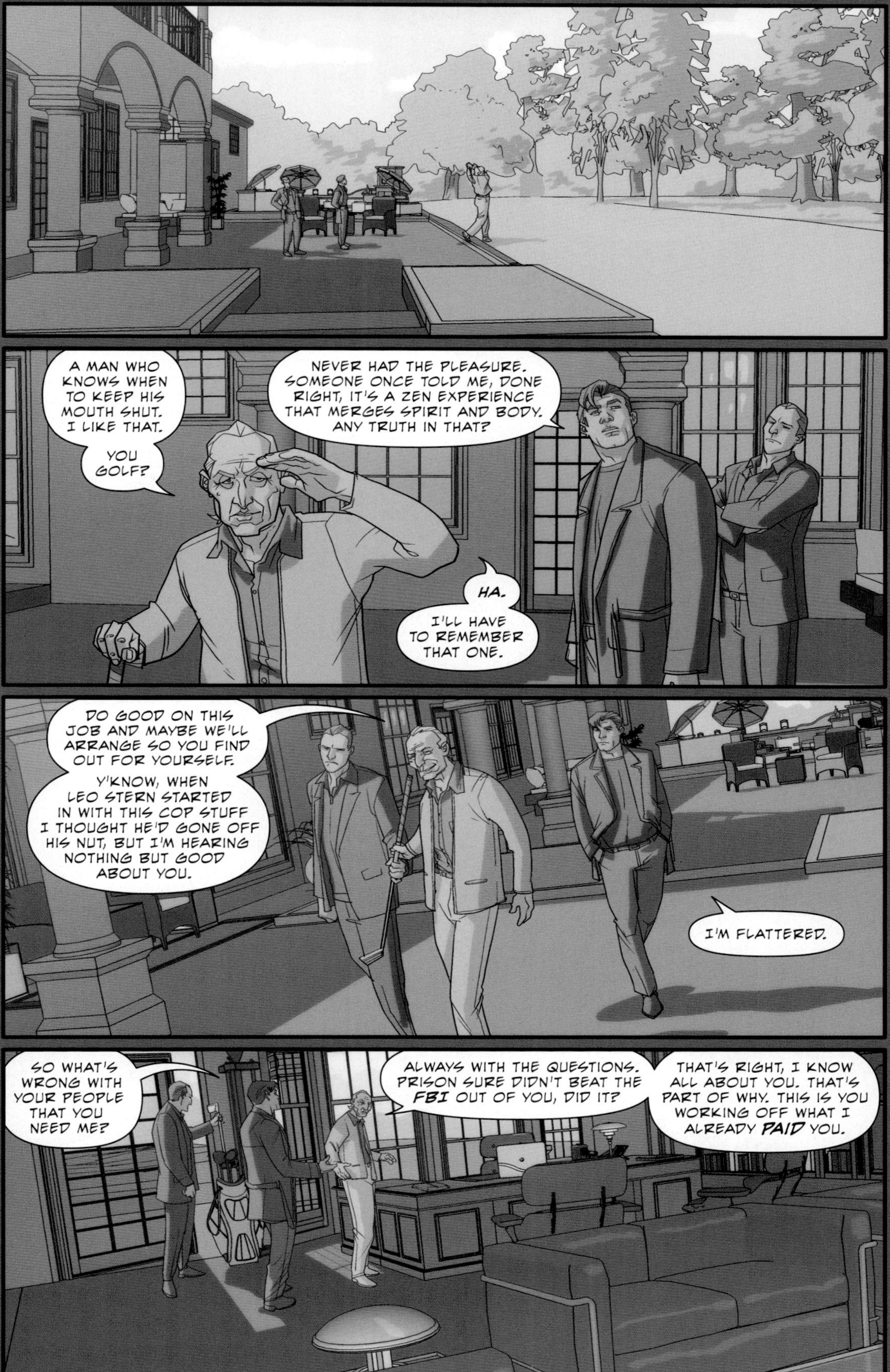
A MAN WHO KNOWS WHEN TO KEEP HIS MOUTH SHUT. I LIKE THAT.
YOU GOLF?
NEVER HAD THE PLEASURE. SOMEONE ONCE TOLD ME, DONE RIGHT, IT'S A ZEN EXPERIENCE THAT MERGES SPIRIT AND BODY. ANY TRUTH IN THAT?
HA.
I'LL HAVE TO REMEMBER THAT ONE.
DO GOOD ON THIS JOB AND MAYBE WE'LL ARRANGE SO YOU FIND OUT FOR YOURSELF.
Y'KNOW, WHEN LEO STERN STARTED IN WITH THIS COP STUFF I THOUGHT HE'D GONE OFF HIS NUT, BUT I'M HEARING NOTHING BUT GOOD ABOUT YOU.
I'M FLATTERED.
SO WHAT'S WRONG WITH YOUR PEOPLE THAT YOU NEED ME?
ALWAYS WITH THE QUESTIONS. PRISON SURE DIDN'T BEAT THE FBI OUT OF YOU, DID IT?
THAT'S RIGHT, I KNOW ALL ABOUT YOU. THAT'S PART OF WHY. THIS IS YOU WORKING OFF WHAT I ALREADY PAID YOU.

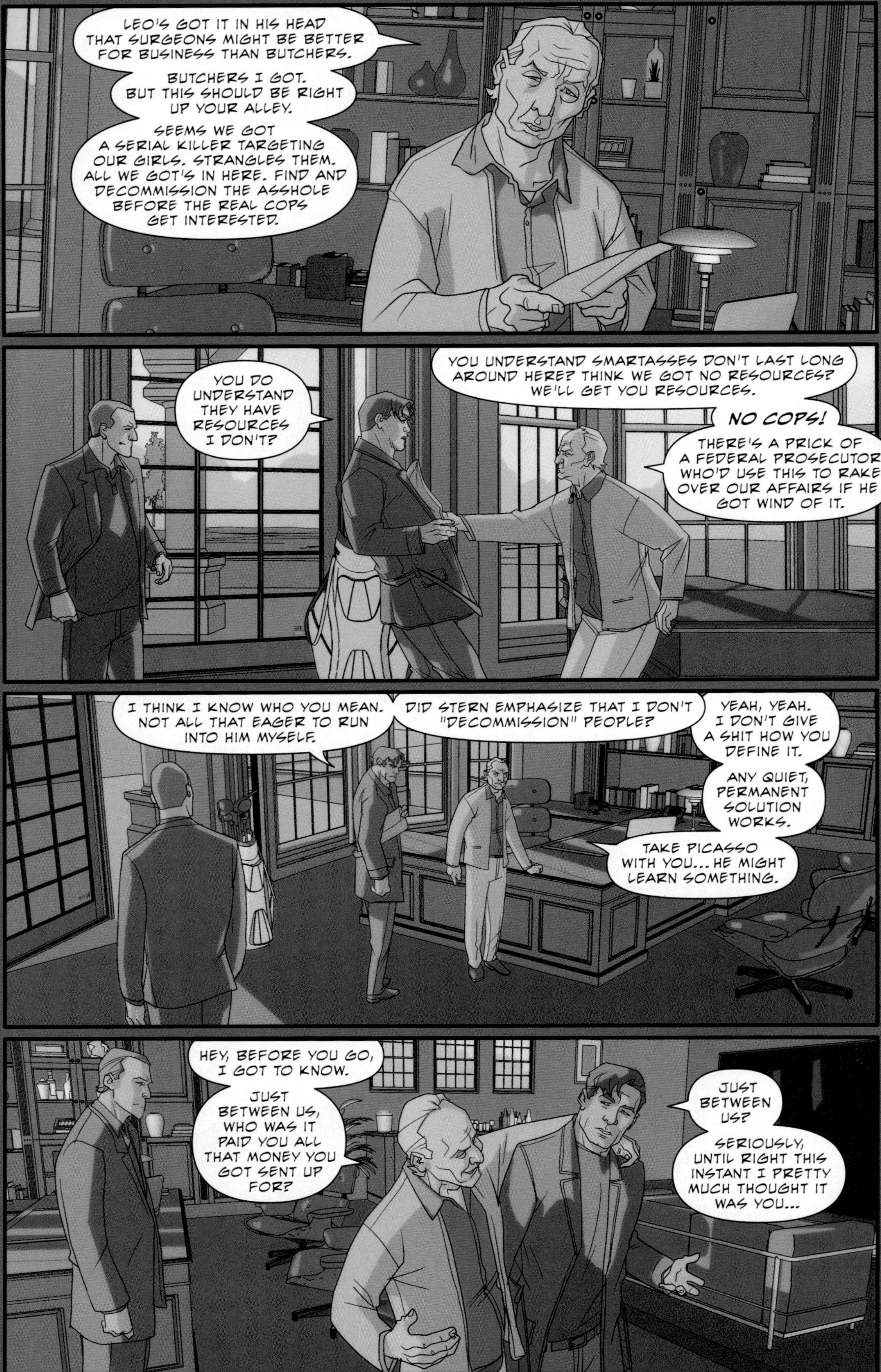
LEO'S GOT IT IN HIS HEAD THAT SURGEONS MIGHT BE BETTER FOR BUSINESS THAN BUTCHERS.
BUTCHERS I GOT. BUT THIS SHOULD BE RIGHT UP YOUR ALLEY.
SEEMS WE GOT A SERIAL KILLER TARGETING OUR GIRLS. STRANGLES THEM. ALL WE GOT'S IN HERE. FIND AND DECOMMISSION THE ASSHOLE BEFORE THE REAL COPS GET INTERESTED.
YOU DO UNDERSTAND THEY HAVE RESOURCES I DON'T?
YOU UNDERSTAND SMARTASSES DON'T LAST LONG AROUND HERE? THINK WE GOT NO RESOURCES? WE'LL GET YOU RESOURCES.
NO COPS!
THERE'S A PRICK OF A FEDERAL PROSECUTOR WHO'D USE THIS TO RAKE OVER OUR AFFAIRS IF HE GOT WIND OF IT.
I THINK I KNOW WHO YOU MEAN. NOT ALL THAT EAGER TO RUN INTO HIM MYSELF.
DID STERN EMPHASIZE THAT I DON'T "DECOMMISSION" PEOPLE?
YEAH, YEAH. I DON'T GIVE A SHIT HOW YOU DEFINE IT.
ANY QUIET, PERMANENT SOLUTION WORKS.
TAKE PICASSO WITH YOU... HE MIGHT LEARN SOMETHING.
HEY, BEFORE YOU GO, I GOT TO KNOW.
JUST BETWEEN US, WHO WAS IT PAID YOU ALL THAT MONEY YOU GOT SENT UP FOR?
JUST BETWEEN US?
SERIOUSLY, UNTIL RIGHT THIS INSTANT I PRETTY MUCH THOUGHT IT WAS YOU...

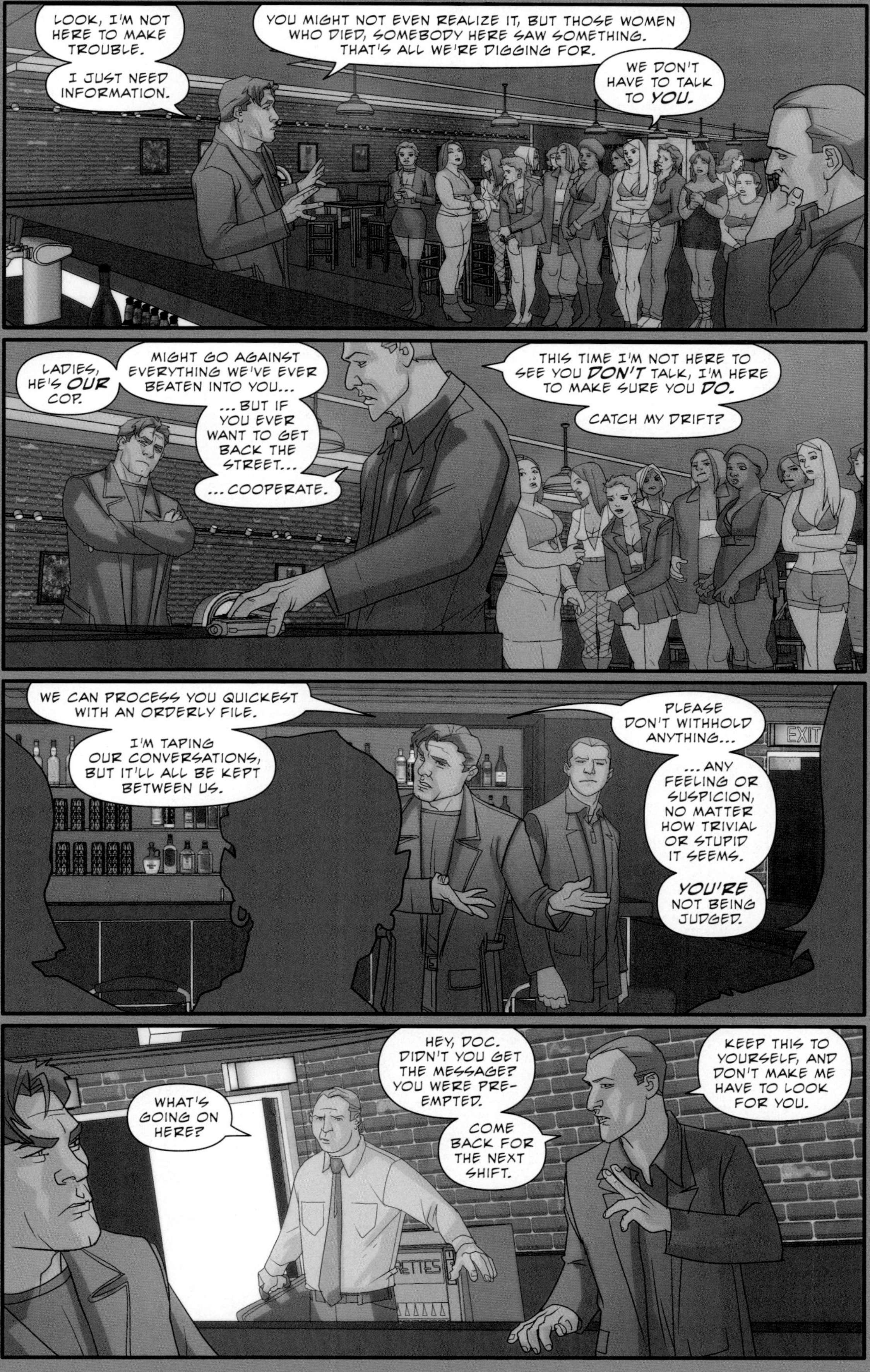
LOOK, I'M NOT HERE TO MAKE TROUBLE.
I JUST NEED INFORMATION.
YOU MIGHT NOT EVEN REALIZE IT, BUT THOSE WOMEN WHO DIED, SOMEBODY HERE SAW SOMETHING. THAT'S ALL WE'RE DIGGING FOR.
WE DON'T HAVE TO TALK TO *YOU.*
LADIES, HE'S *OUR* COP.
MIGHT GO AGAINST EVERYTHING WE'VE EVER BEATEN INTO YOU...
...BUT IF YOU EVER WANT TO GET BACK THE STREET...
...COOPERATE.
THIS TIME I'M NOT HERE TO SEE YOU *DON'T* TALK, I'M HERE TO MAKE SURE YOU *DO.*
CATCH MY DRIFT?
WE CAN PROCESS YOU QUICKEST WITH AN ORDERLY FILE.
I'M TAPING OUR CONVERSATIONS, BUT IT'LL ALL BE KEPT BETWEEN US.
PLEASE DON'T WITHHOLD ANYTHING...
...ANY FEELING OR SUSPICION, NO MATTER HOW TRIVIAL OR STUPID IT SEEMS.
YOU'RE NOT BEING JUDGED.
EXIT
WHAT'S GOING ON HERE?
HEY, DOC. DIDN'T YOU GET THE MESSAGE? YOU WERE PRE-EMPTED.
COME BACK FOR THE NEXT SHIFT.
KEEP THIS TO YOURSELF, AND DON'T MAKE ME HAVE TO LOOK FOR YOU.

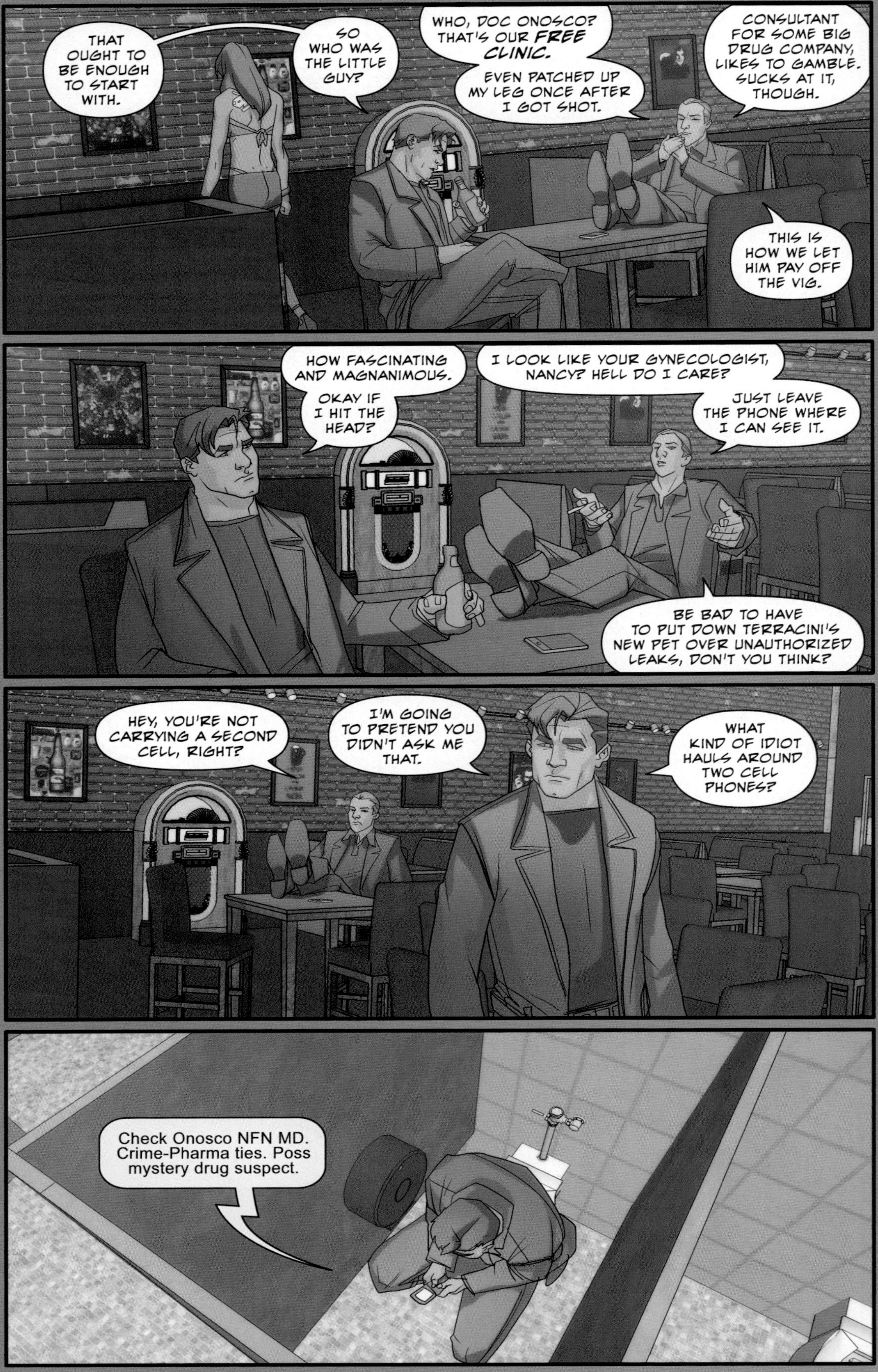
THAT OUGHT TO BE ENOUGH TO START WITH.
SO WHO WAS THE LITTLE GUY?
WHO, DOC ONOSCO? THAT'S OUR FREE CLINIC.
EVEN PATCHED UP MY LEG ONCE AFTER I GOT SHOT.
CONSULTANT FOR SOME BIG DRUG COMPANY, LIKES TO GAMBLE. SUCKS AT IT, THOUGH.
THIS IS HOW WE LET HIM PAY OFF THE VIG.
HOW FASCINATING AND MAGNANIMOUS.
OKAY IF I HIT THE HEAD?
I LOOK LIKE YOUR GYNECOLOGIST, NANCY? HELL DO I CARE?
JUST LEAVE THE PHONE WHERE I CAN SEE IT.
BE BAD TO HAVE TO PUT DOWN TERRACINI'S NEW PET OVER UNAUTHORIZED LEAKS, DON'T YOU THINK?
HEY, YOU'RE NOT CARRYING A SECOND CELL, RIGHT?
I'M GOING TO PRETEND YOU DIDN'T ASK ME THAT.
WHAT KIND OF IDIOT HAULS AROUND TWO CELL PHONES?
Check Onosco NFN MD. Crime-Pharma ties. Poss mystery drug suspect.

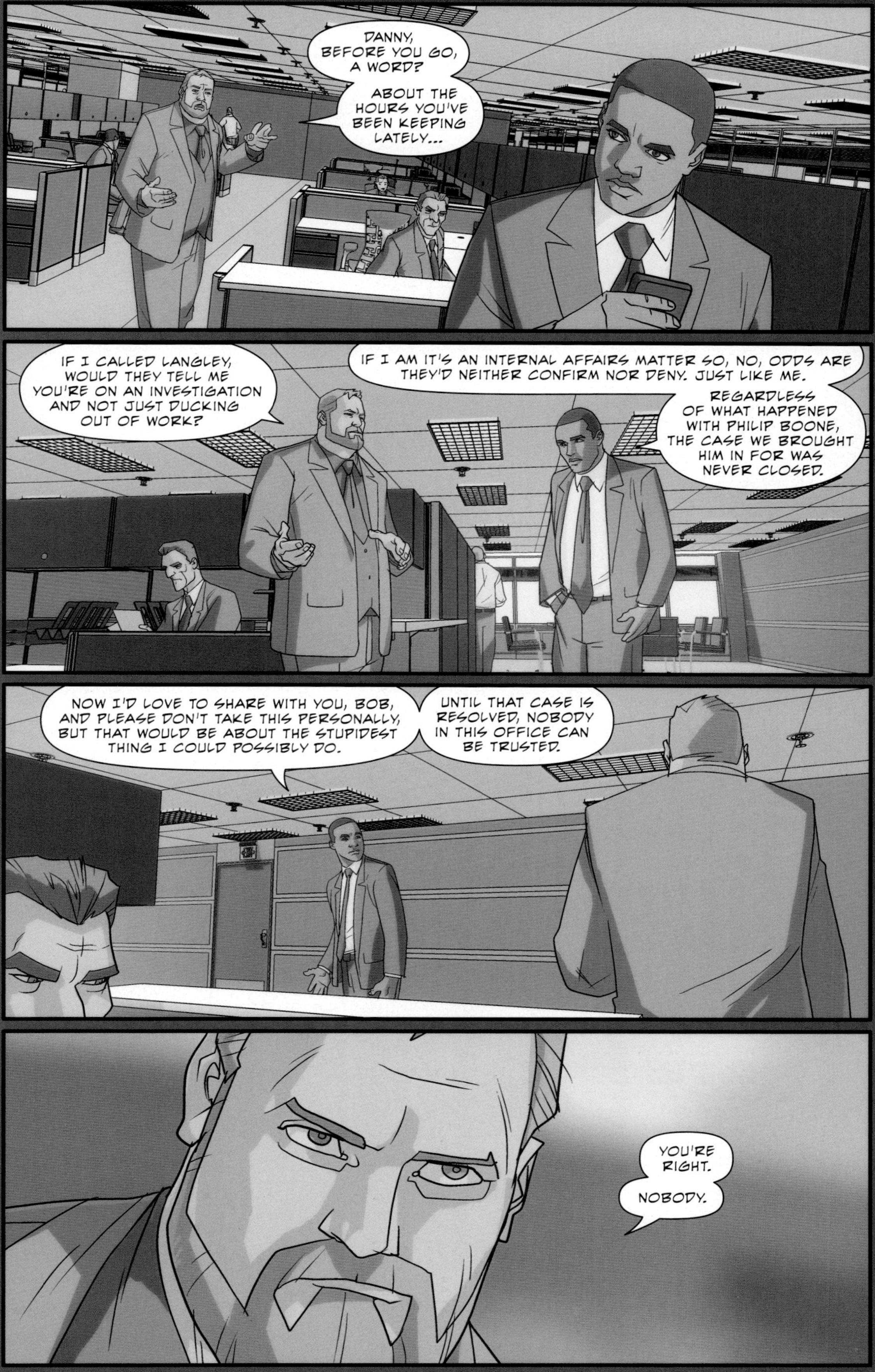
DANNY, BEFORE YOU GO, A WORD?
ABOUT THE HOURS YOU'VE BEEN KEEPING LATELY...
IF I CALLED LANGLEY, WOULD THEY TELL ME YOU'RE ON AN INVESTIGATION AND NOT JUST DUCKING OUT OF WORK?
IF I AM IT'S AN INTERNAL AFFAIRS MATTER SO, NO, ODDS ARE THEY'D NEITHER CONFIRM NOR DENY. JUST LIKE ME.
REGARDLESS OF WHAT HAPPENED WITH PHILIP BOONE, THE CASE WE BROUGHT HIM IN FOR WAS NEVER CLOSED.
NOW I'D LOVE TO SHARE WITH YOU, BOB, AND PLEASE DON'T TAKE THIS PERSONALLY, BUT THAT WOULD BE ABOUT THE STUPIDEST THING I COULD POSSIBLY DO.
UNTIL THAT CASE IS RESOLVED, NOBODY IN THIS OFFICE CAN BE TRUSTED.
YOU'RE RIGHT.
NOBODY.

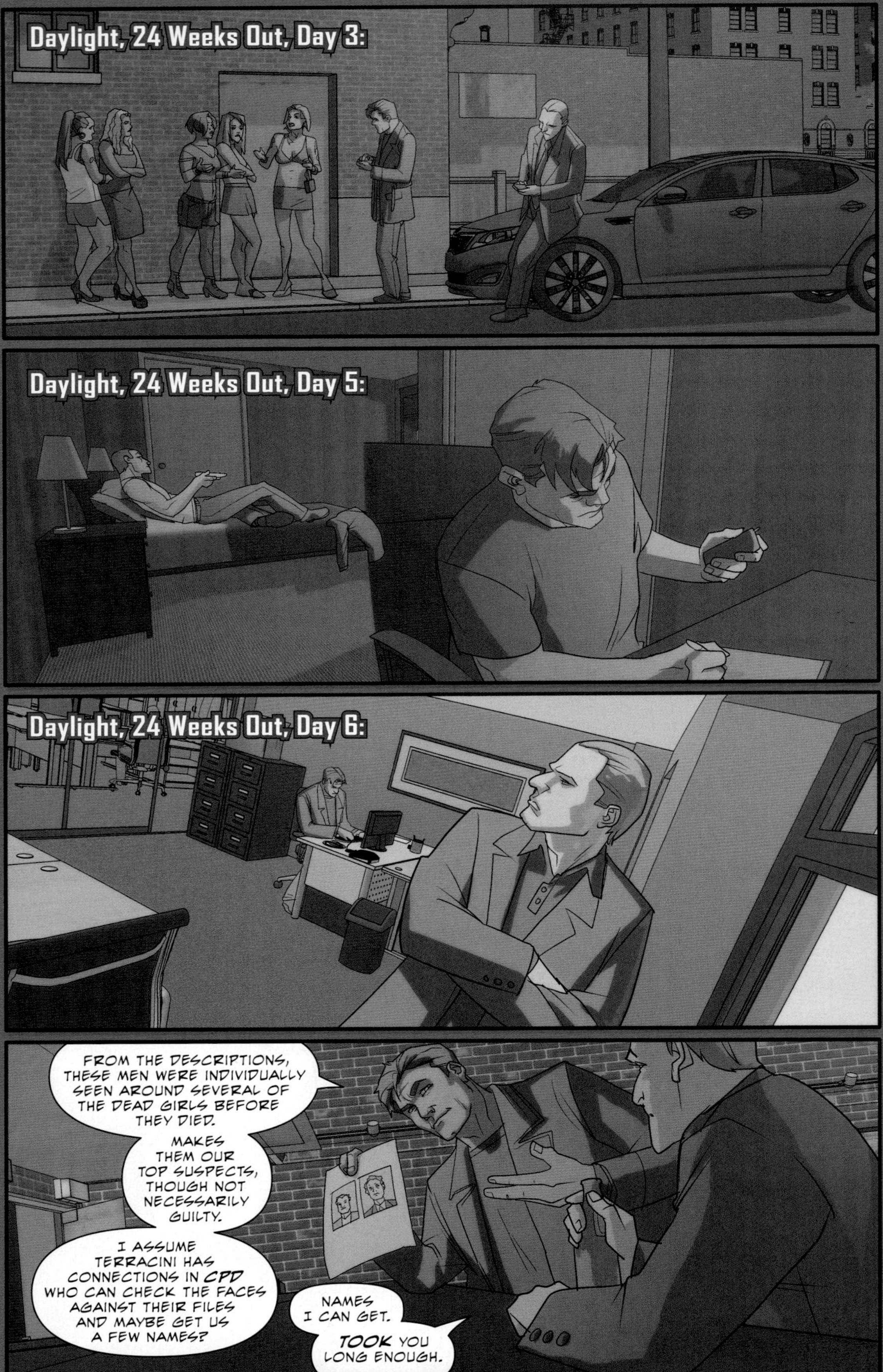

Daylight, 24 Weeks Out, Day 3:
Daylight, 24 Weeks Out, Day 5:
Daylight, 24 Weeks Out, Day 6:
FROM THE DESCRIPTIONS, THESE MEN WERE INDIVIDUALLY SEEN AROUND SEVERAL OF THE DEAD GIRLS BEFORE THEY DIED.
MAKES THEM OUR TOP SUSPECTS, THOUGH NOT NECESSARILY GUILTY.
I ASSUME TERRACINI HAS CONNECTIONS IN CPD WHO CAN CHECK THE FACES AGAINST THEIR FILES AND MAYBE GET US A FEW NAMES?
NAMES I CAN GET.
TOOK YOU LONG ENOUGH.

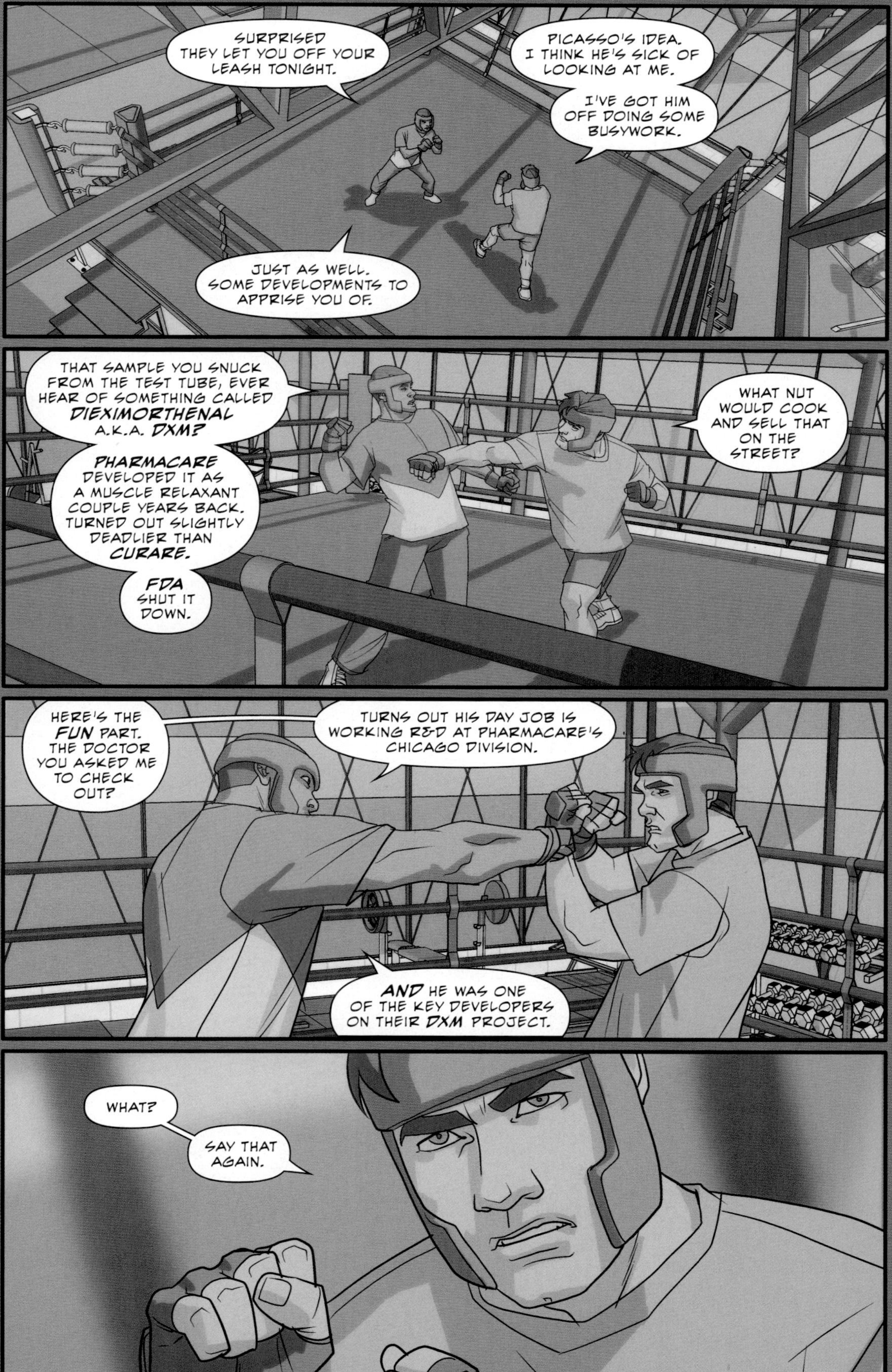
SURPRISED THEY LET YOU OFF YOUR LEASH TONIGHT.
PICASSO'S IDEA. I THINK HE'S SICK OF LOOKING AT ME.
I'VE GOT HIM OFF DOING SOME BUSYWORK.
JUST AS WELL. SOME DEVELOPMENTS TO APPRISE YOU OF.
THAT SAMPLE YOU SNUCK FROM THE TEST TUBE, EVER HEAR OF SOMETHING CALLED DIEXIMORTHENAL A.K.A. DXM?
PHARMACARE DEVELOPED IT AS A MUSCLE RELAXANT COUPLE YEARS BACK. TURNED OUT SLIGHTLY DEADLIER THAN CURARE.
FDA SHUT IT DOWN.
WHAT NUT WOULD COOK AND SELL THAT ON THE STREET?
HERE'S THE FUN PART. THE DOCTOR YOU ASKED ME TO CHECK OUT?
TURNS OUT HIS DAY JOB IS WORKING R&D AT PHARMACARE'S CHICAGO DIVISION.
AND HE WAS ONE OF THE KEY DEVELOPERS ON THEIR DXM PROJECT.
WHAT?
SAY THAT AGAIN.

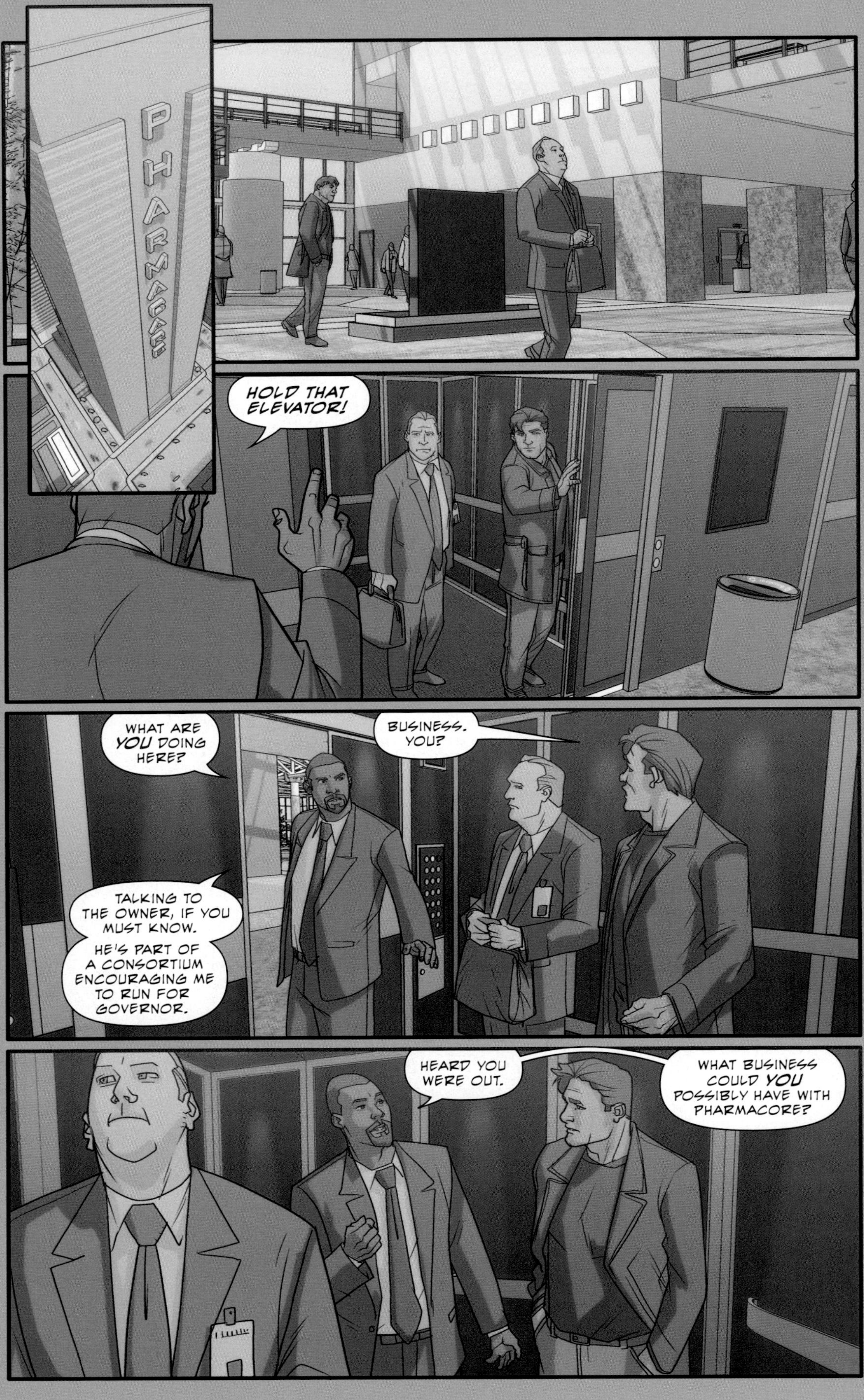
PHARMACORE
HOLD THAT ELEVATOR!
WHAT ARE YOU DOING HERE?
BUSINESS. YOU?
TALKING TO THE OWNER, IF YOU MUST KNOW.
HE'S PART OF A CONSORTIUM ENCOURAGING ME TO RUN FOR GOVERNOR.
HEARD YOU WERE OUT.
WHAT BUSINESS COULD YOU POSSIBLY HAVE WITH PHARMACORE?

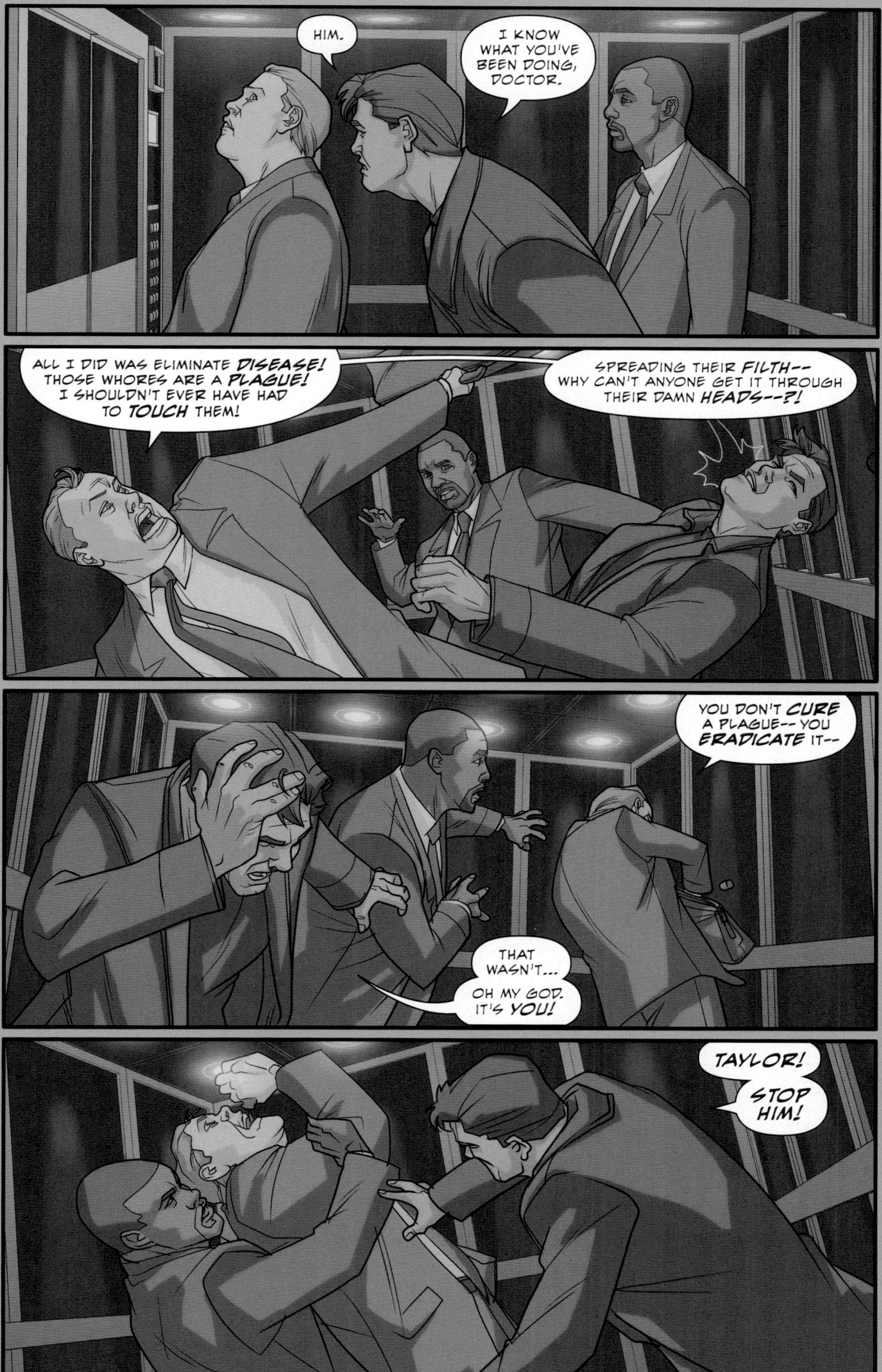
HIM.
I KNOW WHAT YOU'VE BEEN DOING, DOCTOR.
ALL I DID WAS ELIMINATE DISEASE! THOSE WHORES ARE A PLAGUE! I SHOULDN'T EVER HAVE HAD TO TOUCH THEM!
SPREADING THEIR FILTH-- WHY CAN'T ANYONE GET IT THROUGH THEIR DAMN HEADS--?!
YOU DON'T CURE A PLAGUE-- YOU ERADICATE IT--
THAT WASN'T...
OH MY GOD. IT'S YOU!
TAYLOR!
STOP HIM!

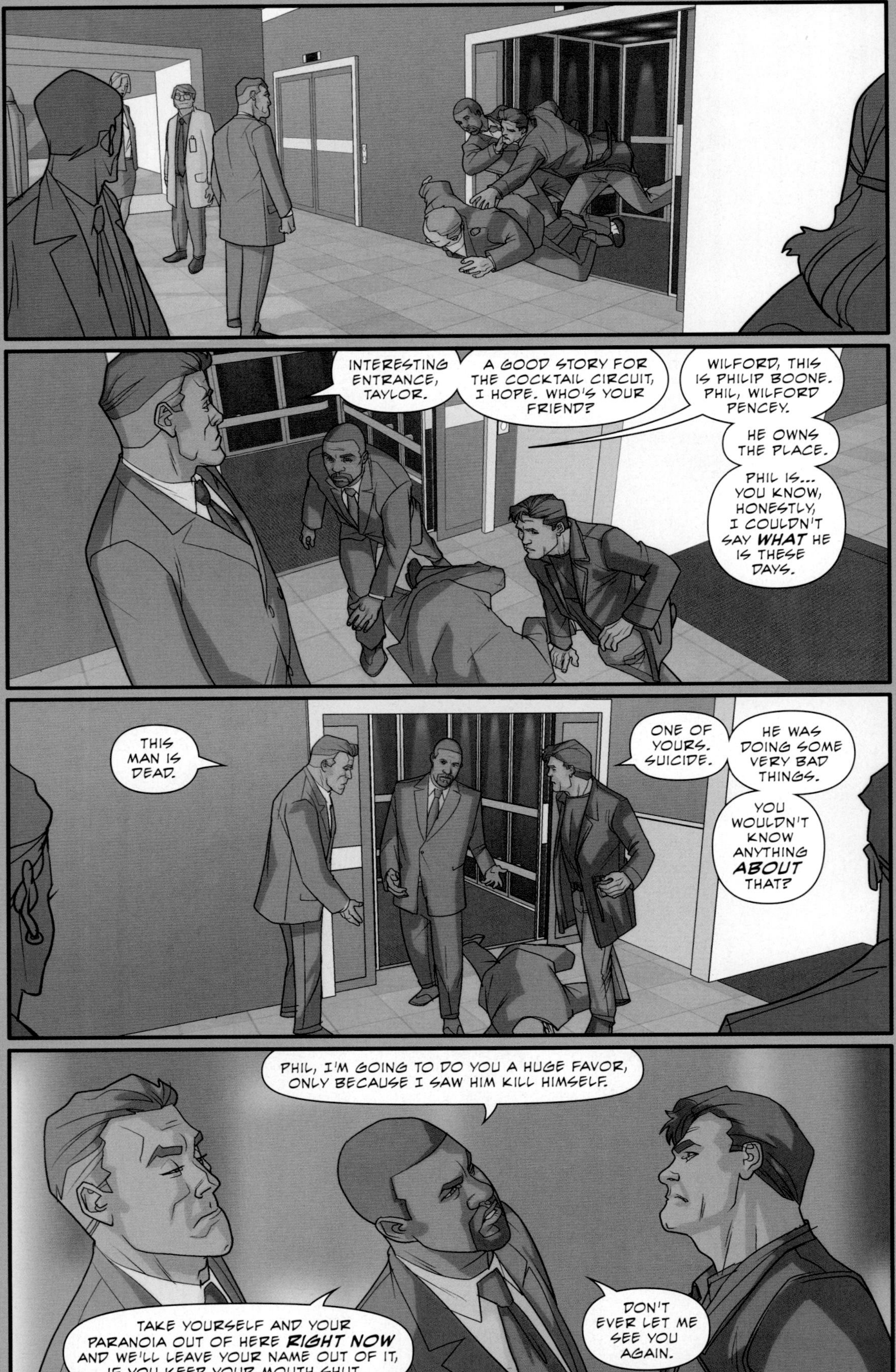
INTERESTING ENTRANCE, TAYLOR.
A GOOD STORY FOR THE COCKTAIL CIRCUIT, I HOPE. WHO'S YOUR FRIEND?
WILFORD, THIS IS PHILIP BOONE. PHIL, WILFORD PENCEY.
HE OWNS THE PLACE.
PHIL IS... YOU KNOW, HONESTLY, I COULDN'T SAY **WHAT** HE IS THESE DAYS.
THIS MAN IS DEAD.
ONE OF YOURS. SUICIDE.
HE WAS DOING SOME VERY BAD THINGS.
YOU WOULDN'T KNOW ANYTHING **ABOUT** THAT?
PHIL, I'M GOING TO DO YOU A HUGE FAVOR, ONLY BECAUSE I SAW HIM KILL HIMSELF.
TAKE YOURSELF AND YOUR PARANOIA OUT OF HERE **RIGHT NOW** AND WE'LL LEAVE YOUR NAME OUT OF IT, IF YOU KEEP YOUR MOUTH SHUT.
DON'T EVER LET ME SEE YOU AGAIN.

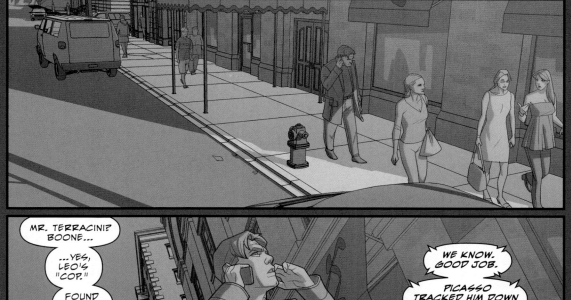

MR. TERRACINI? BOONE...

...YES, LEO'S "COP."

FOUND THE KILLER.

WE KNOW. GOOD JOB.

PICASSO TRACKED HIM DOWN THIS MORNING.

HE'S WORKING ON HIM NOW.

WHAT?

THAT'S NOT--

I JUST--

WHAT?

WHERE ARE THEY?

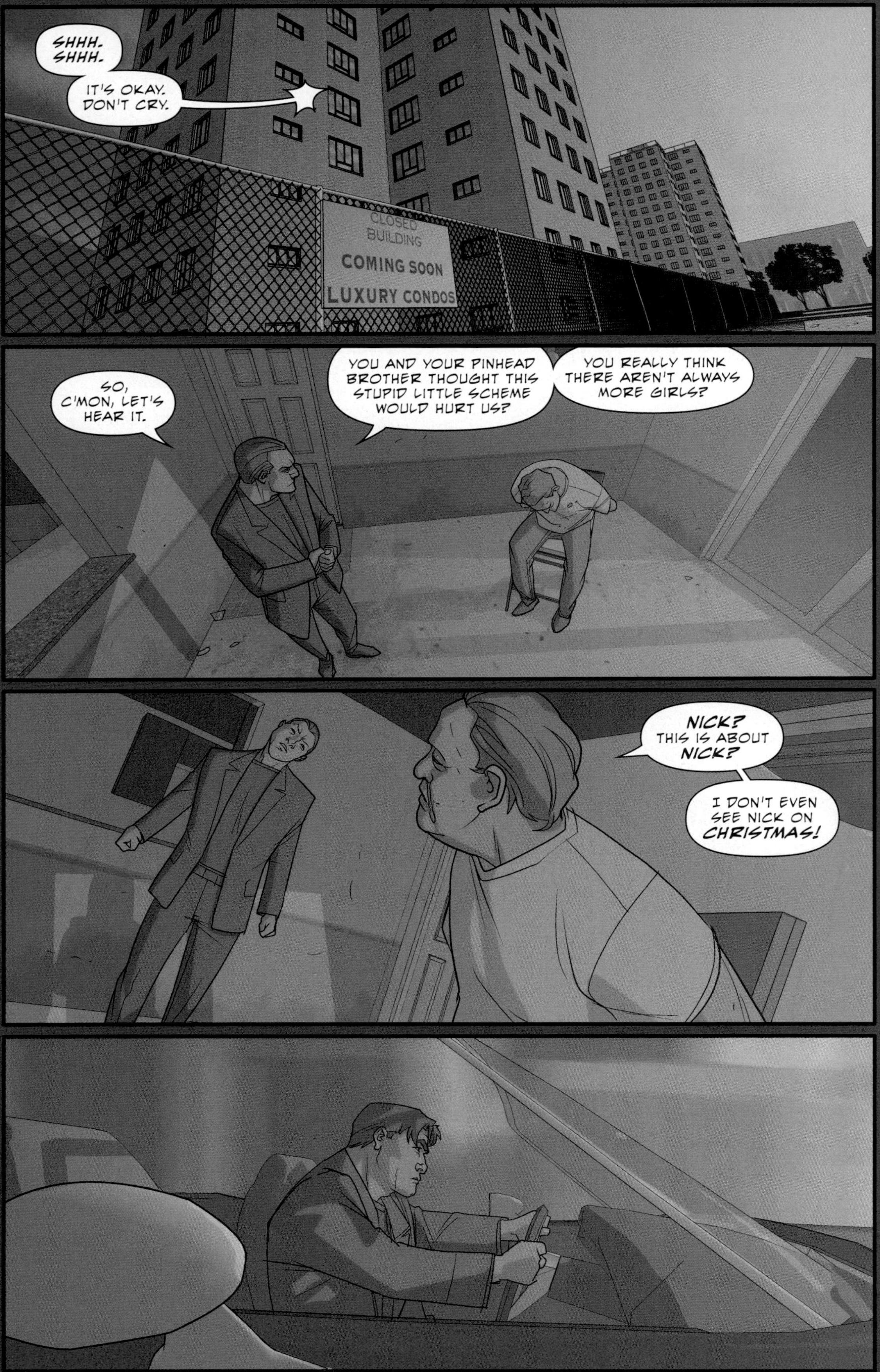
SHHH. SHHH.
IT'S OKAY. DON'T CRY.
CLOSED BUILDING
COMING SOON
LUXURY CONDOS
SO, C'MON, LET'S HEAR IT.
YOU AND YOUR PINHEAD BROTHER THOUGHT THIS STUPID LITTLE SCHEME WOULD HURT US?
YOU REALLY THINK THERE AREN'T ALWAYS MORE GIRLS?
NICK? THIS IS ABOUT NICK?
I DON'T EVEN SEE NICK ON CHRISTMAS!

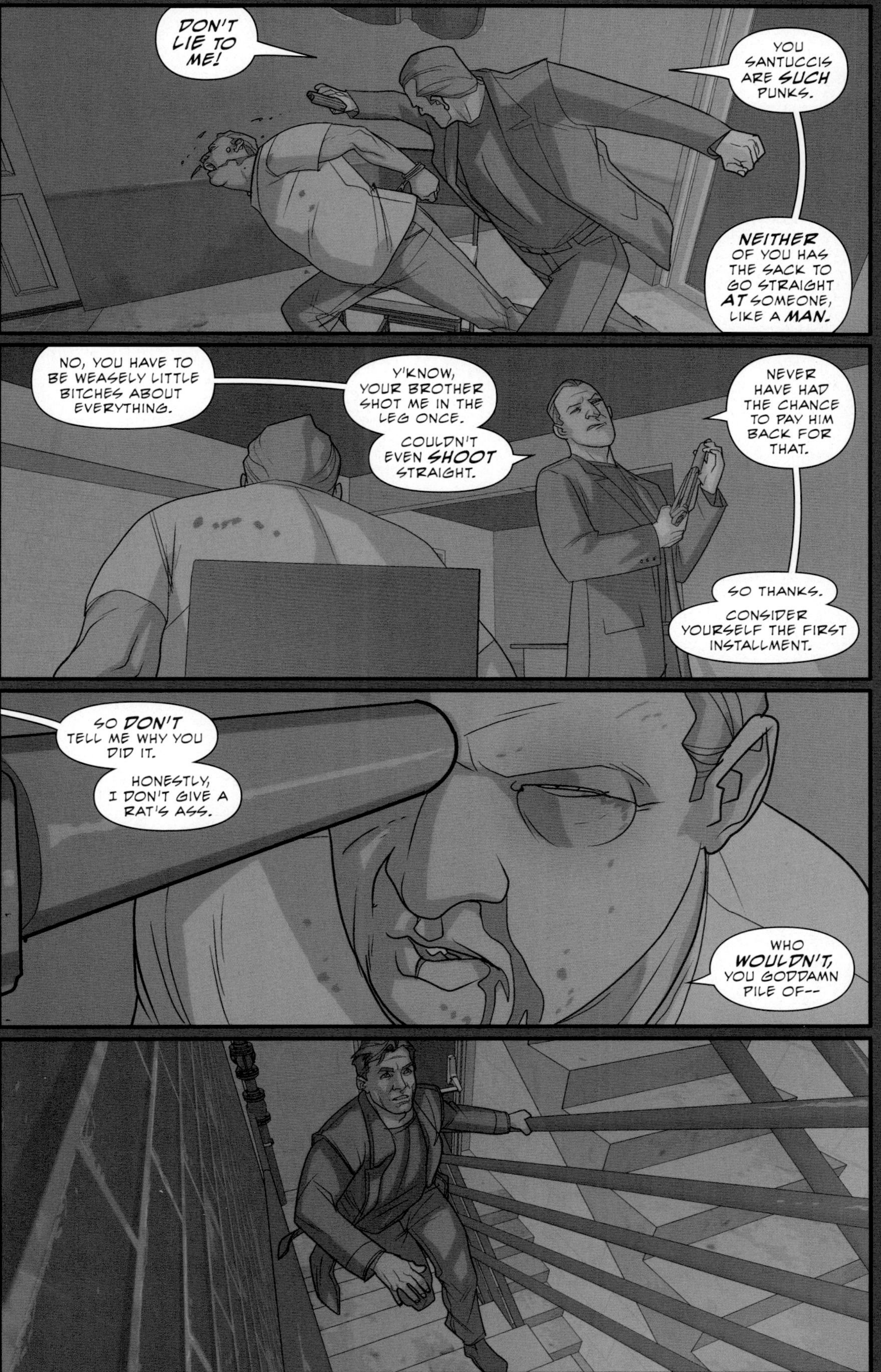
DON'T LIE TO ME!
YOU SANTUCCIS ARE SUCH PUNKS.
NEITHER OF YOU HAS THE SACK TO GO STRAIGHT AT SOMEONE, LIKE A MAN.
NO, YOU HAVE TO BE WEASELY LITTLE BITCHES ABOUT EVERYTHING.
Y'KNOW, YOUR BROTHER SHOT ME IN THE LEG ONCE.
COULDN'T EVEN SHOOT STRAIGHT.
NEVER HAVE HAD THE CHANCE TO PAY HIM BACK FOR THAT.
SO THANKS.
CONSIDER YOURSELF THE FIRST INSTALLMENT.
SO DON'T TELL ME WHY YOU DID IT.
HONESTLY, I DON'T GIVE A RAT'S ASS.
WHO WOULDN'T, YOU GODDAMN PILE OF--

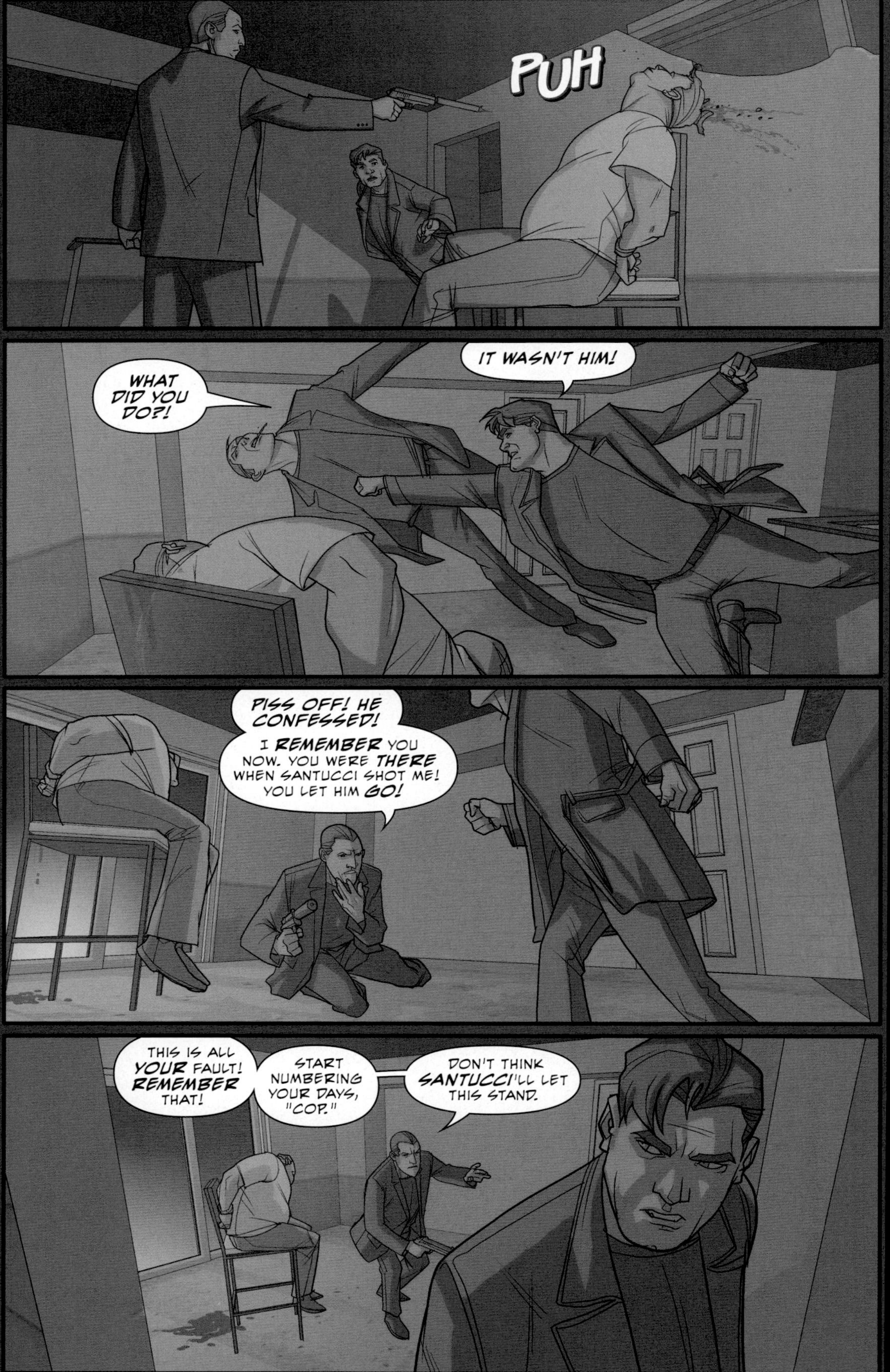
PUH
WHAT DID YOU DO?!
IT WASN'T HIM!
PISS OFF! HE CONFESSED!
I REMEMBER YOU NOW. YOU WERE THERE WHEN SANTUCCI SHOT ME! YOU LET HIM GO!
THIS IS ALL YOUR FAULT! REMEMBER THAT!
START NUMBERING YOUR DAYS, "COP."
DON'T THINK SANTUCCI'LL LET THIS STAND.

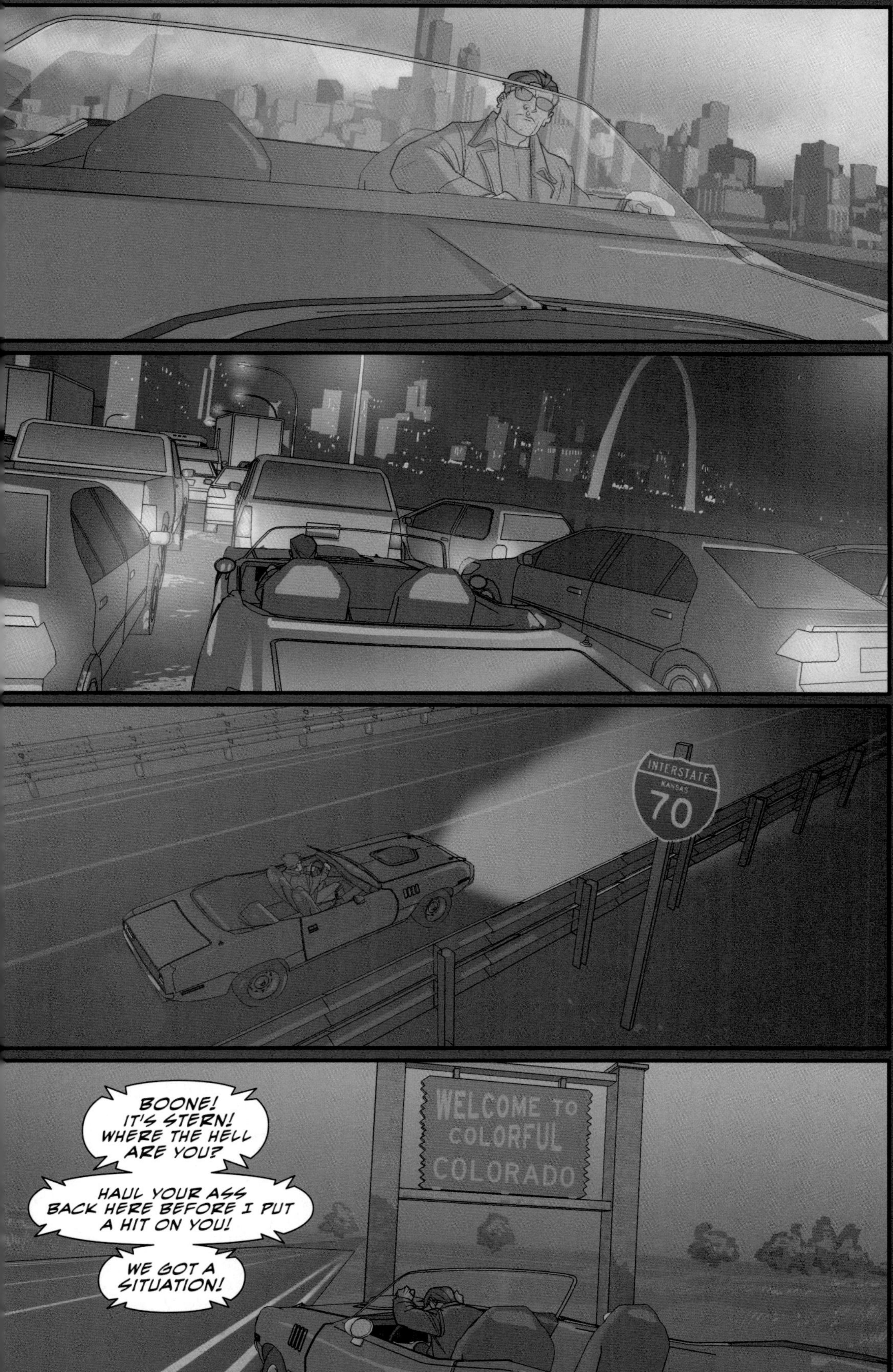
INTERSTATE
KANSAS
70
WELCOME TO COLORFUL COLORADO
BOONE! IT'S STERN! WHERE THE HELL ARE YOU?
HAUL YOUR ASS BACK HERE BEFORE I PUT A HIT ON YOU!
WE GOT A SITUATION!

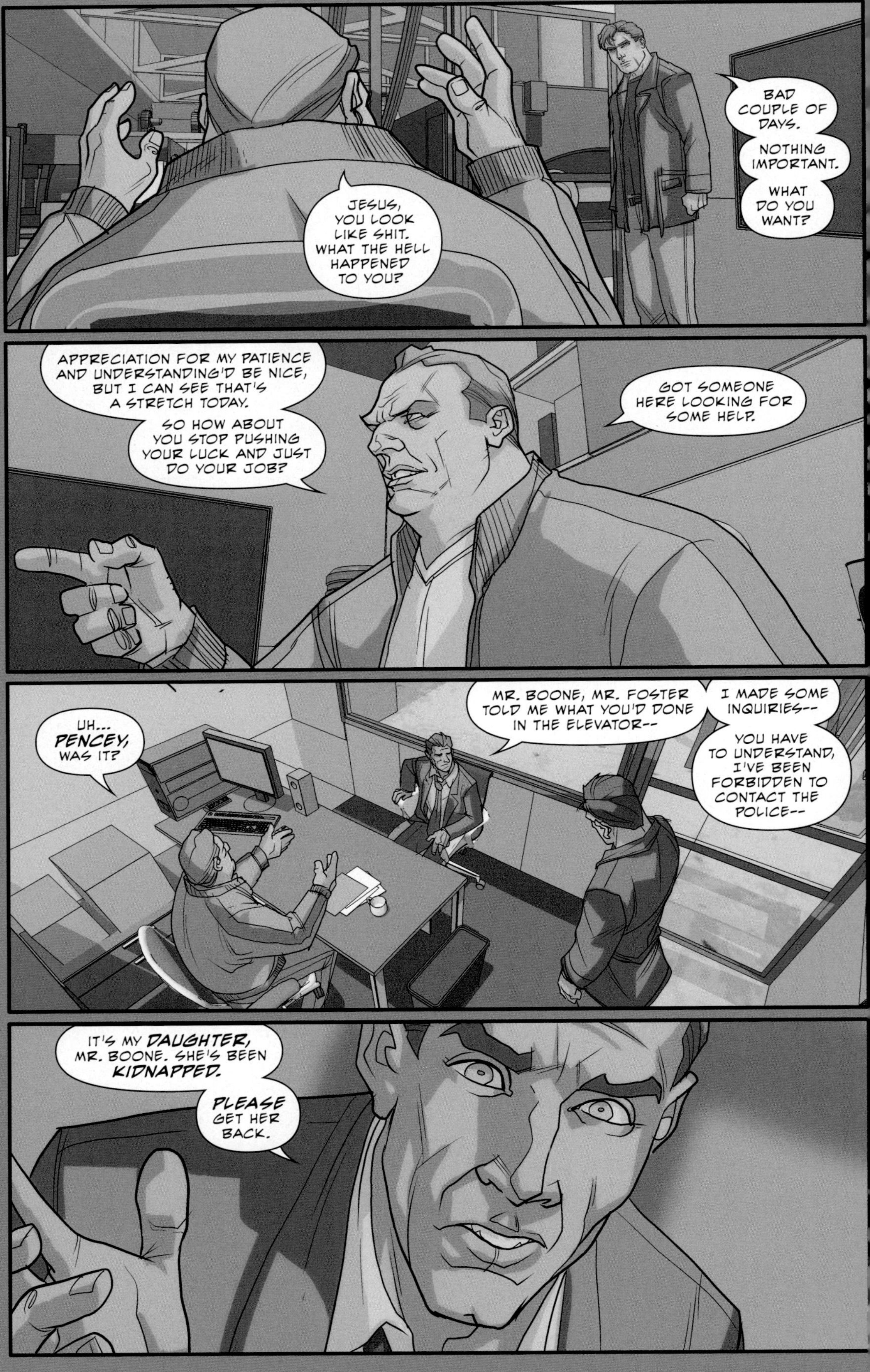
JESUS, YOU LOOK LIKE SHIT. WHAT THE HELL HAPPENED TO YOU?
BAD COUPLE OF DAYS.
NOTHING IMPORTANT.
WHAT DO YOU WANT?
APPRECIATION FOR MY PATIENCE AND UNDERSTANDING'D BE NICE, BUT I CAN SEE THAT'S A STRETCH TODAY.
SO HOW ABOUT YOU STOP PUSHING YOUR LUCK AND JUST DO YOUR JOB?
GOT SOMEONE HERE LOOKING FOR SOME HELP.
UH... PENCEY, WAS IT?
MR. BOONE, MR. FOSTER TOLD ME WHAT YOU'D DONE IN THE ELEVATOR--
I MADE SOME INQUIRIES--
YOU HAVE TO UNDERSTAND, I'VE BEEN FORBIDDEN TO CONTACT THE POLICE--
IT'S MY DAUGHTER, MR. BOONE. SHE'S BEEN KIDNAPPED.
PLEASE GET HER BACK.

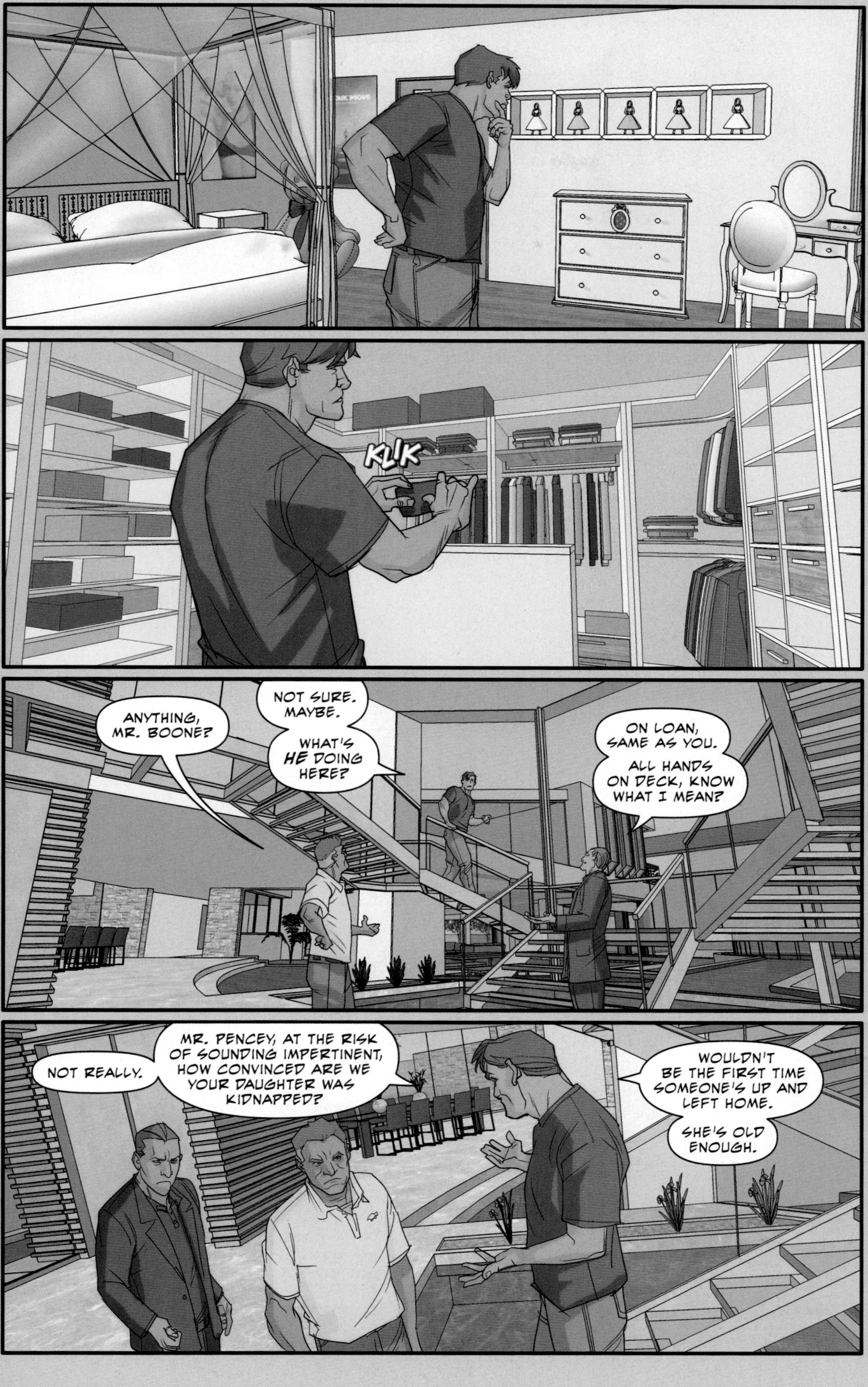
KLIK
ANYTHING, MR. BOONE?
NOT SURE. MAYBE.
WHAT'S HE DOING HERE?
ON LOAN, SAME AS YOU.
ALL HANDS ON DECK, KNOW WHAT I MEAN?
NOT REALLY.
MR. PENCEY, AT THE RISK OF SOUNDING IMPERTINENT, HOW CONVINCED ARE WE YOUR DAUGHTER WAS KIDNAPPED?
WOULDN'T BE THE FIRST TIME SOMEONE'S UP AND LEFT HOME.
SHE'S OLD ENOUGH.

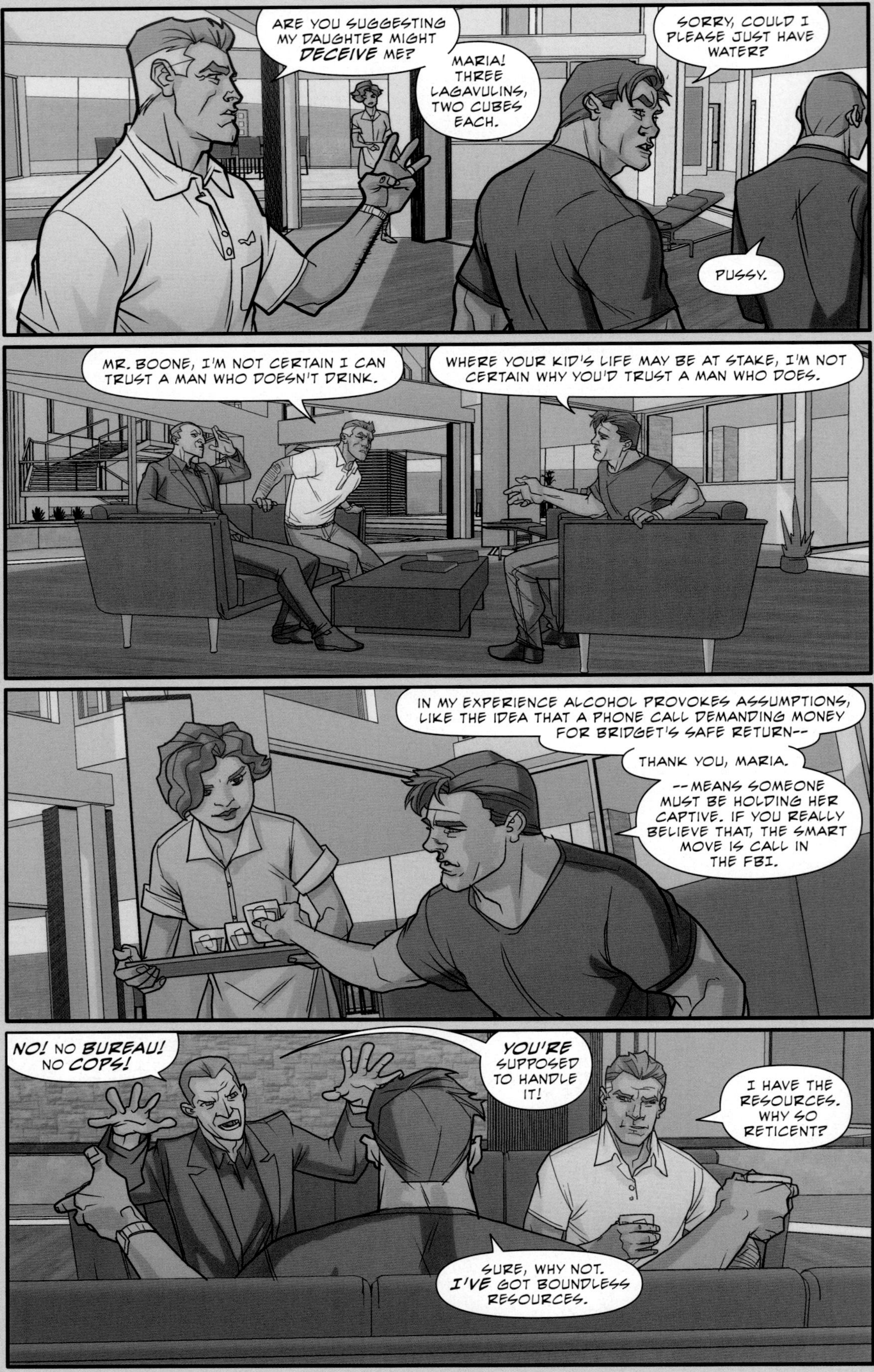

ARE YOU SUGGESTING MY DAUGHTER MIGHT DECEIVE ME?
MARIA! THREE LAGAVULINS, TWO CUBES EACH.
SORRY, COULD I PLEASE JUST HAVE WATER?
PUSSY.
MR. BOONE, I'M NOT CERTAIN I CAN TRUST A MAN WHO DOESN'T DRINK.
WHERE YOUR KID'S LIFE MAY BE AT STAKE, I'M NOT CERTAIN WHY YOU'D TRUST A MAN WHO DOES.
IN MY EXPERIENCE ALCOHOL PROVOKES ASSUMPTIONS, LIKE THE IDEA THAT A PHONE CALL DEMANDING MONEY FOR BRIDGET'S SAFE RETURN--
THANK YOU, MARIA.
--MEANS SOMEONE MUST BE HOLDING HER CAPTIVE. IF YOU REALLY BELIEVE THAT, THE SMART MOVE IS CALL IN THE FBI.
NO! NO BUREAU! NO COPS!
YOU'RE SUPPOSED TO HANDLE IT!
I HAVE THE RESOURCES. WHY SO RETICENT?
SURE, WHY NOT. I'VE GOT BOUNDLESS RESOURCES.

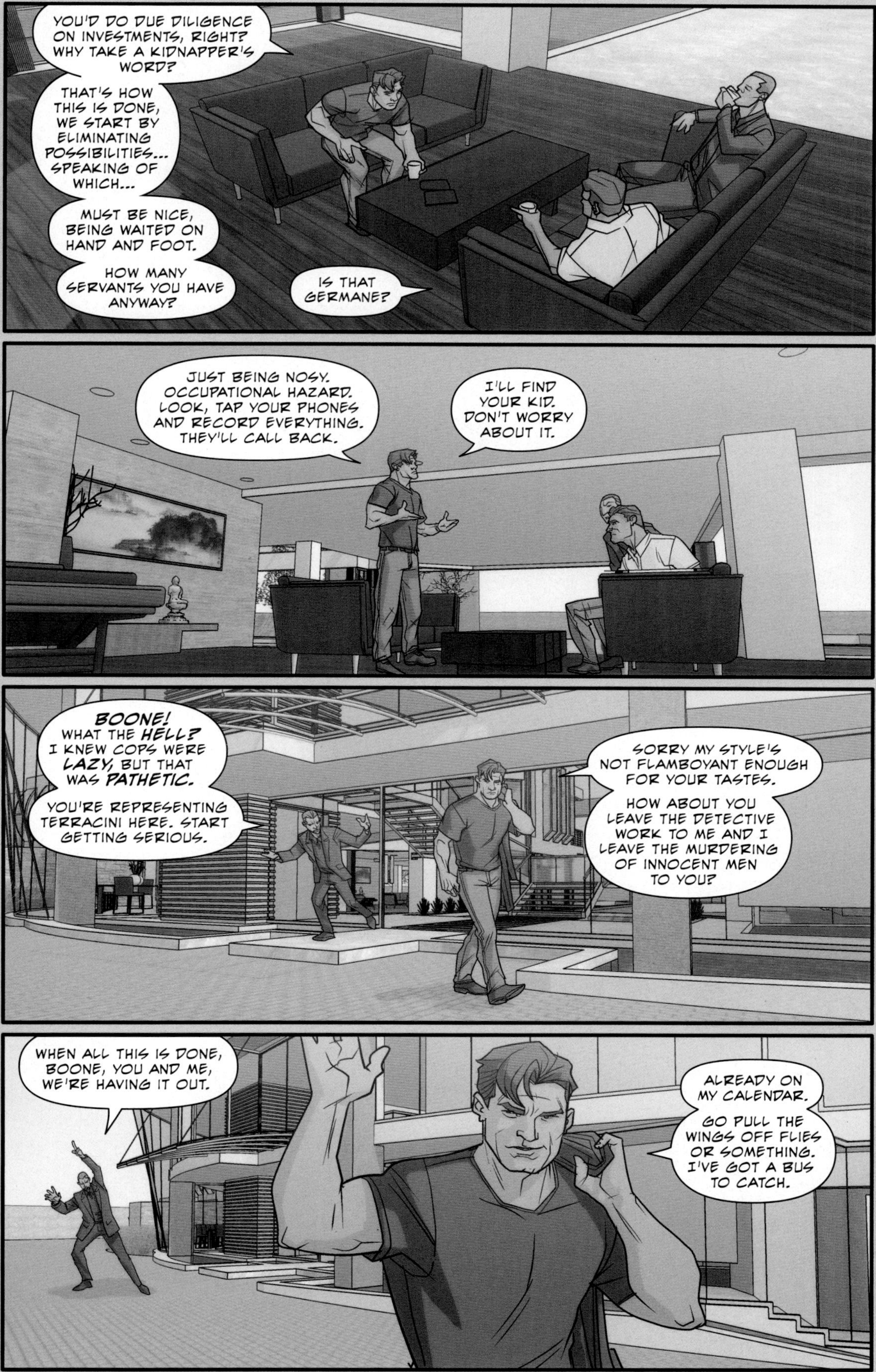
YOU'D DO DUE DILIGENCE ON INVESTMENTS, RIGHT? WHY TAKE A KIDNAPPER'S WORD?
THAT'S HOW THIS IS DONE, WE START BY ELIMINATING POSSIBILITIES... SPEAKING OF WHICH...
MUST BE NICE, BEING WAITED ON HAND AND FOOT.
HOW MANY SERVANTS YOU HAVE ANYWAY?
IS THAT GERMANE?
JUST BEING NOSY. OCCUPATIONAL HAZARD. LOOK, TAP YOUR PHONES AND RECORD EVERYTHING. THEY'LL CALL BACK.
I'LL FIND YOUR KID. DON'T WORRY ABOUT IT.
BOONE! WHAT THE HELL? I KNEW COPS WERE LAZY, BUT THAT WAS PATHETIC.
YOU'RE REPRESENTING TERRACINI HERE. START GETTING SERIOUS.
SORRY MY STYLE'S NOT FLAMBOYANT ENOUGH FOR YOUR TASTES.
HOW ABOUT YOU LEAVE THE DETECTIVE WORK TO ME AND I LEAVE THE MURDERING OF INNOCENT MEN TO YOU?
WHEN ALL THIS IS DONE, BOONE, YOU AND ME, WE'RE HAVING IT OUT.
ALREADY ON MY CALENDAR.
GO PULL THE WINGS OFF FLIES OR SOMETHING. I'VE GOT A BUS TO CATCH.

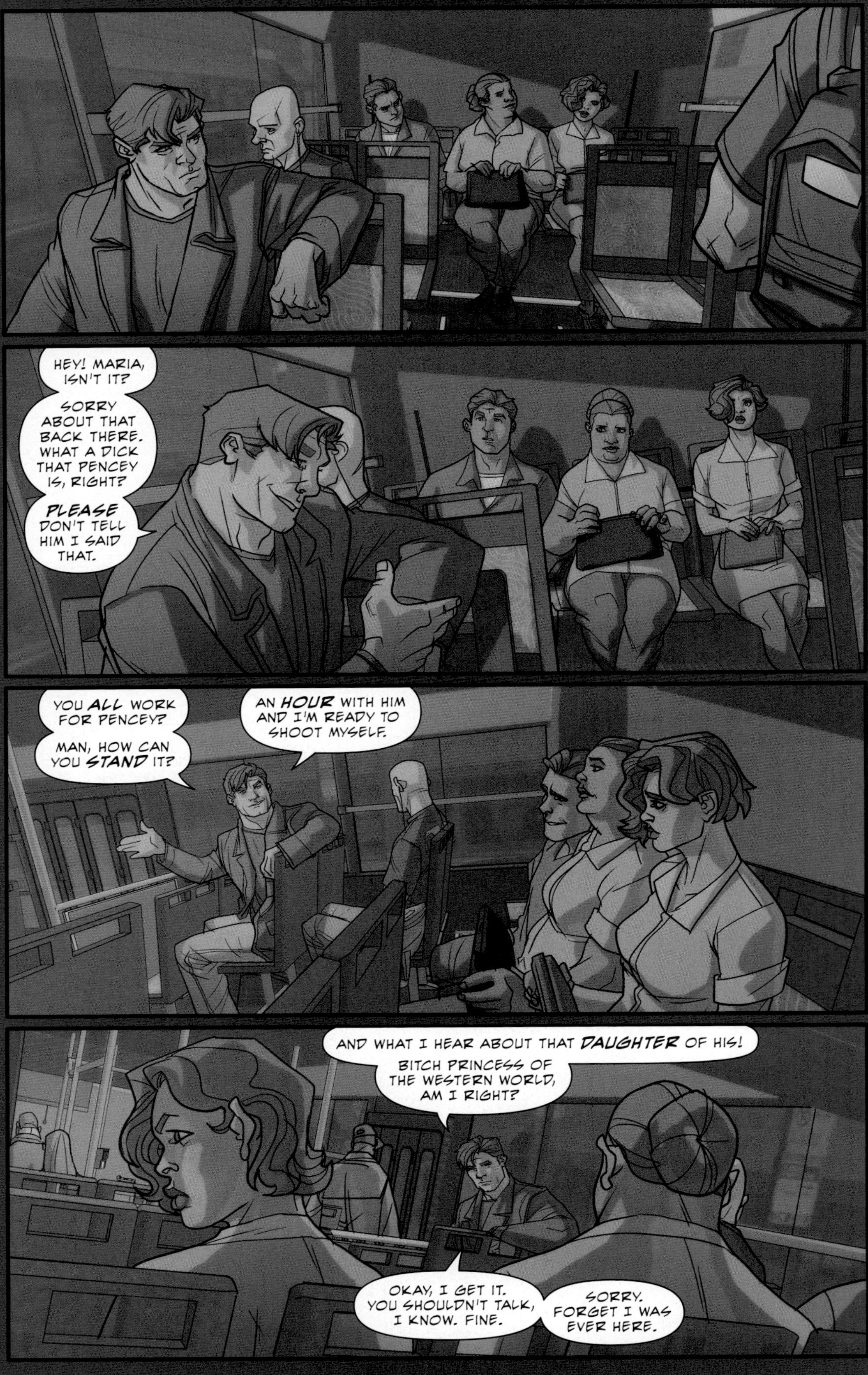
HEY! MARIA, ISN'T IT?
SORRY ABOUT THAT BACK THERE. WHAT A DICK THAT PENCEY IS, RIGHT?
PLEASE DON'T TELL HIM I SAID THAT.
YOU ALL WORK FOR PENCEY?
MAN, HOW CAN YOU STAND IT?
AN HOUR WITH HIM AND I'M READY TO SHOOT MYSELF.
AND WHAT I HEAR ABOUT THAT DAUGHTER OF HIS!
BITCH PRINCESS OF THE WESTERN WORLD, AM I RIGHT?
OKAY, I GET IT. YOU SHOULDN'T TALK, I KNOW. FINE.
SORRY. FORGET I WAS EVER HERE.

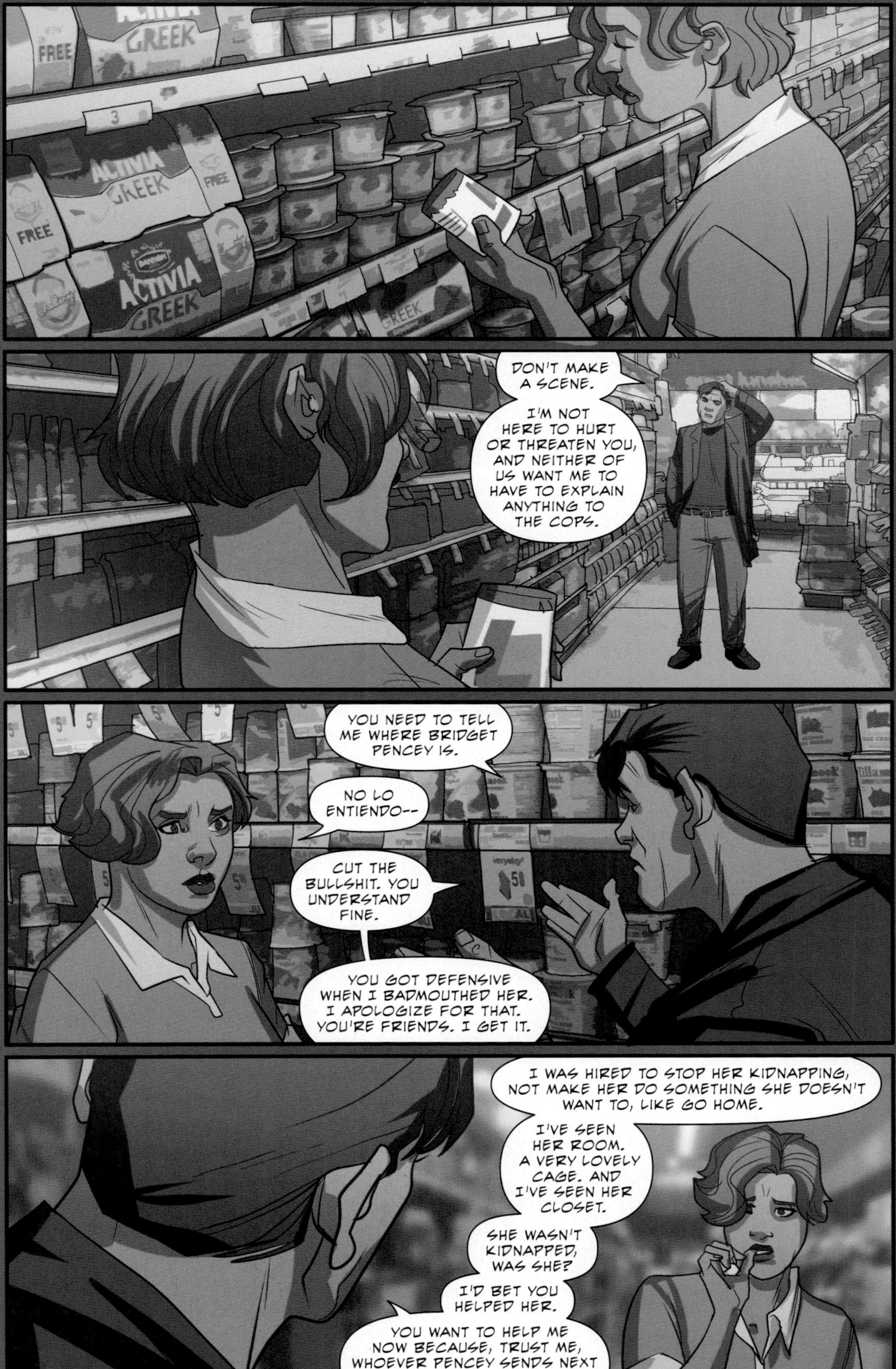
DON'T MAKE A SCENE.
I'M NOT HERE TO HURT OR THREATEN YOU, AND NEITHER OF US WANT ME TO HAVE TO EXPLAIN ANYTHING TO THE COPS.
YOU NEED TO TELL ME WHERE BRIDGET PENCEY IS.
NO LO ENTIENDO--
CUT THE BULLSHIT. YOU UNDERSTAND FINE.
YOU GOT DEFENSIVE WHEN I BADMOUTHED HER. I APOLOGIZE FOR THAT. YOU'RE FRIENDS. I GET IT.
I WAS HIRED TO STOP HER KIDNAPPING, NOT MAKE HER DO SOMETHING SHE DOESN'T WANT TO, LIKE GO HOME.
I'VE SEEN HER ROOM. A VERY LOVELY CAGE. AND I'VE SEEN HER CLOSET.
SHE WASN'T KIDNAPPED, WAS SHE?
I'D BET YOU HELPED HER.
YOU WANT TO HELP ME NOW BECAUSE, TRUST ME, WHOEVER PENCEY SENDS NEXT WON'T BE CONVERSATIONAL.

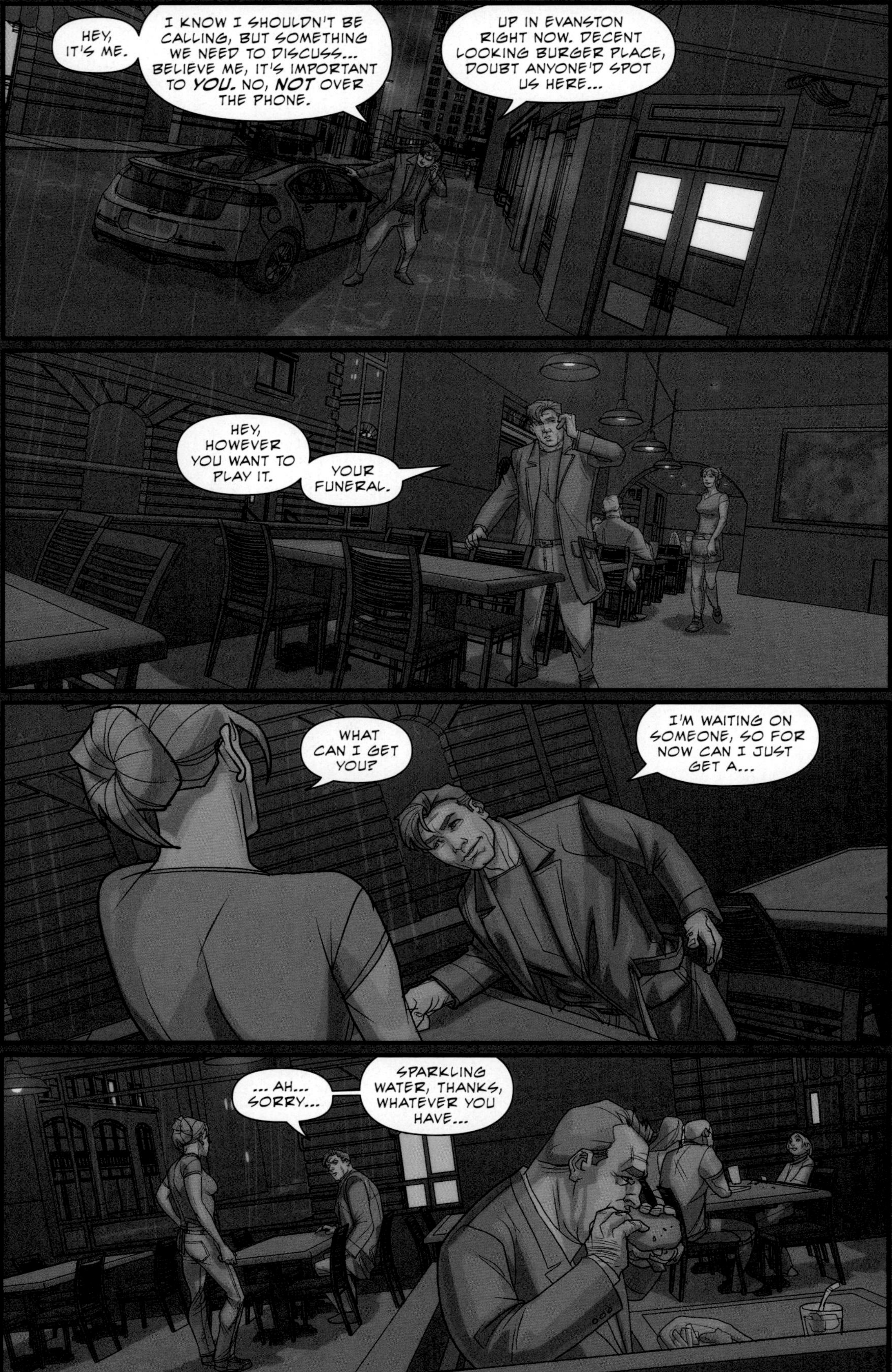
HEY, IT'S ME.
I KNOW I SHOULDN'T BE CALLING, BUT SOMETHING WE NEED TO DISCUSS... BELIEVE ME, IT'S IMPORTANT TO *YOU.* NO, ***NOT*** OVER THE PHONE.
UP IN EVANSTON RIGHT NOW. DECENT LOOKING BURGER PLACE, DOUBT ANYONE'D SPOT US HERE...
HEY, HOWEVER YOU WANT TO PLAY IT.
YOUR FUNERAL.
WHAT CAN I GET YOU?
I'M WAITING ON SOMEONE, SO FOR NOW CAN I JUST GET A...
...AH... SORRY...
SPARKLING WATER, THANKS, WHATEVER YOU HAVE...

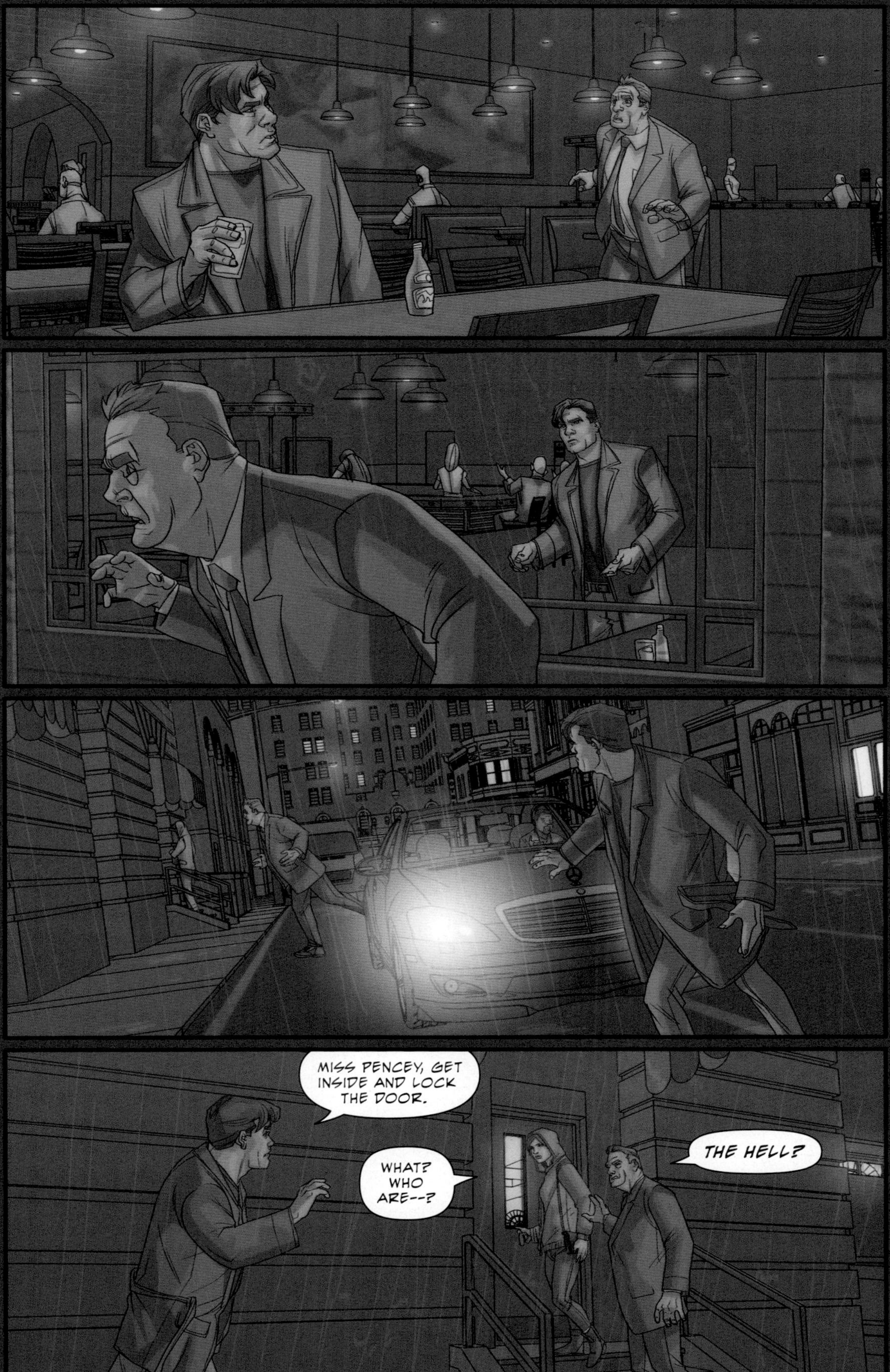
MISS PENCEY, GET INSIDE AND LOCK THE DOOR.
WHAT? WHO ARE--?
THE HELL?

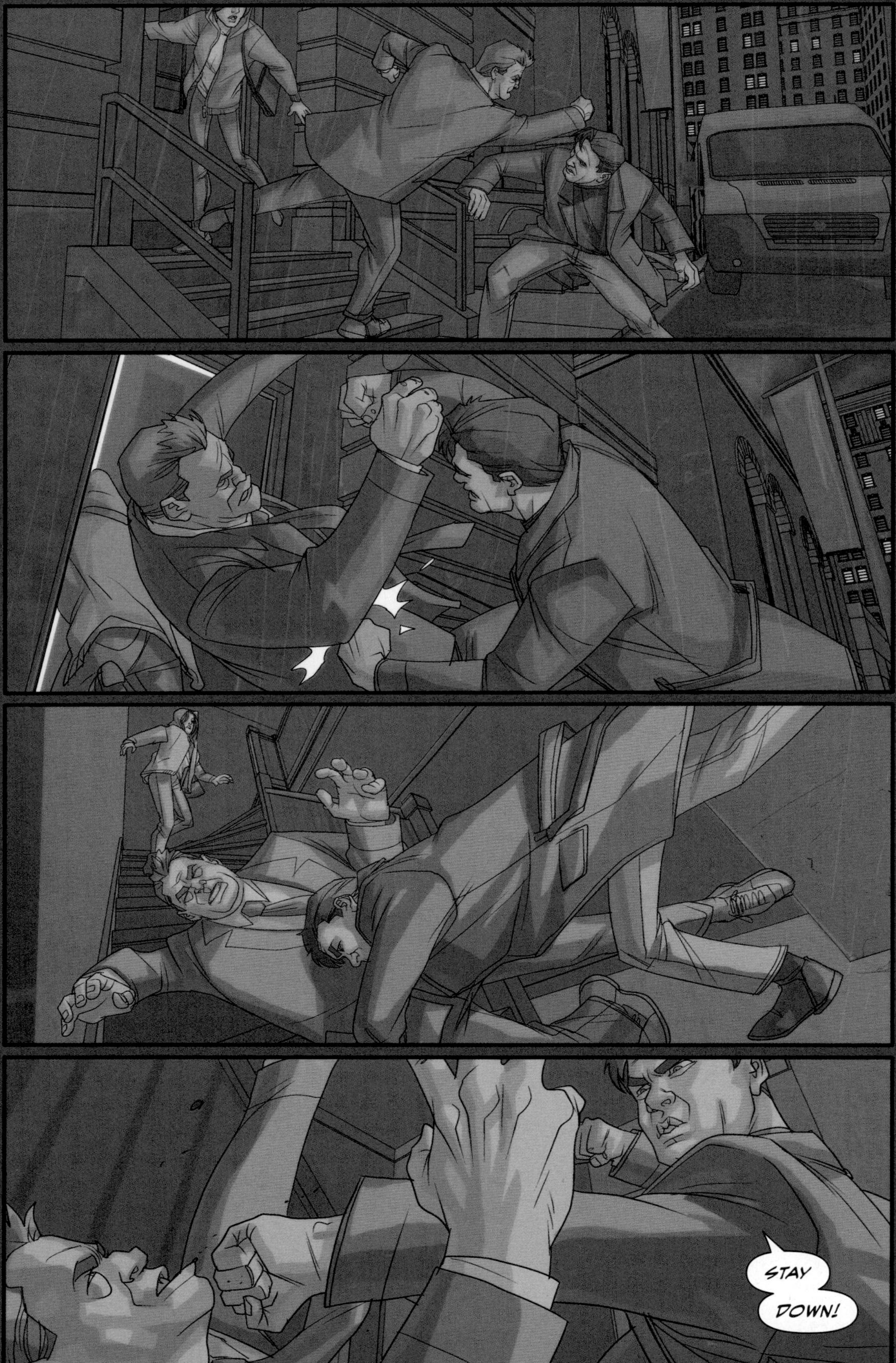
STAY DOWN!

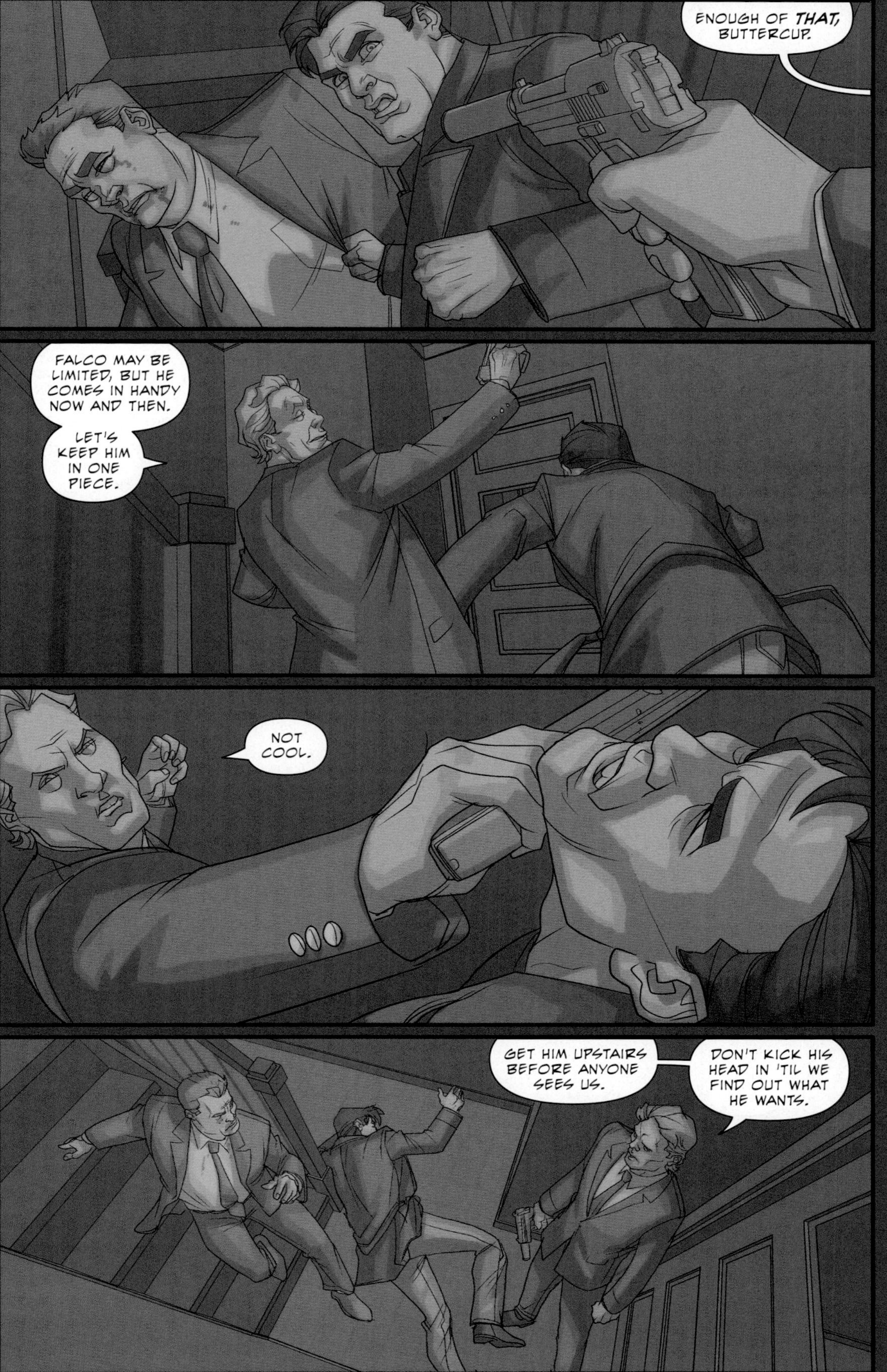
ENOUGH OF *THAT,* BUTTERCUP.
FALCO MAY BE LIMITED, BUT HE COMES IN HANDY NOW AND THEN.
LET'S KEEP HIM IN ONE PIECE.
NOT COOL.
GET HIM UPSTAIRS BEFORE ANYONE SEES US.
DON'T KICK HIS HEAD IN 'TIL WE FIND OUT WHAT HE WANTS.

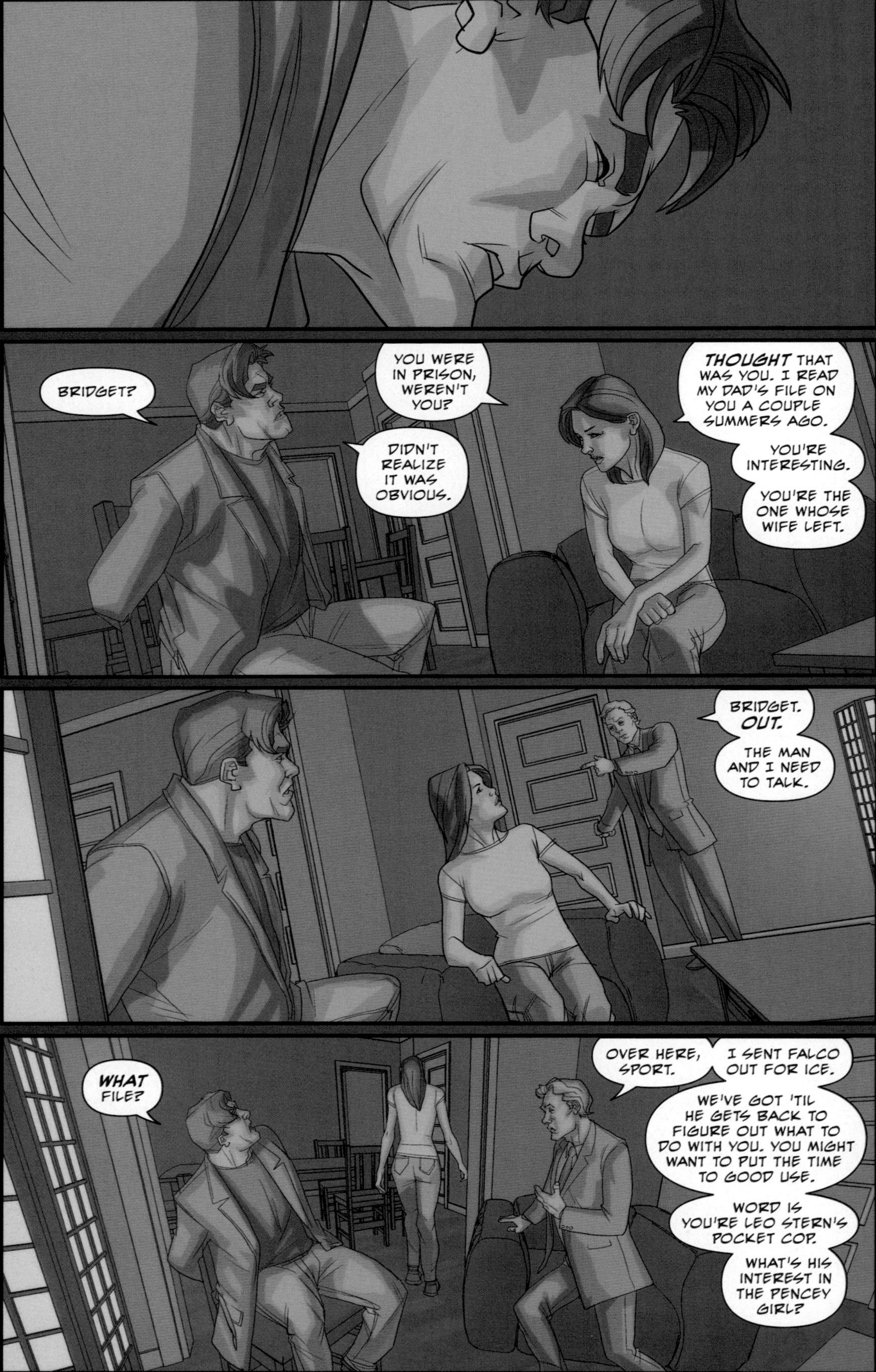
BRIDGET?
YOU WERE IN PRISON, WEREN'T YOU?
DIDN'T REALIZE IT WAS OBVIOUS.
THOUGHT THAT WAS YOU. I READ MY DAD'S FILE ON YOU A COUPLE SUMMERS AGO.
YOU'RE INTERESTING.
YOU'RE THE ONE WHOSE WIFE LEFT.
BRIDGET. OUT.
THE MAN AND I NEED TO TALK.
WHAT FILE?
OVER HERE, SPORT.
I SENT FALCO OUT FOR ICE.
WE'VE GOT 'TIL HE GETS BACK TO FIGURE OUT WHAT TO DO WITH YOU. YOU MIGHT WANT TO PUT THE TIME TO GOOD USE.
WORD IS YOU'RE LEO STERN'S POCKET COP.
WHAT'S HIS INTEREST IN THE PENCEY GIRL?

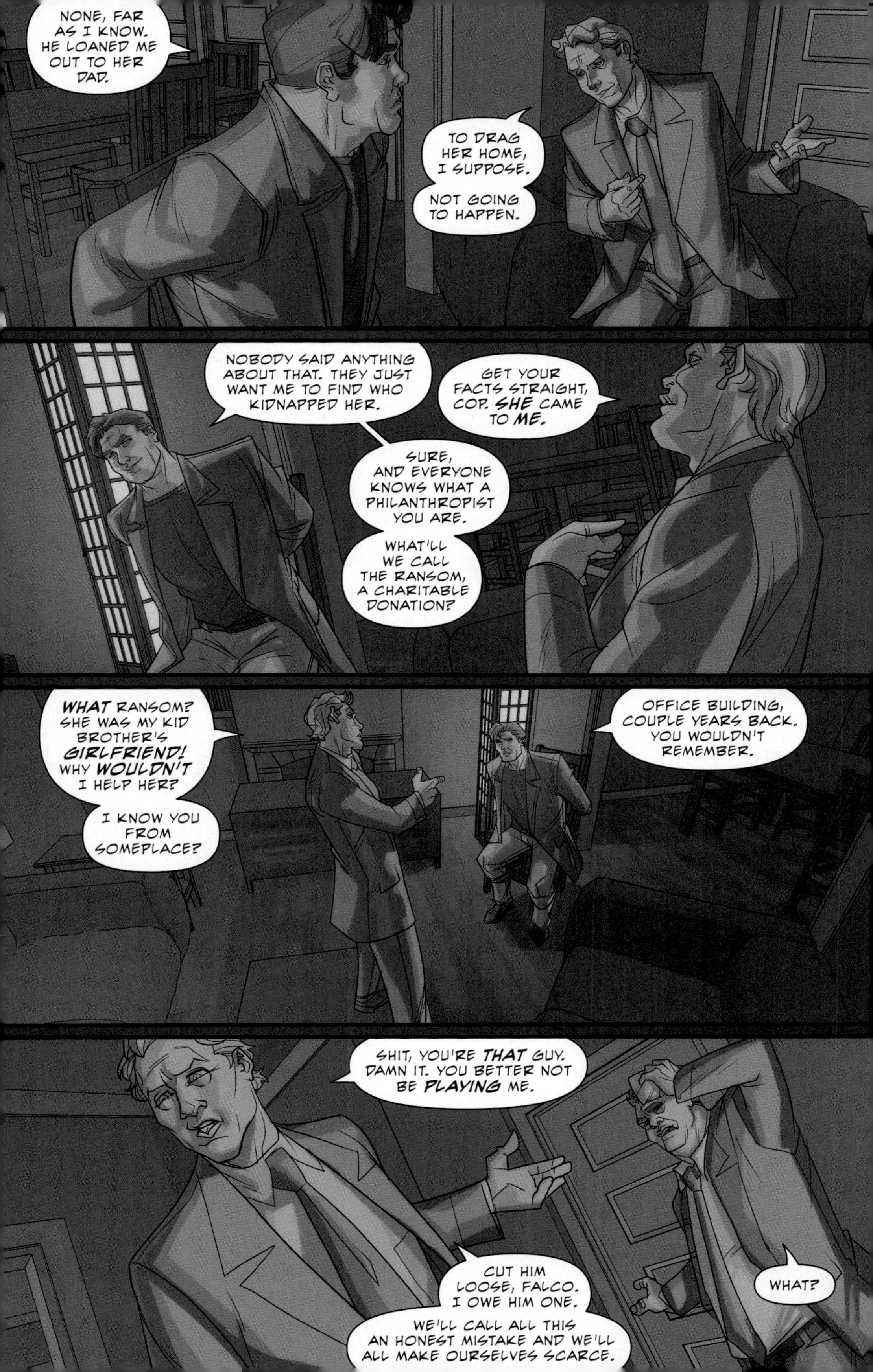
NONE, FAR AS I KNOW. HE LOANED ME OUT TO HER DAD.
TO DRAG HER HOME, I SUPPOSE.
NOT GOING TO HAPPEN.
NOBODY SAID ANYTHING ABOUT THAT. THEY JUST WANT ME TO FIND WHO KIDNAPPED HER.
GET YOUR FACTS STRAIGHT, COP. SHE CAME TO ME.
SURE, AND EVERYONE KNOWS WHAT A PHILANTHROPIST YOU ARE.
WHAT'LL WE CALL THE RANSOM, A CHARITABLE DONATION?
WHAT RANSOM? SHE WAS MY KID BROTHER'S GIRLFRIEND! WHY WOULDN'T I HELP HER?
I KNOW YOU FROM SOMEPLACE?
OFFICE BUILDING, COUPLE YEARS BACK. YOU WOULDN'T REMEMBER.
SHIT, YOU'RE THAT GUY. DAMN IT. YOU BETTER NOT BE PLAYING ME.
CUT HIM LOOSE, FALCO. I OWE HIM ONE.
WE'LL CALL ALL THIS AN HONEST MISTAKE AND WE'LL ALL MAKE OURSELVES SCARCE.
WHAT?

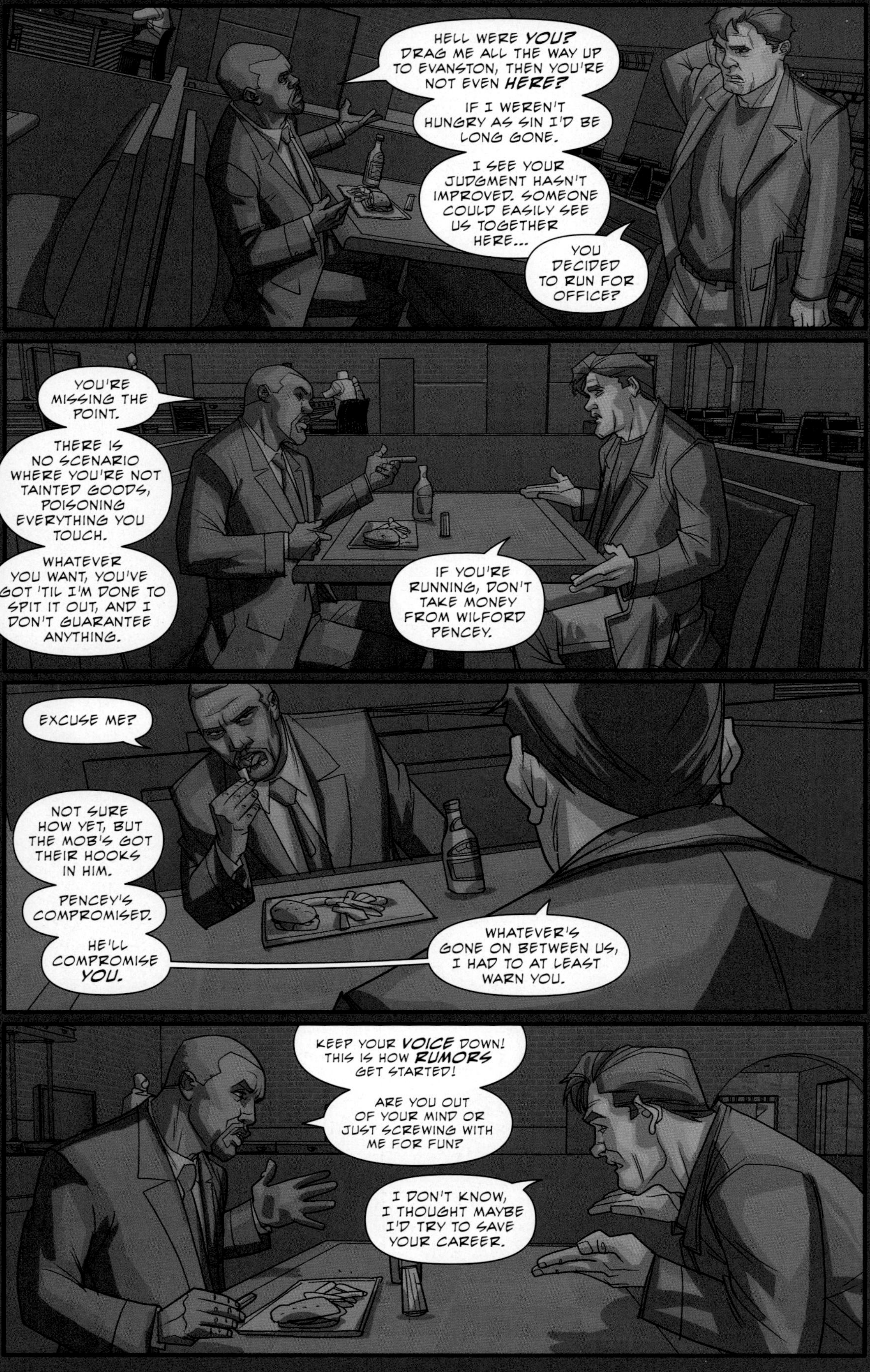
HELL WERE YOU? DRAG ME ALL THE WAY UP TO EVANSTON, THEN YOU'RE NOT EVEN HERE?
IF I WEREN'T HUNGRY AS SIN I'D BE LONG GONE.
I SEE YOUR JUDGMENT HASN'T IMPROVED. SOMEONE COULD EASILY SEE US TOGETHER HERE...
YOU DECIDED TO RUN FOR OFFICE?
YOU'RE MISSING THE POINT.
THERE IS NO SCENARIO WHERE YOU'RE NOT TAINTED GOODS, POISONING EVERYTHING YOU TOUCH.
WHATEVER YOU WANT, YOU'VE GOT 'TIL I'M DONE TO SPIT IT OUT, AND I DON'T GUARANTEE ANYTHING.
IF YOU'RE RUNNING, DON'T TAKE MONEY FROM WILFORD PENCEY.
EXCUSE ME?
NOT SURE HOW YET, BUT THE MOB'S GOT THEIR HOOKS IN HIM.
PENCEY'S COMPROMISED.
HE'LL COMPROMISE YOU.
WHATEVER'S GONE ON BETWEEN US, I HAD TO AT LEAST WARN YOU.
KEEP YOUR VOICE DOWN! THIS IS HOW RUMORS GET STARTED!
ARE YOU OUT OF YOUR MIND OR JUST SCREWING WITH ME FOR FUN?
I DON'T KNOW, I THOUGHT MAYBE I'D TRY TO SAVE YOUR CAREER.

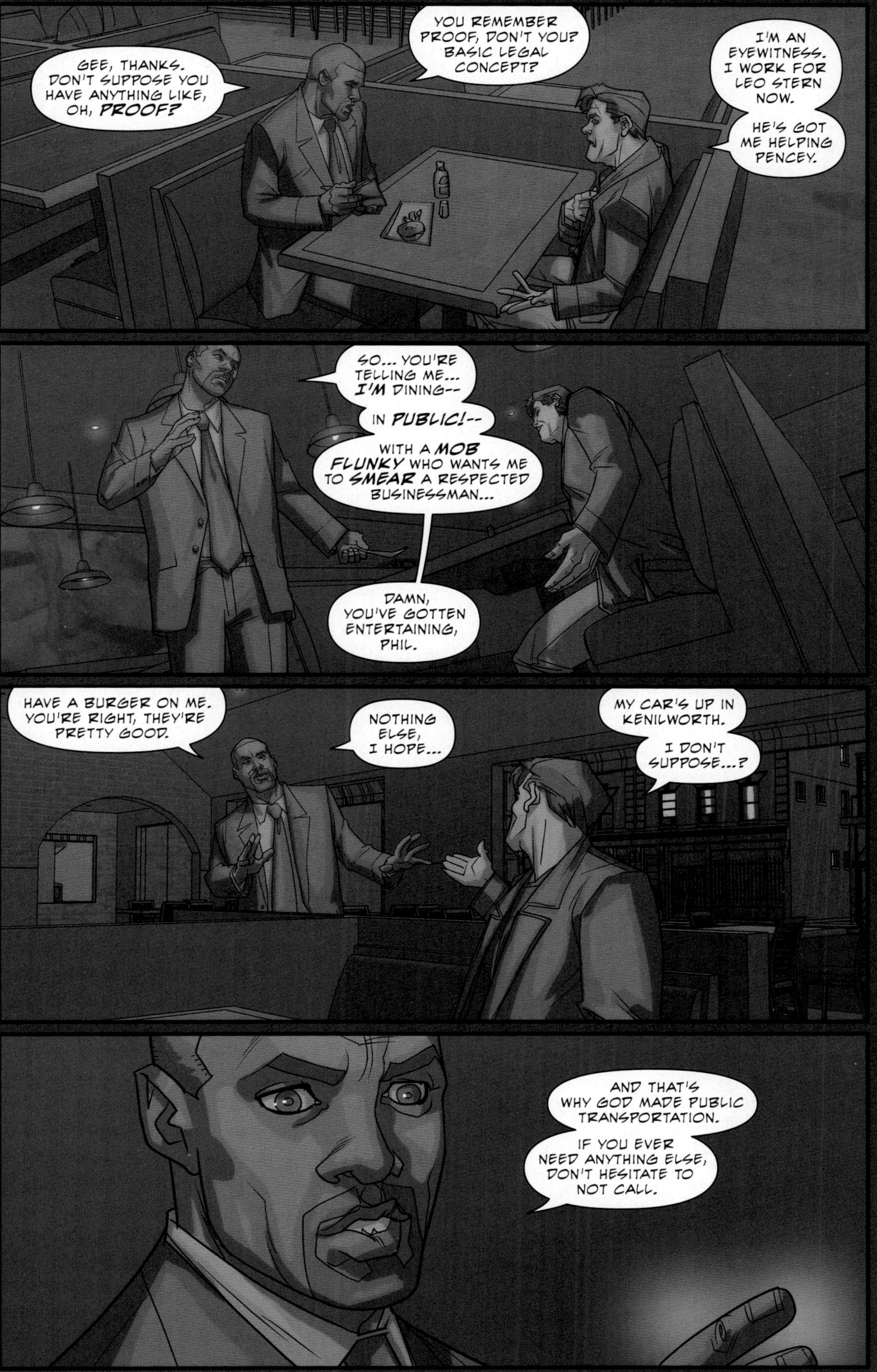
GEE, THANKS. DON'T SUPPOSE YOU HAVE ANYTHING LIKE, OH, PROOF?
YOU REMEMBER PROOF, DON'T YOU? BASIC LEGAL CONCEPT?
I'M AN EYEWITNESS. I WORK FOR LEO STERN NOW.
HE'S GOT ME HELPING PENCEY.
SO... YOU'RE TELLING ME... I'M DINING--
IN PUBLIC!--
WITH A MOB FLUNKY WHO WANTS ME TO SMEAR A RESPECTED BUSINESSMAN...
DAMN, YOU'VE GOTTEN ENTERTAINING, PHIL.
HAVE A BURGER ON ME. YOU'RE RIGHT, THEY'RE PRETTY GOOD.
NOTHING ELSE, I HOPE...
MY CAR'S UP IN KENILWORTH.
I DON'T SUPPOSE...?
AND THAT'S WHY GOD MADE PUBLIC TRANSPORTATION.
IF YOU EVER NEED ANYTHING ELSE, DON'T HESITATE TO NOT CALL.

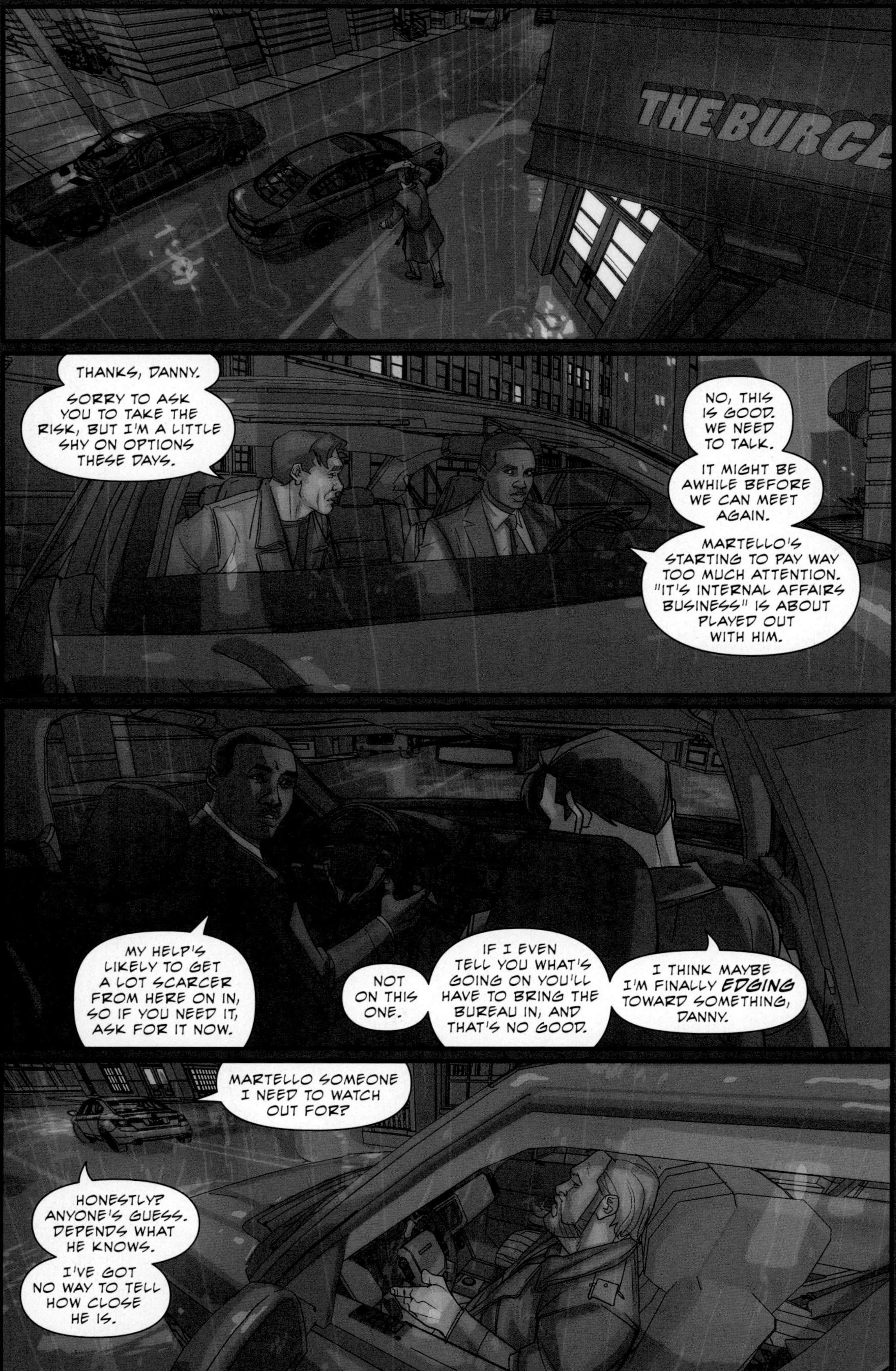
THE BURGE
THANKS, DANNY.
SORRY TO ASK YOU TO TAKE THE RISK, BUT I'M A LITTLE SHY ON OPTIONS THESE DAYS.
NO, THIS IS GOOD. WE NEED TO TALK.
IT MIGHT BE AWHILE BEFORE WE CAN MEET AGAIN.
MARTELLO'S STARTING TO PAY WAY TOO MUCH ATTENTION. "IT'S INTERNAL AFFAIRS BUSINESS" IS ABOUT PLAYED OUT WITH HIM.
I THINK MAYBE I'M FINALLY EDGING TOWARD SOMETHING, DANNY.
MY HELP'S LIKELY TO GET A LOT SCARCER FROM HERE ON IN, SO IF YOU NEED IT, ASK FOR IT NOW.
NOT ON THIS ONE.
IF I EVEN TELL YOU WHAT'S GOING ON YOU'LL HAVE TO BRING THE BUREAU IN, AND THAT'S NO GOOD.
MARTELLO SOMEONE I NEED TO WATCH OUT FOR?
HONESTLY? ANYONE'S GUESS. DEPENDS WHAT HE KNOWS.
I'VE GOT NO WAY TO TELL HOW CLOSE HE IS.

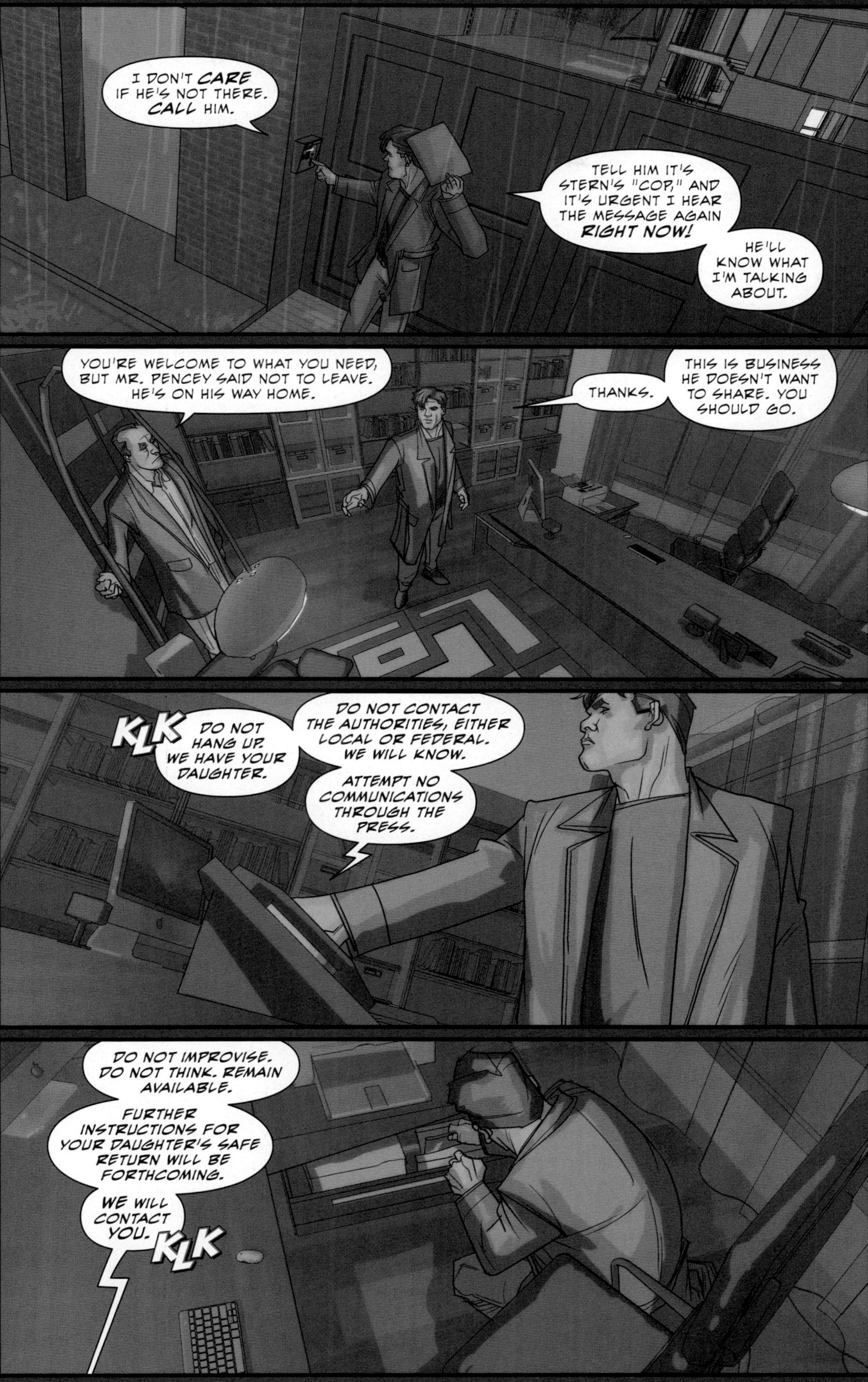
I DON'T CARE IF HE'S NOT THERE. CALL HIM.
TELL HIM IT'S STERN'S "COP," AND IT'S URGENT I HEAR THE MESSAGE AGAIN RIGHT NOW!
HE'LL KNOW WHAT I'M TALKING ABOUT.
YOU'RE WELCOME TO WHAT YOU NEED, BUT MR. PENCEY SAID NOT TO LEAVE. HE'S ON HIS WAY HOME.
THANKS.
THIS IS BUSINESS HE DOESN'T WANT TO SHARE. YOU SHOULD GO.
KLK
DO NOT HANG UP. WE HAVE YOUR DAUGHTER.
DO NOT CONTACT THE AUTHORITIES, EITHER LOCAL OR FEDERAL. WE WILL KNOW.
ATTEMPT NO COMMUNICATIONS THROUGH THE PRESS.
DO NOT IMPROVISE. DO NOT THINK. REMAIN AVAILABLE.
FURTHER INSTRUCTIONS FOR YOUR DAUGHTER'S SAFE RETURN WILL BE FORTHCOMING.
WE WILL CONTACT YOU.
KLK

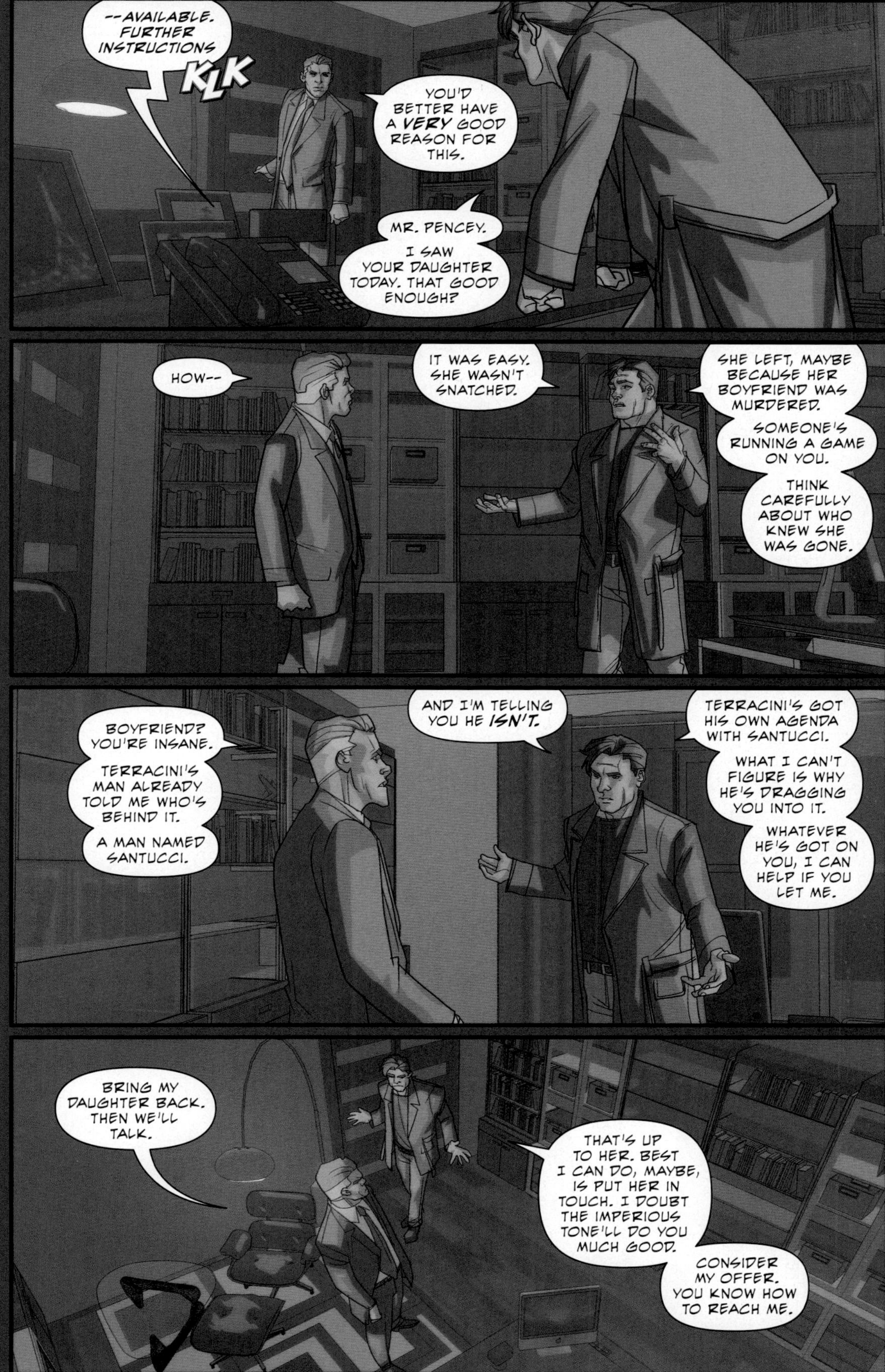
--AVAILABLE. FURTHER INSTRUCTIONS
KLK
YOU'D BETTER HAVE A VERY GOOD REASON FOR THIS.
MR. PENCEY.
I SAW YOUR DAUGHTER TODAY. THAT GOOD ENOUGH?
HOW--
IT WAS EASY. SHE WASN'T SNATCHED.
SHE LEFT, MAYBE BECAUSE HER BOYFRIEND WAS MURDERED.
SOMEONE'S RUNNING A GAME ON YOU.
THINK CAREFULLY ABOUT WHO KNEW SHE WAS GONE.
BOYFRIEND? YOU'RE INSANE.
TERRACINI'S MAN ALREADY TOLD ME WHO'S BEHIND IT.
A MAN NAMED SANTUCCI.
AND I'M TELLING YOU HE ISN'T.
TERRACINI'S GOT HIS OWN AGENDA WITH SANTUCCI.
WHAT I CAN'T FIGURE IS WHY HE'S DRAGGING YOU INTO IT.
WHATEVER HE'S GOT ON YOU, I CAN HELP IF YOU LET ME.
BRING MY DAUGHTER BACK. THEN WE'LL TALK.
THAT'S UP TO HER. BEST I CAN DO, MAYBE, IS PUT HER IN TOUCH. I DOUBT THE IMPERIOUS TONE'LL DO YOU MUCH GOOD.
CONSIDER MY OFFER. YOU KNOW HOW TO REACH ME.

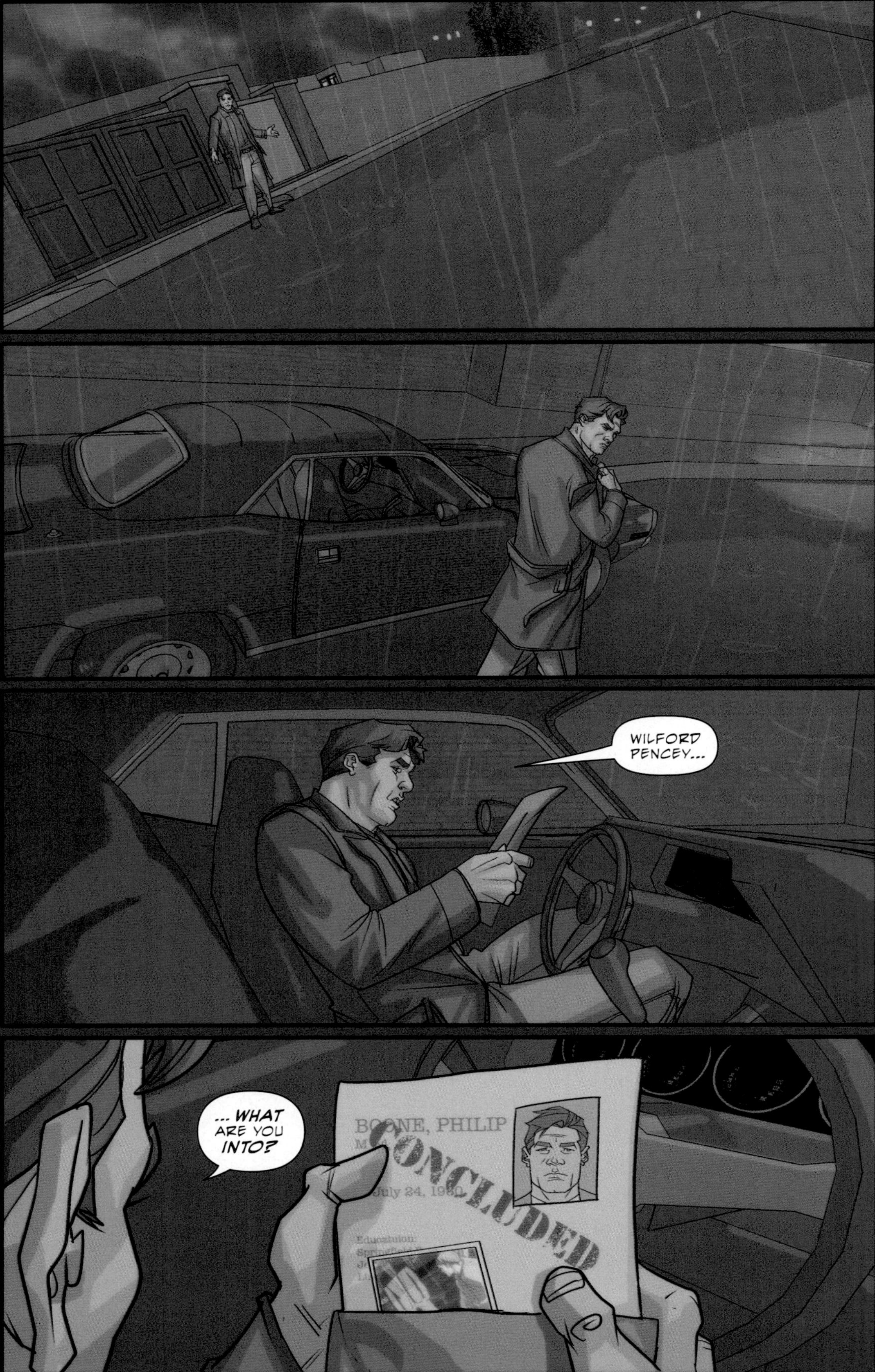
WILFORD PENCEY...
...WHAT ARE YOU INTO?
BOONE, PHILIP
CONCLUDED

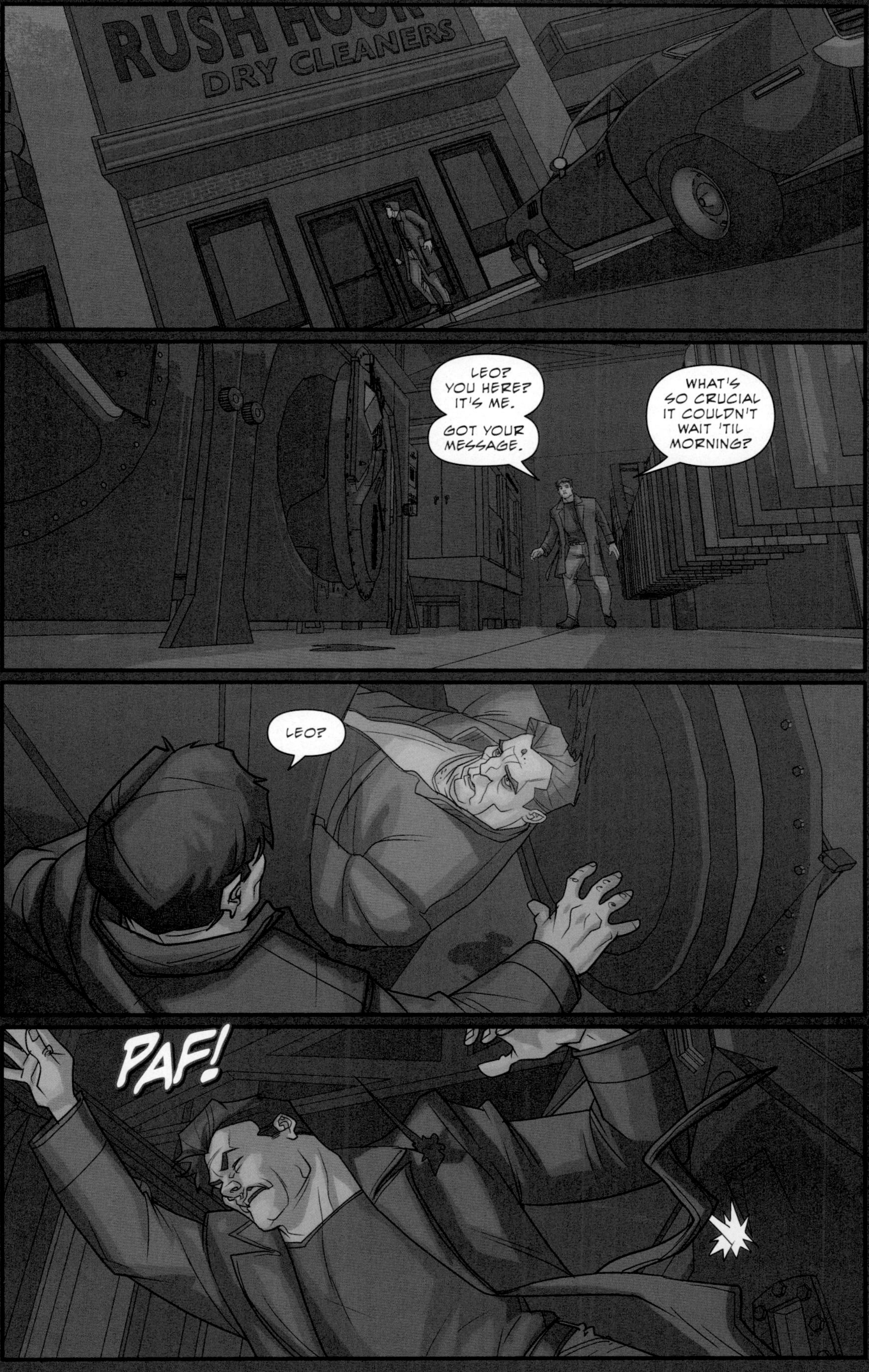
RUSH HOUR
DRY CLEANERS
LEO? YOU HERE? IT'S ME.
GOT YOUR MESSAGE.
WHAT'S SO CRUCIAL IT COULDN'T WAIT 'TIL MORNING?
LEO?
PAF!

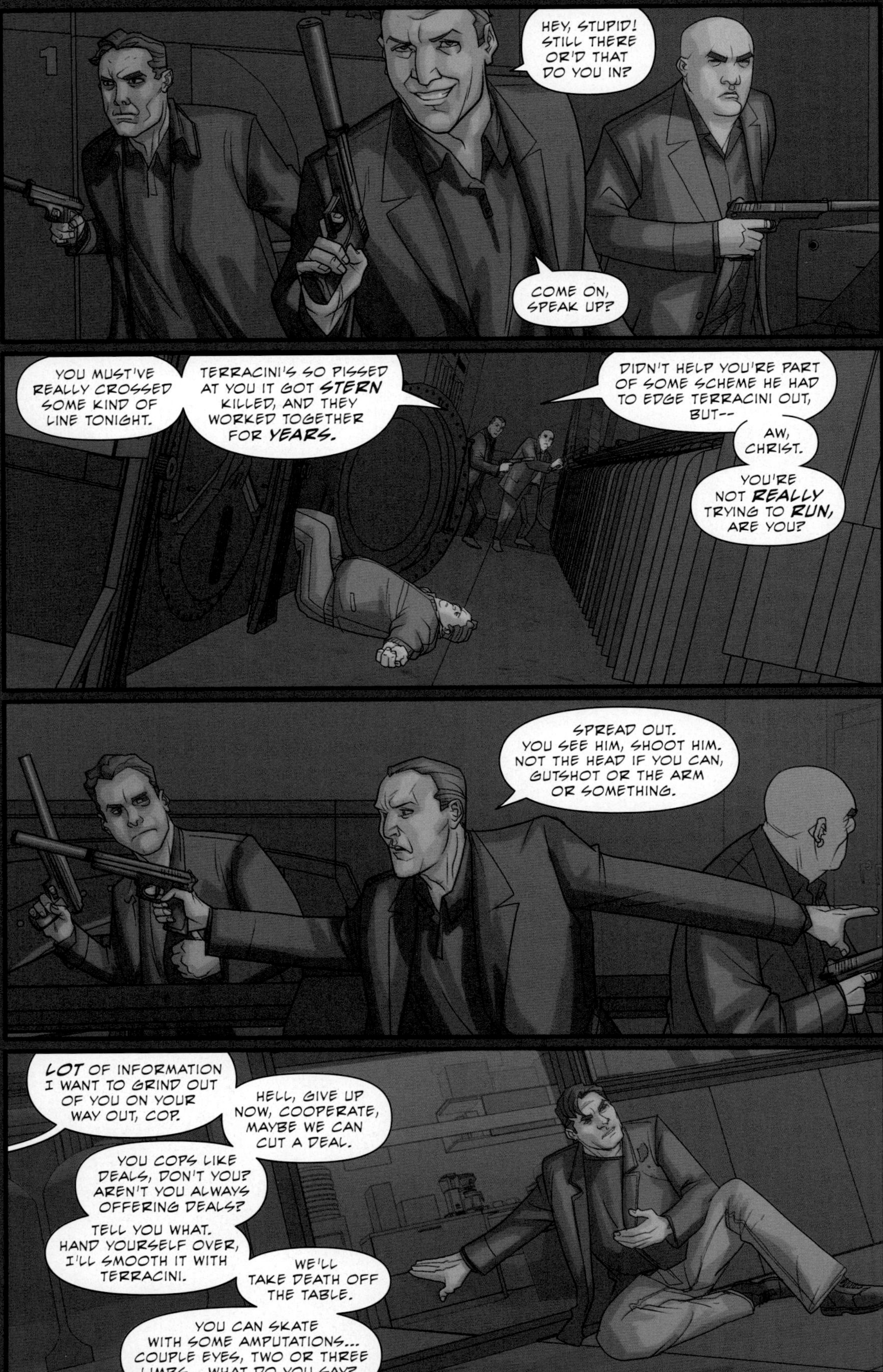
1
HEY, STUPID! STILL THERE OR'D THAT DO YOU IN?
COME ON, SPEAK UP?
YOU MUST'VE REALLY CROSSED SOME KIND OF LINE TONIGHT.
TERRACINI'S SO PISSED AT YOU IT GOT STERN KILLED, AND THEY WORKED TOGETHER FOR YEARS.
DIDN'T HELP YOU'RE PART OF SOME SCHEME HE HAD TO EDGE TERRACINI OUT, BUT--
AW, CHRIST.
YOU'RE NOT REALLY TRYING TO RUN, ARE YOU?
SPREAD OUT. YOU SEE HIM, SHOOT HIM. NOT THE HEAD IF YOU CAN, GUTSHOT OR THE ARM OR SOMETHING.
LOT OF INFORMATION I WANT TO GRIND OUT OF YOU ON YOUR WAY OUT, COP.
HELL, GIVE UP NOW, COOPERATE, MAYBE WE CAN CUT A DEAL.
YOU COPS LIKE DEALS, DON'T YOU? AREN'T YOU ALWAYS OFFERING DEALS?
TELL YOU WHAT. HAND YOURSELF OVER, I'LL SMOOTH IT WITH TERRACINI.
WE'LL TAKE DEATH OFF THE TABLE.
YOU CAN SKATE WITH SOME AMPUTATIONS... COUPLE EYES, TWO OR THREE LIMBS... WHAT DO YOU SAY?

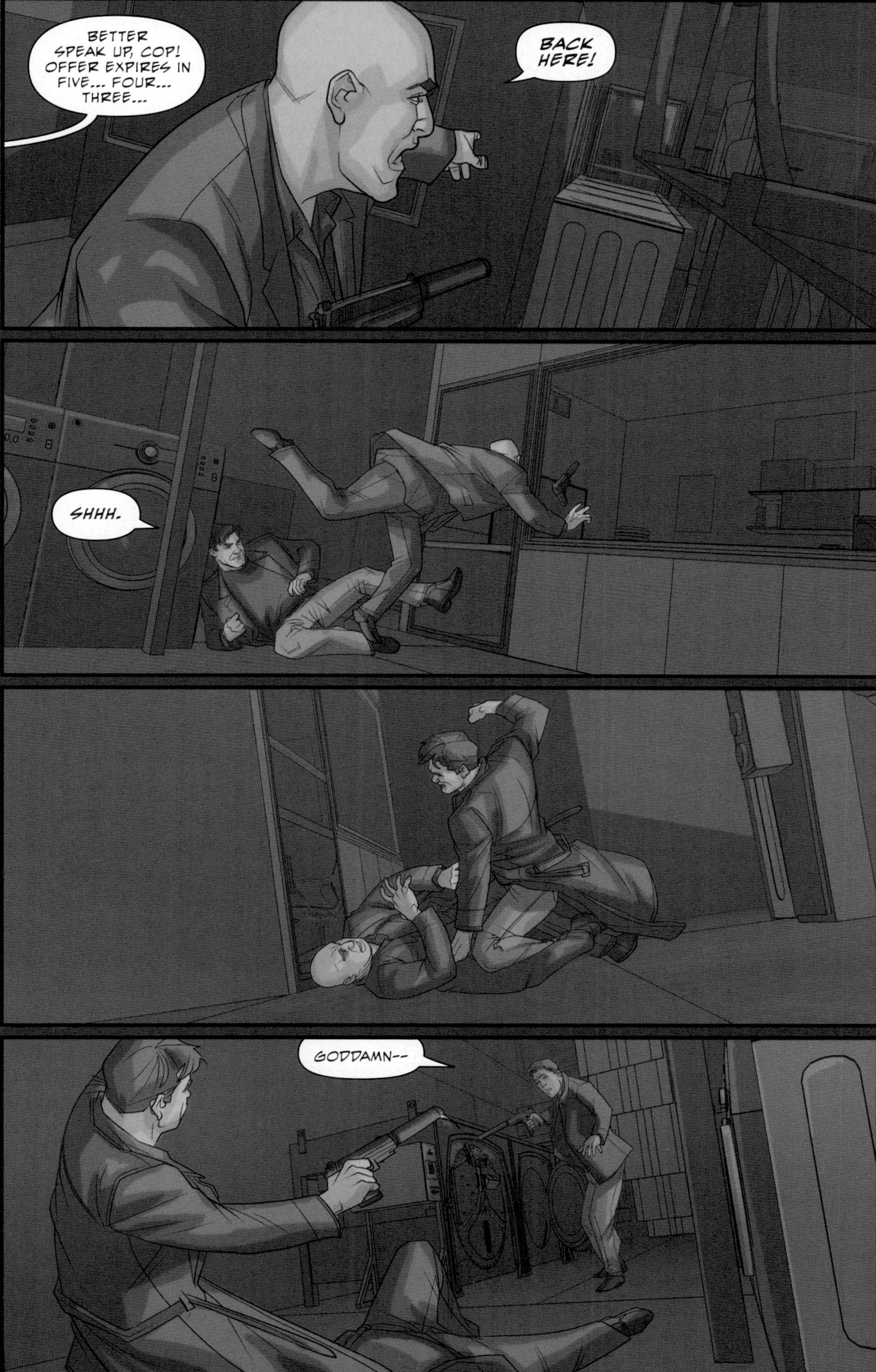
BETTER SPEAK UP, COP! OFFER EXPIRES IN FIVE... FOUR... THREE...
BACK HERE!
SHHH.
GODDAMN--

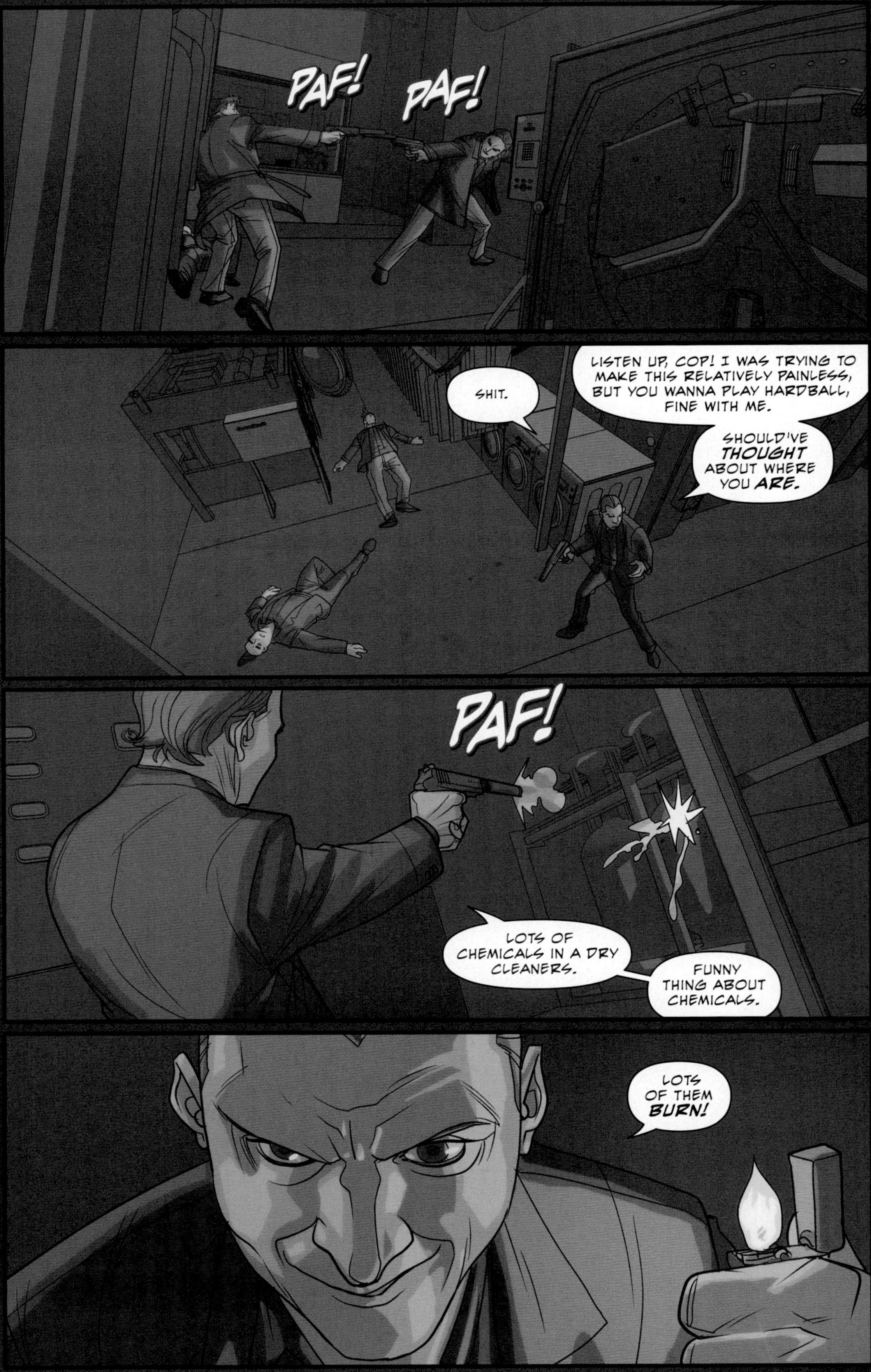
PAF! PAF!
SHIT.
LISTEN UP, COP! I WAS TRYING TO MAKE THIS RELATIVELY PAINLESS, BUT YOU WANNA PLAY HARDBALL, FINE WITH ME.
SHOULD'VE THOUGHT ABOUT WHERE YOU ARE.
PAF!
LOTS OF CHEMICALS IN A DRY CLEANERS.
FUNNY THING ABOUT CHEMICALS.
LOTS OF THEM BURN!

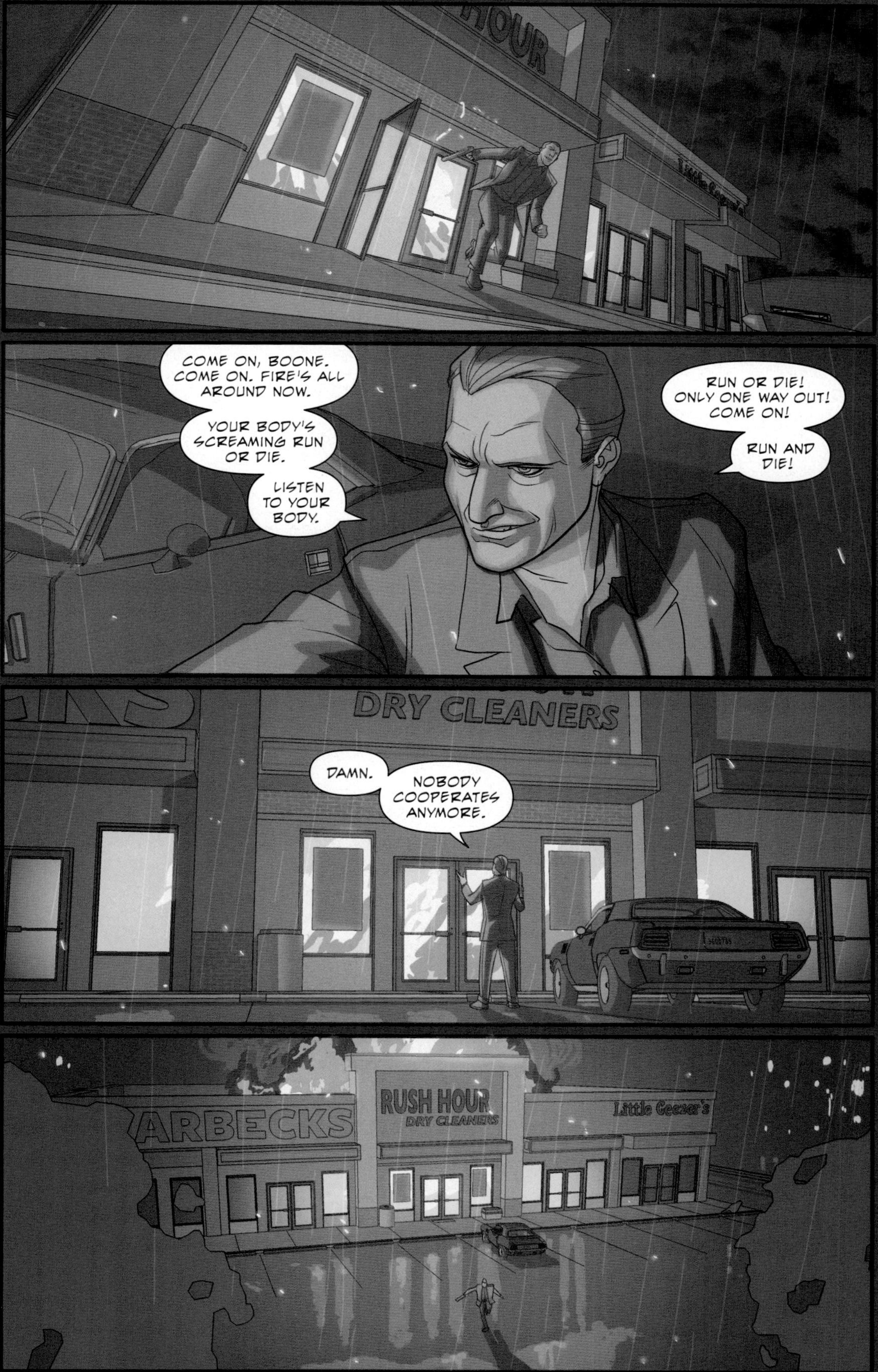
HOUR
COME ON, BOONE. COME ON. FIRE'S ALL AROUND NOW.
YOUR BODY'S SCREAMING RUN OR DIE.
LISTEN TO YOUR BODY.
RUN OR DIE! ONLY ONE WAY OUT! COME ON!
RUN AND DIE!
DRY CLEANERS
DAMN.
NOBODY COOPERATES ANYMORE.
ARBECKS
RUSH HOUR
DRY CLEANERS
Little Geezer's

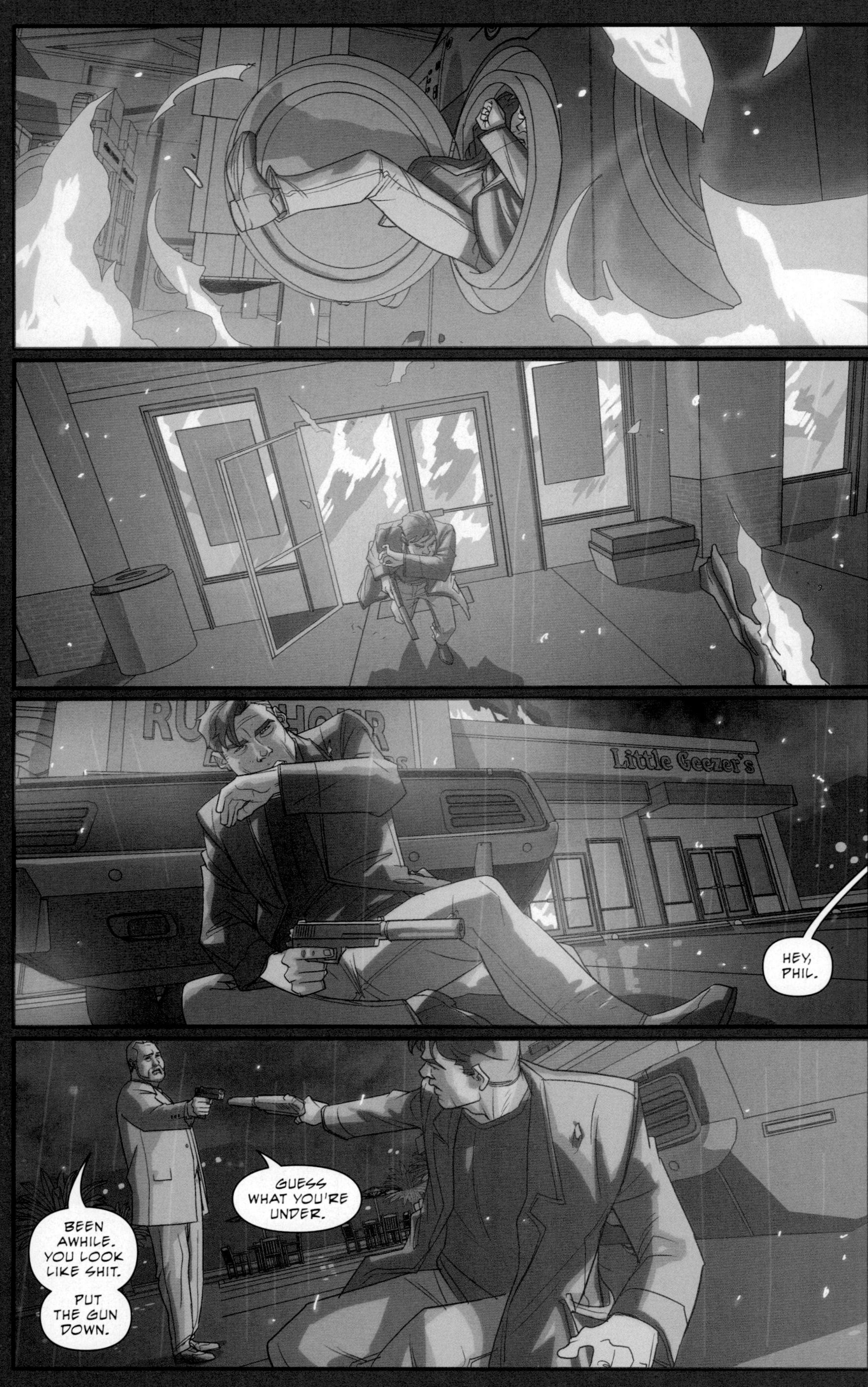
Little Geezer's
HEY, PHIL.
BEEN AWHILE. YOU LOOK LIKE SHIT.
PUT THE GUN DOWN.
GUESS WHAT YOU'RE UNDER.

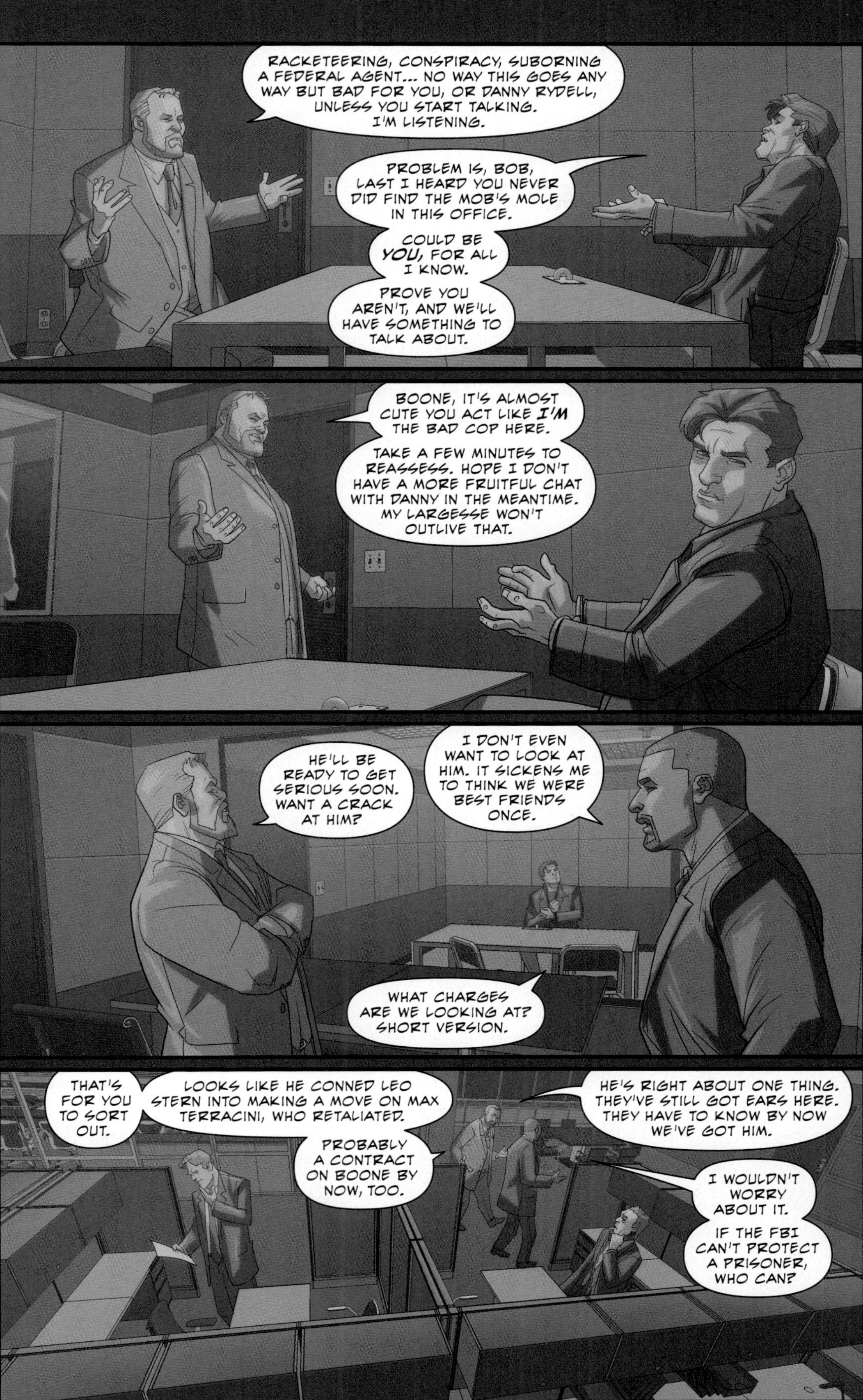
RACKETEERING, CONSPIRACY, SUBORNING A FEDERAL AGENT... NO WAY THIS GOES ANY WAY BUT BAD FOR YOU, OR DANNY RYDELL, UNLESS YOU START TALKING. I'M LISTENING.
PROBLEM IS, BOB, LAST I HEARD YOU NEVER DID FIND THE MOB'S MOLE IN THIS OFFICE.
COULD BE YOU, FOR ALL I KNOW.
PROVE YOU AREN'T, AND WE'LL HAVE SOMETHING TO TALK ABOUT.
BOONE, IT'S ALMOST CUTE YOU ACT LIKE I'M THE BAD COP HERE.
TAKE A FEW MINUTES TO REASSESS. HOPE I DON'T HAVE A MORE FRUITFUL CHAT WITH DANNY IN THE MEANTIME. MY LARGESSE WON'T OUTLIVE THAT.
HE'LL BE READY TO GET SERIOUS SOON. WANT A CRACK AT HIM?
I DON'T EVEN WANT TO LOOK AT HIM. IT SICKENS ME TO THINK WE WERE BEST FRIENDS ONCE.
WHAT CHARGES ARE WE LOOKING AT? SHORT VERSION.
LOOKS LIKE HE CONNED LEO STERN INTO MAKING A MOVE ON MAX TERRACINI, WHO RETALIATED.
PROBABLY A CONTRACT ON BOONE BY NOW, TOO.
THAT'S FOR YOU TO SORT OUT.
HE'S RIGHT ABOUT ONE THING. THEY'VE STILL GOT EARS HERE. THEY HAVE TO KNOW BY NOW WE'VE GOT HIM.
I WOULDN'T WORRY ABOUT IT.
IF THE FBI CAN'T PROTECT A PRISONER, WHO CAN?

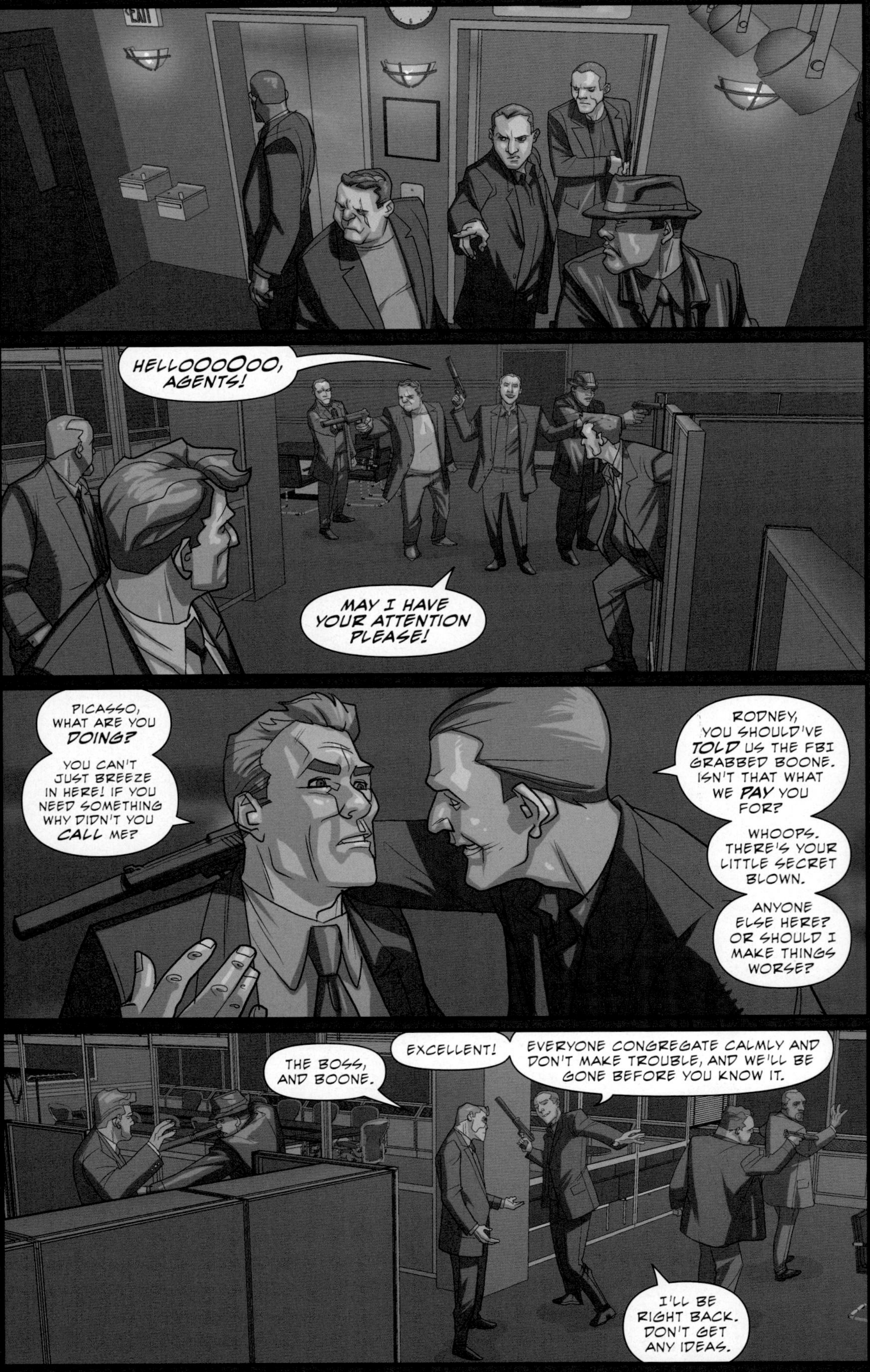
EXIT
HELLOOOOOO, AGENTS!
MAY I HAVE YOUR ATTENTION PLEASE!
PICASSO, WHAT ARE YOU DOING?
YOU CAN'T JUST BREEZE IN HERE! IF YOU NEED SOMETHING WHY DIDN'T YOU CALL ME?
RODNEY, YOU SHOULD'VE TOLD US THE FBI GRABBED BOONE. ISN'T THAT WHAT WE PAY YOU FOR?
WHOOPS. THERE'S YOUR LITTLE SECRET BLOWN.
ANYONE ELSE HERE? OR SHOULD I MAKE THINGS WORSE?
THE BOSS, AND BOONE.
EXCELLENT!
EVERYONE CONGREGATE CALMLY AND DON'T MAKE TROUBLE, AND WE'LL BE GONE BEFORE YOU KNOW IT.
I'LL BE RIGHT BACK. DON'T GET ANY IDEAS.

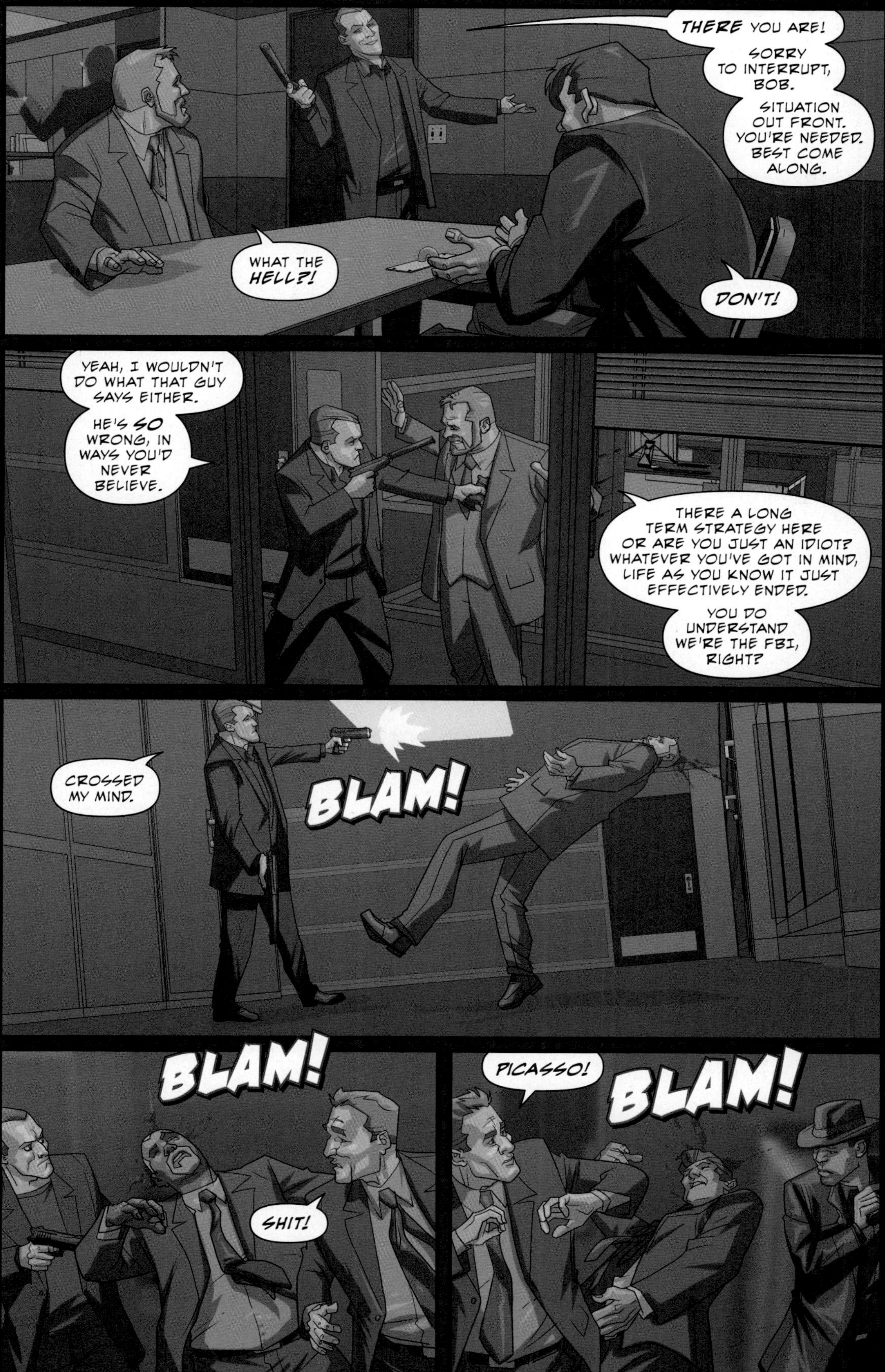
THERE YOU ARE!
SORRY TO INTERRUPT, BOB.
SITUATION OUT FRONT. YOU'RE NEEDED. BEST COME ALONG.
WHAT THE HELL?!
DON'T!
YEAH, I WOULDN'T DO WHAT THAT GUY SAYS EITHER.
HE'S SO WRONG, IN WAYS YOU'D NEVER BELIEVE.
THERE A LONG TERM STRATEGY HERE OR ARE YOU JUST AN IDIOT? WHATEVER YOU'VE GOT IN MIND, LIFE AS YOU KNOW IT JUST EFFECTIVELY ENDED.
YOU DO UNDERSTAND WE'RE THE FBI, RIGHT?
CROSSED MY MIND.
BLAM!
BLAM!
SHIT!
PICASSO!
BLAM!

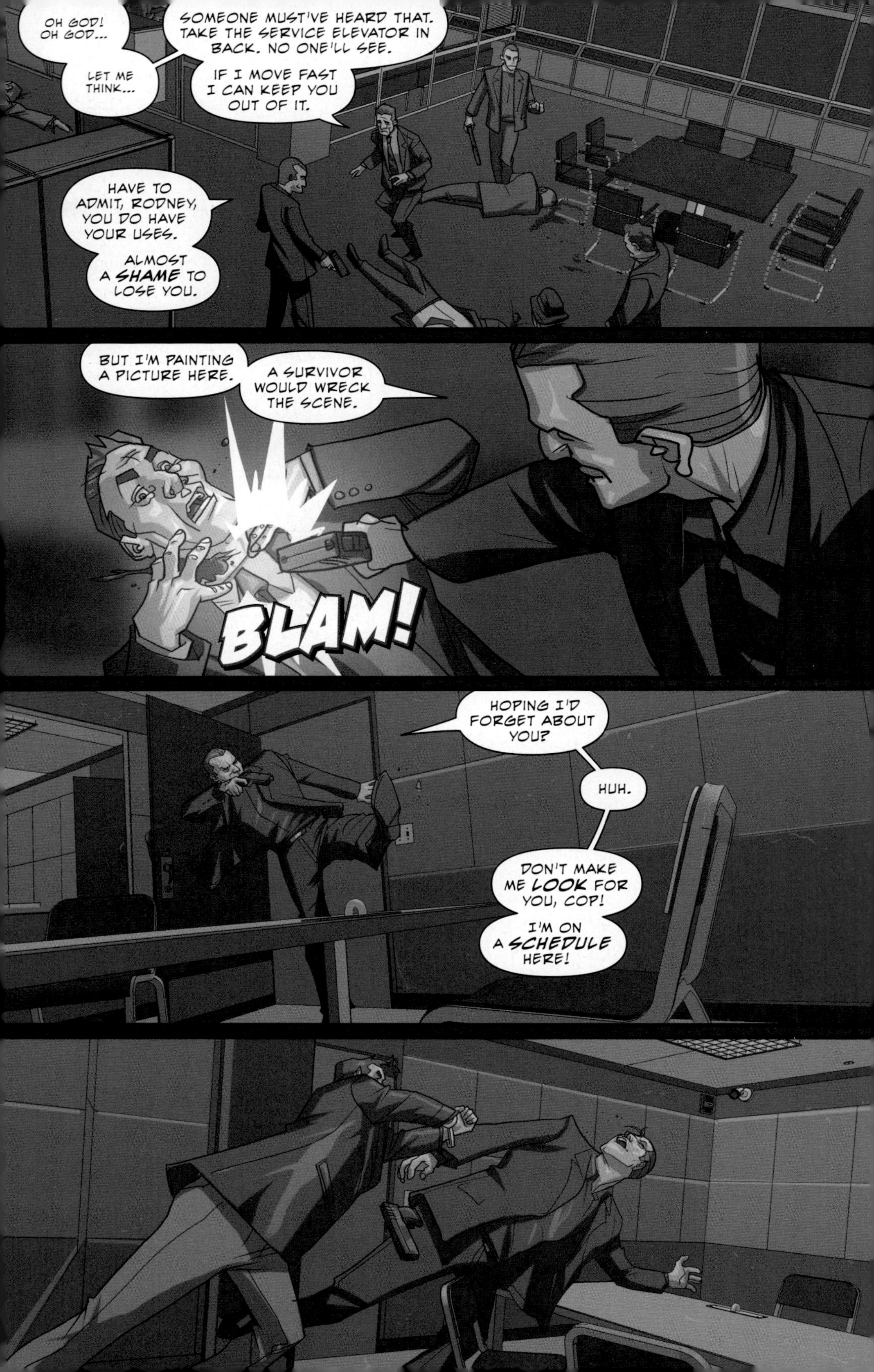
OH GOD! OH GOD...
LET ME THINK...
SOMEONE MUST'VE HEARD THAT. TAKE THE SERVICE ELEVATOR IN BACK. NO ONE'LL SEE.
IF I MOVE FAST I CAN KEEP YOU OUT OF IT.
HAVE TO ADMIT, RODNEY, YOU DO HAVE YOUR USES.
ALMOST A SHAME TO LOSE YOU.
BUT I'M PAINTING A PICTURE HERE.
A SURVIVOR WOULD WRECK THE SCENE.
BLAM!
HOPING I'D FORGET ABOUT YOU?
HUH.
DON'T MAKE ME LOOK FOR YOU, COP!
I'M ON A SCHEDULE HERE!

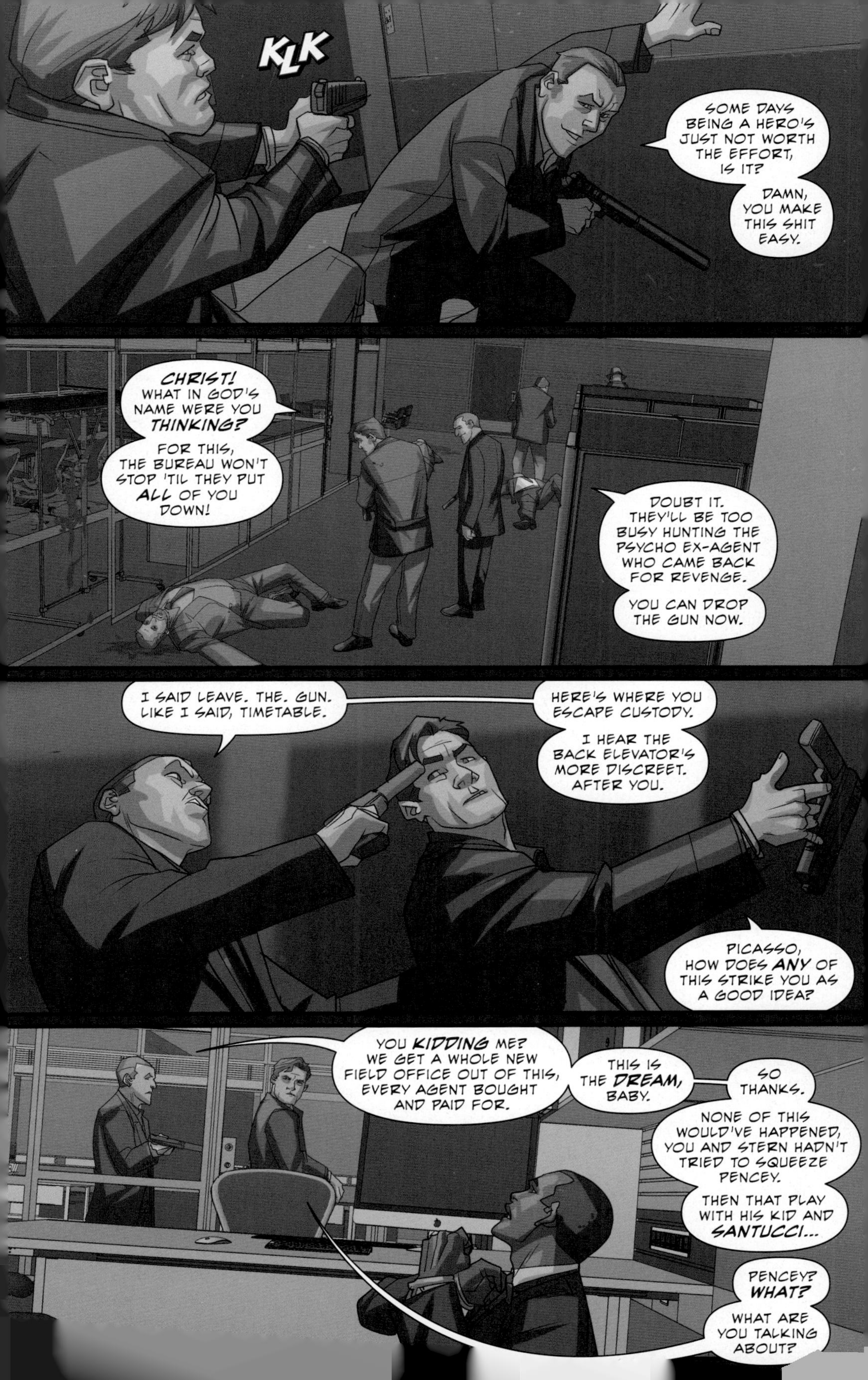
KLK
SOME DAYS BEING A HERO'S JUST NOT WORTH THE EFFORT, IS IT?
DAMN, YOU MAKE THIS SHIT EASY.
CHRIST! WHAT IN GOD'S NAME WERE YOU THINKING?
FOR THIS, THE BUREAU WON'T STOP 'TIL THEY PUT ALL OF YOU DOWN!
DOUBT IT. THEY'LL BE TOO BUSY HUNTING THE PSYCHO EX-AGENT WHO CAME BACK FOR REVENGE.
YOU CAN DROP THE GUN NOW.
I SAID LEAVE. THE. GUN. LIKE I SAID, TIMETABLE.
HERE'S WHERE YOU ESCAPE CUSTODY.
I HEAR THE BACK ELEVATOR'S MORE DISCREET. AFTER YOU.
PICASSO, HOW DOES ANY OF THIS STRIKE YOU AS A GOOD IDEA?
YOU KIDDING ME? WE GET A WHOLE NEW FIELD OFFICE OUT OF THIS, EVERY AGENT BOUGHT AND PAID FOR.
THIS IS THE DREAM, BABY.
SO THANKS.
NONE OF THIS WOULD'VE HAPPENED, YOU AND STERN HADN'T TRIED TO SQUEEZE PENCEY.
THEN THAT PLAY WITH HIS KID AND SANTUCCI...
PENCEY? WHAT?
WHAT ARE YOU TALKING ABOUT?

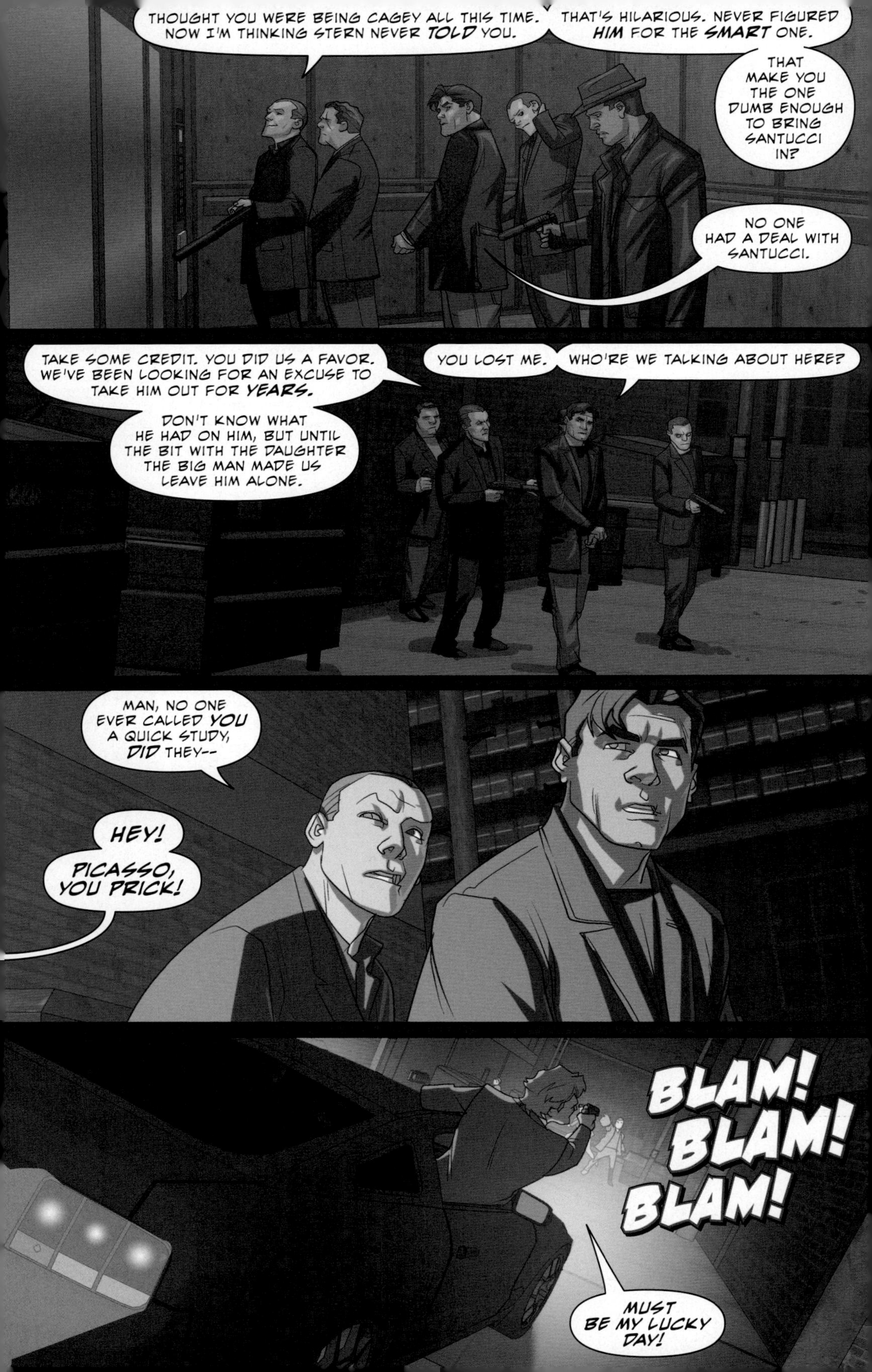
THOUGHT YOU WERE BEING CAGEY ALL THIS TIME. NOW I'M THINKING STERN NEVER TOLD YOU.
THAT'S HILARIOUS. NEVER FIGURED HIM FOR THE SMART ONE.
THAT MAKE YOU THE ONE DUMB ENOUGH TO BRING SANTUCCI IN?
NO ONE HAD A DEAL WITH SANTUCCI.
TAKE SOME CREDIT. YOU DID US A FAVOR. WE'VE BEEN LOOKING FOR AN EXCUSE TO TAKE HIM OUT FOR YEARS.
DON'T KNOW WHAT HE HAD ON HIM, BUT UNTIL THE BIT WITH THE DAUGHTER THE BIG MAN MADE US LEAVE HIM ALONE.
YOU LOST ME.
WHO'RE WE TALKING ABOUT HERE?
MAN, NO ONE EVER CALLED YOU A QUICK STUDY, DID THEY--
HEY!
PICASSO, YOU PRICK!
BLAM! BLAM! BLAM!
MUST BE MY LUCKY DAY!

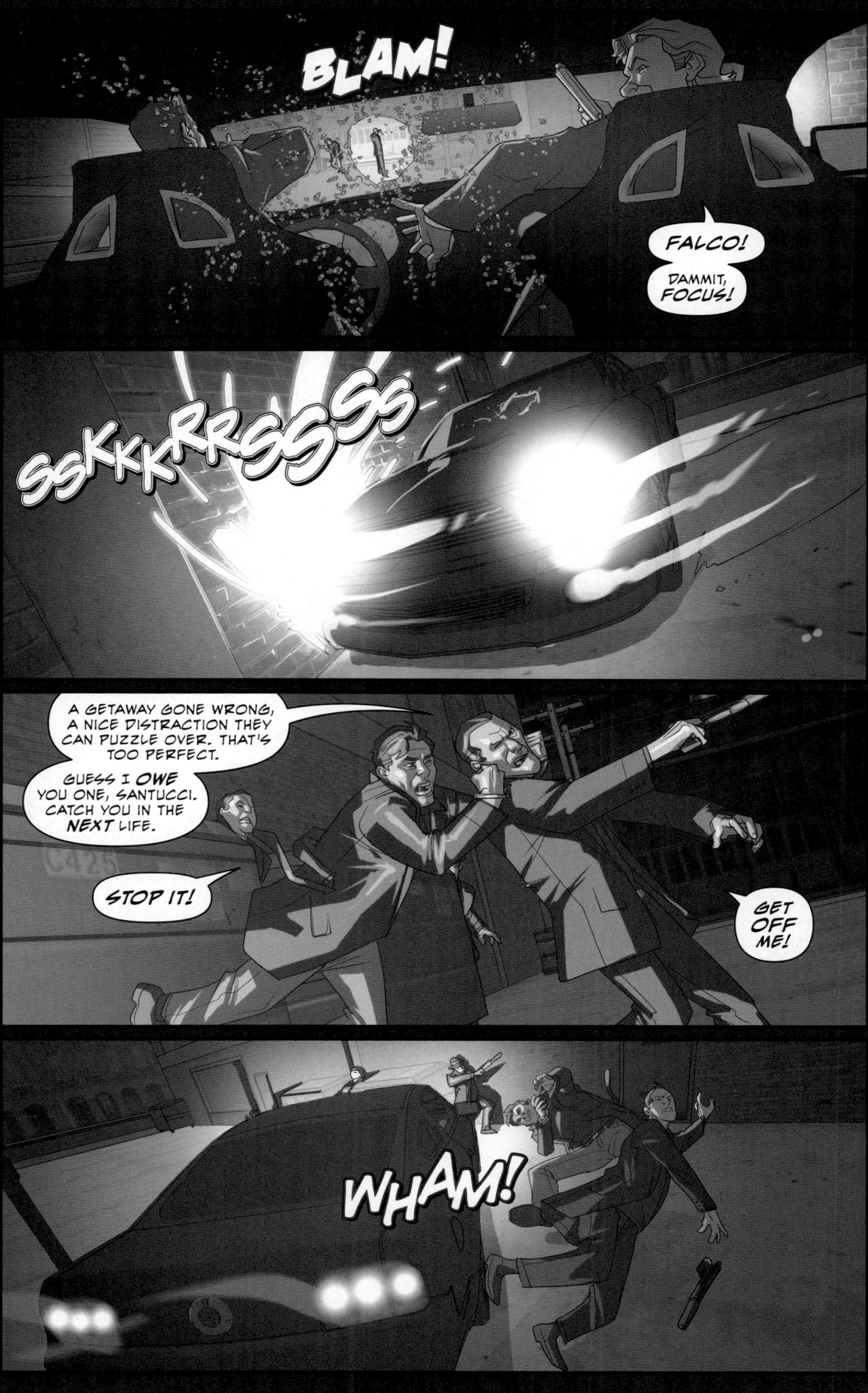
BLAM!
FALCO!
DAMMIT, FOCUS!
SSKKKRRSSSSS
A GETAWAY GONE WRONG, A NICE DISTRACTION THEY CAN PUZZLE OVER. THAT'S TOO PERFECT.
GUESS I OWE YOU ONE, SANTUCCI. CATCH YOU IN THE NEXT LIFE.
STOP IT!
GET OFF ME!
WHAM!

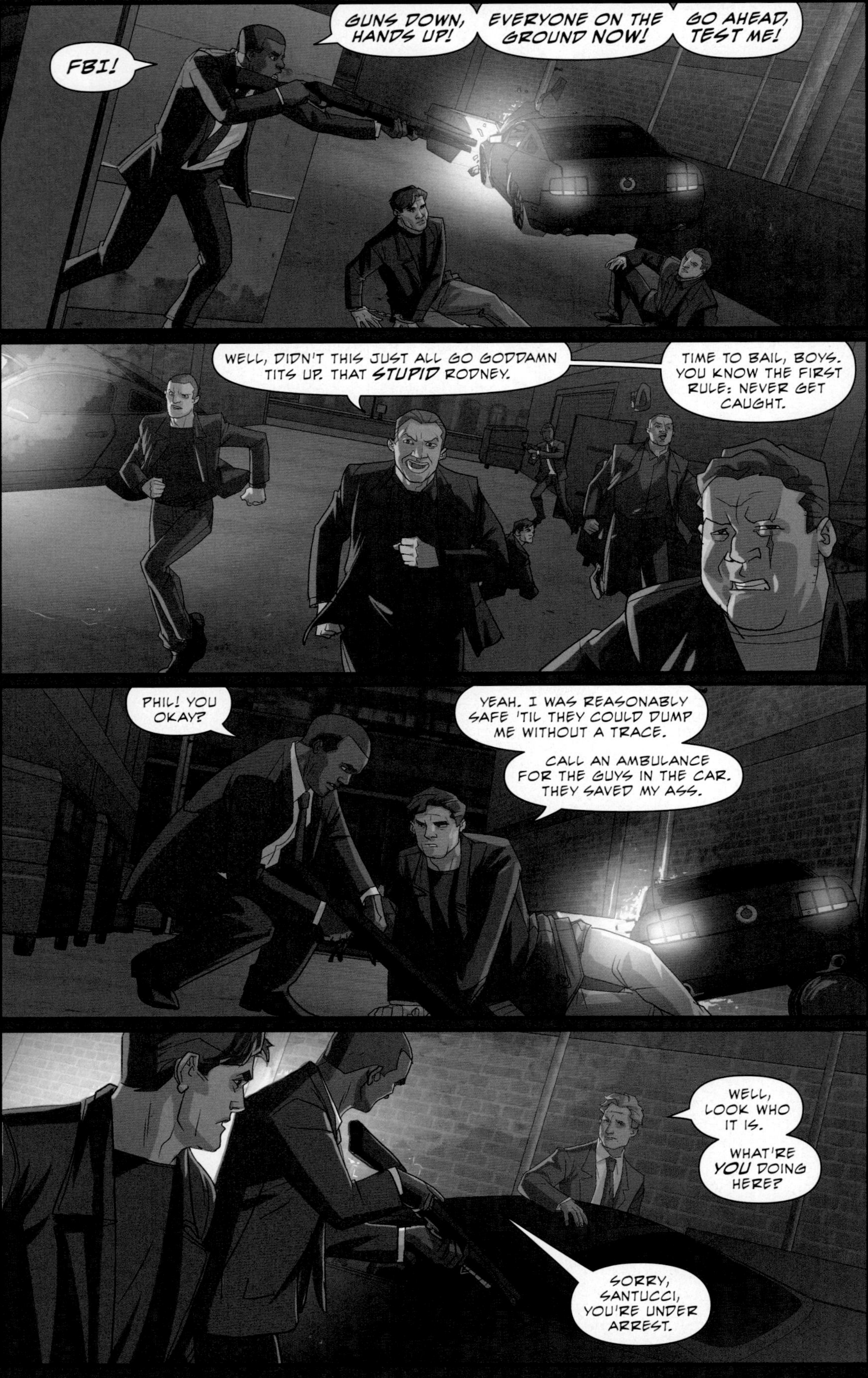
FBI!
GUNS DOWN, HANDS UP!
EVERYONE ON THE GROUND NOW!
GO AHEAD, TEST ME!
WELL, DIDN'T THIS JUST ALL GO GODDAMN TITS UP. THAT STUPID RODNEY.
TIME TO BAIL, BOYS. YOU KNOW THE FIRST RULE: NEVER GET CAUGHT.
PHIL! YOU OKAY?
YEAH. I WAS REASONABLY SAFE 'TIL THEY COULD DUMP ME WITHOUT A TRACE.
CALL AN AMBULANCE FOR THE GUYS IN THE CAR. THEY SAVED MY ASS.
WELL, LOOK WHO IT IS.
WHAT'RE YOU DOING HERE?
SORRY, SANTUCCI, YOU'RE UNDER ARREST.

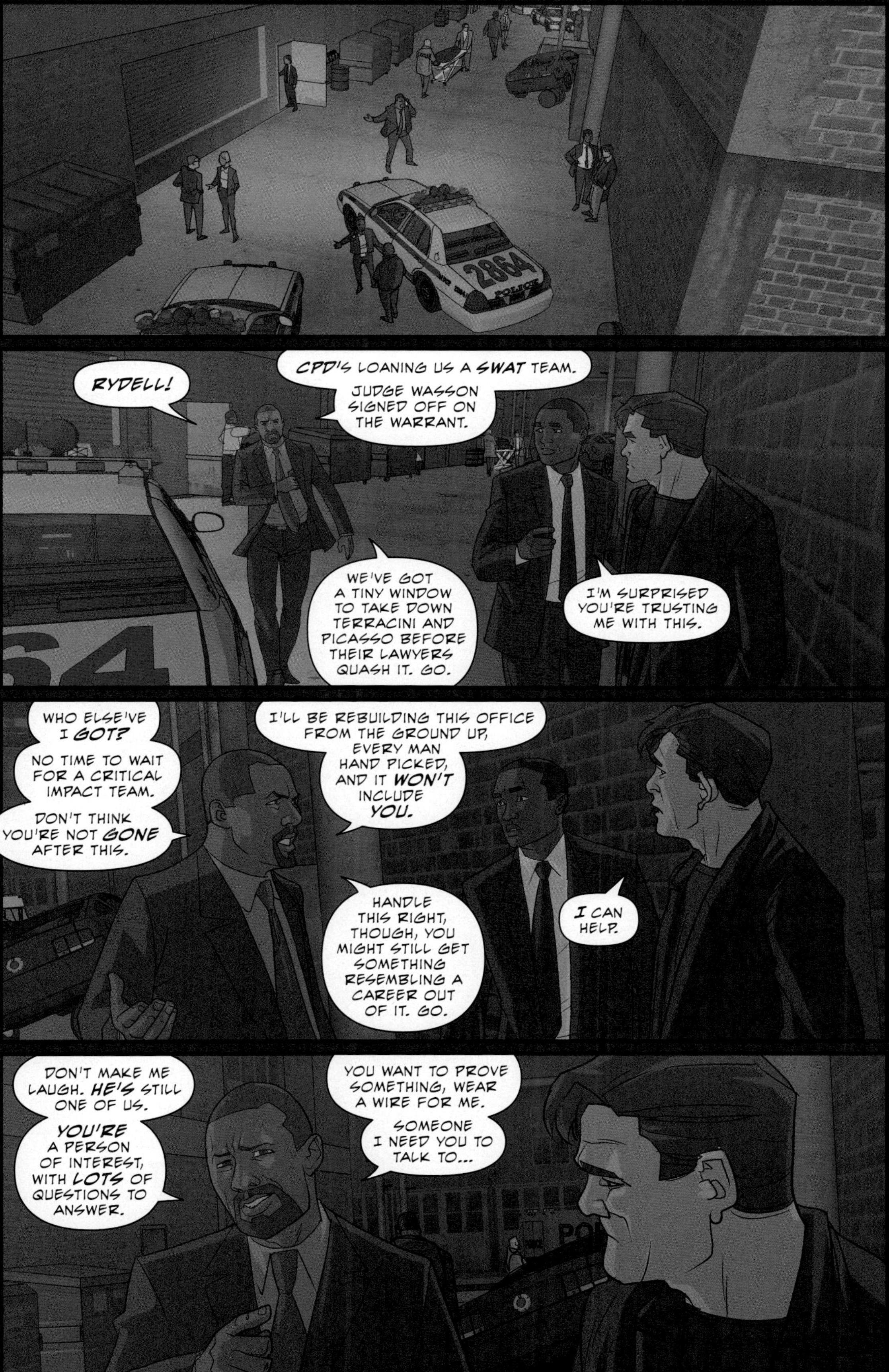
RYDELL!
CPD'S LOANING US A SWAT TEAM.
JUDGE WASSON SIGNED OFF ON THE WARRANT.
WE'VE GOT A TINY WINDOW TO TAKE DOWN TERRACINI AND PICASSO BEFORE THEIR LAWYERS QUASH IT. GO.
I'M SURPRISED YOU'RE TRUSTING ME WITH THIS.
WHO ELSE'VE I GOT?
NO TIME TO WAIT FOR A CRITICAL IMPACT TEAM.
DON'T THINK YOU'RE NOT GONE AFTER THIS.
I'LL BE REBUILDING THIS OFFICE FROM THE GROUND UP, EVERY MAN HAND PICKED, AND IT WON'T INCLUDE YOU.
HANDLE THIS RIGHT, THOUGH, YOU MIGHT STILL GET SOMETHING RESEMBLING A CAREER OUT OF IT. GO.
I CAN HELP.
DON'T MAKE ME LAUGH. HE'S STILL ONE OF US.
YOU'RE A PERSON OF INTEREST, WITH LOTS OF QUESTIONS TO ANSWER.
YOU WANT TO PROVE SOMETHING, WEAR A WIRE FOR ME.
SOMEONE I NEED YOU TO TALK TO...

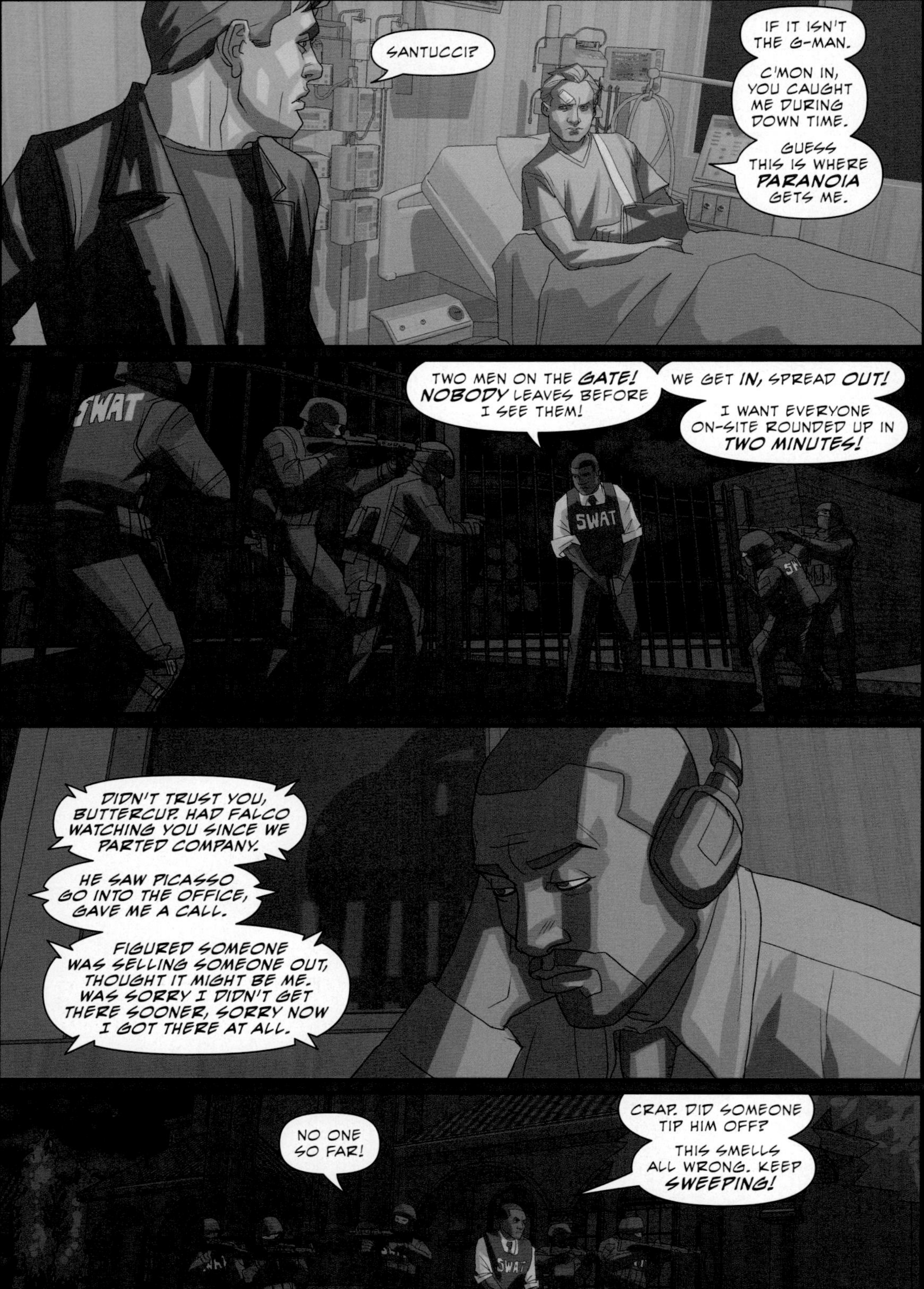

SANTUCCI?
IF IT ISN'T THE G-MAN.
C'MON IN, YOU CAUGHT ME DURING DOWN TIME.
GUESS THIS IS WHERE **PARANOIA** GETS ME.
TWO MEN ON THE ***GATE! NOBODY*** LEAVES BEFORE I SEE THEM!
WE GET ***IN***, SPREAD ***OUT!***
I WANT EVERYONE ON-SITE ROUNDED UP IN ***TWO MINUTES!***
DIDN'T TRUST YOU, BUTTERCUP. HAD FALCO WATCHING YOU SINCE WE PARTED COMPANY.
HE SAW PICASSO GO INTO THE OFFICE, GAVE ME A CALL.
FIGURED SOMEONE WAS SELLING SOMEONE OUT, THOUGHT IT MIGHT BE ME. WAS SORRY I DIDN'T GET THERE SOONER, SORRY NOW I GOT THERE AT ALL.
NO ONE SO FAR!
CRAP. DID SOMEONE TIP HIM OFF?
THIS SMELLS ALL WRONG. KEEP ***SWEEPING!***

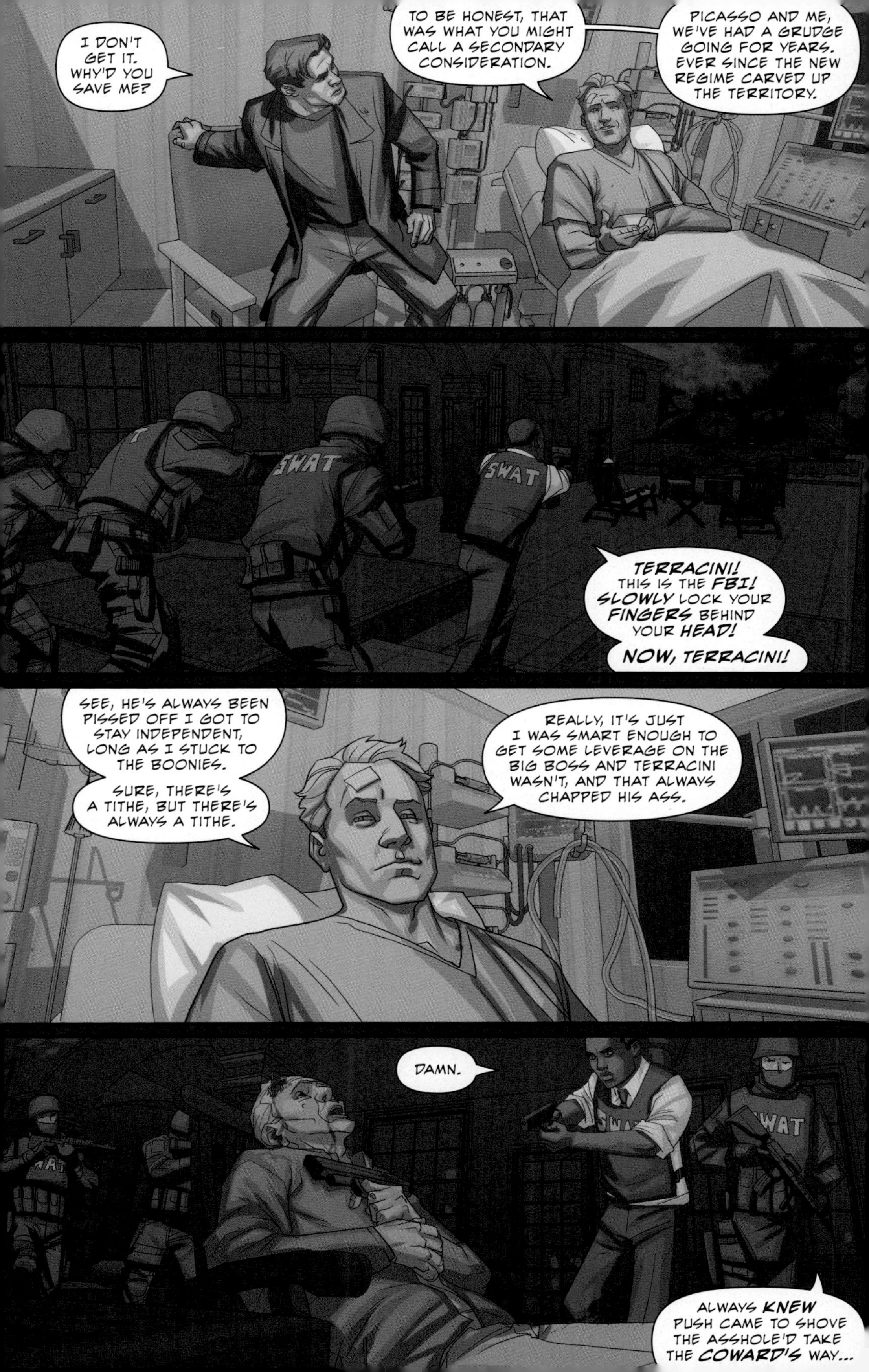
I DON'T GET IT. WHY'D YOU SAVE ME?
TO BE HONEST, THAT WAS WHAT YOU MIGHT CALL A SECONDARY CONSIDERATION.
PICASSO AND ME, WE'VE HAD A GRUDGE GOING FOR YEARS. EVER SINCE THE NEW REGIME CARVED UP THE TERRITORY.
SWAT
SWAT
TERRACINI! THIS IS THE FBI! SLOWLY LOCK YOUR FINGERS BEHIND YOUR HEAD!
NOW, TERRACINI!
SEE, HE'S ALWAYS BEEN PISSED OFF I GOT TO STAY INDEPENDENT, LONG AS I STUCK TO THE BOONIES.
SURE, THERE'S A TITHE, BUT THERE'S ALWAYS A TITHE.
REALLY, IT'S JUST I WAS SMART ENOUGH TO GET SOME LEVERAGE ON THE BIG BOSS AND TERRACINI WASN'T, AND THAT ALWAYS CHAPPED HIS ASS.
DAMN.
SWAT
WAT
ALWAYS KNEW PUSH CAME TO SHOVE THE ASSHOLE'D TAKE THE COWARD'S WAY...

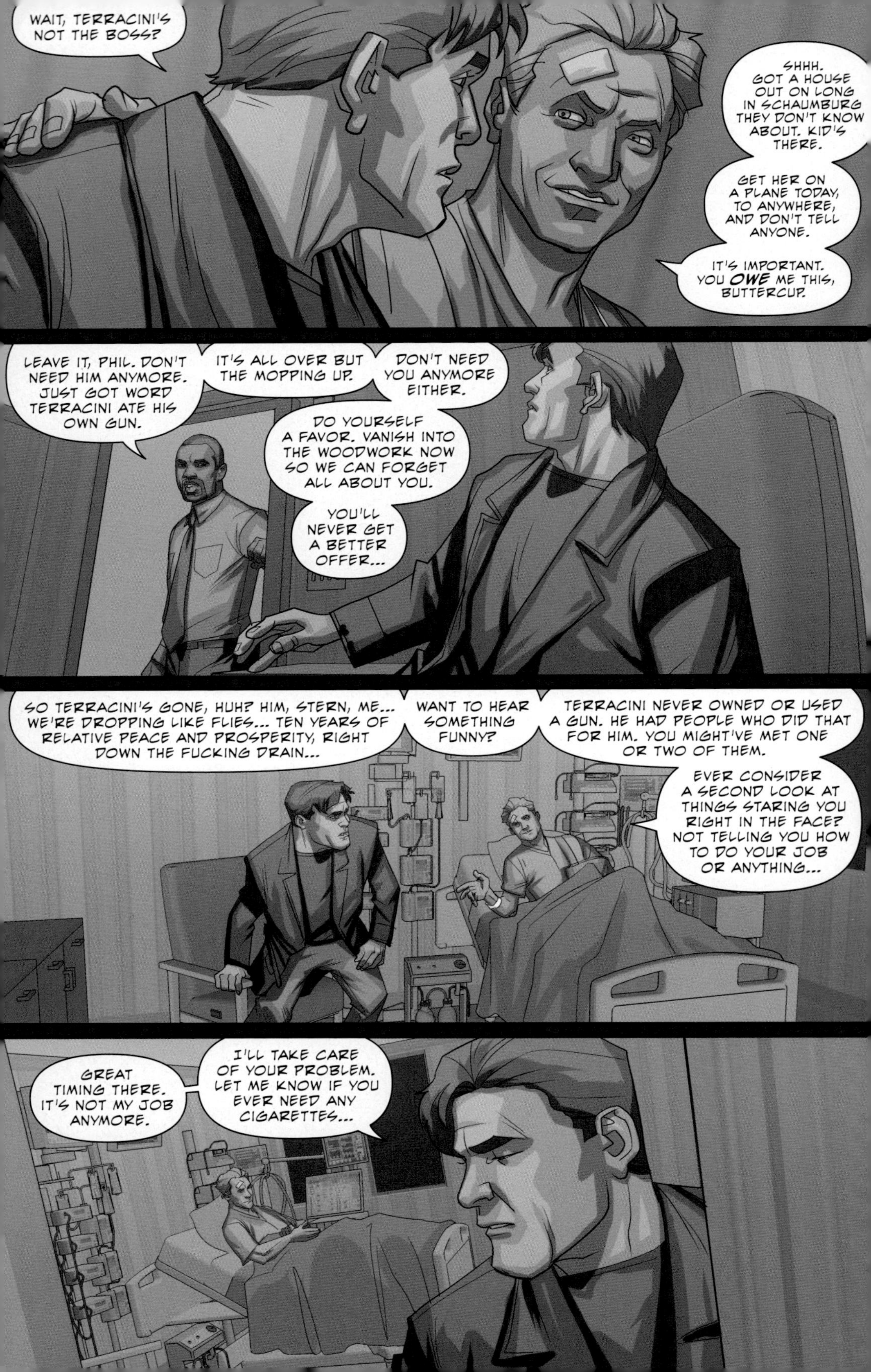
WAIT, TERRACINI'S NOT THE BOSS?
SHHH. GOT A HOUSE OUT ON LONG IN SCHAUMBURG THEY DON'T KNOW ABOUT. KID'S THERE.
GET HER ON A PLANE TODAY, TO ANYWHERE, AND DON'T TELL ANYONE.
IT'S IMPORTANT. YOU OWE ME THIS, BUTTERCUP.
LEAVE IT, PHIL. DON'T NEED HIM ANYMORE. JUST GOT WORD TERRACINI ATE HIS OWN GUN.
IT'S ALL OVER BUT THE MOPPING UP.
DON'T NEED YOU ANYMORE EITHER.
DO YOURSELF A FAVOR. VANISH INTO THE WOODWORK NOW SO WE CAN FORGET ALL ABOUT YOU.
YOU'LL NEVER GET A BETTER OFFER...
SO TERRACINI'S GONE, HUH? HIM, STERN, ME... WE'RE DROPPING LIKE FLIES... TEN YEARS OF RELATIVE PEACE AND PROSPERITY, RIGHT DOWN THE FUCKING DRAIN...
WANT TO HEAR SOMETHING FUNNY?
TERRACINI NEVER OWNED OR USED A GUN. HE HAD PEOPLE WHO DID THAT FOR HIM. YOU MIGHT'VE MET ONE OR TWO OF THEM.
EVER CONSIDER A SECOND LOOK AT THINGS STARING YOU RIGHT IN THE FACE? NOT TELLING YOU HOW TO DO YOUR JOB OR ANYTHING...
GREAT TIMING THERE. IT'S NOT MY JOB ANYMORE.
I'LL TAKE CARE OF YOUR PROBLEM. LET ME KNOW IF YOU EVER NEED ANY CIGARETTES...

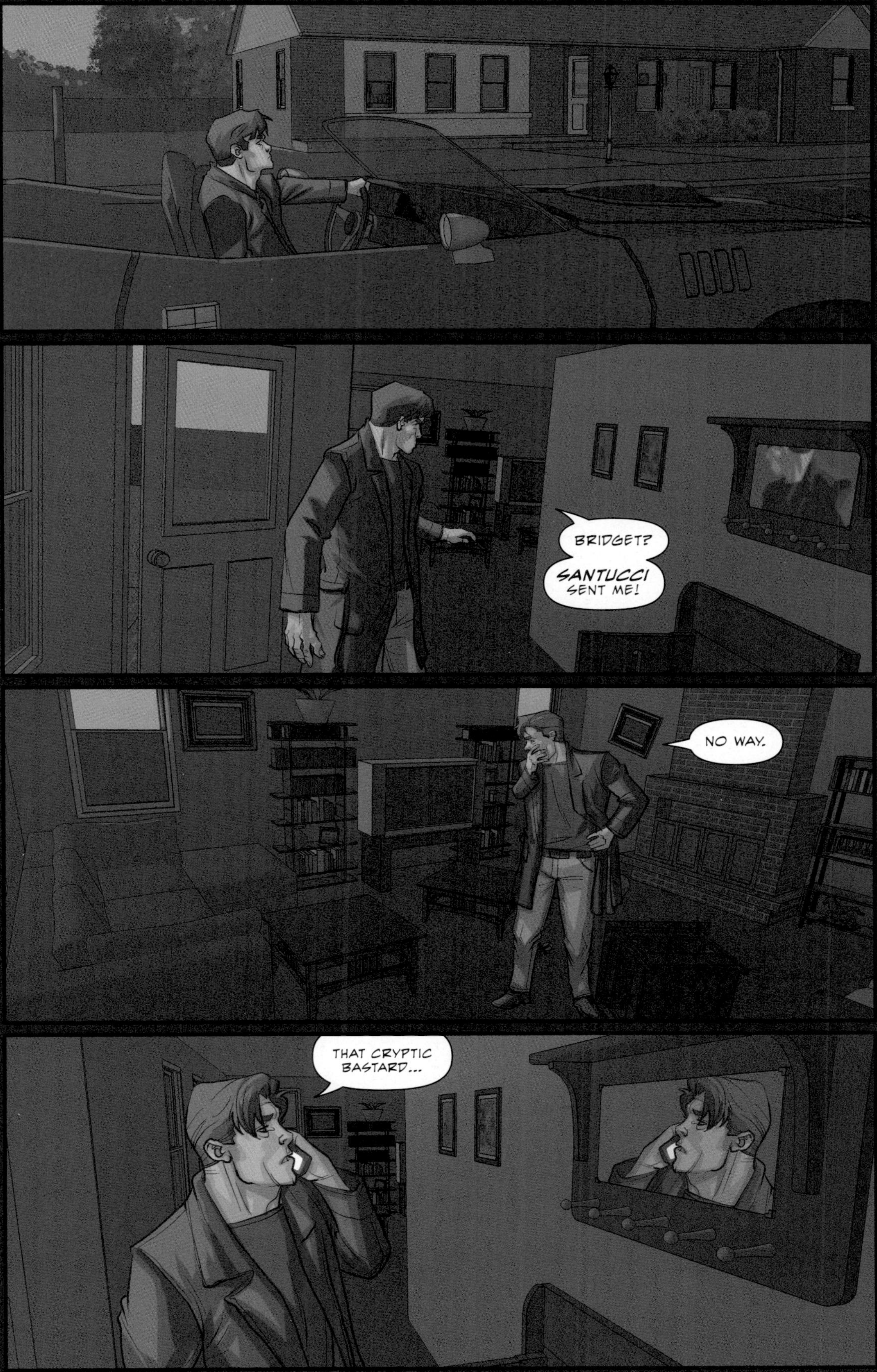
BRIDGET?
SANTUCCI SENT ME!
NO WAY.
THAT CRYPTIC BASTARD...

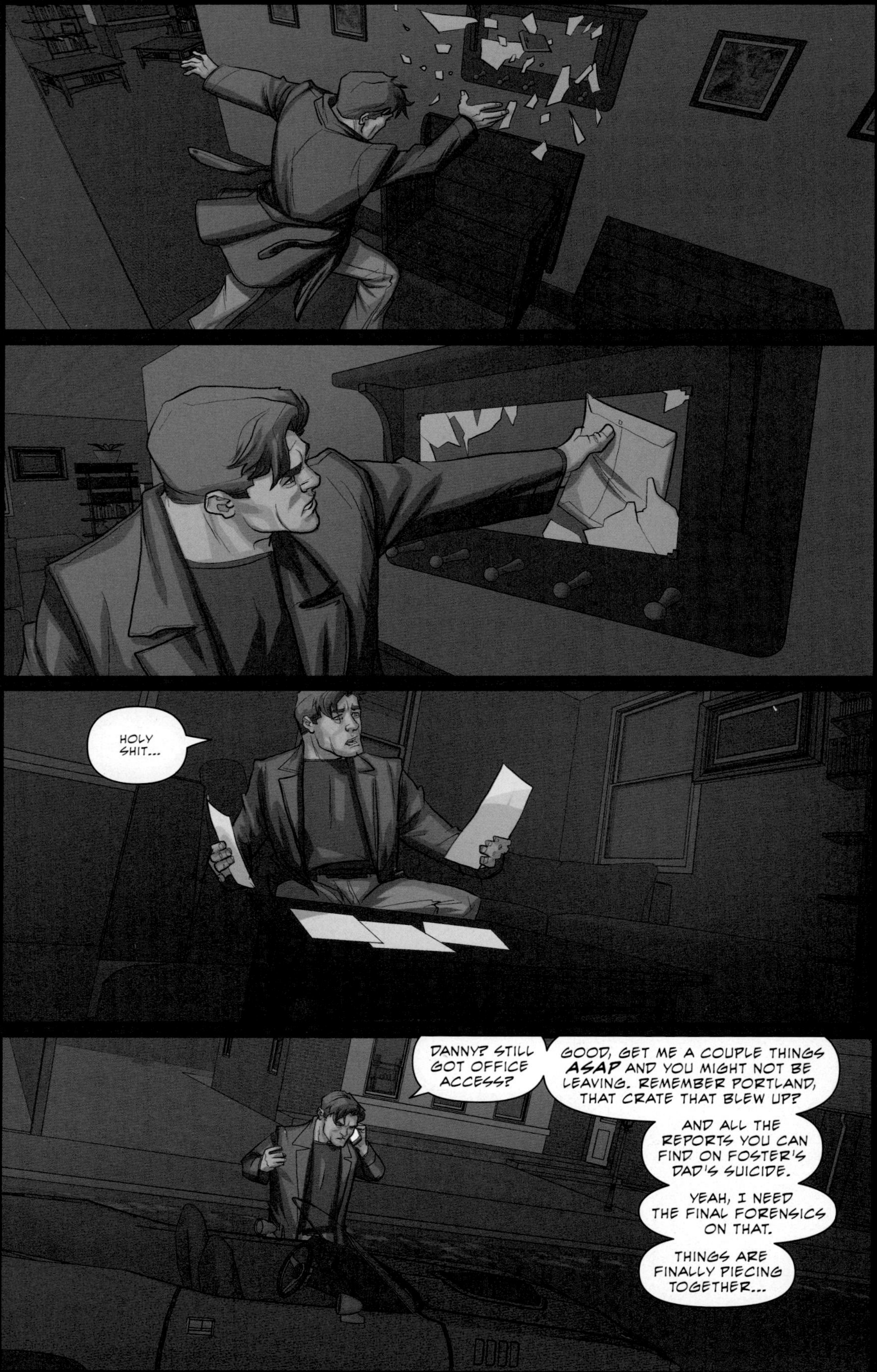
HOLY SHIT...
DANNY? STILL GOT OFFICE ACCESS?
GOOD, GET ME A COUPLE THINGS ASAP AND YOU MIGHT NOT BE LEAVING. REMEMBER PORTLAND, THAT CRATE THAT BLEW UP?
AND ALL THE REPORTS YOU CAN FIND ON FOSTER'S DAD'S SUICIDE.
YEAH, I NEED THE FINAL FORENSICS ON THAT.
THINGS ARE FINALLY PIECING TOGETHER...

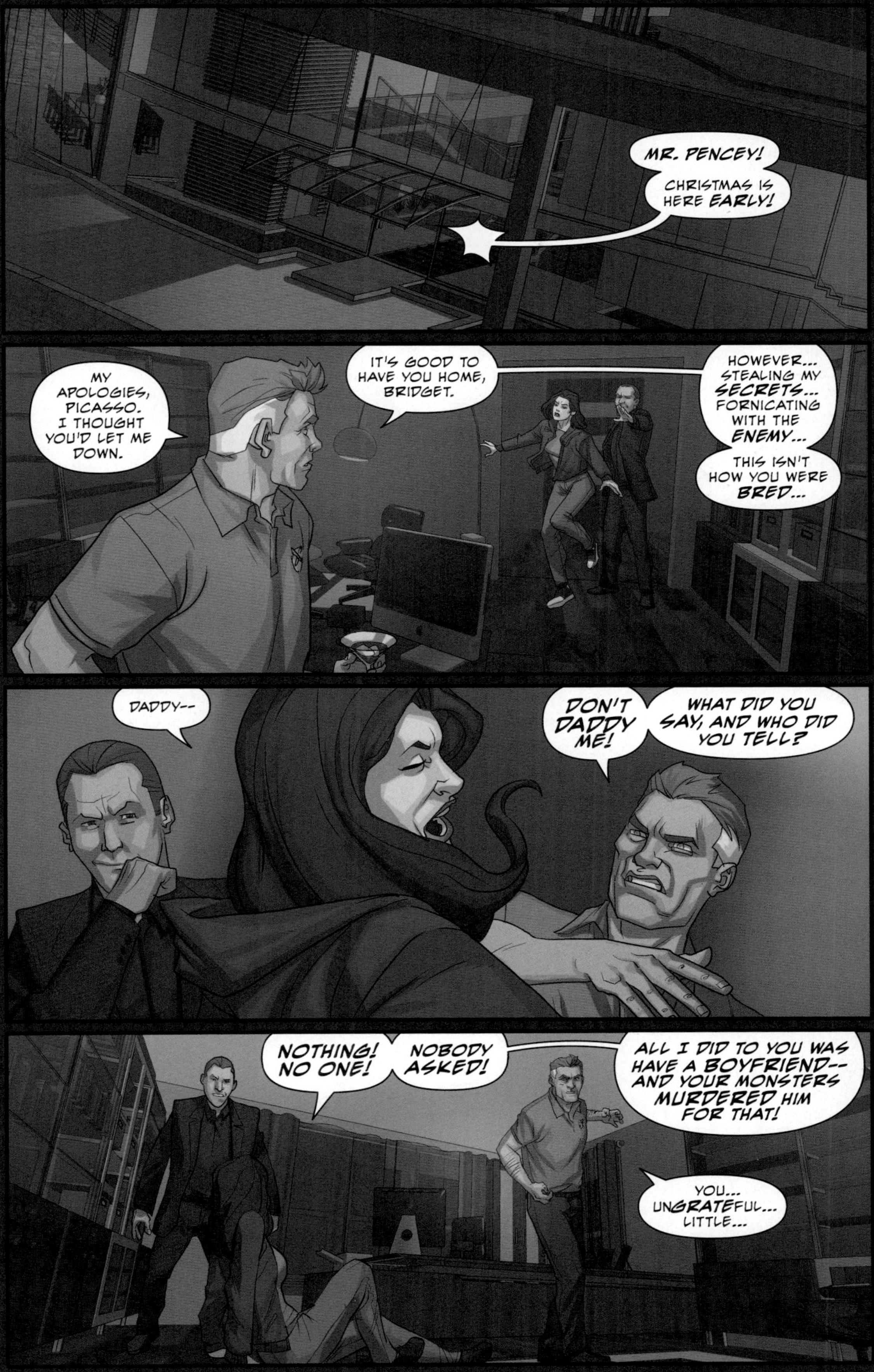
MR. PENCEY!
CHRISTMAS IS HERE EARLY!
MY APOLOGIES, PICASSO. I THOUGHT YOU'D LET ME DOWN.
IT'S GOOD TO HAVE YOU HOME, BRIDGET.
HOWEVER... STEALING MY SECRETS... FORNICATING WITH THE ENEMY...
THIS ISN'T HOW YOU WERE BRED...
DADDY--
DON'T DADDY ME!
WHAT DID YOU SAY, AND WHO DID YOU TELL?
NOTHING! NO ONE!
NOBODY ASKED!
ALL I DID TO YOU WAS HAVE A BOYFRIEND-- AND YOUR MONSTERS MURDERED HIM FOR THAT!
YOU... UNGRATEFUL... LITTLE...

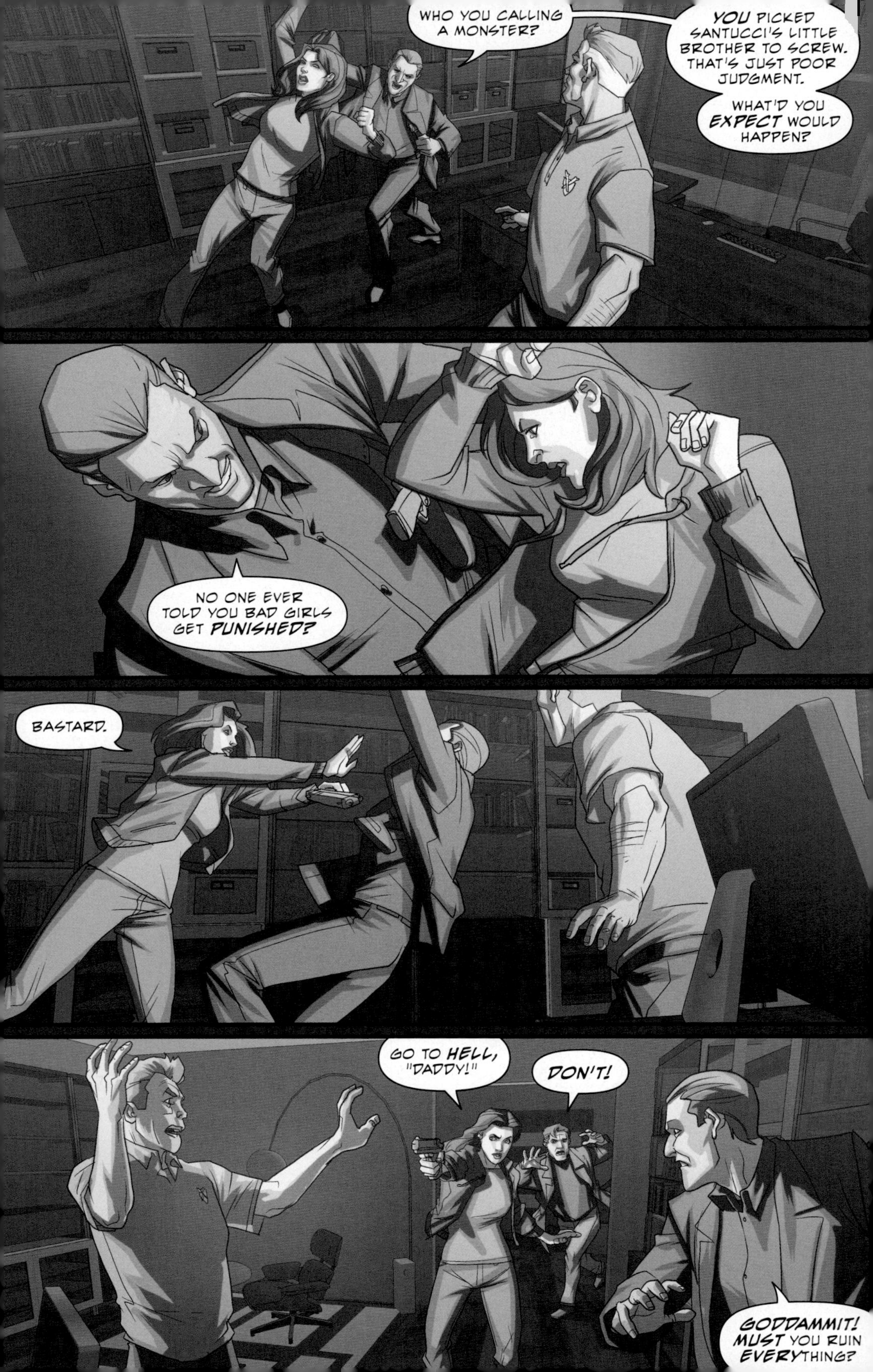
WHO YOU CALLING A MONSTER?
YOU PICKED SANTUCCI'S LITTLE BROTHER TO SCREW. THAT'S JUST POOR JUDGMENT.
WHAT'D YOU EXPECT WOULD HAPPEN?
NO ONE EVER TOLD YOU BAD GIRLS GET PUNISHED?
BASTARD.
GO TO HELL, "DADDY!"
DON'T!
GODDAMMIT! MUST YOU RUIN EVERYTHING?

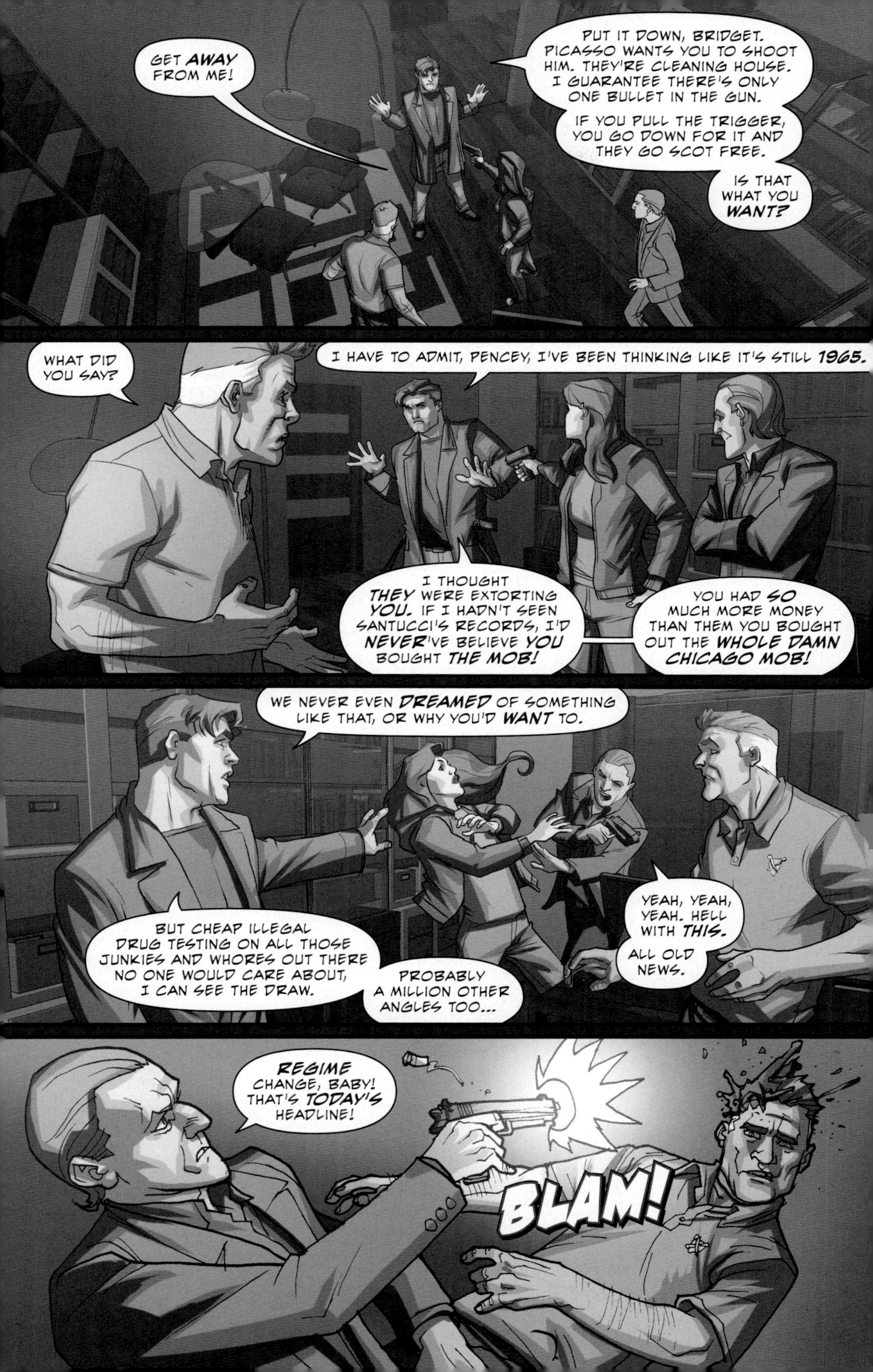
GET AWAY FROM ME!
PUT IT DOWN, BRIDGET. PICASSO WANTS YOU TO SHOOT HIM. THEY'RE CLEANING HOUSE. I GUARANTEE THERE'S ONLY ONE BULLET IN THE GUN.
IF YOU PULL THE TRIGGER, YOU GO DOWN FOR IT AND THEY GO SCOT FREE.
IS THAT WHAT YOU WANT?
WHAT DID YOU SAY?
I HAVE TO ADMIT, PENCEY, I'VE BEEN THINKING LIKE IT'S STILL 1965.
I THOUGHT THEY WERE EXTORTING YOU. IF I HADN'T SEEN SANTUCCI'S RECORDS, I'D NEVER'VE BELIEVE YOU BOUGHT THE MOB!
YOU HAD SO MUCH MORE MONEY THAN THEM YOU BOUGHT OUT THE WHOLE DAMN CHICAGO MOB!
WE NEVER EVEN DREAMED OF SOMETHING LIKE THAT, OR WHY YOU'D WANT TO.
BUT CHEAP ILLEGAL DRUG TESTING ON ALL THOSE JUNKIES AND WHORES OUT THERE NO ONE WOULD CARE ABOUT, I CAN SEE THE DRAW.
PROBABLY A MILLION OTHER ANGLES TOO...
YEAH, YEAH, YEAH. HELL WITH THIS.
ALL OLD NEWS.
REGIME CHANGE, BABY! THAT'S TODAY'S HEADLINE!
BLAM!

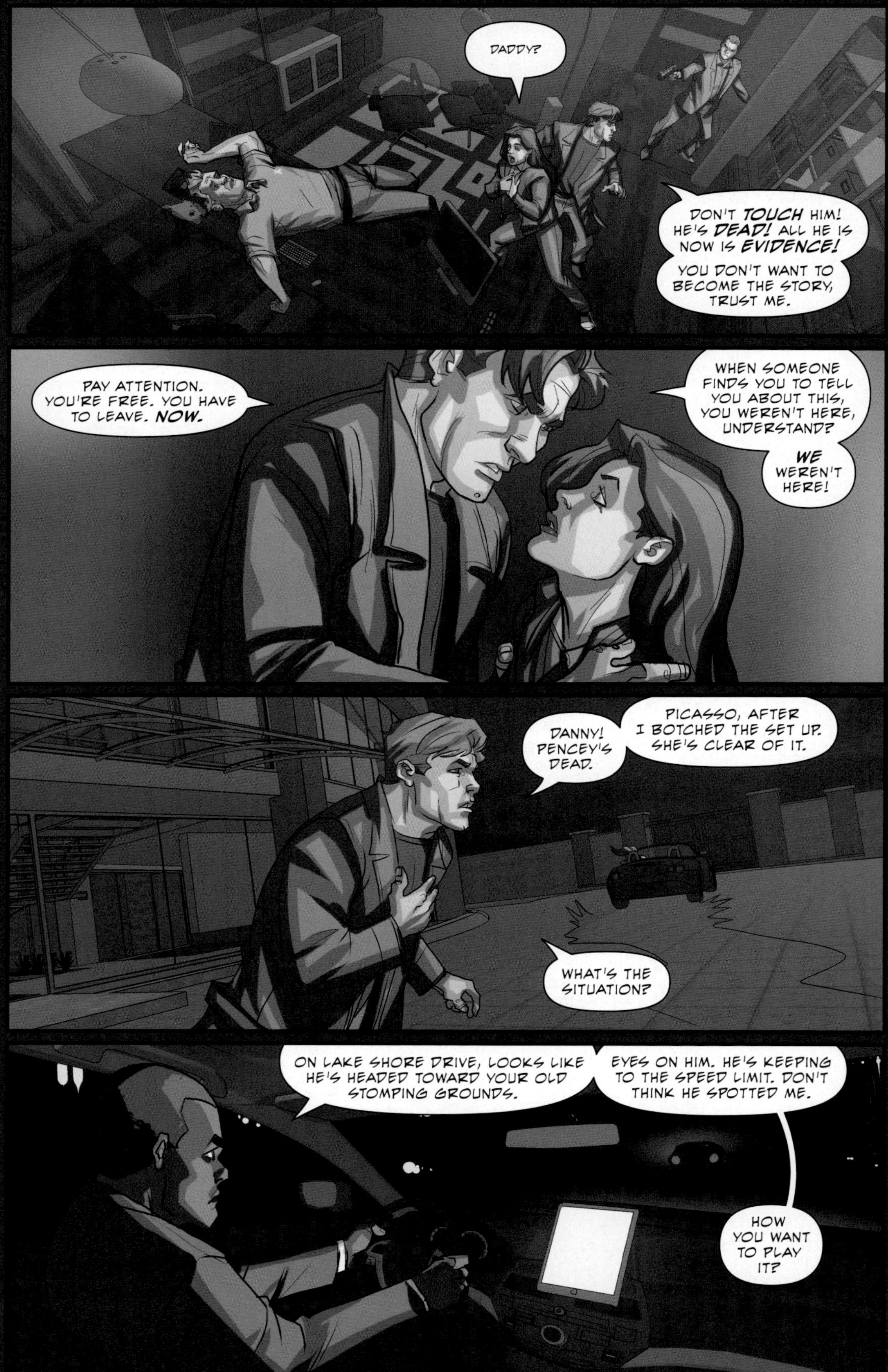
DADDY?
DON'T TOUCH HIM! HE'S DEAD! ALL HE IS NOW IS EVIDENCE!
YOU DON'T WANT TO BECOME THE STORY, TRUST ME.
PAY ATTENTION. YOU'RE FREE. YOU HAVE TO LEAVE. NOW.
WHEN SOMEONE FINDS YOU TO TELL YOU ABOUT THIS, YOU WEREN'T HERE, UNDERSTAND?
WE WEREN'T HERE!
DANNY! PENCEY'S DEAD.
PICASSO, AFTER I BOTCHED THE SET UP. SHE'S CLEAR OF IT.
WHAT'S THE SITUATION?
ON LAKE SHORE DRIVE, LOOKS LIKE HE'S HEADED TOWARD YOUR OLD STOMPING GROUNDS.
EYES ON HIM. HE'S KEEPING TO THE SPEED LIMIT. DON'T THINK HE SPOTTED ME.
HOW YOU WANT TO PLAY IT?

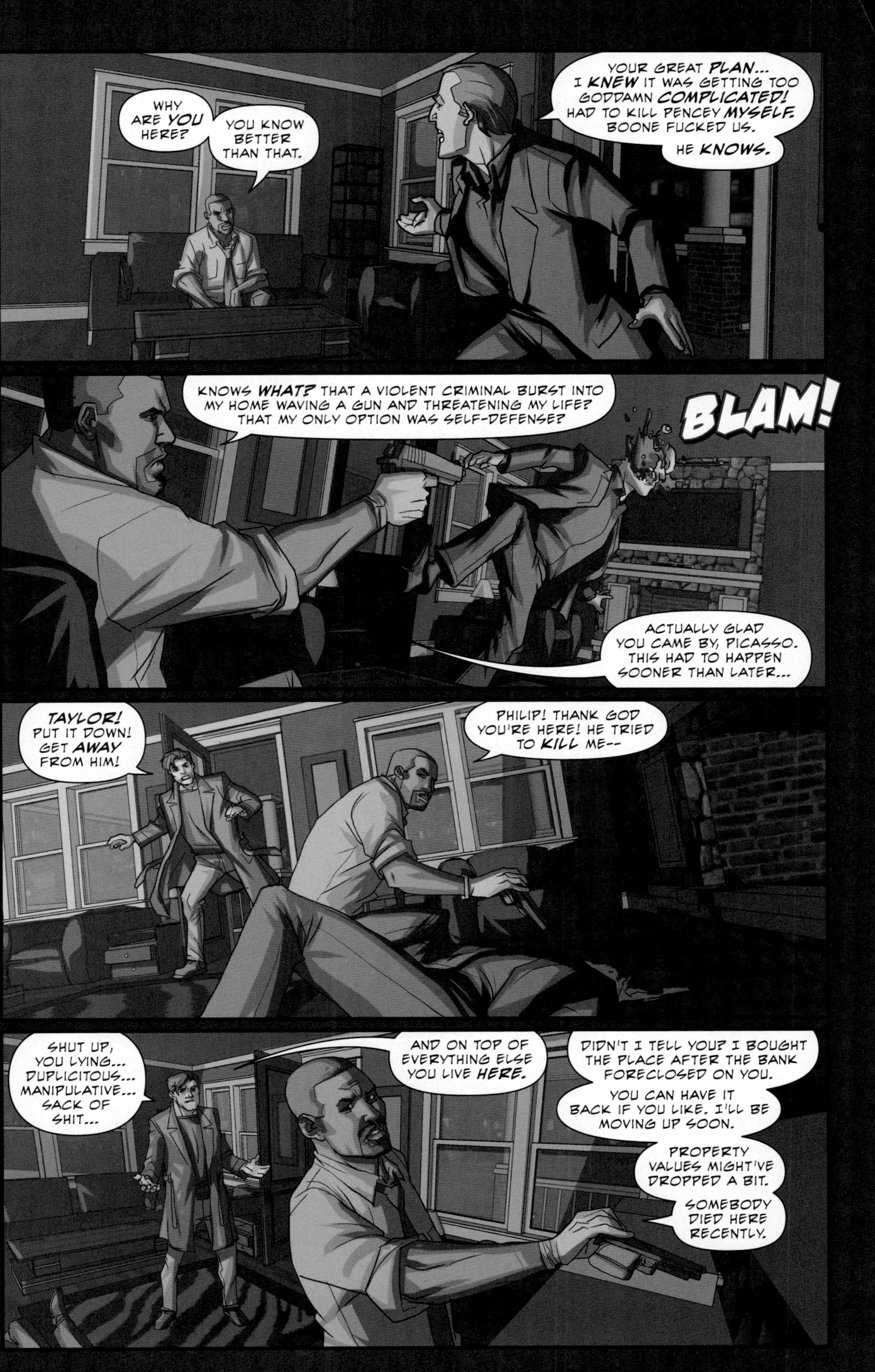
WHY ARE YOU HERE?
YOU KNOW BETTER THAN THAT.
YOUR GREAT PLAN... I KNEW IT WAS GETTING TOO GODDAMN COMPLICATED! HAD TO KILL PENCEY MYSELF. BOONE FUCKED US.
HE KNOWS.
KNOWS WHAT? THAT A VIOLENT CRIMINAL BURST INTO MY HOME WAVING A GUN AND THREATENING MY LIFE? THAT MY ONLY OPTION WAS SELF-DEFENSE?
BLAM!
ACTUALLY GLAD YOU CAME BY, PICASSO. THIS HAD TO HAPPEN SOONER THAN LATER...
TAYLOR! PUT IT DOWN! GET AWAY FROM HIM!
PHILIP! THANK GOD YOU'RE HERE! HE TRIED TO KILL ME--
SHUT UP, YOU LYING... DUPLICITOUS... MANIPULATIVE... SACK OF SHIT...
AND ON TOP OF EVERYTHING ELSE YOU LIVE HERE.
DIDN'T I TELL YOU? I BOUGHT THE PLACE AFTER THE BANK FORECLOSED ON YOU.
YOU CAN HAVE IT BACK IF YOU LIKE. I'LL BE MOVING UP SOON.
PROPERTY VALUES MIGHT'VE DROPPED A BIT.
SOMEBODY DIED HERE RECENTLY.

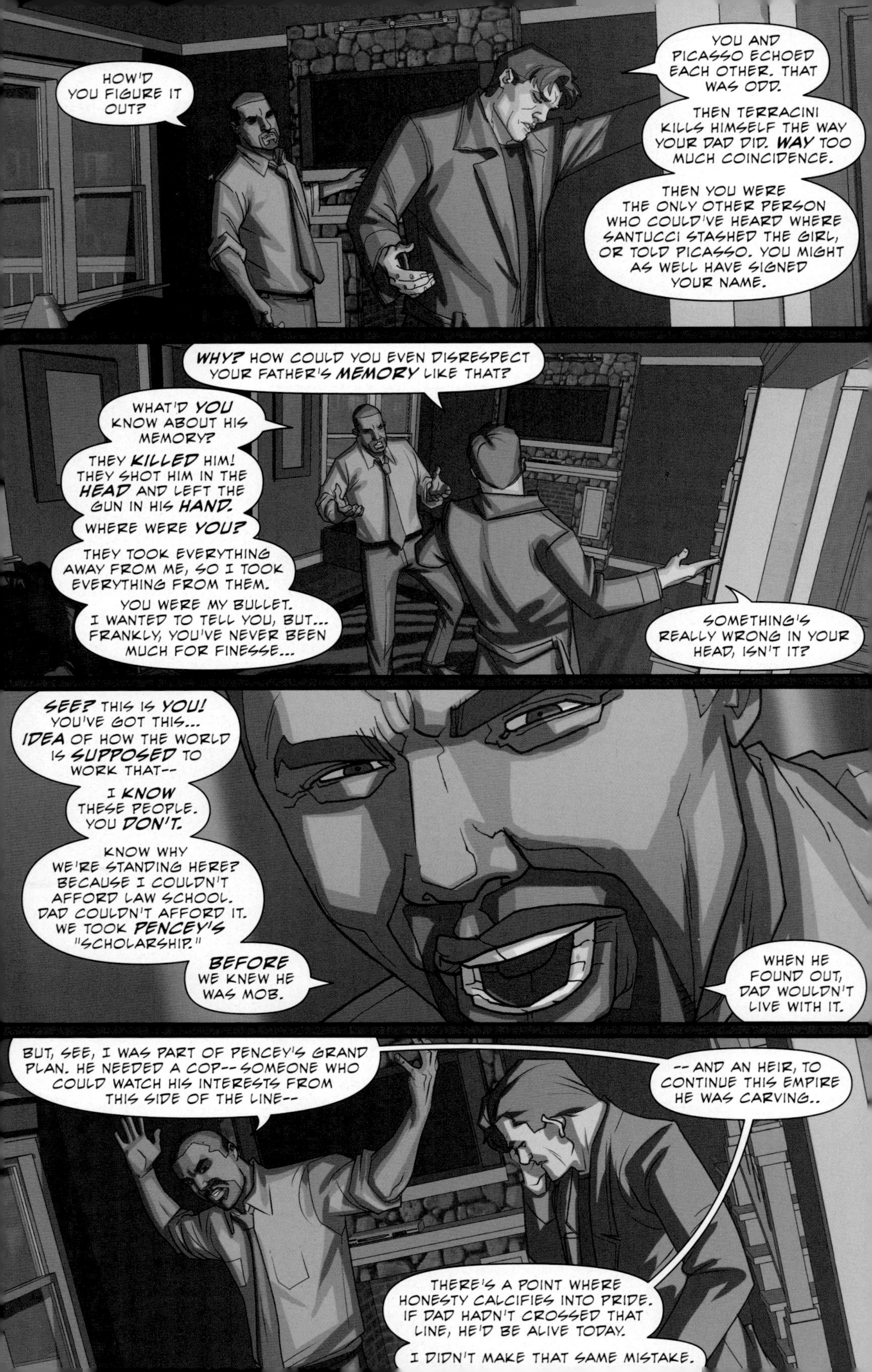
HOW'D YOU FIGURE IT OUT?
YOU AND PICASSO ECHOED EACH OTHER. THAT WAS ODD.
THEN TERRACINI KILLS HIMSELF THE WAY YOUR DAD DID. WAY TOO MUCH COINCIDENCE.
THEN YOU WERE THE ONLY OTHER PERSON WHO COULD'VE HEARD WHERE SANTUCCI STASHED THE GIRL, OR TOLD PICASSO. YOU MIGHT AS WELL HAVE SIGNED YOUR NAME.
WHY? HOW COULD YOU EVEN DISRESPECT YOUR FATHER'S MEMORY LIKE THAT?
WHAT'D YOU KNOW ABOUT HIS MEMORY?
THEY KILLED HIM! THEY SHOT HIM IN THE HEAD AND LEFT THE GUN IN HIS HAND.
WHERE WERE YOU?
THEY TOOK EVERYTHING AWAY FROM ME, SO I TOOK EVERYTHING FROM THEM.
YOU WERE MY BULLET. I WANTED TO TELL YOU, BUT... FRANKLY, YOU'VE NEVER BEEN MUCH FOR FINESSE...
SOMETHING'S REALLY WRONG IN YOUR HEAD, ISN'T IT?
SEE? THIS IS YOU! YOU'VE GOT THIS... IDEA OF HOW THE WORLD IS SUPPOSED TO WORK THAT--
I KNOW THESE PEOPLE. YOU DON'T.
KNOW WHY WE'RE STANDING HERE? BECAUSE I COULDN'T AFFORD LAW SCHOOL. DAD COULDN'T AFFORD IT. WE TOOK PENCEY'S "SCHOLARSHIP."
BEFORE WE KNEW HE WAS MOB.
WHEN HE FOUND OUT, DAD WOULDN'T LIVE WITH IT.
BUT, SEE, I WAS PART OF PENCEY'S GRAND PLAN. HE NEEDED A COP-- SOMEONE WHO COULD WATCH HIS INTERESTS FROM THIS SIDE OF THE LINE--
-- AND AN HEIR, TO CONTINUE THIS EMPIRE HE WAS CARVING..
THERE'S A POINT WHERE HONESTY CALCIFIES INTO PRIDE. IF DAD HADN'T CROSSED THAT LINE, HE'D BE ALIVE TODAY.
I DIDN'T MAKE THAT SAME MISTAKE.

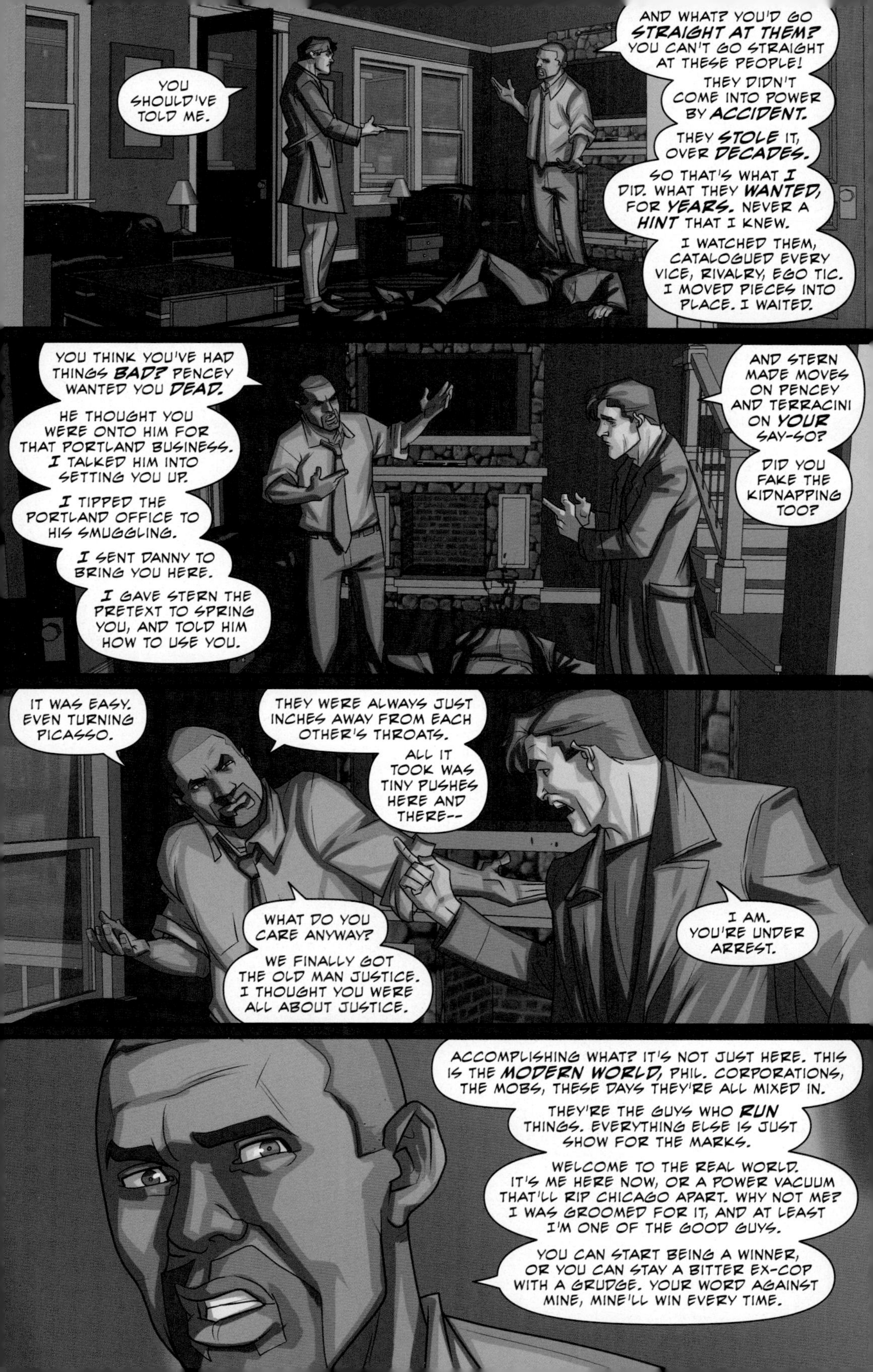
YOU SHOULD'VE TOLD ME.
AND WHAT? YOU'D GO STRAIGHT AT THEM? YOU CAN'T GO STRAIGHT AT THESE PEOPLE!
THEY DIDN'T COME INTO POWER BY ACCIDENT.
THEY STOLE IT, OVER DECADES.
SO THAT'S WHAT I DID. WHAT THEY WANTED, FOR YEARS. NEVER A HINT THAT I KNEW.
I WATCHED THEM, CATALOGUED EVERY VICE, RIVALRY, EGO TIC. I MOVED PIECES INTO PLACE. I WAITED.
YOU THINK YOU'VE HAD THINGS BAD? PENCEY WANTED YOU DEAD.
HE THOUGHT YOU WERE ONTO HIM FOR THAT PORTLAND BUSINESS. I TALKED HIM INTO SETTING YOU UP.
I TIPPED THE PORTLAND OFFICE TO HIS SMUGGLING.
I SENT DANNY TO BRING YOU HERE.
I GAVE STERN THE PRETEXT TO SPRING YOU, AND TOLD HIM HOW TO USE YOU.
AND STERN MADE MOVES ON PENCEY AND TERRACINI ON YOUR SAY-SO?
DID YOU FAKE THE KIDNAPPING TOO?
IT WAS EASY. EVEN TURNING PICASSO.
THEY WERE ALWAYS JUST INCHES AWAY FROM EACH OTHER'S THROATS.
ALL IT TOOK WAS TINY PUSHES HERE AND THERE--
WHAT DO YOU CARE ANYWAY?
WE FINALLY GOT THE OLD MAN JUSTICE. I THOUGHT YOU WERE ALL ABOUT JUSTICE.
I AM. YOU'RE UNDER ARREST.
ACCOMPLISHING WHAT? IT'S NOT JUST HERE. THIS IS THE MODERN WORLD, PHIL. CORPORATIONS, THE MOBS, THESE DAYS THEY'RE ALL MIXED IN.
THEY'RE THE GUYS WHO RUN THINGS. EVERYTHING ELSE IS JUST SHOW FOR THE MARKS.
WELCOME TO THE REAL WORLD. IT'S ME HERE NOW, OR A POWER VACUUM THAT'LL RIP CHICAGO APART. WHY NOT ME? I WAS GROOMED FOR IT, AND AT LEAST I'M ONE OF THE GOOD GUYS.
YOU CAN START BEING A WINNER, OR YOU CAN STAY A BITTER EX-COP WITH A GRUDGE. YOUR WORD AGAINST MINE, MINE'LL WIN EVERY TIME.

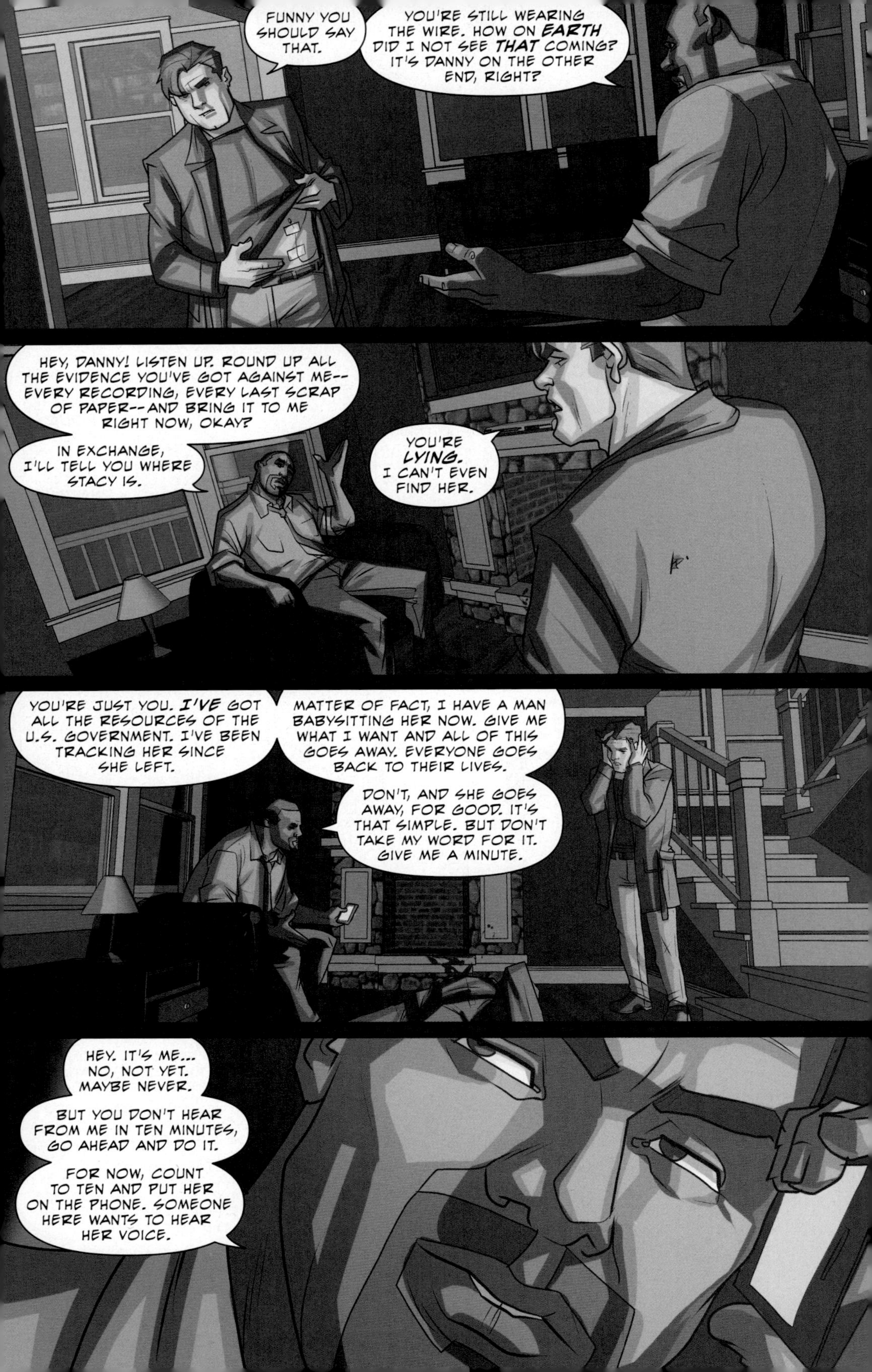
FUNNY YOU SHOULD SAY THAT.
YOU'RE STILL WEARING THE WIRE. HOW ON EARTH DID I NOT SEE THAT COMING? IT'S DANNY ON THE OTHER END, RIGHT?
HEY, DANNY! LISTEN UP. ROUND UP ALL THE EVIDENCE YOU'VE GOT AGAINST ME-- EVERY RECORDING, EVERY LAST SCRAP OF PAPER--AND BRING IT TO ME RIGHT NOW, OKAY?
IN EXCHANGE, I'LL TELL YOU WHERE STACY IS.
YOU'RE LYING. I CAN'T EVEN FIND HER.
YOU'RE JUST YOU. I'VE GOT ALL THE RESOURCES OF THE U.S. GOVERNMENT. I'VE BEEN TRACKING HER SINCE SHE LEFT.
MATTER OF FACT, I HAVE A MAN BABYSITTING HER NOW. GIVE ME WHAT I WANT AND ALL OF THIS GOES AWAY. EVERYONE GOES BACK TO THEIR LIVES.
DON'T, AND SHE GOES AWAY, FOR GOOD. IT'S THAT SIMPLE. BUT DON'T TAKE MY WORD FOR IT. GIVE ME A MINUTE.
HEY. IT'S ME... NO, NOT YET. MAYBE NEVER.
BUT YOU DON'T HEAR FROM ME IN TEN MINUTES, GO AHEAD AND DO IT.
FOR NOW, COUNT TO TEN AND PUT HER ON THE PHONE. SOMEONE HERE WANTS TO HEAR HER VOICE.

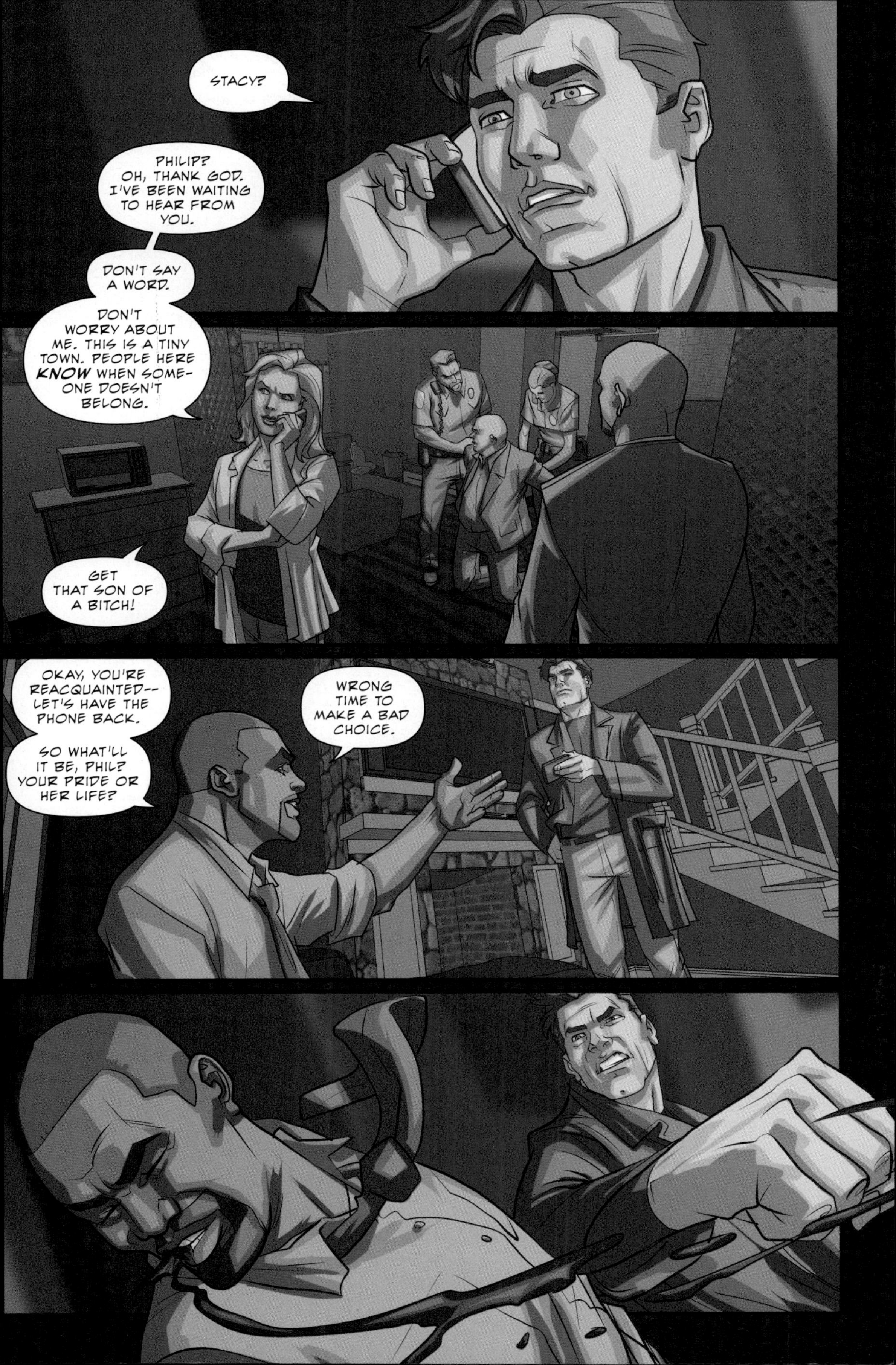
STACY?
PHILIP? OH, THANK GOD. I'VE BEEN WAITING TO HEAR FROM YOU.
DON'T SAY A WORD.
DON'T WORRY ABOUT ME. THIS IS A TINY TOWN. PEOPLE HERE KNOW WHEN SOME-ONE DOESN'T BELONG.
GET THAT SON OF A BITCH!
OKAY, YOU'RE REACQUAINTED--LET'S HAVE THE PHONE BACK.
SO WHAT'LL IT BE, PHIL? YOUR PRIDE OR HER LIFE?
WRONG TIME TO MAKE A BAD CHOICE.

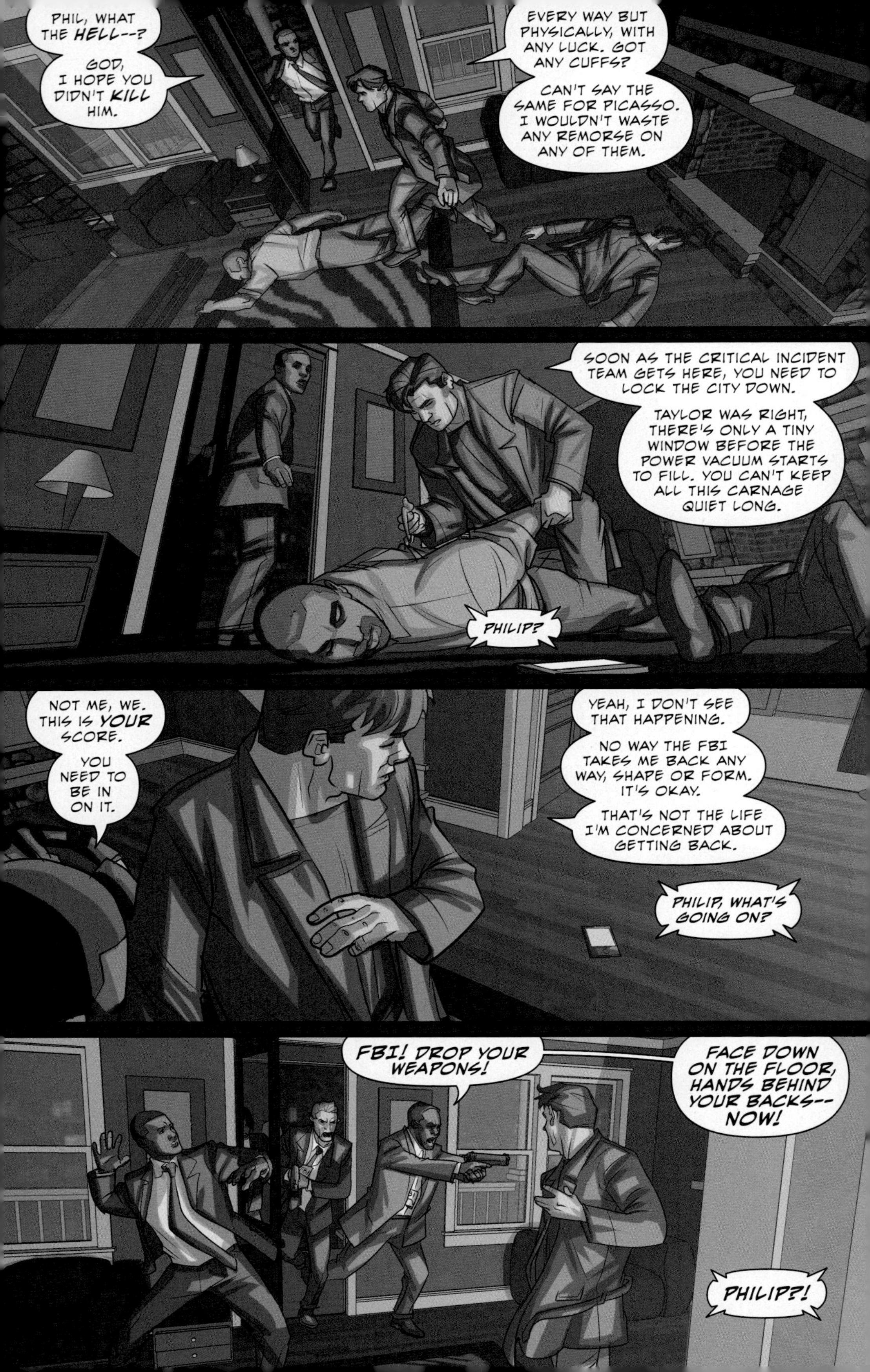
PHIL, WHAT THE HELL--? GOD, I HOPE YOU DIDN'T KILL HIM.
EVERY WAY BUT PHYSICALLY, WITH ANY LUCK. GOT ANY CUFFS?
CAN'T SAY THE SAME FOR PICASSO. I WOULDN'T WASTE ANY REMORSE ON ANY OF THEM.
SOON AS THE CRITICAL INCIDENT TEAM GETS HERE, YOU NEED TO LOCK THE CITY DOWN.
TAYLOR WAS RIGHT, THERE'S ONLY A TINY WINDOW BEFORE THE POWER VACUUM STARTS TO FILL. YOU CAN'T KEEP ALL THIS CARNAGE QUIET LONG.
PHILIP?
NOT ME, WE. THIS IS YOUR SCORE.
YOU NEED TO BE IN ON IT.
YEAH, I DON'T SEE THAT HAPPENING.
NO WAY THE FBI TAKES ME BACK ANY WAY, SHAPE OR FORM. IT'S OKAY.
THAT'S NOT THE LIFE I'M CONCERNED ABOUT GETTING BACK.
PHILIP, WHAT'S GOING ON?
FBI! DROP YOUR WEAPONS!
FACE DOWN ON THE FLOOR, HANDS BEHIND YOUR BACKS-- NOW!
PHILIP?!

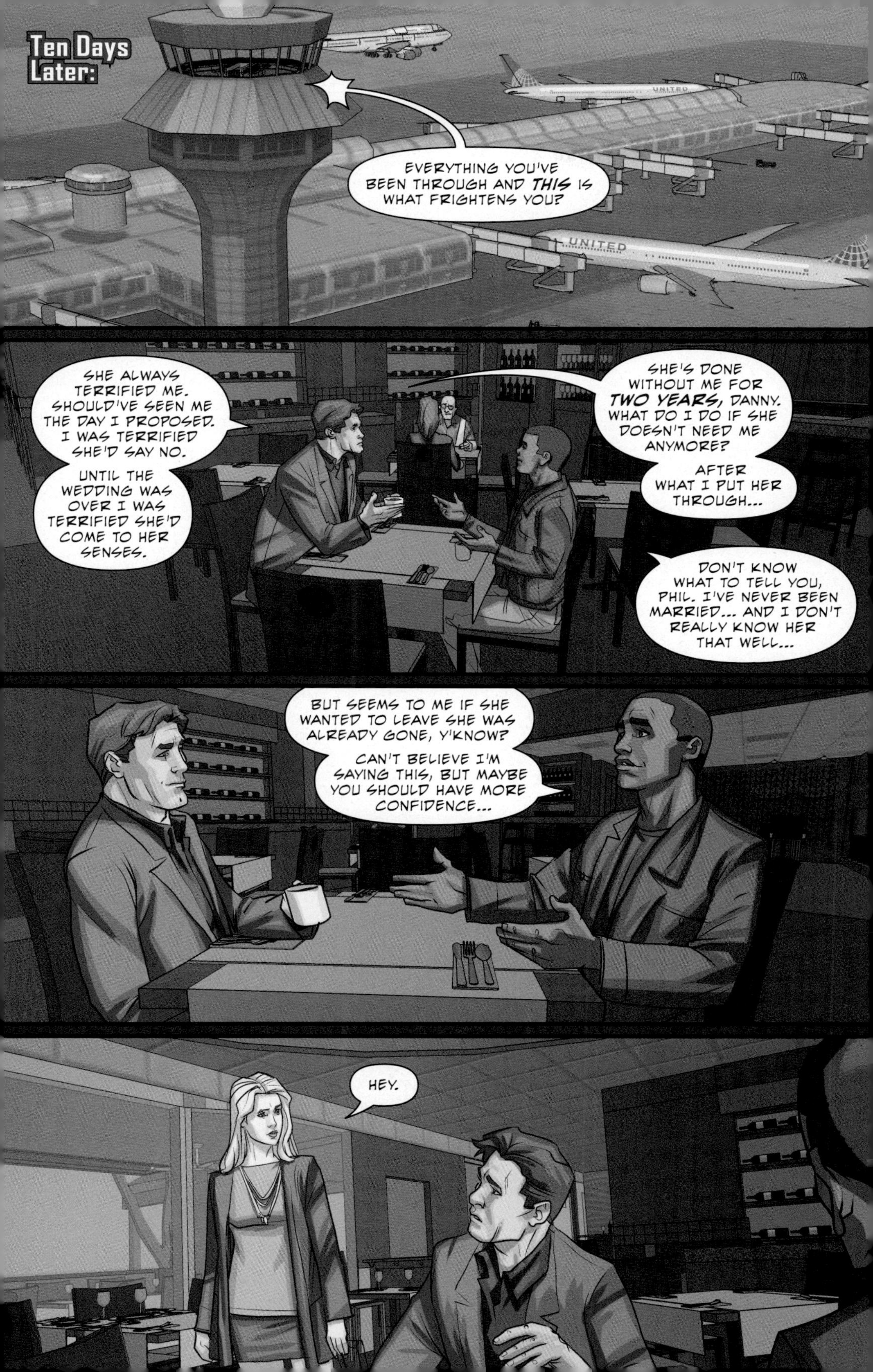
Ten Days Later:
EVERYTHING YOU'VE BEEN THROUGH AND THIS IS WHAT FRIGHTENS YOU?
SHE'S DONE WITHOUT ME FOR TWO YEARS, DANNY. WHAT DO I DO IF SHE DOESN'T NEED ME ANYMORE?
AFTER WHAT I PUT HER THROUGH...
SHE ALWAYS TERRIFIED ME. SHOULD'VE SEEN ME THE DAY I PROPOSED. I WAS TERRIFIED SHE'D SAY NO.
UNTIL THE WEDDING WAS OVER I WAS TERRIFIED SHE'D COME TO HER SENSES.
DON'T KNOW WHAT TO TELL YOU, PHIL. I'VE NEVER BEEN MARRIED... AND I DON'T REALLY KNOW HER THAT WELL...
BUT SEEMS TO ME IF SHE WANTED TO LEAVE SHE WAS ALREADY GONE, Y'KNOW?
CAN'T BELIEVE I'M SAYING THIS, BUT MAYBE YOU SHOULD HAVE MORE CONFIDENCE...
HEY.

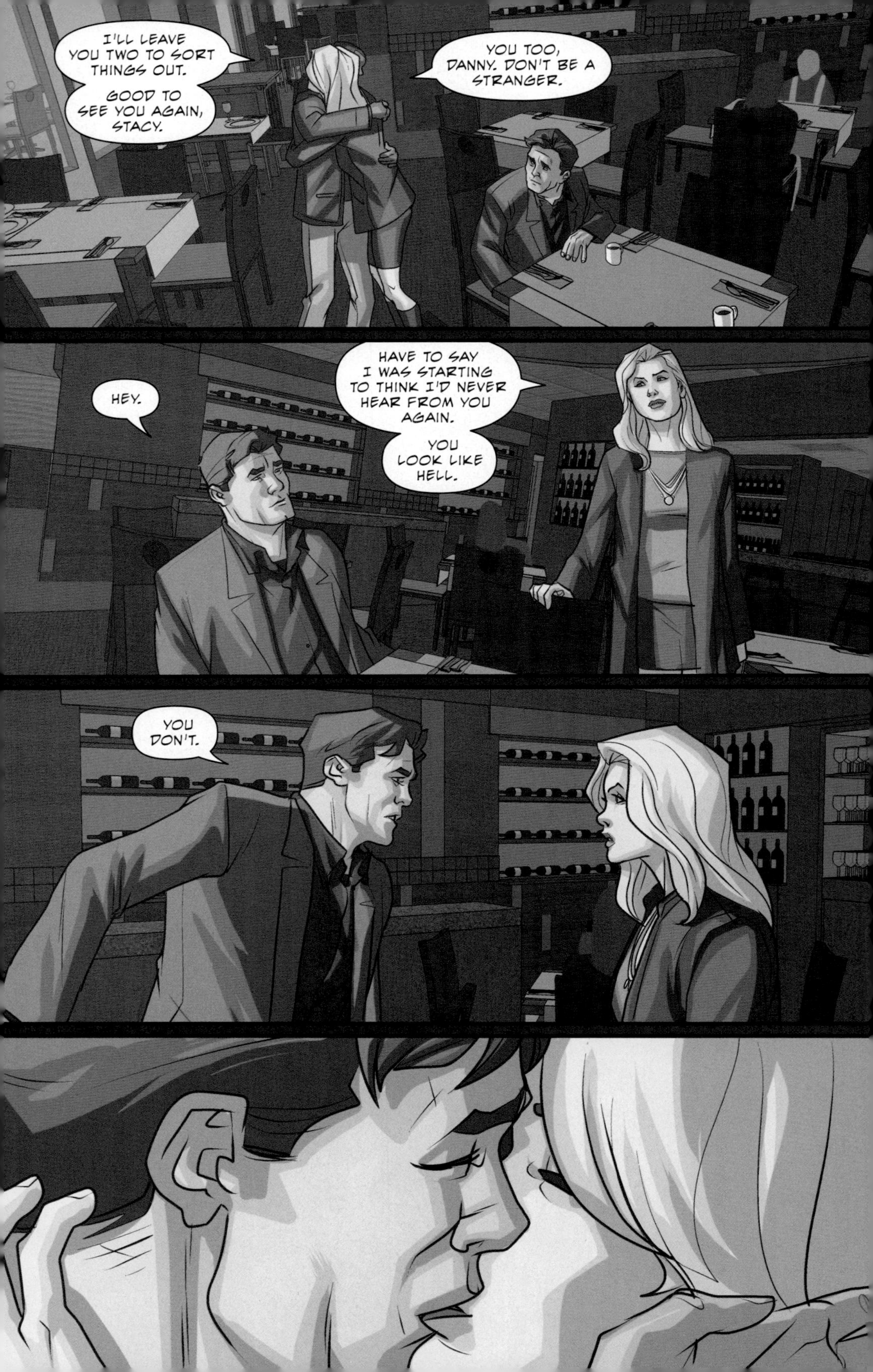
I'LL LEAVE YOU TWO TO SORT THINGS OUT.
GOOD TO SEE YOU AGAIN, STACY.
YOU TOO, DANNY. DON'T BE A STRANGER.
HEY.
HAVE TO SAY I WAS STARTING TO THINK I'D NEVER HEAR FROM YOU AGAIN.
YOU LOOK LIKE HELL.
YOU DON'T.

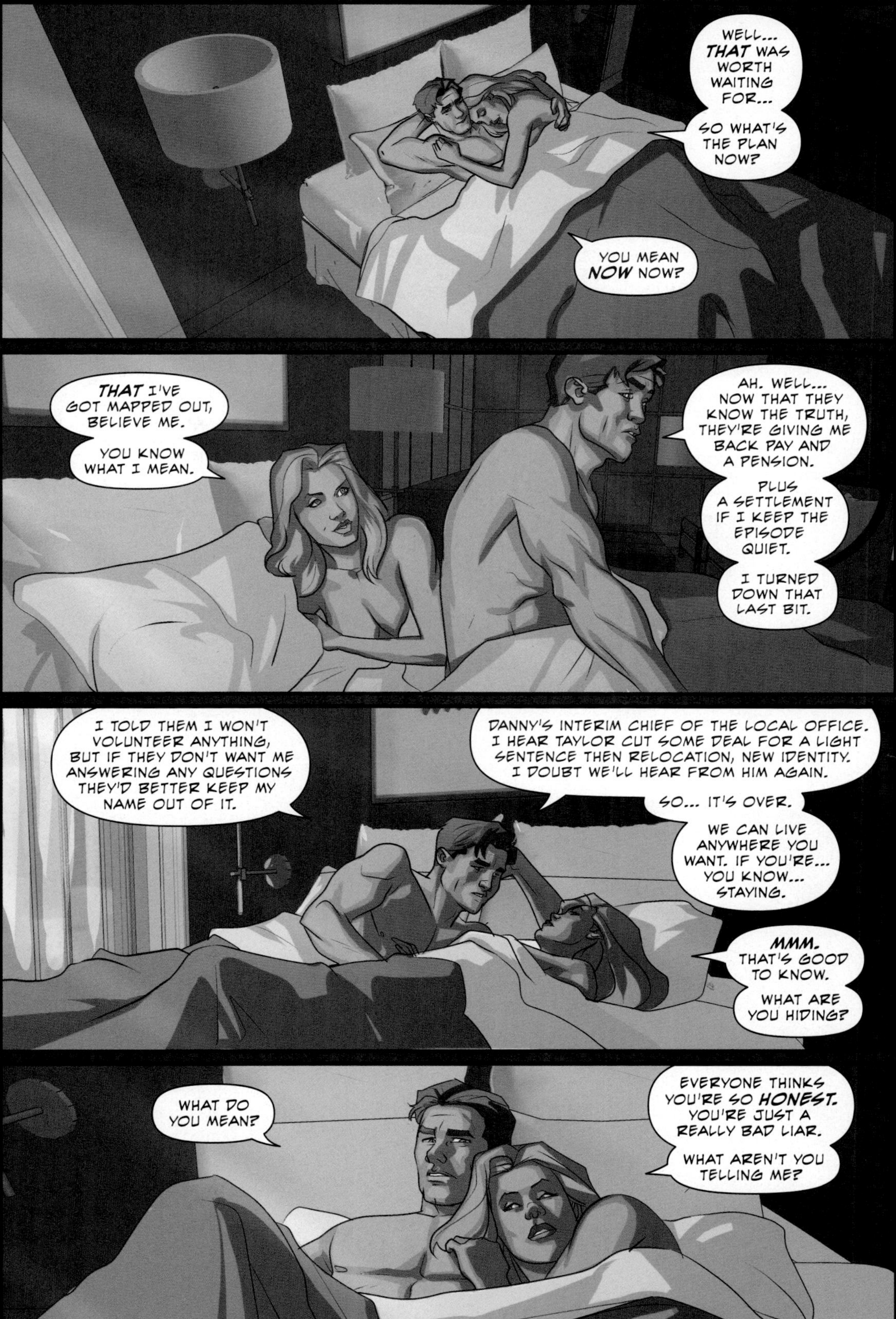
WELL... THAT WAS WORTH WAITING FOR...
SO WHAT'S THE PLAN NOW?
YOU MEAN NOW NOW?
THAT I'VE GOT MAPPED OUT, BELIEVE ME.
YOU KNOW WHAT I MEAN.
AH. WELL... NOW THAT THEY KNOW THE TRUTH, THEY'RE GIVING ME BACK PAY AND A PENSION.
PLUS A SETTLEMENT IF I KEEP THE EPISODE QUIET.
I TURNED DOWN THAT LAST BIT.
I TOLD THEM I WON'T VOLUNTEER ANYTHING, BUT IF THEY DON'T WANT ME ANSWERING ANY QUESTIONS THEY'D BETTER KEEP MY NAME OUT OF IT.
DANNY'S INTERIM CHIEF OF THE LOCAL OFFICE. I HEAR TAYLOR CUT SOME DEAL FOR A LIGHT SENTENCE THEN RELOCATION, NEW IDENTITY. I DOUBT WE'LL HEAR FROM HIM AGAIN.
SO... IT'S OVER.
WE CAN LIVE ANYWHERE YOU WANT. IF YOU'RE... YOU KNOW... STAYING.
MMM. THAT'S GOOD TO KNOW.
WHAT ARE YOU HIDING?
WHAT DO YOU MEAN?
EVERYONE THINKS YOU'RE SO HONEST. YOU'RE JUST A REALLY BAD LIAR.
WHAT AREN'T YOU TELLING ME?

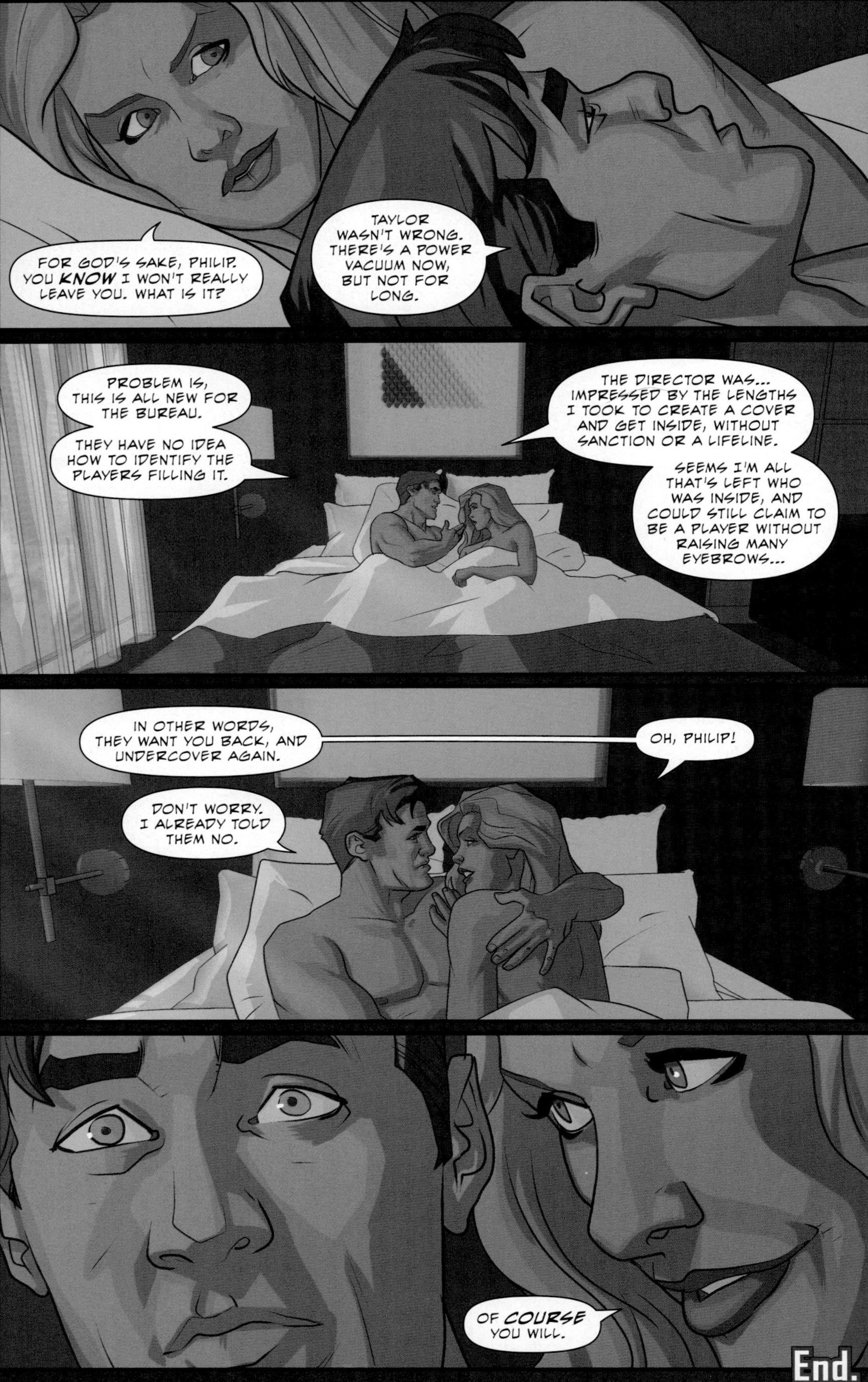
FOR GOD'S SAKE, PHILIP. YOU **KNOW** I WON'T REALLY LEAVE YOU. WHAT IS IT?
TAYLOR WASN'T WRONG. THERE'S A POWER VACUUM NOW, BUT NOT FOR LONG.
PROBLEM IS, THIS IS ALL NEW FOR THE BUREAU.
THEY HAVE NO IDEA HOW TO IDENTIFY THE PLAYERS FILLING IT.
THE DIRECTOR WAS... IMPRESSED BY THE LENGTHS I TOOK TO CREATE A COVER AND GET INSIDE, WITHOUT SANCTION OR A LIFELINE.
SEEMS I'M ALL THAT'S LEFT WHO WAS INSIDE, AND COULD STILL CLAIM TO BE A PLAYER WITHOUT RAISING MANY EYEBROWS...
IN OTHER WORDS, THEY WANT YOU BACK, AND UNDERCOVER AGAIN.
OH, PHILIP!
DON'T WORRY. I ALREADY TOLD THEM NO.
OF **COURSE** YOU WILL.
End.

COVER GALLERY

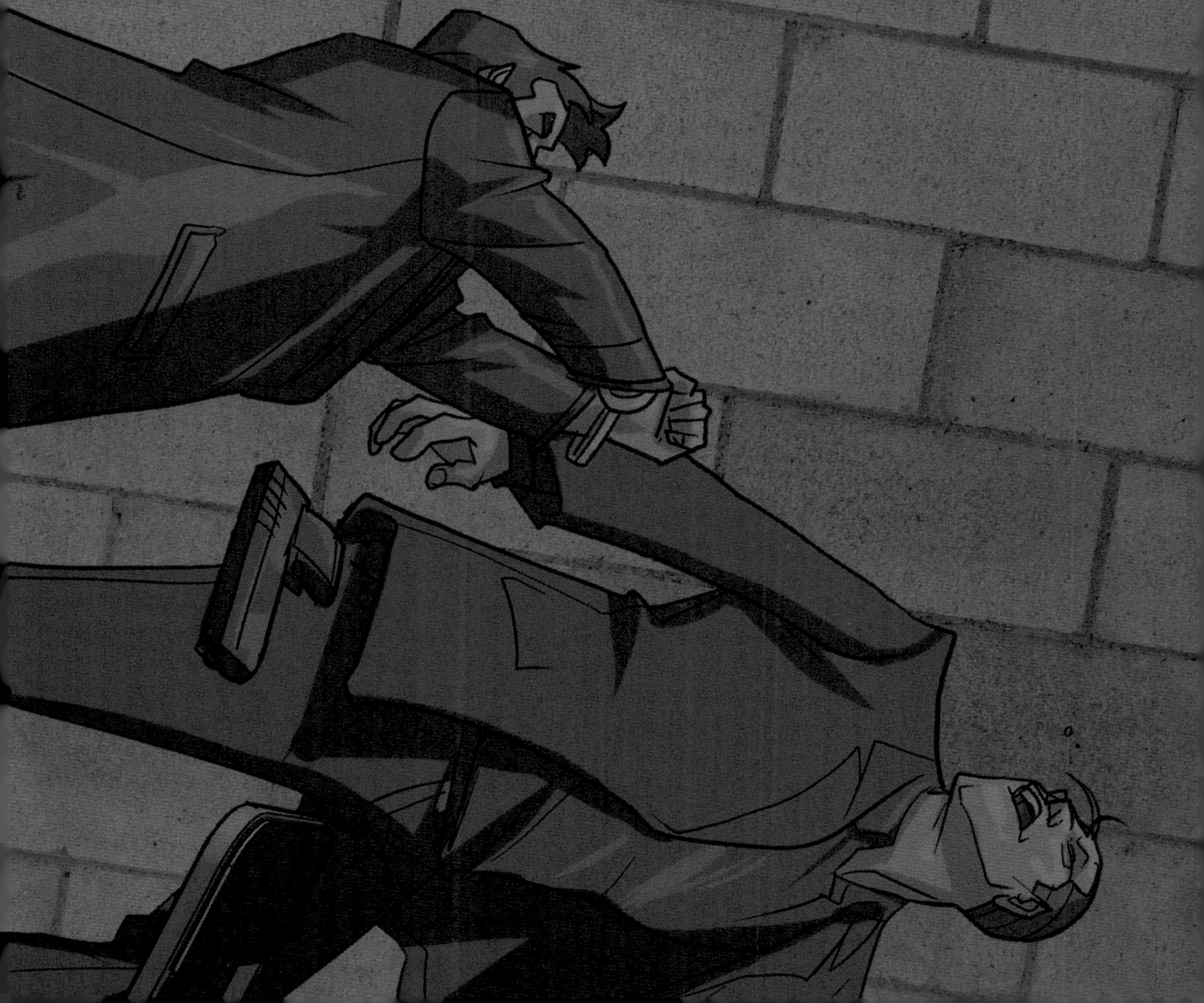

#1 COVER | DAVE JOHNSON

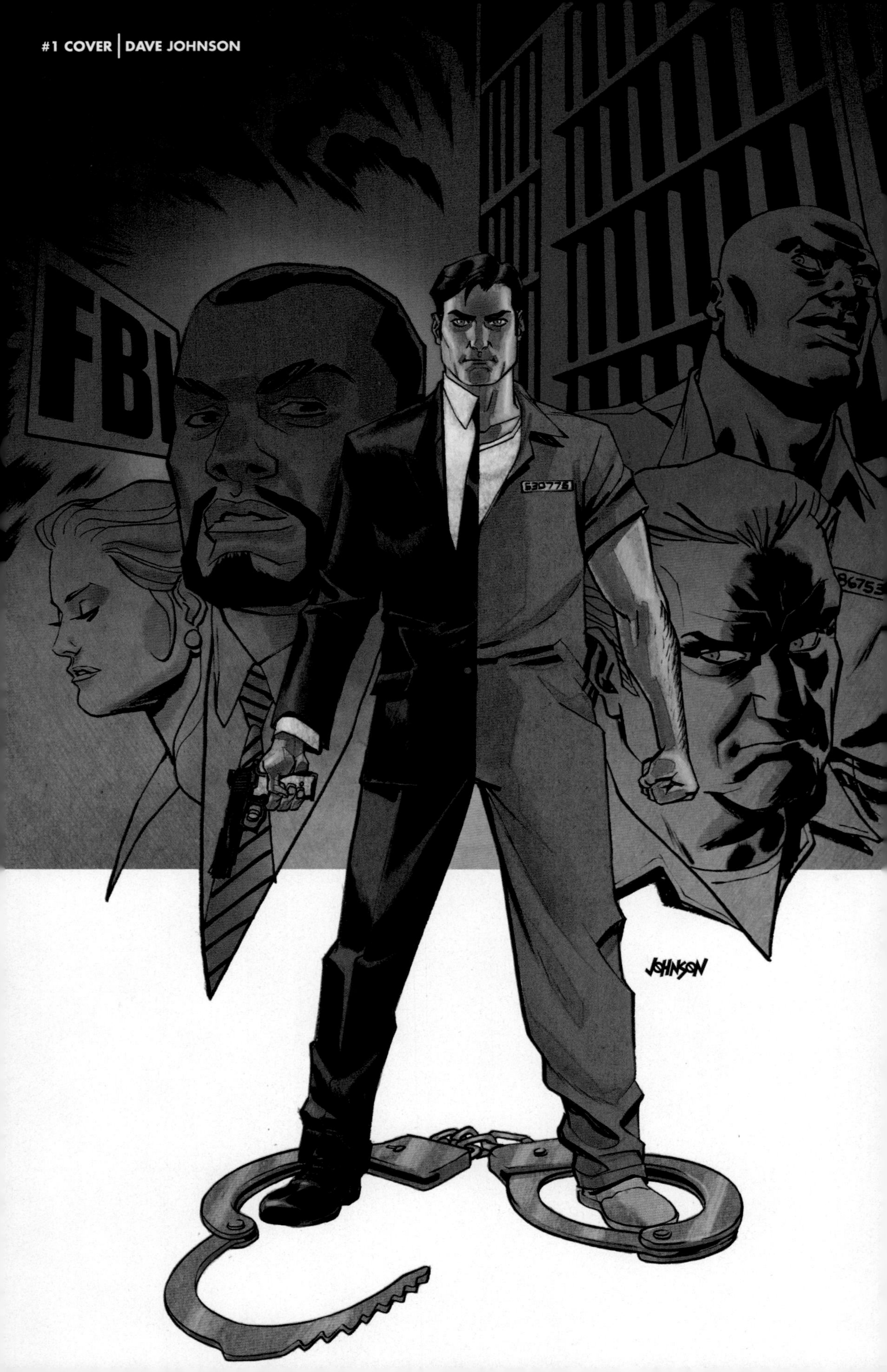
FBI
JOHNSON

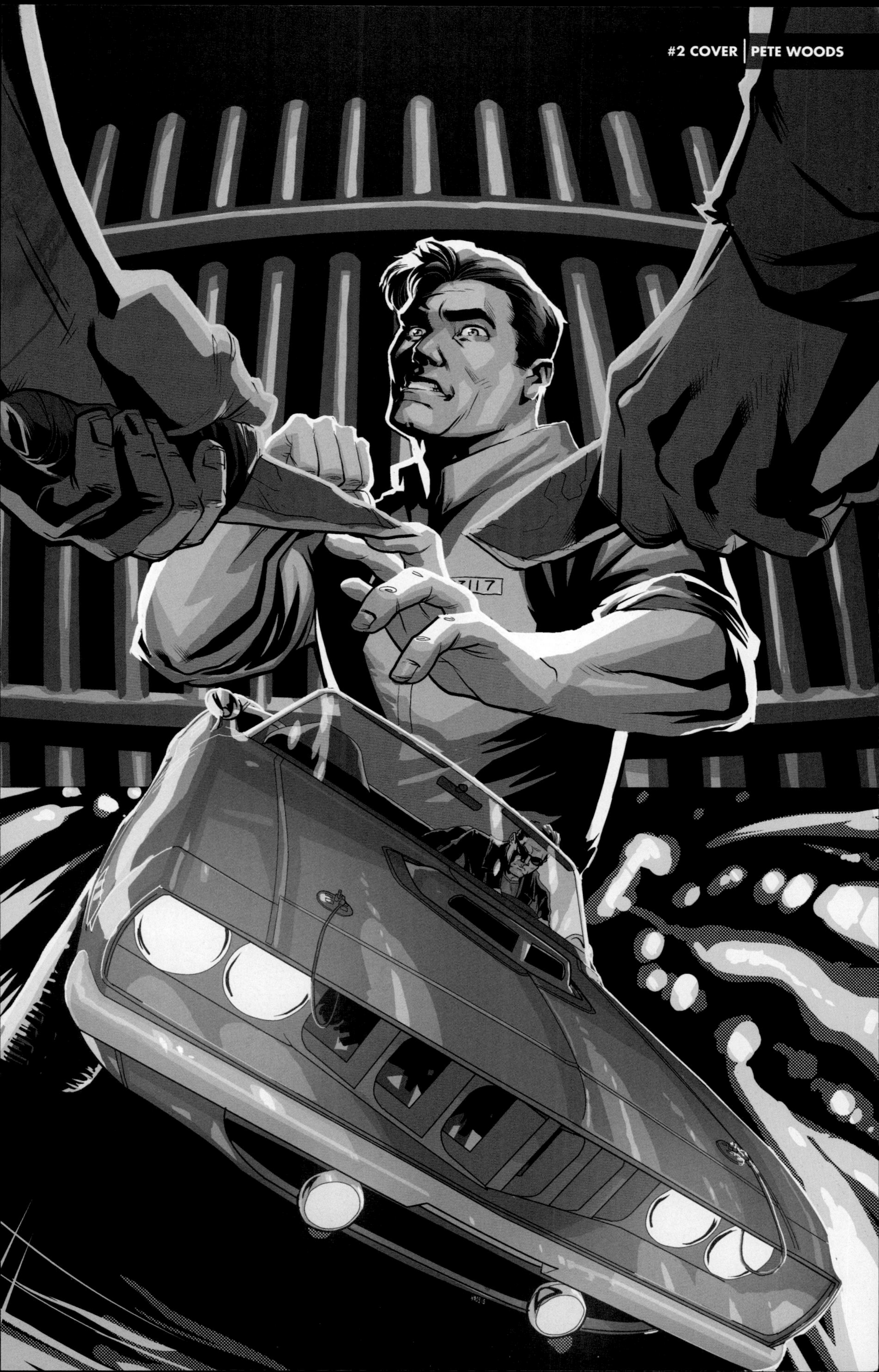

#2 COVER | PETE WOODS

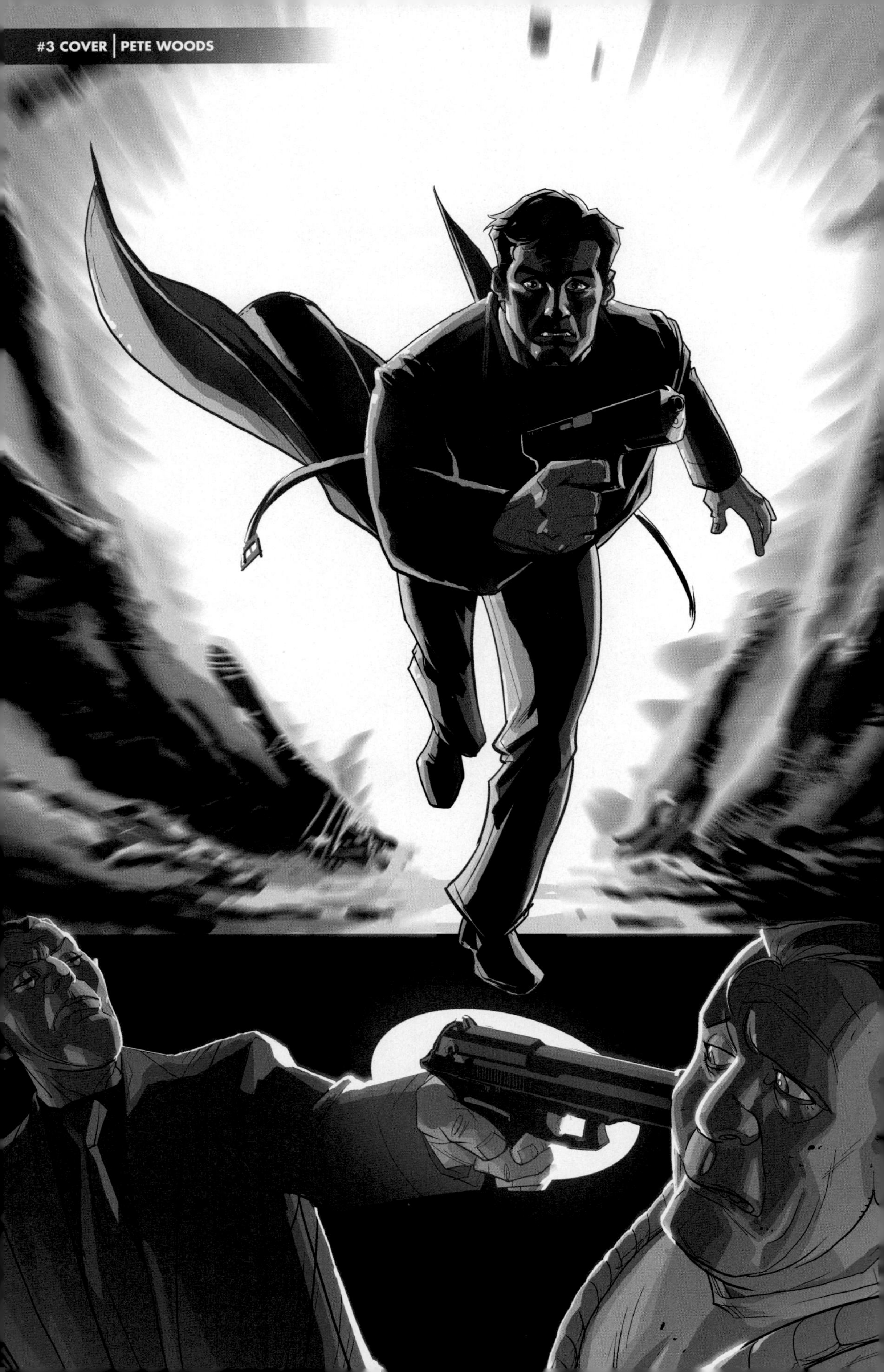

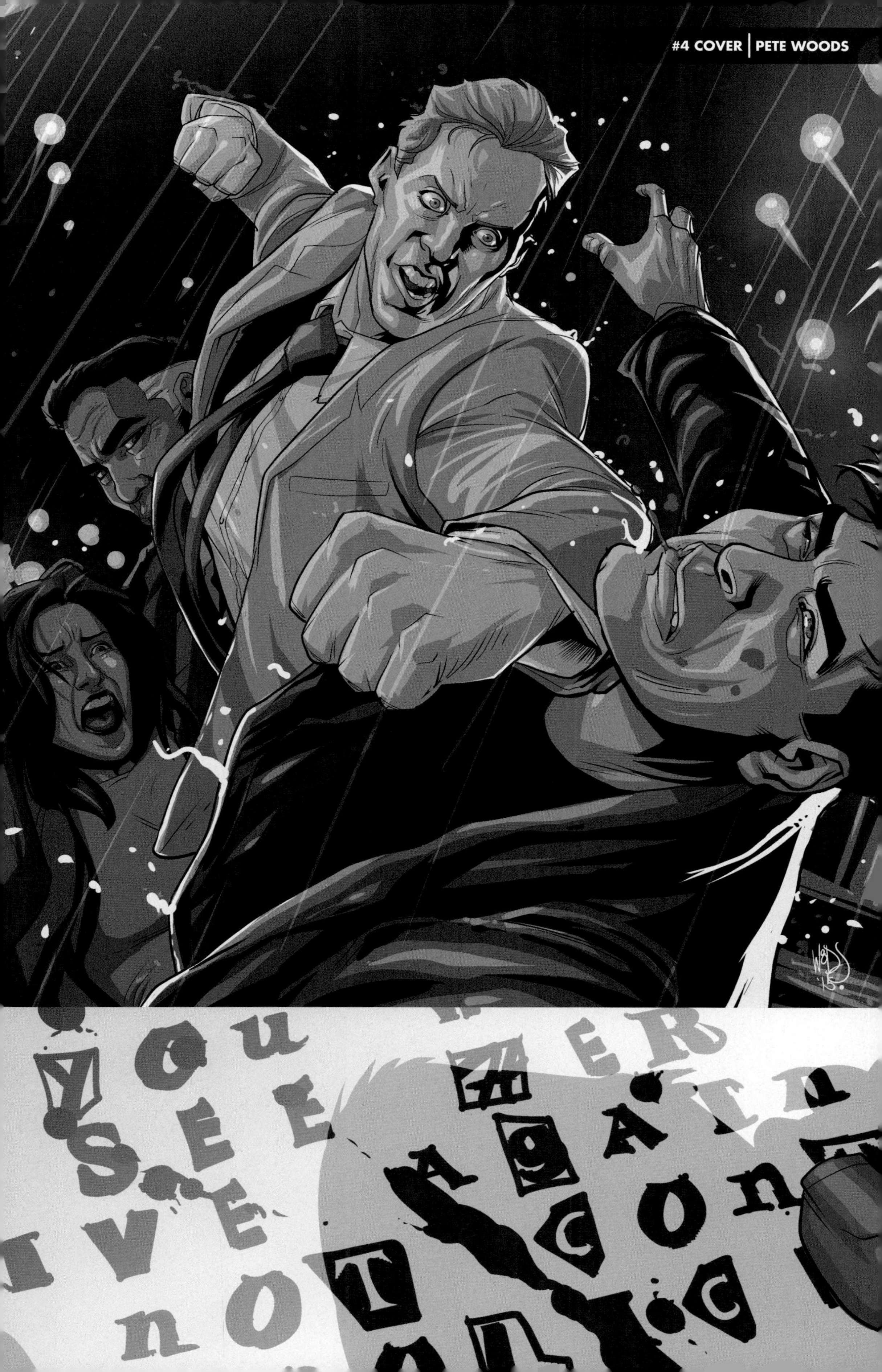

#5 COVER | PETE WOODS

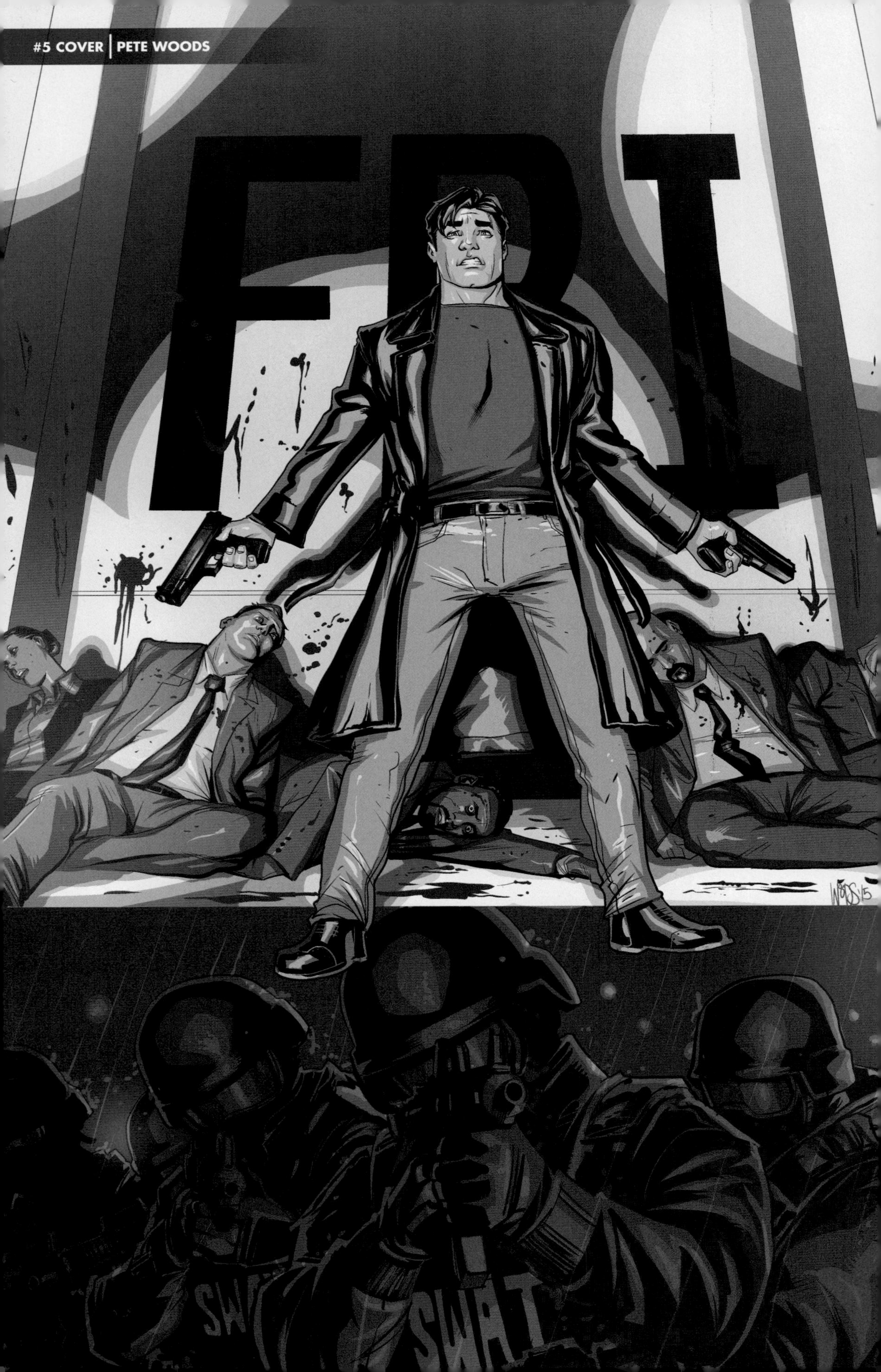
FBI
SWAT

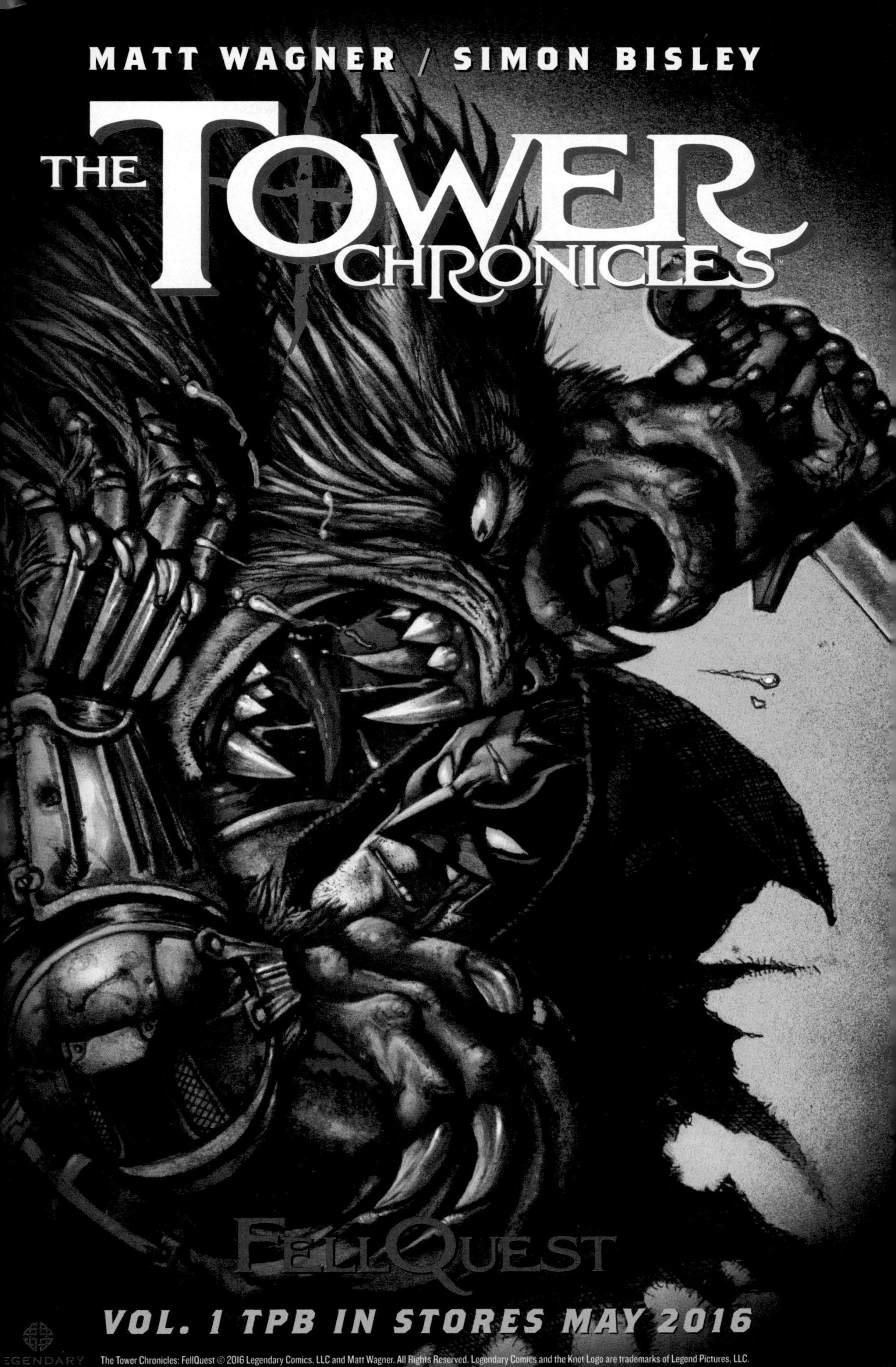
MATT WAGNER / SIMON BISLEY
THE TOWER CHRONICLES
FELLQUEST
VOL. 1 TPB IN STORES MAY 2016

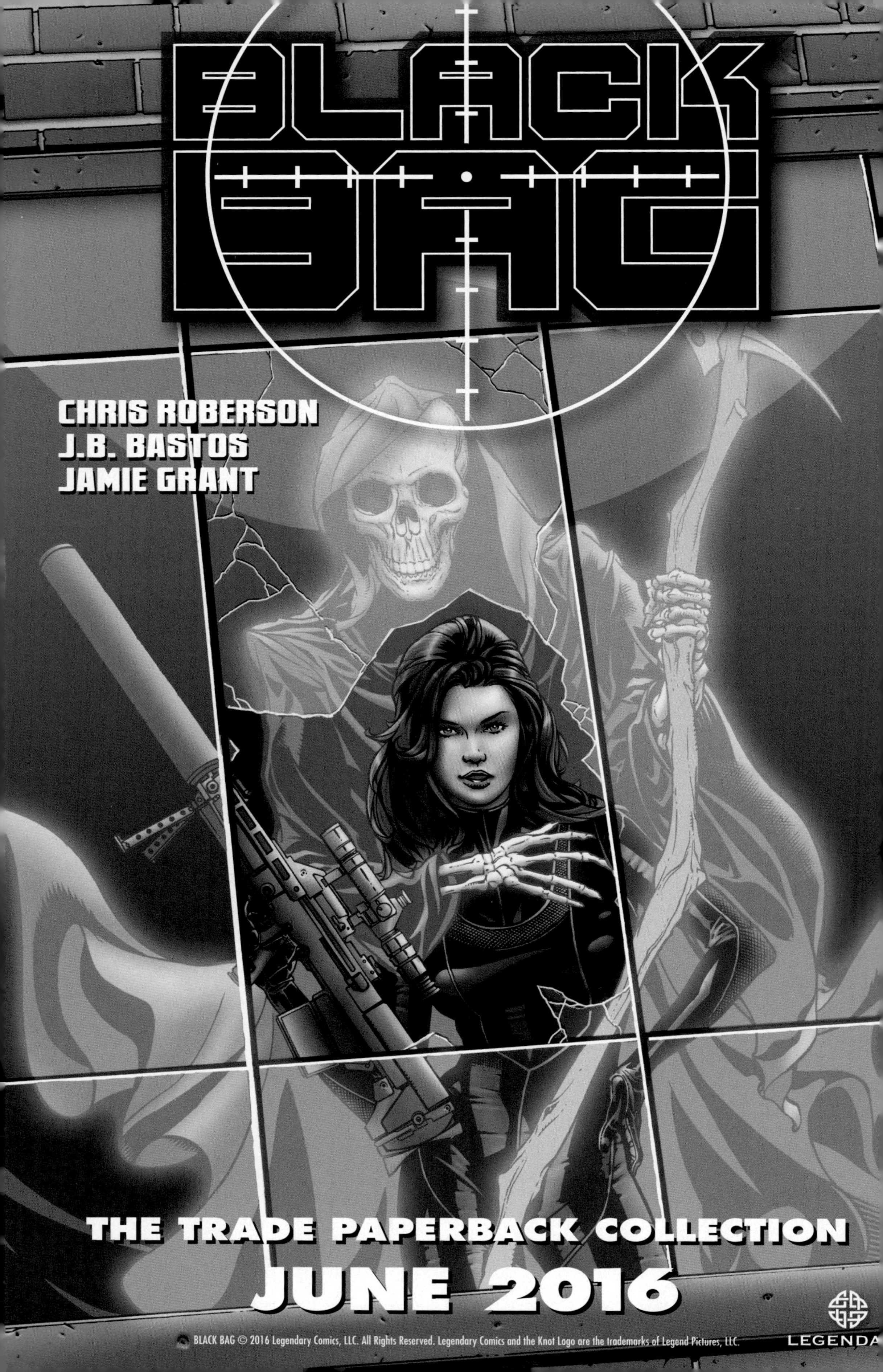
BLACK BAG
CHRIS ROBERSON
J.B. BASTOS
JAMIE GRANT
THE TRADE PAPERBACK COLLECTION
JUNE 2016
BLACK BAG © 2016 Legendary Comics, LLC. All Rights Reserved. Legendary Comics and the Knot Logo are the trademarks of Legend Pictures, LLC.
LEGENDA